The Spiritual Brain:
Science and Religious Experience

Andrew Newberg, M.D.

THE
GREAT
COURSES®

PUBLISHED BY:

THE GREAT COURSES
Corporate Headquarters
4840 Westfields Boulevard, Suite 500
Chantilly, Virginia 20151-2299
Phone: 1-800-832-2412
Fax: 703-378-3819
www.thegreatcourses.com

Andrew Newberg, M.D.
Director of Research
Myrna Brind Center of Integrative Medicine
at Thomas Jefferson University Hospital

Dr. Andrew Newberg is the Director of Research at the Myrna Brind Center of Integrative Medicine at Thomas Jefferson University Hospital. He is also a Professor in the Departments of Emergency Medicine and Radiology at Thomas Jefferson University, and he teaches undergraduate courses at the University of Pennsylvania. Dr. Newberg received his medical degree in 1993 from the University of Pennsylvania School of Medicine. He completed his residency in Internal Medicine at the Graduate Hospital in Philadelphia, and he completed a fellowship in Nuclear Medicine at the University of Pennsylvania. He is board certified in Internal Medicine and Nuclear Medicine.

Dr. Newberg has actively pursued neuroimaging research projects, including studies of aging and dementia, epilepsy, and other neurological and psychiatric disorders. He has been particularly involved in the study of religious and spiritual experiences and the relationship among the brain, religion, and health. Dr. Newberg's research has included analyzing brain scans of people in prayer, meditation, rituals, and various trance states. His research also has included understanding the physiological correlates of acupuncture therapy, massage, and other types of alternative therapies.

Dr. Newberg has taught medical students, undergraduate and graduate students, and medical residents about stress management, spirituality and health, and the neurophysiology of religious experience. In 2010, he was named Teacher of the Year for the University of Pennsylvania's Biological Basis of Behavior Program.

Dr. Newberg has published numerous articles and chapters on brain function, brain imaging, and the study of religious and spiritual experiences. He is the author of *Principles of Neurotheology*, a culmination of ideas based on his research over the past 10 years. He is a coauthor of the best-selling books *How God Changes Your Brain* and *Why God Won't Go Away: Brain Science and the Biology of Belief*. His most recent book, *Words Can Change Your Brain*, was published in June 2012. Dr. Newberg is also a coauthor of *Born to Believe: God, Science, and the Origin of Ordinary and Extraordinary Beliefs* and *The Mystical Mind: Probing the Biology of Religious Experience*, both of which explore the relationship between neuroscience and spiritual experience. The latter book received the 2000 award for Outstanding Books in Theology and the Natural Sciences presented by the Center for Theology and the Natural Sciences.

Dr. Newberg has presented his work at scientific and religious meetings around the world and has appeared on *Good Morning America*, *Nightline*, CNN, and ABC's *World News Tonight*. His research also has appeared in *Newsweek*; *TIME*; *The New York Times*; *Los Angeles Times*; *Scientific American*; *O, The Oprah Magazine*; and *Reader's Digest*. ∎

Table of Contents

Table of Contents

Table of Contents

The Spiritual Brain:
Science and Religious Experience

Scope:

Human beings appear to have spiritual brains—brains that are capable of feeling deeply connected to something greater than themselves and that can develop intense beliefs about religion and God. The human brain can engage in practices such as prayer or meditation that result in powerful spiritual experiences that have been described in every tradition and society. Spirituality also appears to have positive, and sometimes negative, effects on people's mental and physical health. Spiritual practices, beliefs, and phenomena are expressed and experienced in all kinds of ways, but no matter how human beings are spiritual, modern neuroscience can offer new insights into the meaning and nature of spirituality.

This set of 24 lectures examines the fascinating relationship between the human brain and spirituality. Relying on the latest theories and research from neuroscience, psychology, and other behavioral sciences, each lecture in this course addresses provocative questions about human spirituality.

After an introductory lecture that sets the stage for the course, the lectures examine what is known about all aspects of spiritual phenomena, including the study of practices such as prayer or meditation, spiritual development, the differences between atheists and believers, the effects of spirituality and religion on health and well-being, the nature of near-death experiences, the human urge to create myths and rituals, and the biological correlates of specific religious ideas such as revelation. The final lectures examine some of the most fascinating philosophical and theological implications of the field of scholarship that is sometimes referred to as neurotheology—the study of how the brain and spirituality are linked.

In this course, you will learn about many of the latest brain-imaging studies of different spiritual practices that peer into the brain during intense prayer, meditation, or speaking in tongues. You will explore how the effects of these different practices change not only the brain, but the body as well. In addition, you will consider how spiritual and religious beliefs might affect mental health as well as physical health. You will also consider the reverse relationship, in which patients with disorders such as seizures or schizophrenia manifest strong and sometimes bizarre religious experiences. Along the way, you will learn about a wide variety of religious experiences, ranging from basic rituals to the most profound mystical experiences.

A major element of this course is to explore where spiritual beliefs come from. You will consider how the brain develops biologically across the lifespan and how this reflects a person's spiritual growth and development. In addition, you will try to understand why the brains of some people are intensely religious while the brains of others completely reject the notion of God. You will also explore when religion and spirituality have a positive impact on a person's life and when such beliefs turn the brain hateful and destructive. You will learn about the impact of neurological and psychological disorders on spiritual beliefs and about how certain drugs that affect specific neurotransmitter systems in the brain lead to amazing spiritual-like experiences. Near-death experiences, rituals, and myths all have the potential to affect the brain, and of course, the brain's functions are likely involved in helping human beings have such experiences.

In this course, you will learn how thoughts, feelings, and experiences are associated with specific brain areas and how these are related to different aspects of religious and spiritual phenomena. Such phenomena frequently have extremely strong emotions of love or awe, amazing sensory elements such as intense light, and transformative thought processes that change a person's life. Along the way, you will explore the many research studies that are currently helping people understand the nature of all of these aspects of the spiritual brain.

As this course addresses many mysteries of spirituality, you will learn about how neuroscientists are beginning to study these phenomena and why certain questions about spiritual thoughts, emotions, and behaviors have been particularly difficult to evaluate using scientific methods. You will also learn that many popular and widely held explanations for human spiritual behaviors are far more complicated when you begin to incorporate a scientific perspective as well as a spiritual one.

In the process of discussing the spiritual brain, you will ultimately consider the implications for religion, philosophy, and theology. Thus, you can consider how the spiritual brain addresses some of the big questions about why human beings exist, what the nature of truth is, and how people can know what is really real.

Drawing upon the latest research linking modern neuroscience and spirituality, this course shines a light into the deepest parts of the human mind and spirit, giving you deep insights into why people believe what they do and revealing the fascinating relationship between the universal spiritual urge and the intricate workings of the human brain. ■

A New Perspective on Ancient Questions
Lecture 1

The purpose of this course is to understand how and why the mind moves human beings to be spiritual, to contemplate God, and to develop and follow religions. Because religion and spirituality can have a tremendous effect on people, there should be some physiological manifestation of that effect in the most important organ in our body—the brain. If we can study the human brain, then by extension, we can also study how religion and spirituality affect the human brain. If we can measure or quantify that effect, then perhaps we can even learn something about how and why we are spiritual.

Brain Scans of Franciscan Nuns

- In 1993, a study was conducted at the University of Pennsylvania that focused on the examination of brain activity while participants engaged in a type of Christian meditative prayer called centering prayer. The religious participants were a group of cloistered Franciscan nuns.

- To prepare for the study, the nuns allowed researchers to put intravenous catheters into their arms so that the researchers could inject a small amount of radioactive material, which would allow researchers to scan the brains of the nuns and determine which areas were more or less active during prayer.

- The researchers wanted to make sure that each person had enough experience doing the centering prayer, so they set a lower limit of 15 years to qualify.

- One by one, each nun engaged in a prayer session for 45 minutes. The tracer was injected in the last five minutes of the practice to capture the peak of the practice. When the tracer is injected, it circulates for a few minutes and gets locked in the brain, so it captures a snapshot at a particular moment in time.

- The brain scans showed many different changes, including changes in the parts of the brain that are involved in the sense of self, the ability to focus attention, and emotions—evidence that prayer has a measurable effect on the human brain.

- One of the things that scientific experiments do is, as you pursue the answer to one question, the experiment opens your mind to a slew of great questions you hadn't thought of before. In this case, the questions that the brain scans raised were even more fascinating than the conclusions that could be drawn from the preliminary data.

- If prayer causes a very specific pattern of activity in the brain—a pattern that can be detected by scanning technology—the sort of questions that are raised are as follows.
    - Are these changes in brain activity just for prayer, or do they apply to other practices as well?

    - If researchers compare the brain scans of different individuals, can they learn anything about the different ways the individuals conceptualize God?

    - What might these brain scans tell us about the relationship between spirituality and health?

- Are these the kinds of questions that science can actually answer? Researchers can use the latest and greatest in medical technology to see which brain areas are more or less active during prayer, but can that really tell them anything about the spirituality of the person who does the praying? Is spirituality even a proper subject for scientific examination?

- Science is all about understanding the world and ourselves, and few things seem more persistent and fundamental to the study of ourselves than human spirituality.

The History of Religion

- Human beings have pursued religion from our earliest origins. For example, 70,000 to 100,000 years ago, Neanderthals were burying their dead—and not only the bodies. Some graves also included various instruments, jewelry, and other adornments. This suggests, at the very least, that they had some belief that the dead went somewhere and may need those objects. However, it was not the body that had departed, so it must be something nonmaterial—a soul, perhaps.

- About 30,000 years ago, people were painting detailed scenes on cave walls in France and Southern Africa. These scenes included unusual figures that combined humans and animals. Several scholars suggest that these paintings actually represent mystical experiences. If they are correct, then human beings were already capable of profound spiritual states.

- Roughly 11,000 years ago, a temple was constructed at Göbekli Tepe in southeastern Turkey. The temple is comprised of large circular structures with walls made of unworked drystone and numerous T-shaped monolithic pillars of limestone that are up to 10 feet high. A bigger pair of pillars is placed in the center of the structures. There is evidence that the structures had a roof. Perhaps most interesting are the reliefs on the pillars, which include all sorts of animals, including foxes, lions, cattle, hyenas, wild boars, herons, ducks, scorpions, ants, spiders, snakes, and a small number of human-looking figures.

- The temple at Göbekli Tepe suggests that civilization did not precede religion, but that religion preceded civilization. In other words, it is a religious temple that was built thousands of years before the first cities began to appear, which seems to show that cities arose around the temple.

- The ancient Egyptians, 5,000 to 6,000 years ago, developed a rich mythology with many types of gods that helped control the world and especially the afterworld.

- When you consider the origins of monotheistic religions 5,000 years ago—as well as the emergence of Buddhism and Hinduism and the later development of Christianity, Islam, and other religions—all of this clearly demonstrates that throughout time and across the globe, human beings have thought about and struggled with the notion of a spiritual realm or God.

- One way to look at this long history is that religion is just the way things get explained before science comes along, but as a scientist, you might also look at this and see an undeniable pattern. Humans exhibit a persistent tendency to believe in things like God, the afterlife, and the soul. Maybe there's something in the way our brains are put together—the way we're wired—that makes us believe.

- In the 19th century, thinkers such as Nietzsche told us that God was dead, and many people thought that the development of science and universal education would lead people away from religious and spiritual ideas

Many years ago, the ancient Egyptians believed in the existence of many gods and that the gods helped them in their journey into the afterworld. This led to the building of pyramids and all of the accoutrements that went along with them.

- However, despite those thinkers, large percentages of people throughout the world still describe themselves as religious. Depending on the survey, about 85 to 90 percent of people in the United States believe in God, and surveys of the world population usually put the percentage of religious individuals between about 80 and 85 percent.

- Even agnostics and atheists are defined by their beliefs about God—or a lack of God. Almost everyone has thought about this topic at one point in their lives and has come to some conclusion about what belief, or nonbelief, to incorporate into their lives.

The Intersection of the Brain and Spirituality

- Science has to play a role in the exploration of spirituality. Given the universality of the human impulse to believe, how can science really understand our species unless it's willing to explore the spiritual brain? Studies like the one involving the Franciscan nuns aren't scientific sideshows; they can actually help us get to the core of what it means to be human.

- In fact, some of the most exciting research in all of science is occurring in a new field known as neurotheology, which is essentially the study of the relationship between the brain and spirituality.

- The tools of neurotheology are brain-imaging techniques and other physiological measures of the brain and body, such as changes in blood pressure, heart rate, or immune function. Other tools include studies and experiments that measure subjective experience, including thoughts, feelings, and perceptions.

- Neurotheology is a new and expanding field of research that has certainly caught the attention of both scientists and religious scholars in addition to the public at large.

- Of course, neurotheology isn't the first attempt to describe the links between the brain and spirituality. In fact, the wisdom of many ancient traditions includes powerful intuitions and surprising insights about the nature of these elusive links.

- For example, Eastern religious traditions have long shown significant interest in psychology. Buddhist and Hindu writings made extensive evaluations of the experience of the self, our emotional attachment to that self, and how the human psyche can be altered through various practices. These traditions recognized the importance of using the brain to help us achieve spiritual enlightenment.

- Ayurvedic medical practices were developed in India with an emphasis on the body's energy. According to this tradition, the brain, body, and spirit are intimately connected by an energy, or a force, known as Chi. Ayurvedic medicine long ago incorporated a concept that the material brain is deeply connected to the spiritual experiences of the mind.

- Ancient religious texts in the Western world did not deal with the brain's relationship to spirituality per se. The Bible speaks little about specific body physiology or mental processes. However, the description of human beings, their frailties, and the evil actions they commit clearly signifies deep interest in human psychology.

- The Ten Commandments are basically a treatise on moral psychology. They specify what we are to think and how we are to behave. However, we must remember that it is the brain that makes moral guidelines intelligible to us. Furthermore, it is the brain that drives us to behave in ways that either satisfy or violate those intelligible guidelines.

- Questions about the relationship between body and soul, and brain and mind, have been central to the Western philosophical tradition. From Descartes to Spinoza to Kant, people have wondered whether there is something inherent in the human mind that allows it access to ultimate reality.

- People have argued for centuries about how we can have knowledge of ultimate reality, recognizing that such knowledge is the key to understanding the nature of the universe. This is one of humanity's ultimate goals—to explore and understand how the universe works—and we must realize the critical role our mind plays in achieving this understanding.

- Science is constantly giving us new techniques to address the great questions of human life—questions relating to God, the soul, and the nature of belief—and this research is beginning to shed light on the questions regarding the relationship between the brain and human spirituality.

Suggested Reading

Ashbrook and Albright, *The Humanizing Brain*.

Beauregard and O'Leary, *The Spiritual Brain*.

McNamara, ed, *Where God and Science Meet*.

Newberg and Waldman, *How God Changes Your Brain*.

Newberg, d'Aquili, and Rause, *Why God Won't Go Away*.

Questions to Consider

1. Over the centuries, how have we, as human beings, come to understand the persistence and nature of our religious and spiritual beliefs?

2. How can a scientific perspective of the human brain provide a new and deeper understanding of how and why human beings have religious and spiritual beliefs?

A New Perspective on Ancient Questions
Lecture 1—Transcript

Ever since I can remember, I've been interested in questions related to religion and God. This hardly makes me unusual, of course; but because I'm also a scientist, I'm often around people who think that my interest is a little strange, or a little misguided. I won't speculate about the reasons why they might have that opinion of me; but for me, there's never been a disconnect between the pursuit of knowledge and an interest in God.

When I was a child, I liked to ask a lot of questions—just like any good scientist should—and, of course, many of those questions had to do with God: Does God exist? If God does exist, is God loving or vindictive? Does a belief in God have any benefits, either here on Earth or later on; maybe after we die? As I got older, instead of these questions going away, these questions actually took on a new depth; they took on new dimensions for me. I went to college and then on to medical school, and I began to wonder how I might be able to use my scientific background—my scientific training—to address these big questions.

Then one day, as I was engaged in some of my research looking at the brain, it occurred to me: Since religion and spirituality can have a tremendous effect on people, then there should be some kind of physiological manifestation of that effect, and it should be in the most important organ in our body, the human brain. People's lives are changed by their faith in God; their habits and choices are shaped by spiritual practices like prayer and meditation; so surely there's something happening in the brain, something that we should be able to measure, which reflects what spirituality and religion does for us as human beings.

This was something of a revelation for me. We can study the human brain, right? Nobody doubts that. But if we can study the human brain, then by extension we can also study how religion and spirituality affect the brain. Moreover, maybe this would even tell us something about how and why we as human beings are spiritual.

I have to admit that, as a neuroscientist, part of me just thought, "I just want to take a religious person and stick them in a brain scanner and see where religion is in their brain." Of course, that's a little simplistic in looking at things that way; and over the years, I've definitely come to realize that you can't just rely on a brain scan to explain religion. Even so, I thought then and I do think now that using brain imaging technology is a fruitful place to start this whole exploration of the relationship between spirituality and the human brain.

In 1993, I decided to design the first study that we did looking at religion and the human brain. It was to be a small study that we were going to conduct in my lab at the time at the University of Pennsylvania, and the goal was to examine brain activity while various participants (subjects) were engaged in a type of Christian prayer called Centering Prayer. This is a kind of meditative prayer where they continue to come back to the particular idea—a phrase from the Bible; a particular prayer that they like—and reflect on this. What this ultimately would involve was to bring people into our lab who were very religious people and to have them actually engage in this particular practice.

I was fortunate to come across a group of Franciscan nuns who lived nearby—lived in the Philadelphia area—who were very willing to come in and do this kind of prayer. In fact, they were very pleasant to work with, they were very supportive of the research that we were trying to do, and they kind of actually liked the idea of scanning their brains while they prayed.

In and of itself, it was kind of interesting to me to see how willing and interested they were in participating in this study, because, after all, we didn't know what we were going to find; we didn't know if we might find something that seemed to run contrary to their religious or spiritual beliefs, maybe it would be something that the nuns didn't like. But in they came, very cheery and very excited about being a part of our study, and allowing me to put an IV catheter into their arm—a needle into their arm—so that we could inject a very small amount of a radioactive material that would allow us to see the areas of their brain that were active, and particularly the areas of the brain that were active during the centering prayer.

Of course, there are always issues with any study, and particularly the study of religion. To begin with, we wanted to make sure that each person had enough experience doing the centering prayer; in fact, we decided to arbitrarily set a lower limit of 15 years to qualify. We thought that it would be enough time to allow someone to really be able to engage the practice effectively, and one of the things that we kept having to think about in the back of our minds was the idea that we're not asking them to do this practice in their usual setting—they're not going to be in a church or in their home environment that's a comfortable place for them to do this practice—they're going to be in a laboratory setting, with a needle shoved into their arm and all kinds of people around them, now asking them to engage in this very spiritual practice. That seems like it's a little of an unusual kind of thing to ask somebody to do, and therefore we wanted to make sure that the people who were going to come in to do this study had enough experience; that they'd be able to engage the practice because it's just something that's so natural for them to do.

When I asked the first nun how much she'd actually been doing this prayer and how long she'd been doing the prayer, she just looked at me with a very kind of blank expression and said, "I've been doing this for 57 years."

"You're qualified," I quickly thought to myself.

At least we felt very comfortable with the fact that these nuns who'd been doing this practice for many, many years wouldn't have a problem being able to engage in the centering prayer practice while they were in our research laboratory while they were getting their brains canned.

The next potentially problematic issue, which I'd never really considered before, was that the regulations that we have for doing these brain scans— because they do involve some radiation—is that we're supposed to obtain a pregnancy test on every woman who's of childbearing potential. Suddenly, I realized that I wasn't going to be very comfortable with the idea of having to ask a nun to actually take a pregnancy test. I thought that would seem a little strange and maybe a little insulting to them. But, fortunately, we dodged that bullet because all of them were over the age of 60 years old; they were outside the possibility of ever getting pregnant, and therefore we dodged this theological bullet.

When we brought them into our lab, we had to do a couple of things. As I mentioned, first we had to put a small IV or intravenous catheter into their arm. This allows us to have access to their bodies so that we can put in a small amount of a radioactive tracer. The reason that we have to put this tracer into them is that we need to look at what's going on in the brain. In fact, this particular tracer is a very special tracer because it allows us to measure blood flow in the brain. What happens is once I inject the tracer, after about two or three minutes it circulates in the body and gets up into the brain and actually gets locked into the brain. The really neat thing about how this particular type of scan works is that, for example, if I were to come over to where you are right now as you're listening to my talk, and I were to put an IV in your arm and inject you with the radioactive tracer, and then you finished listening to what I have to say, maybe you grab a quick bite to eat, get into the car and go down to your local hospital to actually have the scan done, it would tell me what was happening at the moment that I did the injection, while you were actually listening to me talk; and all the other things that went on in between—having something to eat, driving the car— all of that wouldn't have an impact on what the scan actually showed. This is a very elegant way for us to be able to get at what's going on at the brain at a particular moment in time; and in this case, at the time of doing the prayer.

As I mentioned, one of the things that was very nice about the centering prayer is that they were able to engage it for a period of time; we actually had them doing this particular practice for about 45 minutes. What they'd do is that they'd begin to take this particular phrase, this particular prayer; they'd concentrate on it, focus on it; and as they got into this focusing— this deep experience—they started to notice a variety of different changes going on. They'd start to feel different emotions, a feeling of calmness and blissfulness come over them; and they'd start to feel an unusual loss of the sense of their self. They felt that they became one with the prayer, and if the prayer focused on God they actually could perceive themselves to becoming one with God.

I was very curious to see what was going to go on in the scans of their brains when they actually took part in this particular meditation practice. When we actually did look at the scans of their brains, we saw lots of different kinds of things going on. In fact, we could look at all the different colors that lit up in the brain on the basis of where that radioactive material went and see what areas of the brain were actually turned on and what areas of the brain were actually turned off. We're able to see actual changes that were going on in the areas of the brain that are involved in some of those emotional experiences that they had. They felt calmness; they felt blissfulness; and the areas of their brain that are involved in emotional feelings—a part of the brain that we'll talk about in much more detail in later lectures—is the limbic system. This part of the brain enables us to feel these emotions, and we saw some very extreme changes going on in this area of the brain. The other kind of experience that we saw is where they begin to lose their sense of self; and as they lose their sense of self, we see changes going on in the area of the brain that helps us to feel our sense of self: an area of the brain called the parietal lobe; and this is located towards the back part of the brain.

Again, we're going to be returning to these scans and all the different details of what these scans can show and the changes that we saw during this entire course, and we'll begin to develop based on this research a very detailed picture of what's going on in the brain when people engage in prayer practices, meditation practices, or maybe just have religious and spiritual thoughts and beliefs.

I want to use the centering prayer study as a way of introducing some of the cutting-edge questions that we'll be addressing in this course; because as I look through these scans and the data that the first study with the nuns actually provided, I realized that the results were actually creating many more questions that were every bit as fascinating as the answers that I'd begun to start with. With any good scientific experiment, this is usually what you find: You actually have more questions after the experiment than you actually are able to answer. But as we pursued the different questions—as we pursued them one after the other—we found that there were so many really terrific questions that we'd never even thought of before.

Let's stop for a moment and reflect on the study that I've just been describing. If prayer—and particularly the centering prayer—causes a very specific pattern of activity in the brain, something that we may actually be able to see with our scanning technology, then what sort of questions does it raise in your own mind? What questions would you ask if you were a scientist performing this study?

Here are a few questions that I, as the scientist doing this study, am inclined to ask: First of all, I'd like to know whether the changes that we see in this particular prayer are specific to this prayer, or do they apply to other practices as well? Here's another question that occurs to me: If I compare the brain scans of different individuals, can I learn something about the different ways in which they might actually conceptualize God? I might even want to explore the question: What might these brain scans tell me about the relationship between spirituality and health? As we'll see in later lectures, if spirituality helps us with our feelings of anxiety and depression, then there should be changes going on in the brain that help us to feel that way. You can probably think of many other questions that are just as intriguing as the ones that I've offered.

But wait a minute, some of you are probably already wondering: Are these the kind of questions that science can even answer? Sure, we can use the latest and greatest medical technology to see which areas of the brain are more or less active during a practice like prayer; but does this really tell us something about the spirituality of the person who does the praying? Or to put it succinctly: Is spirituality even a proper subject for scientific examination?

Of course, I wouldn't be teaching this entire course if I didn't answer that question with a resounding "yes." For me, science is all about understanding the world and ourselves; and when it comes to ourselves, few things seem to be more persistent and fundamental than human spirituality. In fact, when you ask the question "who cares about God," the answer seems to be "Pretty much everybody!"

Think about it for a moment: Human beings have pursued religion from our earliest origins. For example, if we go back in time about 70–100,000 years ago, we find that Neanderthals were burying their dead; and they didn't just bury the bodies, but in the graves they actually included various instruments, jewelry, weapons, and other adornments. Why did they do this? Certainly it suggests that there was some belief that these dead friends may go somewhere and may actually need these objects in the afterlife, in some other realm that they travel to. But clearly the body was there; and therefore if the body was still there, and yet somehow they went somewhere else, then there must be some other part of us—something that's non-material; maybe even a soul perhaps—that travels beyond the body after we die.

If we fast forward to about 30,000 years ago, we find some very fascinating paintings going on, on cave walls, in a variety of locations including Europe—places like France—and a variety of places throughout Africa, and particularly Southern Africa. What's interesting about these cave drawings is that they included some very unusual figures that combined human beings and animals; and several scholars have suggested that these paintings actually represented mystical experiences. In fact, part of what led them to this idea was the notion that why would they be in this cave that's dark and you can't see anything, and there seems to be no particular reason to actually be in there in the first place, other than perhaps some kind of ritual—some kind of spiritual practice—that created these experiences for them, and then they drew these experiences in the paintings on the walls.

About 11,000 years ago, a temple was actually constructed at a place called Gobekli Tepe in southeastern Turkey. This temple was recently discovered and it's been an absolutely fascinating find because it appears to be a religious temple that's comprised of these very large circular structures that have walls with these huge monolithic pillars on them. In fact, some of them are as high as 10 feet tall, and there are even larger pairs of pillars that are placed in the center of the structures. What many people are thinking is going on is that this is actually a type of temple for a religious tradition that we've never found or never heard about before. In fact, on a lot of the different rocks and pillars, we find all kinds of drawings of animals such as fox, lions, different birds, even insects like ants and spiders, as well as some human-looking figures.

But why was this find so important? The prevailing idea about when and how religious and spiritual ideas came about was that we needed to create a more central structure to our society, and that this didn't happen until we actually had agriculture so that we could settle down, form societies, and from there we created religious. But what this temple at Gobekli Tepe tells us is that it actually predates any evidence that we have of societies or civilizations; and it's been quite uncertain to people as to how these hunter-gatherers, who really weren't very well settled down, actually developed this type of very complex and intricate type of temple. It suggests that actually religion came even before agriculture, farming, and cities, and that religion was something that actually allowed our first civilizations to come about. It seems like religion is something that's been there from the very beginning of human life, from the beginning even before we had the first cities; and therefore religion is something that's been one of the most powerful forces that's shaped human history.

As we move further through time, we see the ancient Egyptians, who maybe 5,000 or 6,000 years ago developed a very rich mythology that we know a lot about. We know about the different gods that helped them to control the world and especially their journey into the afterworld, which is what led to the pyramids and all of the accoutrements that went along with them to help prepare them for that journey into the future. When we consider some of the monotheistic religions, as well as Buddhist and Hindu thoughts, we see that all of these different religions become such a powerful force in human history, that religions are something that have followed human civilization throughout time, and therefore probably had one of the most important influences on the human brain and on human behavior throughout history.

Even though we've always struggled with the notion of God and have beliefs about God, I want you to stop for a minute and think like a scientist. Why does all of this matter? Sure, we can say, "The religious impulse is very ancient," but so what? Isn't religion just a way of explaining things, maybe before science actually came along and gave us information about the world? That's certainly one way you could look at it. But as a scientist you might also look at this long history and think, "Hmm, there's an undeniable pattern here: Humans exhibit this persistent tendency to believe in things like God, and the afterlife, and a soul; maybe there's something in the way our brains are actually put together, the way that we're wired, that makes us, well, believe." That's the sort of question that we'll be exploring in this course: What is it about human beings that makes us believe?

Notice that I say "makes us believe," not "made us believe"; because, after all, religious beliefs didn't stop 5,000 or even 1,000 years ago. Sure, maybe about 150 years ago, philosophers such as Nietzsche were trying to tell us that God was going to die; that we weren't going to need any more of this archaic belief system in religion or God. With the development of education of the masses and the scientific methodology that was helping us to explain our world, some people really did think that religion wasn't going to be here much longer.

But despite these people who thought that religion and God were going to go away, if we look around us today we see just the opposite has occurred: People throughout the world describe themselves as being religious. Depending on the survey that you want to look at, about 85–90 percent of people in the United States describe themselves as being religious, and surveys of the world's population usually put the percentage of religious individuals somewhere between 80 and 85 percent. Even those people who don't believe—agnostics and atheists—are typically defined by their beliefs about God, or in this case a lack of a belief in God.

Ultimately, we're all interested in this topic of spirituality, religion, and God. Almost everyone has thought about it at one point in their lives and come to some conclusion about what belief system—or non-belief system—that they should incorporate into their lives. That's why I personally feel so strongly that science has to play a role in the exploration of human spirituality. Given the universality of the human impulse to believe, how can science really understand our species unless it also helps us to understand the spiritual brain? It therefore seems crucial to find a way of integrating scientific ideas with spiritual ones.

In fact, some of the most exciting research in this field right now is occurring in a new field that some people have referred to as neurotheology. Neurotheology is essentially the study of the relationship between the brain and spirituality. The tools of neurotheology are some of the brain imaging techniques that we talked about earlier with our study of centering prayer, but also other measures of the physiological processes in our body, and also measures of our immune system, our heart rate, and all the different processes that go on inside of us that make us work. We also have to think about subjective measures: What are people actually thinking, or feeling, or perceiving when they engage in their religious or spiritual traditions? Of course, ultimately it's very important for researchers in this field of neurotheology to strive for a very thorough understanding of what religious, theological, and spiritual phenomena are actually all about.

We'll be returning to the topic of neurotheology in later lectures; but I wanted to introduce it here because it's a new and expanding field of research, and has certainly caught the attention of scientists, religious scholars, and the public at large. Moreover, we'll be employing many of the tools of neurotheology in this course; so it's certainly a term that I want you to be familiar with.

But, of course, neurotheology isn't really the first attempt that we've ever seen that describes the links between the brain and spirituality; in fact, the wisdom of many ancient traditions includes powerful intuitions and surprising insights about the nature of these elusive links.

For example, Eastern traditions have long shown significant interest in psychology. Buddhist and Hindu writings have made extensive evaluations of the experience of our "self": the emotions of our self, how we're attached to our self, and how the human psyche can be altered through different practices, like meditation. These traditions have recognized the importance of using our mind and our brain to help us achieve spiritual enlightenment. In fact, a quote attributed to Buddha states that: "All wrong-doing arises because of mind. If the mind is transformed can wrong-doing remain?" Clearly, Buddha is recognizing the importance of the mind and how it drives our spiritually and our behavior. Similarly, in this course we're going to evaluate the many ways in which the brain helps us to be spiritual, and how it guides us and shapes our religious and spiritual traditions.

Also, in that same area of the world as we look at the Hindu tradition, Ayurvedic medical practices were developed in India with an emphasis on the body's energy. According to this tradition, the brain, body, and spirit are all intimately interconnected by an energy or a force that's called Qi. Even Ayurvedic medicine long ago incorporated a concept that we'll be exploring with the tools of modern science; namely, the concept that the material brain is deeply connected to the spiritual experiences of the mind.

As we look at the Western traditions—the monotheistic traditions of Christianity, Judaism, Islam—we see that even though they may not have directly looked at the relationship between the brain and spirituality, that there was a great deal of interest into how the human person works. The Bible really speaks very little, again, about exactly what's going on in the brain and how that brain is related to our sense of spirituality, but the Bible does give us a lot of information about how to act as human beings. It teaches us about our frailties, about morality, about the evil actions that we might do to other people, and therefore it signifies a very deep interest in human psychology. If you think about the 10 Commandments for a moment, this is basically a treatise on moral psychology. They specify what we're to think and how we're to behave as human beings. But we must also remember that it's the brain that helps to make these moral guidelines intelligible to us. More than this, it's the brain that drives us to behave in the ways that we do, either to satisfy or violate these particular guidelines.

In a sense, the moral psychology of the Bible leads us to a topic that will be central to some of the later lectures of this course: We'll see how the capabilities and the limitations of the human brain relate to our spiritual and moral beliefs, and the behaviors that ultimately grow out of those beliefs.

Of course, questions about the relationship between body, soul, brain, and mind have been central to Western philosophical tradition. From Descartes to Baruch Spinoza to Immanuel Kant, we've always wondered whether there was something inherent within us—something inherent within the human mind—that allowed it access to ultimate reality. People have argued for centuries about how we can have knowledge of ultimate reality, recognizing that such knowledge is the key to understanding the nature of the universe. This, to me, is one of humanity's ultimate goals, to explore and understand how the universe works; and we must realize the critical role our mind plays in achieving this understanding.

It actually reminds me of the story of the two monks who were looking up at the temple flag waving in the wind and one of the monks said, "Look at the flag and see how the flag is moving," and the other monk said, "No, no, no, it's not the flag that's moving, it's the wind that's moving." They debated about this back and forth for many hours, and finally Queen Eng, who was their spiritual leader, came to them and said, "Gentlemen, it's not the flag that moves, and it's not the wind that moves, it's your mind that moves."

This is the purpose of this course: to understand how and why the mind moves human beings to be spiritual, to contemplate God, and to develop and follow our religious traditions. But just like the monks, we can wonder what creates what: Does the brain create God or does God create the brain? Are we biological beings who are spiritual or spiritual beings who are biological? Of course, this relates to the story of the monks, who were debating about what causes what to happen and how we can understand the true nature of our reality.

As we saw in the study with the Franciscan nuns, science is giving us new techniques to address these great questions of human life; questions relating to God and the soul and the nature of belief. This research is just beginning to shed light on the questions regarding the relationship between the brain and human spirituality. We're certainly not the first to consider such questions, but now we can turn to biology and neuroscience to gain a new perspective on some of these very ancient questions. We can consider the brain's many functions and processes in terms of how they relate to spirituality. Just like the monks, we can explore what is inside of us, inside of our brains, that's actually moving us to be spiritual

So let us begin our journey into the spiritual brain. I hope that you will find it as challenging and as exciting as I do.

Why Do We Have a Spiritual Brain?
Lecture 2

I t is undeniable that many people classify certain feelings and experiences as "spiritual." People talk about feeling God's presence or experiencing a peace that goes beyond any physical explanation. However, do these spiritual experiences—or these perceptions of spiritual experience—have a purpose? Do they exist because they do some good for the individual or even for the species as a whole? Why do we have a brain that is capable of spirituality? Many great philosophers and theologians have pondered these questions from a religious or spiritual perspective, but in this lecture, you will consider them from a neuroscientific and evolutionary perspective as well.

Defining Religion and Spirituality

- Historically, many thinkers have tried to define the essence of religion and spirituality. German theologian Friedrich Schleiermacher (1768–1834) placed an emphasis on religion to a more cognitive, visceral, or intuitive sense—"a feeling of absolute dependence." Rudolf Otto's *The Idea of the Holy* (1917) defined the essence of religious awareness as awe that is a mixture of fear and fascination.

- In the past several decades, the meaning and purpose of religion has become a subject not only for theologians like Schleiermacher and Otto, but for scientists as well.

- In the early 1970s, research psychiatrist Eugene d'Aquili began to look at spirituality. He wanted to try to find how brain functions—which appear to have evolved over time—were related to the development of human spirituality.

- In the 1990s, scientist James Austin wrote a book called *Zen and the Brain*. In it, Austin explored how brain functions, particularly those associated with neurotransmitters, were related to meditation practices.

- More recently, scientists have developed improved methodologies for studying the brain, and these methodologies have opened a multitude of avenues for exploring the neurological and physiological aspects of spirituality.

- As scientists explore these new frontiers, they need definitions for the terms "spirituality" and "religion"—just as Schleiermacher and Otto did. However, as they look for definitions that will work for them, scientists are confronted with an interesting issue—one that's probably not as critical to theologians and philosophers.

- Scientists have to define these terms in such a way that the definitions are experimentally useful. In other words, they must develop operational definitions of both religion and spirituality. The definition of spirituality as simply the human experience of the soul is too vague and too difficult to ever apply any kind of scientific analysis to.

- Scientists have to avoid narrow definitions of these terms that might impede research. In addition, they have to avoid broad definitions that cannot be measured and develop appropriate measurement tools.

- Spirituality can be defined as the subjective feelings, thoughts, experiences, and behaviors that arise from a search or quest for the sacred.

- In this definition, the term "search" refers to attempts to identify, articulate, maintain, or transform. Think about how you may have engaged in this search throughout your life. How have you identified yourself from a spiritual perspective? Do you agree with the notion that spirituality is a search?

- In addition, the term "sacred" refers to what the individual perceives as a divine being, ultimate reality, or ultimate truth. For most people in the United States, the sacred relates to God in the Judeo-Christian tradition, but there are many ideas about what is sacred.

- Religiousness can be defined as the search for sacred goals or for nonsacred goals—such as identity, belonging, meaning, or health—in the context of spiritual criteria. The means and methods of the search receive general validation and support from within an identifiable group of people.

- With these operational definitions in mind, consider why humans have a spiritual brain. To put it another way, why do we have a brain that is so strongly disposed to search for sacred objects and goals, such as God or ultimate truth? There are several main ways of approaching this question, including from evolutionary, neuroscientific, and religious standpoints.

Evolutionary Reasons for a Spiritual Brain

- Several evolutionary scientists have argued that religion is adaptive. The argument is that given certain adaptive aspects of religion, the brain continued to evolve in order to maintain these elements that were ultimately expressed in religious or spiritual concepts. In particular, there is a correlation between the evolutionary development of the human brain and religious and spiritual activity.

- By exploring the shape and size of the skull of different species, scientists can determine the size of different parts of the brain. The first evidence of religious activity appears in Neanderthals, who lived 70,000 to 100,000 years ago. Neanderthals had a much larger brain than prior human ancestors; particularly, the cortex, or the outer part of the brain, was responsible for much of the higher thought processes.

- The existence of a larger brain coincided with the beginning of burials involving tools, flowers, or painting on the body. We don't know the real meaning of these burials, and we also don't know if brain size is the same as brain complexity.

- Cro-Magnon, the precursor to modern *Homo sapiens*, had a larger overall brain size, but size does not necessarily relate to complexity—even though there usually is a relationship. Given the size of the Cro-Magnon brain being similar to modern human beings, it would be interesting to see how they may have expressed spiritual beliefs.

- There are several lines of evidence that Cro-Magnon did have spiritual beliefs. In ancient caves, they painted figures of animals that appeared to be killed during the hunt. Perhaps this was related to the notion that if they envisioned a certain future outcome—a successful hunt, for example—that it would come true.

- Cro-Magnon also made the first sculptures, or figurines, which were usually in the shape of a fertile female. The implication is that this is the first evidence of worshiping a female or fertility god.

- Religious and spiritual phenomena are highly complex—involving emotions, thoughts, perceptions, and behaviors—so they probably require a highly complex brain.

- The emergence of spirituality seems to have coincided with an increase in brain size. From an evolutionary standpoint, this is quite intriguing. What survival value might religion have? Did spirituality give our ancestors some evolutionary edge? Was it in some ways adaptive? Some evolutionary theorists think so.

- Religion fosters social cohesion. One line of evidence for the link between religion and social cohesion is historical. For example, the temple at Göbekli Tepe suggests that religious beliefs preceded social structure.

- Many anthropologists have pointed out that no civilization has arisen without religion. From Mesopotamia, to Egypt, to Greece, to Easter Island, different spiritual beliefs have always existed.

- Religions also create a set of morals and laws that can be followed by a society. For example, the Ten Commandments of the Bible provide many rules by which to live.

- Religion also provides a basis for authority. Most leaders, especially historically, were considered to be descended from God or given leadership by divine process. This is the case in ancient Egypt, where the Pharaohs were essentially considered to be gods. In fact, Julius Caesar took on the name "Divine Julius," and the Dalai Lama is supposedly the reincarnation of the Amitabha buddha.

- Furthermore, most moral codes ask people to respect authority, including parents and elders, such as what is written in the Bible. These processes help to create a cohesive society. In addition, religious rituals are social activities that bind people together; they provide a sense of control and comfort.

Historically, many rulers were viewed as dieties, including celebrated Roman ruler Julius Caesar.

- The argument is that our evolutionary ancestors lived in a very dangerous and capricious world with death always lurking around the corner. Religion may have evolved as a way of providing them with an answer to the finality of death and also as a way of providing our species with a sense of control.

- Sometimes this control is real. For agrarian societies, the earth and seasons were part of religious beliefs and activities. Thus, many ancient cultures used the fertile earth mother or earth goddess as a religious figure.

- Sometimes the sense of control is perceived, but it still settles the mind in order to have the person do what they need to in order to survive. According to some evolutionary theorists, this ultimately led to more successful survival.

Neuroscientific Reasons for a Spiritual Brain

- A neuroscientific explanation for our spiritual brains can also be considered to be an evolutionary argument, but it is based more on how the brain has come to work.

- If the brain develops to solve important survival questions such as how to develop crops and domesticate animals, it can also comprehend big philosophical questions about the nature of reality and existence and the meaning of human life. The brain will also begin to consider religious and spiritual answers to these questions.

- In this way, religion itself is not adaptive, but it is the natural consequence of the neurobiology that arose for adaptive purposes. This is referred to as an epiphenomenon.

Religious Reasons for a Spiritual Brain

- In addition to the evolutionary and neuroscientific explanations for why we have a spiritual brain, there is also the religious argument, which simply points out that if a God exists, it would make sense that the human brain would be designed to comprehend God.

- No matter how we look at the reason for having a spiritual brain, one conclusion seems clear: The brain appears to be built in such a way that it has an inherent tendency to search for sacred goals and objects. Furthermore, this tendency enables us to have a large range of religious and spiritual experiences.

- Even though we may not be able to ever fully explain why spirituality or religion is built into the brain, the good news is that the fact that we do have spiritual tendencies provides us with many great topics and issues to explore as we continue our journey to understand the spiritual brain.

Suggested Reading

Beauregard and O'Leary, *The Spiritual Brain.*

Boyer, *Religion Explained.*

Dennett, *Breaking the Spell.*

Newberg and d'Aquili, *Why God Won't Go Away.*

Wilson, *Darwin's Cathedral.*

Questions to Consider

1. How have religious and spiritual beliefs become part of the function of the human brain?

2. Is the reason for having a spiritual brain based upon evolution, neuroscience, or religion?

Why Do We Have a Spiritual Brain?

Lecture 2—Transcript

In the first lecture, we discussed the universality of spirituality and religion. But if people have perceived the reality of spiritual phenomena throughout the course of human history, and if this perception has an important connection to the brain, then one of the first questions that I think is raised is: "Why do we have a spiritual brain in the first place?"

It's undeniable that many people classify certain feelings and experiences as "spiritual"; people talk about feeling God's presence or experiencing a peace that goes beyond any kind of physical explanation. But do these spiritual experiences—or these perceptions of spiritual experience—have a purpose? Are they there because they do something good for us, either on an individual level or even for the species as a whole?

These are not merely rhetorical questions; after all, some scholars have questioned whether spirituality is a good thing, especially when religions are often the cause of some great hatred and violence. In fact, the noted evolutionary biologist Richard Dawkins even went so far as to say (and I quote): "Faith can be very, very dangerous, and deliberately to implant it into the … mind of an innocent child is a grievous wrong."

So I don't think we can take spirituality for granted. We really need to ask ourselves: Why do we have a brain capable of spirituality? Of course, many great philosophers and theologians have pondered this from a religious or spiritual perspective; but today, we're going to think about it from a new perspective: We're going to look at it from a neuroscientific and an evolutionary perspective as well.

But before we launch our scientific exploration, we probably should define some terms at first. After all, if we want to understand why we have a spiritual brain, we really need to define what we mean by "spiritual" in the first place. Take a moment to think about these questions: How would you define "religiousness?" How would you define "spirituality?" One of my favorite exercises to do with my classes that I teach on this topic is to spend much of the very first class asking those two questions. I'll even go up onto the board and write up "religiousness" and "spirituality" and throw it out there: What do they think? It's fascinating, because in all of the years that I've been doing this, I don't think we've ever gotten to the same two definitions for both of them. It's fascinating to think about what people actually are thinking about and how they define the terms "spirituality" and "religiousness."

As a neuroscientist, one of the questions that has greatly intrigued me is that people are capable of having so many different kinds of experiences, even though some of them ultimately fall into this realm that they call "spiritual." Some people might look at a beautiful sunset or have a deep feeling of love, or maybe even a mystical experience; a mystical union with God. But there seems to be something fundamentally different about a spiritual experience as compared to our everyday kinds of experiences. They're spiritual; but what about spiritual experiences actually makes them spiritual? Of course, the same question can be applied to religious experiences; in fact, we can even expand the question to: Is there a difference between a spiritual experience and a religious experience? Some people think there is, and other people think there isn't.

Historically, as I mentioned, many people have grappled with these questions—many scholars have thought about this—and have tried to define the essence of what religiousness or spirituality is all about. Friedrich Schleiermacher, in the 18th century, talked about an emphasis of religion on a more cognitive, visceral, or even intuitive level. He actually defined religiousness as "a feeling of absolute dependence." William James, at the turn of the last century, wrote a book called *Varieties of Religious Experience*, in which he considered different forms that religion takes in terms of human experience itself. He actually defined normal experiences, abnormal experiences, and a vast array of different kinds of experiences that people refer to as "religious." In 1917, a book came out called *The Idea of the Holy*, written by Rudolf Otto. He defined the essence of religious awareness as a feeling of awe, which was a mixture of fear and fascination; what he called the *mysterium tremendum et fascinans*.

We were starting to see the beginnings of a kind of experience that has to do with our emotions, our thoughts, and our experiences, which can lead us towards an analysis of these experiences from a neuroscientific perspective. In fact, this led my late colleague and mentor, Doctor Eugene d'Aquili, to begin to explore these issues as early as the 1970s. He approached spirituality and religiousness from both an anthropological perspective as well as a neuroscientific one. He wanted to try and find out where in the brain and which brain functions appear to have evolved over time that were related to the development of human spirituality and religiousness over time . In fact, his work laid some of the important foundations for the development of the entire field studying spirituality and the brain.

Another scholar in the 1990s, named James Ashbrook, wrote a book called *The Humanizing Brain*. In this book, he takes a more Christian perspective in describing how religion maps onto some very basic brain processes. James Austin wrote a book called *Zen and the Brain*, and in this book he talks about how the brain functions in great detail, particularly as it functions in the contexts of meditative practices. He looks at some of the brain scan studies, some of the information about the different chemicals in the brain called neurotransmitters, to talk about how they might actually relate to meditation practices.

More recently, we've developed improved methodologies for studying the brain, and this allows us, in a way that we were never able to do, to be able to look at the nature of spiritual experiences. These brain scans provide us a window into the nature of the spiritual brain. In today's world, we clearly have a multitude of avenues to explore in the future as we consider throughout this course where spirituality and the human brain intersect.

As scientists take a look at these various attempts to define spirituality and religion, we're confronted with an interesting problem. The problem is perhaps not so much critical to theologians and philosophers, but to scientists in particular who want to find a way of measuring something that we can call "religious" or "spiritual." With that in mind, scientists have to define these terms in a way that we can, in fact, study; therefore we have to develop something called an operational definition of religiousness and spirituality. In other words, we need to have a definition that we can grasp onto in some scientific way. After all, if spirituality is only defined only as the human experience of the soul, for example, that's really too vague and too immaterial to ever be able to apply some kind of scientific analysis to. We need some way of trying to get a hold of what religiousness and spirituality are so that we actually can measure them in some kind of reasonable way that gives us information that will be useful in helping us understand the nature of the spiritual brain.

I was very fortunate that about 15 years ago I was part of a consensus conference that brought together about 80 researchers from across the country. It was a very exciting conference; the goal of this was to look at the relationship between spirituality and health. But, of course, as I was talking about, the scientists realized right away that we needed to know what exactly we were talking about in the first place. What did we mean when we said spirituality? What did we mean when we talked about religiousness? We had to figure that out before we could move forward in trying to understand the nature and the relationship between religion, spirituality, and human health.

The group finally settled on several definitions that I'm going to talk to you about in a few moments, and I want to be clear that I'm going to provide these as an example, not because they're necessarily the best or even the most accurate, but they are an excellent way of trying to operationalize the definitions. But some of the things that we struggled with were how broadly should we define these terms, and how narrowly should we define these terms? We thought about different groups of people, and we thought about whether or not they'd fit into our definitions.

Let me give you an example of what I mean by this: If we keep a very narrow definition of religiousness or spirituality, that might be good because we can really hone in on what it is; but let's say the narrow definition says that religion is only about a God. What do you do with the billion or so people who are Buddhist, who don't have the same conception of God as we may have in a Jewish or Christian kind of context? Then we thought, "Let's make this more broad because we want to be inclusive; we want to bring everybody into these discussions, to be able to do research with." But the problem with having too broad of a definition is that you might begin to include things in religiousness or spirituality that aren't really meant to be included. My favorite example is one of my best friends from Philadelphia who claims that his religion is the Philadelphia Eagles. Unfortunately it's a little bit of a depressing religion, but nonetheless I think you get the point that if we keep our definitions too broad, we might wind up including things that aren't really true religions or true spiritual ideas or experiences.

These scientists worked for a while to try to figure out what the best definition would be, and they came to the idea of setting up some criteria for what spirituality was. They described spirituality as the subjective feelings, thoughts, experiences, and behaviors that arise from a search or a quest for the sacred. A "search" referred to the attempts to identify, articulate, maintain, or transform. What they meant by this is it had to do with how you incorporated this search into your life. In fact, think about how you may have engaged in this type of search throughout your life. How did you ask questions? Did you identify yourself with a particular spiritual perspective? Do you even agree with the notion that spirituality is a search? But for the definition, they felt that this was a useful way of talking about the process of what spirituality was.

They also defined "sacred" in very broad terms, and they said that "sacred" referred to whatever the individual perceives as a divine being, ultimate reality, or ultimate truth. For most people in the United States, of course, the sacred relates to God in the Judeo-Christian tradition; but there are many ideas about what's sacred. In fact, spend a few moments and think about what's sacred to you, and whether it relates to something spiritual or perhaps an emotion. The other reason that I liked this particular definition of spirituality is it focused on the thoughts, the feelings, and experiences that people have. Those are things that we can relate to how the brain works. We can see in the brain where our emotions are, where our thought processes are, and where our experiences are; and we'll be spending a lot more detailed time on this in our future lectures. But I like these definitions because it gives us at least a starting point to be able to engage in our neuroscientific investigation of religion and spirituality.

Now that we have an operational definition for spirituality, what about religiousness? These scientists defined religiousness as referring to a search for sacred goals as well as non-sacred goals, but typically in the context of a group of people who identify with that particular approach. Non-sacred goals would include things such as identity, belonging, or perhaps meaning in life or even health. I think a very interesting example in the context of this definition is Judaism, because clearly there are people who are Jewish who have a very deep sense of spirituality and religiousness. If you look at the Orthodox Jews, their entire life is spent praying, meditating, and believing in God and the tenets of the religious tradition. But in the United States, we find a lot of people who refer to themselves as "cultural Jews." They're religious in the sense that they're in search of non-sacred goals, in the context of belonging to a community, belonging to a society, doing charitable works; and in this sense, it's a part of their religiousness even though it may not necessarily be something that's deeply spiritual to them.

One of the things that typically define religion is that the means and the methods of the search receive some kind of general validation and support from an identifiable group of people. This tends to be a very important element of religiousness that can help differentiate religions from, for example, cults, where even though it may be a very small group that will identify their particular belief system, it may not generally be accepted by others. But, again, cults wind up being a very interesting problem in terms of where do we put them in the context of these definitions?

As I mentioned, these definitions are by no means the only or even the best definitions of spirituality and religiousness, and I certainly would suggest that you think about this after the lecture: Talk about it with people; ask them what their definitions of spirituality and religiousness are; write it down; come up with arguments for and against different ways of defining these terms. But from a scientific standpoint, I think the definitions that we just reviewed will at least provide a helpful reference point as we go forward. So when I talk about analyzing spirituality or studying religiousness from a scientific perspective, these are the definitions that we'll at least start with. I will add one other little twist to this: Almost all the definitions that we have today are most likely going to change as we go into the future and learn new kinds of information from the research that we do.

Now that we have a good operational definition of spirituality, let's turn to the primary question of this lecture: Why do humans engage in this search for the sacred? Why are there certain subjective feelings, thoughts, experiences, and behaviors associated with this search? In short, why do humans have a spiritual brain? There are several primary ways of approaching this question. There's an evolutionary approach, a neuroscientific approach, and a religious approach, at least for starters. Let's spend some time talking about religion as an evolutionary adaptation.

There are a number of evolutionary scientists who've argued that religion is, in fact, adaptive. The argument is that given certain adaptive aspects of religion, the brain continued to evolve in order to maintain these elements; that these were ultimately expressed in religious or spiritual concepts, and that's why religion and spirituality became such an intimate part of human life, behavior, and ultimately our biology.

If we look at the correlation between the evolutionary development of the human brain and religious and spiritual activity, we see some interesting things starting to occur. We can actually infer the size and complexity of the human brain by looking at the size of the skull of different species that were part of our evolutionary ladder. In fact, we can determine to some degree the size of different parts of the brain as well, although this doesn't necessarily coincide with the complexity of the inner connections there.

The first evidence of religious activity—as we talked about in the last lecture—seems to appear about 70–100,000 years ago in the Neanderthal burials. As I mentioned, we see the idea that these Neanderthals were burying the dead with some notion that there may be an afterlife, and it's also interesting that Neanderthals had a much larger brain than many of the prior human ancestors. This is particularly true in terms of the cortex or the outer part of the brain; the part of our brain that we normally think of as the human part of the brain: the different folds that form around the outer part of how our brain actually functions and is structured. This part of the brain is responsible for much of our higher thought processes, and it's interesting that we see the development of this higher part of the brain coinciding with the beginning of these burials. There seems to be some evidence to support that as the brain got bigger, especially in the cortical areas, that we started to see the evolution of human spirituality and religion.

Of course, there are some problems with this analysis: We don't know for sure what the meaning of the burials is all about; we don't know exactly whether or not they truly believed in God or in something beyond the life that was here; and, of course, we also don't know if the size of that brain and the size of the structures are actually related to the complexity and the ability to function at a certain level. In fact, one of the precursor species to the modern Homo sapiens, called Cro-Magnon, had an actual larger brain size, skull size, than modern-day humans. Size may be very important, but it doesn't necessarily relate to the complexity, and particularly the functional capacity, of what the brain can do.

On the other hand, given the size of the Cro-Magnon brain being so similar to modern human beings, it would certainly be interesting to see how they may have expressed spiritual beliefs; and there are several lines of evidence that the Cro-Magnon people did have spiritual beliefs. In fact, it's in the ancient cave paintings that we talked about before where we see animals that appeared to be killed during the hunt and other types of interesting figures and pictures that may have had a religious basis to them. The idea that they were drawing pictures of the hunt may have actually been related to the notion that they envisioned a certain future outcome, and that perhaps it would come true by drawing these pictures. The Cro-Magnon also made the first sculptures or figurines that were in the shape of a fertile female. This image, this symbol, is believed to be one of the very earliest types of religious or spiritual symbols for us as human beings because the idea is that they're worshiping a female or fertility god that's going to help them bear children and help them create a fertile agricultural environment so that they can grow the crops and have sufficient food for them. But religious and spiritual phenomena are highly complex and involve many different emotions, thoughts, perceptions, and behaviors, so they probably require a highly complex brain.

What makes religiousness and spirituality adaptive? It certainly appears that the emergence of spirituality coincided with the increase in the brain size; and from an evolutionary perspective, this is very intriguing because we can ask: Why did this get in there? What was the actual survival value that religiousness or spirituality would have? Did spirituality give our ancient ancestors some kind of evolutionary edge? Was it in some way adaptive? Of course, a lot of evolutionary theorists actually think so.

One of the arguments has been that religion fosters social cohesion. It brings people together; it creates a cohesive society; and there are several lines of evidence to support this. One is historical; and, for example, as we saw in our first lecture, at the temple at Gobekli Tepe suggests that religious beliefs actually preceded social structure. Religiousness preceded the ability to form agrarian societies and to settle down into cities, towns, and civilizations. From Mesopotamia, to Egypt, to Greece, to Easter Island, we almost always see some kind of spiritual belief that's part of the development of that particular civilization.

If we look at what religions do, religions also create a set of morals and laws that are followed by a society: The 10 Commandments of the Bible provide many rules by which to live. Religion also provides a certain basis for authority. This is an interesting issue because one of the questions that I think always comes up is: Why do we follow a leader? Why do we follow a pharaoh, a king? Most leaders, especially historically, considered themselves to be either gods themselves or descended from God, and that was what gave them the right to lead over the people. This is certainly the case in ancient Egypt, in which the Pharaohs were essentially considered to be gods; Julius Caesar actually took on the name "Divine Julius"; and even in today's world, the Dalai Lama is supposedly the reincarnation of the Buddha. The notion is that the people who are our leaders are given that authority by God and in so doing create a cohesive hierarchy of the structure of our society. In addition, most moral codes ask for respect of that authority and also respect of our parents and our elders, which is certainly what we see in the Bible as well as many other sacred texts. All of these processes come together to create a cohesive society; and we know that the more we can form a society that's close, and isn't fighting with each other, and is working together, we can function more effectively and create an environment where we can grow, develop, have more children, and live out our lives.

Interestingly, a lot of religious rituals also help to bind and bring people together. In all of these different societies throughout time as well as today, these rituals helped to create a sense of socialization and a group environment of everybody working together. Other people have postulated that religiousness and spirituality provides a sense of control and comfort. The argument is that our evolutionary ancestors lived in a very dangerous and a very capricious world—death was always lurking around the corner for them—so religion may have evolved as a way of providing them with some kind of answer to the finality of their death and perhaps some kind of sense of control over the environment.

Sometimes this control was very real: For example, in agrarian societies, where they were dependent on the earth, the rain, and the whole cycle of the seasons for their sustenance, they frequently had the sense of a fertile Earth Mother or Earth Goddess as a primary figure in their religious tradition; and by creating a religious tradition that enabled them to plant seeds, grow their crops, and harvest at certain times, these different rituals literally gave them control over their environment so that they could actually live their lives as effectively as possible. Sometimes this control is just perceived, but still makes the person feel a little bit better. Maybe it's just the notion that "If I talk to God, I'll feel a little bit better about my situation"; maybe it doesn't really help, but people feel better psychologically and that ultimately quells a lot of their stressors, it makes their body function better, it makes their brain function better, and that's something that can be of benefit in order to keep them alive and to help them survive.

According to a variety of different evolutionary theorists, all of these different forces come together to help to create an adaptive advantage in those people who are religious or spiritual. This leads to more successful survival, and this ultimately incorporates these kinds of belief systems into the brain itself.

Speaking of the brain, we've been talking primarily about evolutionary explanations about why humans have a spiritual brain; but let's think about this a little bit more from a neuroscientific perspective. This can also be considered an evolutionary argument of sorts, but it's based more on how the brain has come to work, not so much the different societal and cultural impacts of these particular processes. If the brain has developed in such a way to solve important survival questions such as how to develop crops, domesticate animals, and so forth—even moral questions that we have to deal with in order to work with each other—then the brain also can comprehend these big philosophical questions about the nature of reality, the nature of existence, and the meaning of human life.

The brain will also begin to consider religious and spiritual answers to these questions. In this way, religion itself is not adaptive per se, but it's the natural consequence of our neurobiology doing the things that it normally does anyway. This is referred to as an epiphenomenon; and, again, if we think about, for example, our original definition of the searching brain, if our brain is developed simply to search so that we can find answers to problems, that we can find ways of creating ways of growing crops and working together, then the ability to do all of this is part of what led us to begin to think about these questions. We didn't think about the questions to create the search, but because we have the search we developed our religious and spiritual ideas around that search.

In addition to the evolutionary and the neuroscientific explanations for why we have a spiritual brain, there's, of course, the religious argument. The religious argument simply points out that if God exists—if there's a God up in Heaven somewhere and we have to as human beings interact with God— then it would be kind of fundamentally silly to not have a brain inside of us that would be able to interact with God and comprehend God.

No matter how we look at the reason for having a spiritual brain, one conclusion seems clear: The brain appears to be built in such a way that it enables us to have a large range of different religious and spiritual experiences. How and why it got that way, we may never know for sure; but it's certainly interesting to try to speculate as to why we have a spiritual brain.

What do you think makes the most sense? What questions might you raise that would challenge each of the arguments for why we have a spiritual brain? The good news is that even though we may not be able to ever fully explain why we have spirituality or religion built into the brain, the fact that we do provides us with many great topics and issues to explore as we continue our journey to understand the spiritual brain.

Brain Function and Religion
Lecture 3

The brain has many different functions, and many of those functions relate to a particular aspect of religion or spirituality. You have to understand where the brain comes from, what it does, and how it works before you can understand what the spiritual brain is all about. In this lecture, you will learn about the brain's basic functions and processes, and you will consider how many of the latest scientific techniques can be used to help study the spiritual brain.

The Brain versus the Mind

- Generally, we think of the brain as the biological structure that is inside our heads. This includes the neurons, neurotransmitters, and electrical connections in the brain. This also includes the connections of the brain to the sensory organs and to the rest of the body.

- Alternatively, we tend to think of the mind as the thoughts, feelings, and experiences we have, but these intangible qualities of the mind must be connected somehow to the biological stuff of the brain.

- Up to the present time, science has not been able to determine exactly where our thoughts and consciousness reside. Are they equivalent to the biological processes, intimately bound to the biological processes, or something completely different?

- Many thinkers have created a dualistic understanding of the mind and brain. For example, Saint Thomas Aquinas referred to the *actus hominis* and the *actus humanus* in differentiating the biological from the intellectual. In addition, René Descartes is famous for creating a dualistic approach to the mind and brain, keeping them in separate domains.

Brain Systems

- If you think about your body and how it works in the context of the brain, there need to be "on" and "off" switches for the body. The "on" switch is typically supplied by the autonomic nervous system, which works automatically.

- The autonomic nervous system is typically regarded as being comprised of two fundamental parts. One of them is the arousal part; in scientific terms, it is called the sympathetic nervous system. The arousal system turns on when something of motivational importance happens in our environment that we need to react to.

- The "off" switch is related to the part of the autonomic nervous system called the parasympathetic nervous system, or the quiescent nervous system, which calms us down.

- To some degree, the arousal system expends energy—to flee or to fight, for example—and the quiescent side enables us to rejuvenate our energy stores.

- Normally, these two systems mutually inhibit each other. In other words, one of the systems of the autonomic nervous system turns on while the other one turns off. However, sometimes, they can mutually excite each other.

- Mutual excitation is important in regard to some very important spiritual experiences that seem to invoke two different kinds of responses: On one hand, they seem to invoke a very powerful calming response—a feeling of blissfulness—but on the other hand, these profound spiritual states are incredibly arousing and alerting.

- The autonomic nervous system ultimately connects the brain and the body. The regulation of that connection takes place in a part of the brain called the limbic system, which may be thought of as the primary emotional controller of the brain.

- The limbic system is comprised of several different structures that enable us to have different emotional responses. The amygdala functions as a watchdog in the brain. It turns on when anything of emotional importance—positive or negative—occurs in our environment.

- If you are engaged in a religious or spiritual practice in which something important is about to happen, perhaps it can be observed that the amygdala will turn on in response.

- Another structure of the limbic system is the hippocampus, which is located behind the amygdala and is kind of a diplomat of the brain. It helps to regulate our emotional responses so that we don't become too extreme in one way or another. The hippocampus helps to write memories into the brain.

- In regard to religion and spirituality, it is important that our memory is related to our emotions. When we think about what we remember and how we remember it and incorporate it into our lives, the limbic system is very important for making religious and spiritual beliefs a part of who we are as human beings.

- Another important structure that is located in the limbic system is the hypothalamus, which is one of the most central structures of the brain and, in many ways, is the master controller of almost every different body function. The hypothalamus regulates our hormone system, so it's very crucial in regulating how our body reacts to the world and to the brain. In fact, the hypothalamus controls which parts of the autonomic nervous system are turned on or off.

- If we think about the nature of religious and spiritual experiences as not only affecting us emotionally, but also as having an effect on the body itself, we can see how the hypothalamus may be a key regulator in translating the information that we're feeling and thinking about in the higher parts of the brain to the rest of the body.

Association Areas of the Brain
- The brain is divided into four basic lobes: the occipital lobe in the back of the brain, the frontal lobe in the front part of the brain,

the temporal lobe along the side of the brain, and the parietal lobe toward the back top part of the brain.

- The brain receives millions of pieces of information and ultimately tries to create a very coherent rendition of what our world is all about. The brain takes what we see, hear, taste, and smell and puts all of that together, making a picture of the world.

- In the visual system, light initially comes in through our eyes and travels to the occipital lobe. In this lobe, instead of perceiving pictures, we see lines, shapes, and colors. Different association areas take information from many different neurons and begin to construct a vivid picture of what the world is all about. Then, these association areas connect with other association areas to attribute a memory to what we see.

- The verbal-conceptual area is located between two of the larger lobes of the brain—the temporal lobe and the parietal lobe. The verbal-conceptual area helps us with language, concepts, and abstract ideas.

- The frontal lobe is also an association area that is sometimes referred to as the attention area. Many brain-scan studies have shown that when we focus our attention on a particular task, the attention area is what turns on. It helps coordinate our thought processes and physical behaviors by linking what we're thinking about with what our body and brain are doing.

- Located in the parietal lobe, the orientation area takes all of our sensory information and helps to orient ourselves in the world.

- This area is relevant to religious or spiritual experiences because when people pray, they often lose their sense of self and feel a sense of spacelessness and timelessness. If that's the case, then perhaps there is something going on in the orientation area that is changing the way they think about themselves.

Complex Cognitive Functions of the Brain

- The quantitative function of the brain helps us with numbers, which abound throughout sacred texts. Numbers are given meaning and importance by the quantitative function of the brain.

- The part of the brain that helps us with binary thinking is important because binary processes set aside opposites for us. In terms of religion and spirituality, binary concepts such as what's right or wrong are set by the binary processes of the brain.

- The causal functioning part of the brain is activated when we think about and see causes and effects in the world. In the context of religious or spiritual ideas, we might think about God as causing the universe to come into existence or causing the universe to exist all the time.

- There is also an existential function in the brain that tells us when something is real and exists. This becomes important when considering the nature and experience of human reality.

- The reductionistic function breaks things down, and the holistic function binds everything together. When people have mystical experiences, they describe a sense of oneness, which might involve this holistic function.

- The abstract function in the brain allows us to think about things abstractly, and this is very crucial for all of the philosophical, religious, and theological ideas that we hold.

Measuring the Brain

- Over the past several decades, neuroscientists have developed amazing tools for peering into the brain, and these tools are starting to be used to study the spiritual brain.

- Subjective measures refer to asking people how they feel, what they think about, and how they understand the experiences that they have. Physiological measures refer to measuring changes in electrical activity in the brain—called electroencephalography—or using different neuroimaging studies to look at activity levels in the brain, or the amount of chemicals in the brain.

- There are many different ways to subjectively measure the brain, including taking psychological inventories, measuring a person's memory, and determining a person's cognitive status. A variety of spiritual scales exist as well.

- Physiologically, what's going on in the brain and what's going on in the body can be analyzed. In terms of autonomic function, heart rate and blood pressure can be measured, and by drawing blood, changes in the immune system and in hormones can be measured. All of these things are important ways of trying to help us establish the link between our spiritual and biological selves.

- Furthermore, there are a few ways to specifically look at the brain. Electroencephalography, which measures the electrical activity in the brain, is a good technique for looking at what's going on from moment to moment, but it doesn't give an accurate determination of where something is happening in the brain. Imaging studies offer the ability to look at the brain structurally or anatomically as well as functionally.

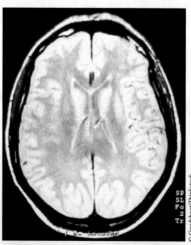
© Goodshoot/Thinkstock.

- Functional imaging—which usually uses magnetic resonance imaging (MRI), positron emission tomography (PET), or single-photon emission computed tomography (SPECT)—involves ways

Researchers have compared the brain scans of religious people to those of nonreligious people.

of looking at the activity levels in the brain. All of these are very important for helping us to assess what spirituality is and how it affects the brain and, ultimately, the body.

Suggested Reading

Austin, *Zen and the Brain.*

Benson, *Timeless Healing.*

Newberg and Iversen, "The Neural Basis of the Complex Mental Task of Meditation."

Newberg and Waldman, *Why We Believe What We Believe.*

Questions to Consider

1. How does the brain work to enable human beings to have religious and spiritual beliefs and experiences?

2. How do each of the different parts of the brain—such as the hypothalamus, limbic system, and cortex—contribute to religious and spiritual phenomena?

Brain Function and Religion

Lecture 3—Transcript

The average human brain weighs about three and a half pounds. It's roughly the size of a large head of cauliflower, and resembles the color and consistency of a generous blob of extra-firm tofu (which actually explains why I don't eat tofu anymore). This blob of matter is moored to the walls of our skull by a bunch of small ligaments and is protected by a thin layer of fluid that provides a cushion between the brain and the inner surface of the skull.

How is it possible that this rather bland-looking organ is the seat of everything we know to be human? The brain is capable of generating our most profound thoughts, our most intense emotions, and our most sacred beliefs. Yet, as neuroscience continues to explore the various parts of the brain that are active when we engage in these processes, we still have no real understanding of how the neurons and their connections ultimately create a thought or a sense of consciousness. In fact, there's been centuries of debate regarding the difference between the mind and the body; or in today's world, between the mind and the brain.

It's always difficult to determine what exactly is the relationship between what people usually refer to as the mind and what people refer to as the brain. Generally, we think of the brain as the biological structure that's inside of our head. This includes the different neurons and cells in the brain, the chemicals or neurotransmitters in the brain, and the various electrical connections that connect the brain parts to each other. We might add to that the connections of the brain to the sensory organs and even to the rest of the body, since the brain and the body are very intimately connected. The mind we tend to think of as the thoughts, the feelings, and the experiences that we have; but these intangible qualities of the mind must be connected somehow to the biological stuff that's in the brain itself.

At the moment, science has really not been able to determine where exactly our thoughts, our consciousness, our mind actually reside. Is the mind equivalent to the biological processes? Is it intimately bound to these biological processes, or is it something completely different altogether?

Many thinkers, scientists, philosophers, and theologians have created a dualistic understanding of the mind and brain. If we go back about 1,000 years, Thomas Aquinas, in his famous book *The Summa Theologica*, refers to the *actus hominis* and the *actus humanus* in differentiating the biological from the intellectual, the part that makes us human. René Descartes, the famous philosopher, is also famous for creating a very dualistic approach to the mind and brain, keeping them in very separate domains. In fact, his dualism was actually the approach that was taken by science up until the past several years; it really pervaded science for over 400 years, even up to the present day.

For the purposes of this course, we'll try to restrict ourselves to the first definitions that I offered. The brain will be thought of as the thing in our head, and the mind is going to be the intangible ideas and experiences. But the mind and brain must always be considered in a fully integrated way; after all, this is what this course is all about: integrating things that don't always go together. Certainly when we think about the mind and the brain, this will be our approach: to bring them together and to think about how they relate to each other.

Let's begin by considering the various functions of the brain. One of the things that I want to say right from the outset is that the brain does a huge number of things for us; there are so many different functions that it has. We're going to focus on some very specific ones, and particularly those that relate to religious and spiritual phenomena and experiences. If you hear me talking about a particular part of the brain and something that it does, we're going to try to relate that to a particular aspect of religion or spirituality even though that part of the brain may do a variety of other things as well.

The other approach that I like to take in terms of thinking about how the brain works is to imagine how I would build a brain if I was going to make one; so we can all pretend to be Doctor Frankenstein's for a moment. How would we put this together? I think we'd have to start from the bottom up; we'd have to think about how we can begin from the bodily parts that connect to our brain, all the way up to the central parts of our brain, and then ultimately to the higher processes of the brain to see how they all would work, how we'd want them to work together, and ultimately how these processes would relate to different aspects of spirituality that we're going to cover in much more detail in future lectures. I think that this discussion is going to be essential in terms of our future considerations of the spiritual brain. We all have to understand where the brain comes from, what it does, and how it works before we can understand what the spiritual brain is all about.

Let's start building our brain from the bottom up. To some degree, if we think about our body and how it's going to work in the context of the brain, there needs to be some kind of on and off switch for the body. This is typically supplied by something called the autonomic nervous system. It's called autonomic because it works very automatically for us, and it's typically regarded as being comprised of two fundamental arms, or two fundamental parts. One of them is called the arousal part; in scientific terms, it's called the sympathetic nervous system. I like to call it the arousal system because that's exactly what it does: it arouses us; it turns us on; it's the "on" switch for the body. Many of you growing up may have heard about the "flight or fight response"; and it's this arousal system that's incredibly important in that flight or fight response. It turns on when something of motivational importance happens in our environment that we need to react to. As I mentioned, it happens automatically; so if you think to a time where maybe you were driving calmly down the highway and suddenly a car cuts you off completely and it's a near-accident, before you even start to think about what's going on, your body has started to react. Your automatic nervous system, your sympathetic nervous system, kicks in and you react; your heart rate and your blood pressure go up before you actually even think about what's going on.

If there's an "on" switch to the body, there's also an "off" switch; and this is related to part of the autonomic nervous system called the parasympathetic nervous system; what I sometimes refer to as the quiescent nervous system. I call it that because that's exactly what the parasympathetic nervous system does: It calms us down; it settles our body down; and it's this part of the autonomic nervous system that kicks in when we're digesting our food, when we're getting ready to go to sleep, so that we can rejuvenate our energy stores. In some degree, the arousal system is what expends energy—to flee or to fight, for example—and the quiescent side is what enables us to rejuvenate those energy stores.

Normally, they mutually inhibit each other. This certainly makes sense: If you have to flee out of a burning building, you'd want your arousal system to kick in; it's not time for your quiescent system to come in and say, "It's time to lie down and take a nap." You have to get out of the building, you have to move, and you have to move now. On the other hand, sometimes if you're trying to go to bed and you're anxious about something that's happening the next day—maybe a big presentation or a test, or something like that—then it's difficult to sleep. Why? Your quiescent system is trying to kick in, trying to get you to sleep, but your arousal system keeps turning on and keeps you awake. In general, we'd like to see one of those sides of the autonomic nervous system turning on while the other one turns off, but sometimes they can actually mutually excite each other.

The reason that this mutual excitation might be important will be later on when we talk about some very important spiritual experiences, which seem to invoke two different kinds of responses: On one hand, they seem to invoke a very powerful calming response, a feeling of blissfulness; and yet on the other hand, they sometimes describe these profound spiritual states as being incredibly arousing and alerting. What's going on in these experiences? Is it possible that both sides of the autonomic nervous system are getting involved and both of them are turning on so that we seem to have an experience of both arousal and calming at the same time? These are questions that we'll take on later on in the course.

The autonomic nervous system is what ultimately connects the brain and the body so that the brain and the body know what each other are doing and the body knows how to respond to whatever the brain is thinking about. But what goes on in the central parts of the brain that help to regulate that? This takes place in a part of the brain called the limbic system, and the limbic system is a very central part of structures in the brain. They're fundamental to how our brain works and, in fact, the limbic system is a part of other animals' nervous systems, as well as the autonomic nervous system. The limbic system may be thought of as the primary emotional controller of the brain.

The limbic system is comprised of several different structures that enable us to have these different emotional responses. One of the first ones that we come to is a structure called the amygdala. Some of you may have heard of the amygdala because it tends to get a lot of attention in the neuroscientific literature. It tends to turn on a lot; and, in fact, it turns on when we experience something of great fear—one of the main reasons why it turns on—so the amygdala kind of functions as a watchdog in the brain. It turns on when anything of emotional importance occurs in our environment.

What's also interesting is that the amygdala occurs not only when it's something to be feared, but something that's very positive. It turns out that if a lion walked into the room, we might see the amygdala lighting up on a brain scan, and if your loved one walked into the room you might see the amygdala lighting up on a brain scan; so the amygdala lights up when something important happens to us. What are things that could be important to us? Religion and spirituality. If you're engaged in a practice where something very important is about to happen, maybe we'll start to see changes going on in the amygdala—the amygdala turning on—in response to this very important thing happening in our environment.

Another structure of the limbic system is called the hippocampus; it's actually located a little bit behind the amygdala, and it functions to help balance what's going on in the amygdala. The hippocampus is kind of a diplomat of the brain; it helps to regulate our emotional responses so that we don't become too extreme one way or another. The other very important aspect of how the hippocampus works is that it actually helps to write memories down into the brain. In fact, when people develop Alzheimer's disease, the hippocampus is one of the primary areas that's affected first in the disease, which explains why they don't remember things.

But why is it important that our memory would be related to our emotions? Think about how the brain would want to work: Do you need to remember something that isn't really that important to you? No; what you want to remember are things that are important to you. In fact, if you think about how you remember things, one of my favorite examples is to take the events that happened on 9/11. Almost everybody remembers what was happening in their day and where they were when they heard about all the horrible things that were going on in 9/11. But almost no one remembers what was going on, on September 10. September 10 happened, we all lived through it; but unless it had some kind of emotional importance to you—maybe a wedding, or a child's birth, or something like that—you don't remember it. What you do remember are the days and the events that have emotional salience to you, because that's what's important for your brain.

Now think about religion and spirituality; are those things that are important to remember? If your amygdala is turning on and your hippocampus is turning on, it's telling you that this is something that's important and something that should be an important part of your memory. That's why when we think about what we remember and how we remember it and incorporate it into our lives, the limbic system is very important for making religious and spiritual beliefs a part of who we are as human beings.

Another structure that's also very important in our limbic system is called the hypothalamus. This is one of the most central structures of the brain and in many ways is the master controller of almost all the different body functions. The hypothalamus regulates our hormone system, it regulates our thyroid, our sex hormones, our stress hormones, so it's very, very crucial in regulating how our body reacts to the world and how our body reacts to the brain. In fact, the hypothalamus controls which arms of the autonomic nervous system are turned on or turned off. The hypothalamus is this master controller, and if we think about the nature of religious and spiritual experiences as not only affecting us emotionally but having an effect on the body itself (as we'll discuss later on), we can see how the hypothalamus may be a key regulator in translating the information that we're feeling about and thinking about in the higher parts of our brain ultimately down to the body.

As we get to the higher parts of the brain, I want you to think about the brain as being a great receiver. The reason I say that is that the brain receives millions of pieces of information and ultimately tries to create for us a very coherent rendition of what our world is all about. it takes what we see, what we hear, what we taste and smell and puts all of that together so that we have some way of understanding the world; making a picture of the world. How does it do this? It actually goes through a series of different processing steps.

When we look at how our brain works, it continues to build from the bottom up. Let's take our visual system for a moment: Initially, the light comes in through our eyes and it actually goes to the very back parts of the brain; a part of the brain called occipital lobe. In the occipital lobe, we don't perceive the pictures of what we see out there, we see lines, shapes, and colors. but if you then go to what are called the association areas that take information from lots of different neurons, it begins to construct for us step by step a very vivid picture of what the world is all about and brings in the different images, colors and then connects with other association areas so that it attributes a memory to whatever it is that we see in front of us. For example, if a dog walks in front of us, the visual system picks up the colors and the lines and the shapes, it kicks that information up to the association areas that put together a picture of what the dog actually looks like, and then that connects with our memory areas to tell us, "Oh, that's a dog." We may have positive emotions to it if we love dogs in our lives; we may have negative if we had a very negative interaction with a dog. The brain works through these different multiple steps and we have what are called association areas that bring together very complex, coordinated processing of all of this different information that comes in to us from the world.

There are a few other association areas that I want us to also keep in mind. These association areas are very relevant in the context of religious and spiritual experiences and practices. One of them is what I like to refer to as the verbal-conceptual area. In terms of where it's located in the brain, it's actually located between two of the larger lobes of the brain. The brain is divided into four basic lobes: I've mentioned the occipital lobe in the back of the brain; we've talked in the first lecture about the frontal lobe, which is in the front part of the brain; along the side of the brain is a part of the brain called the temporal lobe; and the parietal lobe is located towards the back top part of the brain. This verbal-conceptual area is actually somewhere between the temporal lobe and the parietal lobe, and it does just what I suggested it does in terms of its name: It helps us with language and it helps us with concepts, with ideas; abstract ideas. All of these are put together so that we can begin to think about things from a language perspective as well as a conceptual perspective.

The frontal lobe is also a kind of association area that I like to refer to as the attention area because many brain scan studies have shown that when we focus our attention on a particular task, whether it's driving down the street or perhaps in meditation or prayer, the attention areas is what turns on, and it actually helps to coordinate our thought processes and actually our physical behaviors by linking together what we're thinking about, focusing on in an attention way with what our body and our brain are doing.

The final association area that I want to mention is located in the parietal lobe, the back part of the brain. I like to refer to this area as the orientation area because what this part of the brain does is it takes all of our sensory information and actually helps to orient ourselves in the world. If you're going to get up out of your chair at the end of listening to my lecture and walk out of the room and through the doorway, it's this orientation area that enables you to do that. Why would this be relevant to a religious or spiritual experience? We talked about this a little bit with respect to the study of the Franciscan nuns. One of the experiences that they have is that they lose their sense of self and they feel a sense of spacelessness and timelessness. If that's the case, maybe there's something going on in this orientation area of the brain that's changing the way in which they actually think about themselves; and we'll talk about this in more detail in future lectures.

We've talked about the different structures of the brain and the basic functions of what they do, but I'd like to take another step forward think about the more complex cognitive functions of what the brain has to offer us in terms of how it processes our world. I think each of these cognitive functions bears directly on various aspects of religious or spiritual thoughts, ideas, and experiences. One of my favorite ones to think about is actually the one that helps us with numbers; I sometimes refer to this as a quantitative function of the brain. It's probably located in the parietal lobe; probably a little bit towards the back part of the brain, but not quite so far back as the orientation area, and this helps us with numbers.

Obviously it's very helpful for us to be able to look at numbers in the world, but do numbers have anything to do with religion or spirituality? If you've read through different sacred texts, you'll find numbers abound throughout these texts. We'll see, for example, it raining for 40 days and 40 nights in the story of Noah and the flood, or we see Moses and the Jews wandering around the desert for 40 years. Why is 40 important? Are there other numbers that might be important? Maybe 3, for example, as it relates to the Trinity in

Christianity? We can start to see how numbers are actually given meaning and importance, in large part by the quantitative function of the brain.

Another very important part of the brain in terms of its function is the part of the brain that helps us with what I like to refer to as binary thinking, and this is probably also very close to that verbal conceptual area because it helps us with different ideas. But the reason that our binary processes are so important is they set aside opposites for us. Think about religion and spirituality for a moment: What are the opposites that we think about there? We might think about moral opposites: What's right, what's wrong; what are a believer and a nonbeliever; what are the right ways to think about God and the wrong ways to think about God? These different concepts are set for us by the binary process of the brain and therefore become very important in terms of how we think about religious and spiritual ideas.

Another really important part of the brain is the causal functioning part of the brain; and this is interesting because we do perceive cause and effect in the world, and there are parts of our brain that actually are activated when we think about and see causes and effects in the world. In fact, there have been some interesting studies that have shown that even in infants, if they're presented with a series of conditions that don't seem to make sense causally, they stare at that longer than if it does seem to make sense causally; so it seems that even at a very young age, maybe three to six months of age, we have the ability to think about things causally. Again, if we think about this in the context of religious or spiritual ideas, we might think God in a causal perspective; we might think about God as causing the universe to come into existence, or causing the universe to exist all the time. Our causal function of the brain becomes very, very important in terms of our ideas about God.

We have an existential function in the brain that tells us when something is real and exists. I won't spend much time on it now, but this is a fascinating issue that comes up later on when we talk about the nature and the experience of human reality.

Within our brain we also have two opposing functions: one that kind of breaks things down (I like to refer to it as the reductionistic function) and one that seems to bring things together and bind everything into a oneness (what I like to refer to as the holistic function). When people have mystical experiences, they describe as sense of oneness; and if that's the case, how does this holistic function actually start to play a role? Maybe this has something to do with that orientation part of the brain in terms of how we perceive our self and how we relate that self to the rest of the world.

We have an abstract function in the brain so that we can think about things abstractly, and this is very crucial for all of the philosophical, religious, and theological ideas that we hold. As I mentioned, we have a limbic system that enables us to have our emotion and apply those emotions to all of these different thoughts, feelings, and experiences.

But how do we know about all of these functions and how they're tied to the brain? Over the past several decades, neuroscientists have developed amazing tools for peering into the brain, and we've really now begun to use these tools to study the spiritual brain. Of course, this is going to be a very important part of a lot of our course: to try to understand how we can apply these different methods for measuring the brain to look at specific religious and spiritual ideas.

What are the ways of measuring the brain and its function? To some degree, I like to think about this in the context of subjective measures as well as objective measures. Subjective measures refer to asking people how they feel, what do they think about, how they're understanding the experiences that they have? This is very crucial because we need to understand better how we make sense of what the person is actually thinking or feeling. We also have to think about physiological measures, because we have to understand what's going on in the brain itself, in the body itself; and we can measure that through changes in electrical activity in the brain—something called electroencephalography—or using different neuroimaging studies to look at activity levels in the brain, the amount of chemicals in the brain. All of these different things are ways in which we can actually better understand the physiological objective processes of what's going on in the brain and ultimately how they relate to different religious and spiritual experiences.

But let's return for a moment to the subjective measures. There are a lot of different ways of getting at what we understand subjectively. We can take psychological inventories and ask people about the emotions that they have. We can ask them whether they feel depressed, anxious. There are a lot of very elegant ways of trying to do this. We can measure a person's memory, a person's cognitive status; whether they're able to focus attention; and whether they're able to do different tasks better or worse. People have also developed a variety of different spiritual scales, so we can ask people: How important is religion in their lives? What kinds of spiritual experiences might they have had? I think that this is very important for us to look at these kinds of subjective measures so that we can begin to link them better with what we're measuring physiologically.

Again, physiologically, we can look at not only what's going on in the brain itself but what's going on in the body, in terms of our autonomic function; our heart rate, our blood pressure; we can draw blood and measure changes in our immune system, changes in our hormones; and all of these things are important ways of trying to help us establish the link between our spiritual selves and our biological selves.

In terms of the ways of specifically looking at the brain, there are a few very, very good ways of trying to do that. Electroencephalography, I mentioned a few moments ago, measures the electrical activity in the brain. It's a very good technique for looking at what's going on moment to moment, but it kind of looks at general areas of the brain and doesn't really give us an accurate determination of where something is happening in the brain. For that, we really have to turn to imaging studies; and when we look at imaging studies, we generally find the ability to look at the brain structurally or anatomically as well as functionally.

When we look at the brain structurally, it tells us something about the size of the brain, the size of the different parts of the brain, and how different parts of the brain are connected to each other. Functional imaging, what usually uses either a technique called Magnetic Resonance Imaging, or Positon Emission Tomography (PET imaging), or Single-Photon Emission Computed Tomography (SPECT imaging) are ways of looking at the activity levels in the brain. For example, if you're engaged in a prayer practice like our nuns, the structure of their brain didn't change in that moment, but there were a lot of functional changes that were going on. all of that is very important for helping us to assess what spirituality is and how it affects the brain and ultimately the body.

We have now laid the foundation for discussing the spiritual brain in much greater detail. We understand the brain's basic functions and processes, and we've considered how many of the latest techniques can be used to help study the spiritual brain. Given the information we've now reviewed on the brain and the ability to measure the brain, I'd like you to do something before we move on to the next lecture: I'd like you to spend a few moments to think about or even to write down some of the burning questions in your mind. Why were you interested in learning about the spiritual brain, and what research questions do you have? I'm always so pleased when I give a talk to people to hear all of the wonderful questions that come about that challenge different and new ways of thinking about research questions. What questions would you want to answer? Is there a specific question that you think would be a great topic for a research study? Maybe you have a favorite practice that you do and you want to know how it relates to your own brain function. How can your questions be studied with these different neuroscientific techniques? This is the topic that we'll consider in the next lecture.

How Does Science Study Religion?
Lecture 4

In this lecture, you are going to be introduced to some of the elements of a well-designed scientific study. Specifically, you are going to learn about the design elements that need to be considered when science undertakes the study of spirituality. By understanding the principles of research design, you will have a better sense of how this field of research has developed, and you will be able to use this information when reviewing the various studies that are presented in this course. This lecture also offers you the opportunity to think about how you might study the spiritual brain.

Studying Spiritual Phenomena
- Suppose that you have questions regarding spiritual phenomena.
  - Why does religion sometimes result in very positive behavior and sometimes in very negative behavior?

  - How can being religious help someone if he or she has cancer?

  - What happens in the brain during a mystical experience?

- To begin to answer any of these questions, you have to start by designing an experiment. First, what is your question? What is the thing you want to answer? It can't be something too general; you have to be very specific in your goal.

- For example, if you want to study the effects of prayer on the brain, you must first decide what specific type of prayer and what traditions you are going to study.

- The study of the Franciscan nuns that was mentioned in Lecture 1 focused not on prayer in general, but specifically on the Christian centering prayer. The primary question was to determine how prayer affected the brain, but it was debated whether centering prayer was the best type of prayer to study. After all, is centering prayer even something that a person can easily do in a laboratory setting? How would it relate to other types of prayer? Can this prayer be compared to prayer performed by other religions?

Centering prayer is a form of Christian meditation that involves the recitation of sacred words.

- There is a downside to studying one type of prayer because, unfortunately, the more specific you get, the less generalizable the results will be. However, the virtue of specificity is that it makes it easier to know exactly what you are studying. It makes the data stronger, even though the data might not be applicable to other practices.

- As soon as you know what question you want to address with your study, the next thing you need to decide is whom you will study. How religious or spiritual should the participants in your study be, and how will you decide this? Do you want to study people who are very familiar with the practice or people who have never done it before? What questions will you ask to assess their level of expertise?

- Once you figure out the practice to study and the subjects to study, you have more questions to deal with. For example, what instruments or techniques will you use to conduct the study? How do you plan to analyze your data?

- Clearly, studying spirituality with science is not easy. You have to contend with many critical issues if you want to get data that are worthwhile, interesting, and useful.

Issues with Studying Spiritual Phenomena

- One of the biggest issues scientists face when studying spiritual phenomena is the problem of paradigms. When it comes to understanding or explaining reality, science has one perspective, or paradigm—and spirituality has quite another.

- Spirituality is more experience driven than science. For example, a person of faith can usually offer some type of evidence that supports his or her beliefs, but this is usually not tested from the scientific perspective.

- Ultimately, what is evidence? In church, the congregants believe they have lots of evidence that God exists in their lives—but does that constitute as scientific evidence?

- Any scientific study of spirituality has to confront the issue of establishing definitions. In addition to developing an operational definition for spirituality and religiousness, there are many other terms that might need to be defined in any given study of human belief, including prayer, love, forgiveness, and salvation.

- When defining such terms, scientists face a challenge: They must avoid narrow definitions of terms that might impede research, but they also must avoid broad definitions that cannot be measured. Definitions are an issue for all types of studies.

- Measuring spirituality is another critical issue. Researchers must make whatever connections they can between the subjective descriptions of spiritual experiences that people have—of the thoughts and feelings that they have—and the objective measurements of the brain and other physiological processes.

- It is not even clear whether spirituality or religiousness can be isolated for measurement. Researchers can ask people about what they feel, think, or experience, but are feelings, thoughts, and experiences really the essence of what is spiritual?

Lessons from Professor Newberg's Research

In my own research, I decided that we really needed to have more information on the subjective nature of religious and spiritual experiences. If we could get this information, then we could better evaluate and design neuroscientific studies because we would know better about the thoughts, feelings, and experiences of people, and we could directly tie this subjective information together with brain functions.

How could we get this kind of subjective information? We wanted to make sure that we used a variety of different ways to get at what a spiritual experience actually was and what it felt like. We also wanted to get information about the people having the experiences, and we wanted to use different existing measures of spirituality to see how they related to each other.

We decided to turn to the Internet because it would provide a great platform for getting this information, and we could get information from a lot of people in a relatively short period of time.

We started to design a website that was as comprehensive as possible. We started by asking participants about who they were. We asked questions about their religious tradition of origin, current religious belief system, demographic information, and personal history—including medical problems, medications, and history of drug use.

Then, we asked them questions based on a variety of validated questionnaires, including those that get at the importance and meaning of religion in their lives, their openness to other beliefs, and their fear of death. Finally, we provided a box with the simple instruction to write as much as they wanted about their spiritual experience or experiences.

With data from over 2,000 participants, the results have been incredible. We will share some of the results from this study at different points in the course. Some information will be from the narratives of the participants in terms of how they describe their spiritual experiences. Other data relate to how measures of religiosity worked.

For example, we developed a series of questions designed to find out how open people were about different beliefs. Some of the questions were more abstract in terms of what participants believed while others were more practical, such as asking participants if they would marry someone outside of their religion. About 25 percent responded that they would not. Overall, we found out that most people were somewhat open to other belief systems, but very few people were totally open to other beliefs.

As interesting as these data from our web survey are, there are still other fascinating approaches to measuring spirituality that were not used. For example, is it possible to develop an external measure of spirituality? Can priests or spiritual masters evaluate students in some way?

- Some researchers in this field have suggested that a subtraction perspective might be useful. In other words, if we factor everything out, we might be left with something truly spiritual.

- For the time being, however, researchers must make whatever connections they can between the subjective descriptions of spiritual experiences and the objective measurements of physiological and neurological states.

- Spirituality and religiousness are usually described in terms of psychological, emotional, or cognitive processes, and science has developed tools that enable us to measure those processes— at least to some degree. Physiological and neurophysiological measures need to be combined with subjective and phenomenological analysis.

- What type of study do we need to evaluate the spiritual brain? There are advantages and disadvantages to each type. Consider developing a new study in which you want to use imaging to determine which parts of the brain are turned on or off during a specific practice, such as doing the Rosary.

- Longitudinal studies repeatedly evaluate individuals over a period of time (a practice that can also be valuable for experimental studies), but they often take too much time. Cross-sectional studies are, therefore, much easier, but they sometimes miss the transition.

- Correlational research involves studying the relationship between two or more variables—for example, praying the Rosary and alcohol use. This type of research can be valuable, but it has limitations as well.

- There are a few other considerations that you will need to address for your Rosary study. You want to measure brain changes, but you have to decide if you want to measure general activity, specific areas, or specific neurotransmitters (such as serotonin or dopamine).

- You also need to make sure that you compare the measures you get from imaging with something subjective, so you will want to make sure that people do the Rosary correctly and get the experience you expect.

- You have to determine what type of change you are interested in. You may want to determine changes in blood flow or changes in anxiety. You also have to make sure that whatever changes you find are relevant in the sense that they actually mean something to the person.

- In a larger way, you have to think about who should be studied and why each group might be good or bad for studying the Rosary. For example, should you study atheists, members of the general population, or members of the religious population? Should you study novices, experts, or mystics?

- If you find a change, you might want to make sure that the change is directly related to doing the Rosary and not to doing one of hundreds of other types of practices. Therefore, you need to have a good comparison state. However, can there be an adequate placebo? Can subjects act as their own control?

- Study design is important because it tells us something about the capabilities and limitations of science. More importantly, it helps us understand what kind of information regarding religious and spiritual phenomena we can actually obtain.

Suggested Reading

Beauregard and O'Leary, *The Spiritual Brain*.

Gay, ed, *Neuroscience and Religion*.

Grassie, ed, *Advanced Methodologies in the Scientific Study of Religion and Spirituality*.

Koenig, McCullough, and Larson, *Handbook of Religion and Health*.

McNamara, ed, *Where God and Science Meet*.

Questions to Consider

1. What are the capabilities and limitations of using the scientific method to study religious and spiritual phenomena?

2. What are the challenges to science in terms of evaluating spiritual experiences, analyzing the effects of religion on the brain and body, and defining what religion and spirituality actually are?

How Does Science Study Religion?
Lecture 4—Transcript

How might science look at religion?

It turns out that even the authors of the Bible understood the need for good research study design.

I'm thinking in particular of the first chapter of the Book of Daniel, where we have something that looks a lot like a nutritional study. Daniel is talking to an official of King Nebuchadnezzar's court, and the official is worried about Daniel's diet and Daniel says to him:

> Please test your servants for ten days, and let us be given some vegetables to eat and water to drink. Then let our appearance be observed in your presence and the appearance of the youths who are eating the king's choice food; and deal with your servants according to what you see. So he listened to them in this matter and tested them for ten days. At the end of ten days their appearance [Daniel's appearance] seemed better and they were fatter than all the youths who had been eating the king's choice food.

Today we're going to follow in Daniel's footsteps and try to identify some of the elements of a well-designed scientific study. Specifically, we're going talk about the design elements that need to be considered when science undertakes to study spirituality. It's important that we do this, because from this point forward, we're going to be looking at a number of research studies, and we'll appreciate the information that these studies can—and can't—give us if we first take time to understand the principles of research design.

You'll remember in the first lecture we talked about my study of nuns, and nuns in particular doing centering prayer. A study like that doesn't just happen off the cuff; a great deal of thought had to go into design and preparation of a study like that.

In fact, it took a lot of thought and discussion before my colleagues and I came up with the design for these imaging studies. There were so many questions we had to address before we could even get started.

Let's suppose you have your own burning questions regarding spiritual phenomena. In fact, usually when do I give a lecture to my colleagues, students, or even the general public, there are many different study ideas that people keep suggesting during the question and answer period; and to some degree this is what I hope you'll get from this particular lecture: an ability to stretch your own scientific legs, if you will, and think about how you might study the spiritual brain.

Maybe you want to know why religion sometimes results in a very positive thought or behavior, and sometimes in a very negative behavior.

Maybe you want to understand how being religious can help you if you have cancer or some other type of disorder.

Perhaps you want to study intercessory prayer and the ability to actually affect someone at a distance through prayer. Or maybe you want to know, like I did, what happens in the brain during a practice like meditation or a mystical experience.

To get at any of these questions, you have to begin by designing an experiment. Typically, the first question of any scientific experiment is: What's the question? What's the thing that you want to answer?

It can't be too general, because there'd be no way for you to actually get a hold of it and measure it. if you remember back to our definitions of religiousness and spirituality, we talked about whether we can be very specific or very general. When you begin a research study, you have to kind of get down to some specifics.

For example, if you want to study the effects of prayer on the brain, what specific type of prayer are you going to study? Are you going to look at centering prayer, like we did? Maybe you want to look at doing the rosary or some other type of prayer. Which tradition do you use? Do you want to study someone from the Christian tradition, Jewish, Buddhist, Hindu, Muslim, or any of the others?

For example, the study I mentioned in Lecture One focused not on prayer in general but specifically on centering prayer. Our primary question was to determine how prayer affected the brain; but, again, we debated about whether centering prayer was really the best type of prayer to study. These are the kinds of questions that we all have to begin to think about when we look at any study of the spiritual brain. After all, in this case centering prayer on one hand is good because it's something that a person can easily do in a laboratory kind of environment. But, of course, that's one of the questions that we needed to address; because if we look at other practices, which may not be so conducive to being in a laboratory environment, we may not get a good study. In fact, if we talk about trying to scan the brain during these practices, different scans require us to be in different positions. I mentioned in the last lecture one of the modalities of imaging the brain is called functional magnetic resonance imaging (or fMRI). It's a wonderful technique, but you have to be lying down in the scanner; so if you're going to do a practice where you need to be standing up, you can't do it in a MRI machine.

If we think about the kind of prayer that we're going to study, we also have to think about what we compare it to. What are the other types of practices that we might compare it to? Should we compare it to sitting still, resting quietly? Should we compare it to other types of meditation practices? Of course, this creates a great deal of complexity in terms of how we decide to design the study. It's nice if you can focus in on studying one type of prayer because that makes it easier, but the problem is that if you're just looking at the one type of prayer—like centering prayer—then how do we know if the results that we get are generalizable; how do we know that it can be applied to all different kinds of prayer? Again, though, one of the good things about picking one particular type of practice is that it makes it easier to know exactly what we're studying; so it makes the data stronger, even though we may or may not be able to apply it to other kinds of practices.

Now you know what question you want to address with your study, and therefore the next thing you have to ask yourself is: Who are you actually going to do the study with?

Sometimes this is obvious: If you're going to do a Christian prayer such as centering prayer, you probably aren't going to invite a group of Buddhists in to do the centering prayer; you need to find people who know how to do that particular prayer. But who should you actually study as part of your study? Should they be very religious, moderately religious, or only slightly religious; and how do you decide that? Do you want to take people very familiar or expert with the practice or people who've never done it before?

What questions will you ask to assess their level of expertise?

If you remember, in our study of the nuns doing centering prayer, we decided to take people who were very expert at doing this practice. The reason that we decided that is that we wanted people who we felt very comfortable would be able to do the practice, would engage the practice fully, and were comfortable with it. but the downside is the results tell us what an expert does when they do centering prayer and it may not be as useful in telling us what the general public does in their brain when they engage in centering prayer.

So it's helpful to think about very deeply the kinds of individuals who you want to study so that you can actually design the study in as effective way as possible.

Once you decide on which people you're going to study, you have to think about what instruments or techniques you're going to use for the study.

In addressing this particular question, you have to plan not only what types of instruments to use but how you're going to actually analyze your data. Again, let's think about the instruments for a moment. In the study of centering prayer, we could've done Functional Magnetic Resonance Imaging, but most of the nuns felt that they were typically seated when they did the practice. The other problem with the MRI, if you've never had a MRI, is it's very noisy—it's actually about 110 decibels of a lot of banging noises—so it's not a very conducive environment for doing a practice like prayer or meditation, and therefore we might want to make sure that we have a technique that we can use that would make it more accessible for them, easier for them, to do the particular practice. Again, once you have all of this information, you have to combine and analyze the data—the imaging data with the subjective experiences that they had—and think about how you want to do that.

Wow; that's really a lot of questions that you have to think about before you even start doing the study. Clearly, studying spirituality with science isn't very easy to do. You have to contend with so many different critical issues if you want to get data that is ultimately worthwhile, interesting, and useful. So what I'd like to do in the rest of this lecture is to take a closer look at some of the important issues we have to think about in terms of how we design scientific studies to look at spirituality. In the process, we'll circle back on some of the questions and some of the ideas that we've already addressed, and we'll try to look at them in even greater detail.

One of the biggest problems that I as a scientist and perhaps all scientists face in studying spirituality from a neuroscientific perspective is what I call the problem with paradigms.

Here's what I mean: When it comes to understanding or explaining reality, science has a very specific perspective; spirituality and religion has quite another.

For one thing, spirituality is very experience-driven; it doesn't rely on experimentation the way science does.

For example, a person of faith can usually offer some kind of evidence—but usually personal experiential evidence—that supports his or her own belief system, but this isn't tested from the perspective of science; there were no scans that were done to help them to prove that they should be religious or spiritual. Maybe the person actually had an experience, some kind of epiphany when they were in church or watching a beautiful sunset; maybe they had a very intense experience, like a near-death experience; or maybe they just were walking along the street and suddenly everything just felt clear to them.

But as a scientist, I often think: What actually should we accept as evidence? Again, if you go into any church, synagogue, or mosque and ask the congregants who are there if have evidence that God exists in their lives, most of them would say "Absolutely." But does that constitute scientific evidence? A lot of nonbelievers would say, "Absolutely not; we need to have a better way of looking at what spirituality, what religion, is to help to prove whether it's right or wrong."

Then there's another intriguing problem with paradigms, and that relates to studies of intercessory prayer. Over the last 20 years, there have been a number of studies looking at the effect of intercessory prayer on various aspects of human health. One of the earliest studies back in the 1980s asked people to pay for other patients who were in the hospital with heart problems. The reason that this has such a potentially powerful impact on paradigms is if the study actually shows that intercessory prayers works, what does that mean in terms of how we understand the nature of our world? We typically don't think about the possibility that "Somehow in my mind or spirit that I can reach across space and affect somebody else"; and yet some of these intercessory prayer studies have demonstrated results that suggest just such a possibility. Clearly there's a lot of controversy over how these studies were done, how well they were done, and certainly the meaning of these studies; but the implications on the paradigms of how we understand science could be profound.

In addition to the problem of paradigms, any scientific study of spirituality has to confront the issues that we spoke about in the earlier lectures about definitions. In fact, in our last lecture we talked a lot about developing an operational definition for spirituality and religiousness. But think of all the other terms that might need to be defined in any given study of human religious and spiritual beliefs: What does prayer actually mean? There are many different types of prayer. For some people, prayer is just repeating a phrase over and over again or a hymn over and over again. For some people, prayer is conversational; they talk to God. What about other kinds of experiences that are associated with spirituality, like forgiveness, love, or even revelation or salvation? What do we mean by these terms? This list goes on and on; and if we're ever going to look at a study that tries to understand those experiences, then we have to do a better job at defining them.

Definitions are an issue for all types of studies; and certainly for studies of religious or spiritual ideas, we're definitely going to have to try to find our best way of defining these particular terms. That was one of the reasons why we actually studied centering prayer, because it was a very well-defined practice. We knew exactly what the nuns were doing, we knew how they were doing it, we knew what kinds of experiences, feelings, and thoughts they were going to have during the practice; and therefore when we saw the results on the brain scans, it became much easier for us to relate those changes to what we knew they were doing as part of the centering prayer. But if you take a broader perspective on what prayer is or meditation, you may find a chance in the brain and it may have nothing to do with what other people think of as prayer or meditation.

Then there's the critical issue of how do we actually measure spirituality? How do we do this? It was kind of amusing when we first started our studies, like with the Franciscan nuns. I wanted to get a sense as to how spiritual they felt and I designed a questionnaire where the very first question was, "On a scale of 1–10, how spiritual do you feel?" As I started to utter those words to the first nun, I realized how ridiculous-sounding of a question that was. How could you ask that question and put a number on that kind of a feeling? So we try to get at other ways of measuring spirituality—other subjective ways—and these subjective measures usually require some kind of self-reporting. On one hand, this is great because it gives us an opportunity to develop a scale or a list of questions where we can assess what a person feels spiritually or religiously. These measures are sometimes very useful only within a particular tradition, though; for example, we might have questions about beliefs in Christianity, which apply to Christians but may not work so well for a Jewish or Muslim population.

In my own research, I decided that we really needed to have more information on the subjective nature of religious and spiritual experiences. If we could get this information, we could better evaluate and design neuroscientific studies because we'd know a lot more about the thoughts, the feelings, and the experiences that people actually have when something spiritual happens to them and we could therefore directly tie this subjective information into the brain functions that we can study with our scans.

But how can we get this kind of subjective information? We wanted to make sure that we used a variety of different ways to get at what a spiritual experience actually was and what it felt like. We also wanted to get information about the people who were having these experiences, and we wanted to use different existing measures of spirituality to see how they related to each other.

We thought about how we were going to do this for quite some time, and we decided to turn to the internet since this provides a great platform for getting this kind of information and getting it from lots of different people in a relatively short period of time. What did we do?

We began by designing a website that was comprehensive as possible in getting at all the different aspects of what spirituality was for people. We started out by asking some very basic questions about the participants. If somebody came to the website, first they were just asked questions about how old they were, what gender they were; we asked them questions about their religious tradition of origin, how they grew up; and we asked them where they are today. We asked them about other issues related to their lives: What stressors did they have? Did they have any very intense medical problems, for example; maybe they were struggling with terminal cancer. Are they on any different medications or drugs; have they had problems with taking drugs in the past or drinking too much alcohol?

Then we asked them questions based on a variety of well-tested and validated questionnaires. These different questionnaires got at a variety of different aspects of what spirituality and religiousness is for people. It would ask them questions about the meaning of religion in their lives. We asked them questions about their fear of death; about how they applied their religion in their lives. Did they go to church, go to synagogue and partake in a lot of social interactions or did they do something more personal? Ultimately, we asked them to describe their spiritual experiences to us. We just gave them a little box and we said, "Write as much as you want to do"—the box just kept going—and some people wrote a paragraph or two, some people wrote pages. The simple question was, "Describe to us what your spiritual experience was." The results from this survey have been—as far as I'm concerned—absolutely incredible, and we're still going through all of the data from over 2,000 individuals who hit the website. I'm going to share some of the results of this study at different points in the course.

Some of this information—some the most powerful information—came in the form of the narratives; the descriptions that people provided about their spiritual experiences. But other data related to how the different measures of religiosity actually worked.

For example, we developed a series of questions designed to find out how open people were about different religious beliefs. Some of the questions were more abstract; we just said, "Are you open to other people's beliefs?" and we asked them did they agree with that or did they disagree with that? But we realized that people may often say, "Oh, yes, I'm very open to other people's beliefs," but how do they bring that into their actual lives?

So we asked other questions that had a more practical implication. We might ask a question, for example, of, "Would you marry somebody outside of your religious tradition?" and, in fact, about 25 percent of the respondents said that they wouldn't marry somebody outside of their religious tradition. Overall, we found out that most people are at least somewhat open to other belief systems, but very few people are totally open to other beliefs. We were able to then begin to compare openness with other aspects. We found that older people were more open to other people's beliefs than younger people, and we began to even delve into it more deeply in terms of gender, religious traditions; all of these are the kinds of questions that we now have an opportunity to be able to explore in more detail.

Another very interesting possibility that some of my colleagues and I have pondered is whether it's possible to develop some external measure of spirituality. For example, it's possible that we could go to different spiritual teachers—priests, spiritual leaders of a monastery—and ask them to evaluate how their students are doing from a spiritual perspective. Wouldn't it be fascinating to ask the students and ask the teachers and see if they match up? It might be the case that a student feels that they've been completely spiritually enlightened while the master says, "No, no, you're not even close"; and then, of course, we have the even more profound question of which person is actually right?It isn't even clear whether spirituality or religiousness can actually even be isolated for measurement, because we always have to ask the question: How does it make you feel? How does it make you think? Even if we get an external impression, we're asking them:

What do they think? What do they feel? That, to me, is really begging the question: Are we getting to something that's truly spiritual, or are we getting around what spirituality actually is because we always have to ask how it makes you feel, think, or understand the world?

One other possibility—another intriguing suggestion from some of my colleagues—is to use a kind of subtraction technique. What if we could do brain scans, subjective measures, and throw all of that into the mix, and when we look at the data we find out that the person is still feeling something in some way or something's still being measured that nothing else accounts for; so if we factor everything out, we might finally be left with something that's truly inherently spiritual. In fact, in kind of an amusing way of thinking about the research studies that we've done looking at brain scans, I've always argued that perhaps one of the most interesting results that we could've had from our research study of the nuns doing centering prayer is that they would've had an intense spiritual experience and nothing changed on the scan. If this were the case, we may have captured something that wasn't a brain state per se, but something else entirely; something unmeasurable by scientific means, something that might actually be spiritual.

For the time being, however, we researchers must make whatever connections we can between the subjective descriptions of the spiritual experiences and thoughts and feelings that people have and the objective measurements of the brain and other physiological processes.

Spirituality and religiousness are usually described in terms of psychological, emotional, or cognitive processes; and as we began to see in our previous lecture, science has developed some tools that enable us to measure these kinds of processes, at least to some degree.

We can begin to look at different physiological measures in the body; so we can look at changes in heart rate and see how they relate to the positive emotional experiences that a nun might have doing centering prayer. Is that associated with an increase in their heart rate? Is it associated with a decrease in their heart rate? If somebody engages in a prayer practice, does it change their autonomic nervous system activity? Does it change the hormones in their body? Does it change their immune system? There's some evidence to support that some of these practices actually do help to boost the way the immune system works.

Of course, what this whole course is about are the neurophysiological measures. What's going on in the brain in terms of its activity, in terms of the different neurotransmitters, the chemicals that are going on in the brain; can we get that information and combine that with what the person experiences subjectively so that we can find out, for example, that the more active their frontal lobe is on a SPEC scan or a MRI scan, the deeper is their experience of the spiritual. Or perhaps if we see more profound changes going on in the orientation area of the brain that it's associated with experiences where they lose their sense of self, and they lose their sense of space and time. What type of study do we ultimately need to evaluate the spiritual brain? There are all different kinds of advantages and disadvantages to all of these different types. So let's consider developing a new study in which we want to use imaging of the brain to determine which parts of the brain are turned on or off during a specific practice, perhaps the Rosary as one example. Again, we have some important questions: Do we want to make this a longitudinal study—meaning we want to study people over time—so that we take people who maybe have never done the practice before and see how they do over a period of months, or do we just take a cross-section of the population and look at people who are expert at it and those people who are just starting to do it and see where the differences are? Of course, if we take that cross-section, we may miss the transition as to how somebody ultimately comes to do it better and better.

On the other hand, if we want to follow people longitudinally, sometimes that's difficult because we don't know how long we have to follow them and we still may miss the actual transition point of when they start to really get the practice and really feel the intensity of the experience.

We might want to do some kind of relational research: We might want to compare doing the Rosary to mental health issues, maybe alcohol use, depression, or anxiety; but each of these have limitations as well because if we see an effect, how do we know for sure that it was the Rosary and not a variety of other factors that are going on? There are other considerations we'll need to take into consideration for our Rosary study: We want to measure the brain changes, but we have to decide if we want to look at general activity in the brain; maybe focus on specific areas, like the frontal lobes or the amygdala; or maybe even look at neurotransmitters, chemicals like serotonin or dopamine, which have been shown to have very important effects on our emotions.

We also need to make sure that we compare the measures that we get with the imaging with something subjective. This is what I've been saying all along: We want to understand what the people feel; are they doing the Rosary properly, are they getting the experiences that we hoping that they're going to get; and how do we know that they've gotten them?

The American Archbishop, Fulton Sheen, who hosted a nighttime radio program called "The Catholic Hour" for 20 years, described the Rosary this way: He said, "The Rosary is the best therapy for these distraught, unhappy, fearful, and frustrated souls, precisely because it involves the simultaneous use of three powers: the physical, the vocal, and the spiritual, and in that order." If we design a study of the Rosary, do we need to take into consideration the actions, the experiences, and the feelings, and how do we measure them?

We have to determine the type of change that we're interested in. We may want to determine changes in the brain's blood flow or changes in measures of anxiety; but we also have to make sure that whatever changes we find that they're relevant in the sense that they actually mean something to the person. For example, if I find that the person's rain increases its activity by two percent, they may say, "That's great, but so what?" We need to make sure that what we find is true, significant, and also relevant.

In a larger way, we have to think about who should actually be studied; why each group might be good or bad for studying the Rosary. In fact, we might even contemplate the possibility of having atheists try the Rosary, or we might restrict it to those who are truly expert at it in terms of a religious population.

If we find a change, we may want to make sure that it's a change that's directly related to doing the Rosary and not by doing one of hundreds of other types of practices that might be similar; so we need to have a good comparison state.

The problem is that in science we typically like to have what we call the placebo or the control condition. What's a good control condition for doing the Rosary? It involves manipulating your hands; it involves repeating certain things outwardly, internally. Do we want somebody to be doing something with their hands, or do we want somebody to simply be resting there quietly?

All of these are the questions that we really have to take into consideration to make sure that if we find a change it's a real change, it's meaningful in the context of the practice, and it's something that can have some usefulness in terms of understanding its effect on us as human beings.

Why is all of this discussion about study design important?

For one, it tells us something about the capabilities and the limitations of science.

It's something that I've been deeply interested in since I'm a scientist and I want to know how far we can push science; and if we don't ask all of these very compelling questions, we might not understand exactly what science can tell us. But more importantly, it helps us to understand what kind of information regarding religious and spiritual phenomena we can actually obtain.

We now have a better sense of how this entire field of research has developed and we can use this information when we review the array of studies that we'll consider in all of our upcoming lectures

Believers and Atheists

Lecture 5

Religious practices and experiences seem to be universal within the human species, but if all human beings have a spiritual brain, why are there nonbelievers? This question is at the forefront of many atheists' minds. From a neuroscientific perspective, is there a difference in the brains of people who believe and those who do not? The implication is that there might possibly be something distinctive about brain structure or function that influences whether people become either believers or nonbelievers, and that implication is a fascinating component to an even bigger question: Is it the brain or something else that determines whether you believe?

Why Are There Nonbelievers?

- Nonbelievers, like religious individuals, come in many different types. A scientist, for example, might be an atheist because he or she does not believe in any kind of supernatural process of the universe. On the other hand, a Buddhist might look at the world in a very spiritual way but doesn't actually believe in a God. Materialists believe that only the material aspects of the world exist, and agnostics don't really believe in a God but are not sure.

- Not every nonbeliever shares the same epistemological principles, but for the purposes of this course, a nonbeliever is someone who does not believe in a supernatural realm or who does not require a God to explain the existence and nature of the universe.

- There are two broad classes of people in the world—believers and nonbelievers—and science has some tools and techniques for evaluating the difference between them.

- One approach is to take believers and nonbelievers and analyze scans of their brains. A few studies have attempted this in various ways. Several studies have compared those who meditate or pray as part of their spiritual tradition to people who do not meditate or pray. The results have been somewhat striking.

- Several MRI studies have shown that the brains of long-term practitioners are thicker than the brains of nonmeditators. In particular, the frontal lobes appear thicker. Similarly, it has been shown that meditators functionally have more activity in the frontal lobes than nonmeditators.

- Research also points to changes to another central structure in the brain called the thalamus, which controls sensory information, cognition, and consciousness. Basically, it is essential for our experience and understanding of reality.

People who exercise their brains through prayer or meditation tend to have thicker brains.

- The results are intriguing because they show a difference, but they also raise an important question: Did the spiritual people have thicker brains and more active frontal lobes to begin with, and that is what attracted them to spiritual belief and practices, or did their brains change over time as the result of doing these practices and being spiritual?

- Longitudinal studies can help us answer the question of which came first. The basic idea of such studies is to evaluate people over time—months or years.

- If we can evaluate what happens in people's thought processes and spiritual beliefs over time, we might better determine whether the brain causes people to believe or not—or, perhaps, the longer a person believes something, the more their brain changes to accept that belief.

- Unfortunately, at the present time, there are no longitudinal studies that specifically compare the way a believer's brain changes over time versus the way a nonbeliever's brain changes.

- Imaging technology can be used to compare brain activity in believers versus nonbelievers. One study showed that when atheists—all of whom were good at meditating—were asked to meditate on God, their frontal lobes did not turn on like those of the Franciscan nuns in the study from Lecture 1.

- If the frontal lobe helps people concentrate or focus on something and atheists have a real problem with doing so, maybe they are struggling with a sense of cognitive dissonance. They are trying to focus on something that they really don't like very much, and they don't feel comfortable focusing on it. Clearly, the nuns are able to engage the concepts of their prayer, of their meditation, and of the notion of God.

- Several studies have been designed to study how believers and nonbelievers think—or think differently. Syllogisms are typically used to test how people think logically, and some early studies showed that nonbelievers performed better on such tests.

- One clever study used syllogisms that were either proreligious or antireligious. The following is an example of a proreligious syllogism.
    o If to succeed in life you have to be Christian, and if a person named Thomas wants to succeed in life, then Thomas should become a Christian.

- The following is an example of an antireligious syllogism.
    - If being religious is found to be bad for people who have depression, and if you suffer from depression, then you should try to be less religious.

- Participants were asked to evaluate whether the syllogisms were internally logical or not. The results were intriguing. The religious people did better on the proreligious questions, and the nonreligious people did better on the antireligious questions. The results suggest that both groups make logical mistakes, but they make them in the direction of their beliefs.

- Another study also demonstrated the difference between believers and nonbelievers in an intriguing way.

- Believers and nonbelievers were asked to look at distorted photos with some real and some nonreal elements. Believers were more likely to see things that were there, but sometimes they saw things that weren't there. Nonbelievers never saw things that weren't there, but sometimes they missed things that were there. Again, each group made mistakes, but they made them in directions that were consistent with their beliefs.

- Another interesting result from this study is that when nonbelievers were given dopamine, their results were more similar to the results of believers.

- One of the things that dopamine does is help regulate our sensations, and it is also part of the reward system in the brain. In the context of this study, dopamine helps to modify how we interpret our sensory perceptions. It changes our view of reality.

- Perhaps dopamine, or some other neurotransmitter, is crucial for helping a person see the world in a spiritual way or in a nonspiritual way. It would certainly be interesting if there were some relationship between neurotransmitters and various aspects of spirituality.

- The relationship between dopamine and spirituality takes another turn in a study conducted by Dr. Dean Hamer, a behavioral geneticist at the National Institutes of Health.

- Hamer analyzed DNA and personality data from over 1,000 individuals and identified one particular gene as the "God gene," which was found to correlate with people's feelings of self-transcendence. Interestingly, this gene is involved in producing the VMAT2 receptor, which regulates dopamine and serotonin levels in the brain.

- Some scientists note that the effect of this gene on differences in spiritual beliefs is likely very low—perhaps less than 10 percent of the effect. However, Hamer states that the God gene does not imply that it is the only factor in making someone spiritual or religious, but it seems to be involved in the process.

- Some religious people were concerned that religion was being reduced only to genes, ignoring doctrine, culture, traditions, and—most importantly—God. However, Hamer responded that the existence of such a gene would not be incompatible with the existence of a personal God.

- One of the advantages of the Hamer study is that it looked at a relatively large number of people. However, in order to fully answer the questions about believers and nonbelievers, we may need to greatly expand the population of people we are going to study.

- We could study atheists and contrast them against ardent believers, but we might also consider studying the general population to see how spirituality is expressed along a continuum of many different people. It is like trying to study music—one way would be to compare expert musicians to those people who are completely tone deaf.

- We could also compare musicians to the general public, but maybe we should study the general population to find the entire range of musical abilities. What about studying children before their first musical lesson and then seeing which of them become musicians and which don't?

- We could also study relative novices and compare them to experts. Perhaps an even more fascinating approach would be to study the very few people who might be similar to Mozart—those for which musical ability is at an entirely different level.

- Extrapolating this to religion and spirituality, we could study believers and nonbelievers, the general population, or maybe people on an entirely different level, such as Mother Teresa or the Dalai Lama. There are many fascinating possibilities that we can begin to explore to help us better understand what the spiritual brain is, why some people are more spiritual than others, and how spirituality is expressed throughout humanity.

- It appears that there may be some important differences in believers and nonbelievers. The differences are manifested in how they think about and interpret reality. However, the differences are also reflected in the brain. Different parts of the brain react differently in believers and nonbelievers.

- Of course, there is a broad spectrum of belief, and few people are at the extreme of either unshakeable belief or absolute unbelief in spiritual phenomena. As scientific research becomes more sophisticated, we will be better able to analyze the subtle differences on the spectrum of belief. In the meantime, it's fascinating to consider how far belief may be determined from birth by our genes—or acquired through our interactions with other people or perhaps even acquired through an encounter with God.

Suggested Reading

Newberg and Waldman, *Why We Believe What We Believe.*

Shermer, *The Believing Brain.*

1. Why are there believers and atheists, and are there differences in their brains?

2. How are genes and neurotransmitters associated with different belief systems?

Believers and Atheists
Lecture 5—Transcript

I'd like for you to imagine a beautiful starlit night. Two people, Jane and Tom, are sitting near their campsite far from the city, staring up at the stars in silence. Both of them, let's imagine, feel amazement at the beauty and the immensity of the universe; but that's where the shared experience ends. Tom senses a powerful presence in the night; a creator, perhaps, or a spirit that connects him with everything he sees, even the most distant star. Jane, by contrast, enjoys the experience but reflects only on the natural beauty around her. The stars are merely distant suns, fun to look at but nothing more.

So far in this course, we've been talking about the seeming universality of religious practices and experiences in the human species. But our campsite scenario raises a very important question:

If we all have a spiritual brain, why are there nonbelievers?

This question is at the forefront of many atheists' minds.

From a neuroscientific perspective, the question is slightly different: Is there a difference in the brains of people who believe and those who don't?

The implication is that there might possibly be something distinctive about the brain structure or function that influences whether people become either believers or nonbelievers.

That implication in and of itself is a fascinating component to an even bigger question: Is it the brain or something else that determines whether you believe?

But let's get back to the first question: Why are there nonbelievers?

You know already that I'm a stickler for definitions, so first of all: What exactly do we mean when we talk about nonbelievers? After all, atheists, like religious individuals, actually come in many different types and flavors. A scientist, for example, might be an atheist because they don't believe in any kind of supernatural process of the universe; it's all what we can see from a scientific perspective. We can do experiments, understand the physical world around us, and that's it. on the other hand, a Buddhist, for example, might look at the world in a very spiritual way even though ultimately they don't actually believe in a God, at least a God in terms of the monotheistic traditions like Christianity and Judaism. Even though they don't believe in God, they have this very intense sense of spirituality and they believe in an afterlife. This is very different than a scientist who's an atheist or someone who might consider themselves a materialist, both looking at the world in which there's just the material aspects of the world and nothing beyond that. Of course, other people consider themselves to be agnostic. They don't really believe in God, but they're not so sure; maybe there is, maybe there isn't. But if you actually asked them are they religious or not, most of the time they'd say, "No, I'm not that religious or spiritual."

Now we have a pretty clear idea of what we mean by a "nonbeliever." Not every nonbeliever shares the same epistemological principles; but for our purposes, we'll say that, broadly, a nonbeliever is someone who doesn't believe in a supernatural realm. They don't require a notion of God to explain their existence or the existence and nature of the universe.

Given that we have these two broad classes of people in the world— believers and nonbelievers—let's now turn to science to see if it has any tools or techniques for evaluating the differences between them.

One approach is by taking believers and nonbelievers and actually scanning their brains.

A few studies have actually attempted to do this in various ways.

For example, several studies have compared those who meditate or pray as part of their spiritual tradition to people who don't meditate or pray.

The results of these studies have actually been somewhat striking. Most of the studies have actually not measured the function of the brain so much as the size of the brain, and they can actually quantify how big different parts of the brain are. When these studies have looked at the difference between those who've been doing practices like meditation and prayer for many, many years, what they find is that those people who've been doing those practices actually have thicker brains; their brains are actually bigger, and particularly in the part of the brain called the frontal lobe. If you remember from our previous lectures, the frontal lobes are involved in our ability to focus our attention, to concentrate on things, and to control and regulate our emotions and our behaviors. When people engage in prayer or meditation, clearly they are heavily focused in the practice; and therefore it may make sense that, just like exercising a muscle, they've exercised their brain and actually made it thicker.

I've talked to you a little about some of our research. I've been able to study people who are engage in different types of meditation practices, and we talked at the very beginning of the course of our studies looking at Franciscan nuns and prayer. We can actually look at whether or not there aren't just structural changes in the brain, but whether or not there are actually functional changes as well. Our research actually points to several very interesting changes or differences between those people who've been engaged in these practices of prayer and meditation for many years in comparison to those who've never done these practices. Similar to what the MRI studies showed of increased thickness in the frontal lobe of the brain, we've actually found increased blood flow, increased activity, in the frontal lobe of the brain. It suggests that when people do these practices for many years, always drawing on the activity levels of their frontal lobe to engage in that practice, they're actually setting the stage for that frontal lobe to function in a whole different way; it actually even at rest functions in a more active way.

Another very interesting finding that we've found with regard to our studies of people engaged in prayer or meditation has been in a different structure, a very central structure, called the thalamus. We haven't really talked much about the thalamus yet, but the thalamus is actually one of the most critical relays in the brain. The thalamus actually takes in all of our sensory information, and particularly that from our vision and from our hearing, and brings it up to the higher parts of the brain so that we can create a sense of our reality. It also helps different parts of the brain to communicate with each other; so it controls sensory information, it controls our cognitive processes, and some people even think that it's the seat of consciousness. It's essential for our entire experience and understanding of reality.

What did we find when we looked at the long-term meditators? Interestingly, when we look at the long-term meditators, their thalamus is very asymmetric. What I mean by that is we have a thalamus on the left and the right side, and it turns out that long-term meditators tend to have one of those sides be more active than the other. When we look at the general population, they're pretty evenly balanced. If you think about what's going on with regard to the brain, it looks like their brain is looking at the world in a very, very different way because this thalamus that regulates all of their sensory information and the ways in which they think is actually functioning differently than a person who hasn't done this kind of a practice.

These results—the MRI studies showing changes in the thickness of the brain; our studies showing changes in the activity levels of the brain—are very intriguing because they do in fact show a difference between those people who are religious and spiritual and those who aren't (or at least those who've done long-term meditation and prayer practices), but this raises an even more fundamental question, which is a chicken and the egg kind of question. That question is: Did the spiritual people have thicker brains or more active frontal lobes in their brains to begin with and that's what attracted them to their spiritual beliefs and practices, or did their brains change over time as the result of doing these practices and of being spiritual? In other words, what came first?

To answer this chicken and the egg question, we need a longitudinal study. The studies that we've talked about so far are really just taking a one-time look at the people who are religious and the people who aren't and trying to make a comparison; but how have they changed over time? Can we take people who are early on their lives and follow them over time; or can we take people who maybe have never done a practice like meditation or prayer, have them begin to do a practice, and study them for many months or even years?

If we can evaluate what happens in their thought processes and their spiritual beliefs over time, we might better determine whether the brain causes people to believe or not.

It's also possible that the longer a person believes in something, the more their brain changes to accept that belief.

I'm a pretty avid tennis player, and one of the analogies that I always think about is playing tennis in this regard. We all are able to play tennis—if I put a racket in your hands right now, you could probably go out and play tennis, hit the ball—and if all of us went out and practiced for hours and hours every single day, we'd all get a lot better; but we'd also have to acknowledge that some people are just going to naturally be better than others. I think this tennis analogy applies very nicely to the notion of people who are spiritual, because on one hand we might argue that everyone has an ability to be spiritual to some degree, but the more we engage it the more spiritual we can become. It raises some fascinating questions as to if you took somebody who really wasn't that spiritual at least in terms of their predisposition and you had them engage in these practices a lot, they might actually get to a moderate level of spirituality. On the other hand, someone who might be predisposed to being a very spiritual person, if they were never able to engage in any kind of religious or spiritual practices, then perhaps they'd ultimately not be all that spiritual. To some degree, there may be something built in inside of us, but it may also be something that is learned and changed over time.

Unfortunately, at this time in terms of the research, there are no longitudinal studies that have specifically compared the way a believer's brain changes over time and compared that to the way a nonbeliever's brain changes over time. However, we'll be considering some other interesting longitudinal studies later in the course that may shed some light on this fascinating issue.

For now, let's look at another approach that uses imaging technology to compare brain activity in believers and nonbelievers.

As someone studying spirituality and the brain, I was very interested in trying to get at some way of understanding where this difference would actually be in the brain and I started to engage in some kind of fun conversations with some friends of mine who were very staunch atheists. I said to them, "You know, would it be possible for you to actually come into our lab and we could scan your brain when you're meditating perhaps"—these were all people who actually had a fairly active meditation practice even though they were atheists—and I said, "Could you come in and instead of meditating the usual way you did, actually meditate on the idea of God?" Essentially what I was doing was asking an atheist to contemplate God. I thought if we could actually scan their brains while they were contemplating God, I could compare what was going on in their brain to what was going on in the brain of, for example, our Franciscan nuns, who also prayed or meditated on the idea of God. That's exactly what we did: We brought a few of my friends in to actually scan their brains while they contemplated the notion of God, and we scanned them at rest and during this contemplation.

What happened in their brains? We looked at the frontal lobes—which, as we know, turned on in the Franciscan nuns—and what happened to the atheists who were contemplating God? Their frontal lobes actually didn't turn on; in fact, if we looked at the scans, it looked like one side of the frontal lobe actually turned on a little bit and the other side actually turned off a little bit. What's going on here? If the frontal lobes help us to concentrate on something and to focus on something and they're having a real problem in actually doing it, maybe they're struggling with a sense of cognitive dissonance; they're trying to focus on something that they really don't like very much, they don't feel comfortable focusing on it. Clearly the nuns do; they're really able to engage the concepts of their prayer, of their meditation, and of the notion of God. Already we're starting to see where there are certain differences between those people who are atheists and those people who are believers when they actually engage the topic or the concept of God.

What about some other studies that could be done to look at the difference between atheists and believers? In fact, you may actually be able to think of some ways of studying the differences between these two groups of people. One of the arguments has frequently been that those people who are believers are not as logically sound as those people who are nonbelievers; the nonbelievers are more skeptical. Studies have looked at the ability to interpret syllogisms—logical arguments—to see how religious people and nonreligious people actually interpret these logical problems and these different patterns.

Several studies have actually been designed to look at this difference. Syllogisms are usually used in some way of trying to get at how well they're able to think logically; but what one very interesting study decided to do was to kind of tweak these syllogisms from being simply logical questions to being questions that were either pro- or anti-religious. For example, a pro-religious syllogism would be something like the following:

If to succeed in life you have to be Christian, and if a person named Thomas wants to succeed in life, then Thomas should become a Christian. Internally, this is a logically accurate statement. You don't have to necessarily agree with each part of the statement, but if you look at the given first two statements, the third one follows logically. But it's also a pro-religious syllogism because it speaks very positively about religion.

An anti-religious syllogism might be something along the following:

If being religious is found to be bad for people who have depression, and if you suffer from depression, then you should try to be less spiritual or religious. Again, internally this makes logical sense. Whether you believe in those first two statements or not is irrelevant; if you accept them, then logically they make sense.

This study looked at religious and non-religious people and asked them a whole series of these pro- and anti-religious syllogisms.

The results were very intriguing, and perhaps to some degree not surprising. The religious people actually did better on the pro-religious syllogisms than the non-religious people; and, not surprisingly, the atheists—the non-religious people—did better on the anti-religious questions. The result suggests that both groups make logical mistakes, they just happen to make them in the direction of their prevailing belief system. The ways in which we think about ourselves, the ways in which we believe about our world, actually change the way we understand our world.

Another study also demonstrated the difference between believers and nonbelievers in a very intriguing way that also bears directly on our question about how the brain responds differently in one group or the other. But it started out a bit as a non-brain study: They brought believers and nonbelievers in to their lab and they asked them to look at a series of photographs. These photos had been distorted so that they looked a little bit like a Rorschach kind of test; it was very difficult to tell what was actually in the photos. Within the photos, though, there were some real and some non-real elements; so there may be a picture of a dog, for example, which was actually in there and then maybe there were some other pictures of a tree that it kind of looked like a tree but that really wasn't in the picture.

They asked believers and nonbelievers to describe what these photos looked like and the things that they saw in them.

What were the results? They were very interesting. Believers more likely to see things that were there but also sometimes saw things that weren't there. On the other hand, nonbelievers never saw things that weren't there but sometimes did miss the things that were there. Again, each group made mistakes, but in directions that were consistent with their beliefs. The idea is that those people who believe are more willing to accept other pieces of information as part of reality and hence could see other things in those pictures than what were actually there. On the other hand, the nonbelievers tend to have a lower threshold as to what they'll accept as being real, and they cut off where that threshold is so that they don't see some of the things that actually are there.

But there's one other interesting part of this study: The experimenters actually gave to the nonbelievers a drug that helps to increase the amount of the chemical dopamine in the brain. We haven't talked much yet about the neurotransmitters in the brain—we're going to discuss this in much more detail later on in the course—but for now what I want you to know about dopamine is that it's very involved in our ability to perceive the world, it's very involved in our emotional responses, and it's also very involved in our ability to move and to behave properly in the world. What happened when they actually gave a drug that increased the level of dopamine to the nonbelievers and then gave them those same pictures again? The nonbelievers actually responded much more like the believers did now: They actually saw some things that weren't there and they picked up almost all the things that were there. In this context, this study shows that dopamine may be a very important mediator of how we interpret our sensory information and how we may actually turn into somebody who believes in a spiritual way or in a non-spiritual way. It would certainly be interesting to see if there's some deeper relationship between these neurotransmitters and specific aspects of spirituality.

The relationship between dopamine and spirituality actually takes another very interesting turn in a study that was conducted by Dr. Dean Hamer, who was a behavioral geneticist at NIH.

Hamer actually analyzed the DNA from many different people to try to get a sense as to what aspects of DNA affect our personality. The way this study worked was that he gave a whole series of personality tests to over 1,000 individuals—asked them all kinds of questions about their emotions, about their thought processes; all different kinds of things—and he also took blood samples from them to look at all of their different genetic patterns. In this study, he identified one particular gene that he ultimately called the "God gene." This gene was found to correlate with people's feelings of what was called self-transcendence.

What is self-transcendence? It's that feeling of being able to get beyond your self; to connect to something that's simply beyond the material world. Of course, this sounds very much like the spiritual experiences that people often describe. There's this sense that they can go beyond their self, they can get beyond where they are in the everyday reality world, and connect with something that's greater than the self.

What was particularly interesting about this result was that this so-called "God gene" was involved in producing something called the VMAT2 receptor. We know, for example, that the VMAT2 receptor actually regulates the concentration of dopamine, and it also regulates the concentration of another neurotransmitter chemical called serotonin. As I mentioned, dopamine and also serotonin are very involved in our emotions, very involved in our sensory perceptions of the world, and therefore have a great deal to do with how we experience and think about our world.

Some scientists noted that the effect of this gene on the differences in spiritual beliefs is likely to be very, very low; maybe less than about 10 percent of the actual effect. But Doctor Hamer was very quick to point out that this "God gene" doesn't imply that this is the only factor in making someone spiritual or religious, but it does seem to be part of the process. Some religious people, of course, were very concerned that religion was actually being reduced only to our genes; ignoring the spiritual doctrines, our cultural and various traditions that have had an impact on what makes people religious and spiritual; and, of course, most importantly they argue that focusing in on the genes actually ignores even the existence of God. But Hamer responded that the existence of such a gene wouldn't be incompatible with the existence of a personal God. "Religious believers," he said, "can point to the existence of God genes as one more sign of the creator's ingenuity—a clever way to help human [beings] acknowledge and embrace a divine presence."

In fact, Hamer repeatedly notes in his book that, "This book is about whether God genes exist, not about whether there is a God."

One of the advantages of Doctor Hamer's study is that it looked at a relatively large number of people; but in order to fully evaluate and answer this question about believers and nonbelievers, we may need to greatly expand the population of people that we're going to study. We could study—as a bunch of researchers have already done—the contrast between atheists and religious people; that's obviously the most simple way to do it. We take people who are very religious, we take people who are very non-religious, and we look at the differences between them. But we might also try to consider studying the general population, because there we're going to get a much greater range; and we can see how spirituality is expressed along a continuum of many different people and many different cultures and traditions.

It's a little bit like trying to study music. There are a lot of different ways that we could get at how we as human beings process and think and experience music. One way would be to compare the expert musicians to those people who are completely tone deaf. That's a little bit like our comparison of religious people and non-religious people; we're taking those who are and those who really aren't and seeing where the differences are.

We could also compare musical abilities in the general public. We could look at a how huge array of people think about music, from those who are fairly tone deaf, to those who maybe practiced the piano when they were kids, to those who like to sing in the shower, to those who are actually expert musicians. In fact, it might be interesting to study children before they've ever had any kind of musical induction or any kind of musical lesson and see which of them become musicians and which of them don't. Again, it'd be very helpful then to see which of them became novices and experts to see where those differences are. One other possibility—which has always been intriguing to me—is to not just look at the experts and the non-experts, but to look at the people who are truly gifted in this particular practice. Wouldn't it have been fascinating to have been able to study Mozart's brain, for example? Here we have a person who looked at music from an entirely different perspective from almost everyone else who's ever lived; what would that person's brain look like and how would that be different from everyone else? Now extrapolate this to our discussions about religion and spirituality: We could study believers and nonbelievers as we said, we could look at the general population, or maybe we actually focus on those who are at the very pinnacle of spirituality; the Mother Theresa's of the world, the Dalai Lama. There are many different fascinating possibilities that we can begin to explore to help us better understand the spiritual brain, and why some people are more spiritual than others and how spirituality is expressed throughout humanity.

It appears that there may be some very important differences in believers and nonbelievers, and the differences may be manifested in how they think and interpret reality; but ultimately these differences are also reflected in the structure and the function of their brain.

Different parts of the brain react differently in believers and nonbelievers; and, of course, there's probably a broad spectrum of belief and few people are at the extreme of either unshakeable belief or absolute unbelief in a spiritual phenomena or God. As scientific research becomes more sophisticated, we'll be able to better analyze these differences along the entire spectrum of belief. But in the meantime, it's fascinating to consider how far belief may be determined from birth by our genes, acquired through our interactions with other people, or perhaps even acquired through an actual encounter with God.

Spiritual Development

Lecture 6

The brain and spirituality appear to develop in parallel throughout the human life span. It is through this developmental process that we come to our religious and spiritual belief systems—first as children through stories; then as adolescents, when we begin to create our own belief systems; and finally into adulthood, when we consolidate our beliefs. As we grow and develop, our brain grows and develops, and this appears to parallel our spiritual growth.

Fowler's Model of Spiritual Development

- In his book *Stages of Faith*, James Fowler offered a template for spiritual development over the course of a human lifetime. He identified seven stages of development, beginning at stage zero and going through stage six. Each stage corresponds to a particular period in a person's life—from infancy through late adulthood.

- Fowler's model is not meant to be taken too exactly. Not everyone goes through all seven stages—nor does everyone attain the same level of spiritual development on the same chronological schedule. It is also not certain whether different traditions and cultures have different levels of spiritual development.

- The human brain changes and develops throughout life, so perhaps we can learn something about spiritual development by looking at brain development. If we consider spirituality from a neurophysiological perspective, we might expect that spirituality develops along the same lines as the brain. In addition, we might expect that both spirituality and the brain develop in a similar way in all people. In other words, there should be certain universal processes.

- The first stage of Fowler's model is stage zero, which corresponds with infancy. Fowler refers to this as the stage of undifferentiated faith.

- From a neurological standpoint, there is little in the way of higher cognitive functions during infancy, especially with regard to integrating sensory phenomena. As a result, there can be no identifiable or differentiated faith or belief system. The infant operates almost exclusively in a stimulus-response mode.

© Stockbyte/Thinkstock.

- Even if the infant is raised in a highly devoted religious family, he or she cannot cognitively absorb this

It is during childhood when the human brain has the highest metabolism that it will ever have over the lifespan of an individual.

information in order to derive an understanding of any particular religious perspective. This is the stage where the seeds of trust, hope, and love are developed.

- It is imperative that the environment provides enough consistency and nurturance and is not one in which there is deprivation, which—at least in animal models—results in a lack of the neuronal complexity and interconnectedness that lay the foundation for future brain development.

- Such isolation is arguably associated with an overall lack of connections not only between the neurons in the individual's brain, but also between the individual and the rest of his or her environment. If such a lack of connection persists beyond this stage, then the individual's association areas may not form adequately, thus preventing the person from being able to explore spirituality and meaning in the first place. This stage is, therefore, critical for overall development—both psychologically and spiritually.

- A child's pattern of brain function changes throughout the first year of life, with initial increases in the sensorimotor cortex, thalamus, brain stem, and cerebellum. There is no significant higher cortical function and, subsequently, no strong evidence of well-integrated cognitive functioning at this stage.

- At eight to nine months, there is increasing activity in the frontal lobes and other brain association areas, coinciding with the advent of cognitive thinking and social interaction. Brain scans qualitatively begin to resemble the adult brain after one to two years. This sets the stage for future brain and spiritual development.

- The second of Fowler's stages, which is actually stage one, is called the intuitive-projective faith stage. For Fowler, stage one extends from age two to age six.

- During this stage, children are able to gain some control over the world through the use of language and symbolic representation, but their thinking is magical, episodic, and not constrained by stable logical operations.

- During this stage, children have integrated and conceptualized God in the way in which society has ingrained it into them through fantasy, stories, and dramatic representations. Church plays, holiday stories, and simplistic prayers are what children draw on for their information about religious and spiritual ideas.

- Neurophysiological development is associated with a progressive increase in overall brain metabolism, particularly in the neocortex. The initial increase in metabolism is likely associated with the overproduction of neurons and their connections.

- During stage one, the child's brain is constantly establishing so many different connections that there is tremendous expansion and overconnectedness between neurons. The result is that there are few clearly defined rules, and there is a sense of blending many different experiences and ideas.

- The child would, therefore, perceive the world as being comprised of many overlapping ideas, experiences, and feelings and would likely see things in ways that appear to be a fantasy to older individuals. Children in this stage will likely not see any problem blending ideas about God with very mundane issues.

- In this stage, children also have a developing sense of self with increasing activity in the frontal and parietal lobes. With this developing sense of self comes the beginning of experiencing concepts of death, sex, strong taboos within society, and the ultimate conditions of existence. However, children will not likely be able to make sense of these complex issues in the same way a mature adult would.

- Fowler's next stage, stage two, occurs during the school-age years—approximately six to 10 years of age—and is referred to as the mythic-literal faith stage.

- During this stage, a child begins to internalize stories, beliefs, and observances that symbolize belonging to a community or group. This internalization enables the older child to begin to compose a worldview and ideology. Beliefs are related to literal interpretations of religions or doctrines and are usually composed of moral rules and attitudes.

- By removing inappropriate neural connections, the brain allows for the appropriate connections to form. This process likely involves specific neural rules by which some connections are strengthened and others are cut. These rules are likely associated with the elaboration of myth in order to provide information and understanding of the world around us. During stage two, stories, drama, and myth are the primary venues in which ideas are experienced.

- As a child reaches adolescence, he or she enters stage three of the model of spiritual development—a stage that Fowler calls synthetic-conventional faith stage.

- An adolescent's sense of spirituality is likely to be built upon notions of religion and spirituality that were established in the childhood stages. During the synthetic-conventional stage, there is elaboration of basic ideas of the person's overall world perspective.

- This is the period in which the person's basic approach to life, relationships, self, and spirituality are galvanized and fully elaborated. Most religions recognize how a person's spirituality matures at this stage by incorporating specific religious ceremonies such as bar or bat mitzvah in the Jewish tradition and confirmation in the Christian tradition. These ceremonies recognize that the individual has left his or her childhood belief system and is entering into the belief system of adulthood.

- This is also a complex stage due to a variety of factors, including hormonal states and sexual maturation. In addition, the adolescent's world begins to extend beyond the family into peer and other cohort groups.

- Neurophysiologically, this stage corresponds to a time in which the overall metabolism in the brain begins to decrease—probably from the age of 11 to 20. This is associated with the pruning of neuronal connections in order to establish the primary connections that will take the person into adulthood.

- Formal operational thinking and mutual perspective taking characterize this stage. Plasticity of the brain decreases notably during the decreasing metabolism phase of brain development.

- There is still significant room for developing and learning new ideas and concepts, but these ideas are not as likely to be the kind of foundational concepts that were formed in childhood stages.

- Stage four of Fowler's model is the individuative-reflective faith stage, which occurs when there is a break between the person's own belief system and whatever or whoever has been the authority figure in his or her life. There is critical distancing from one's established value system.

- This stage usually occurs during young adulthood but can happen as late as age 30 to 40. It is a time when one begins to take responsibility for his or her choices—irrespective of what others feel.

- Neurophysiologically, this stage is associated with the full development of the cognitive and emotional processes that are now significantly more stable than in all of the previous stages. Few new neuronal connections are established, and the pruning of connections is also limited. This stage becomes the person's state throughout the majority of their life.

- As a person moves into midadulthood, he or she may enter the fifth stage of Fowler's model, which he called the conjunctive faith stage. The initiating factor that propels a person into stage five is disillusionment with one's compromises and recognition that life is more complex than one's ability to use logic and abstract thinking. This leads to the search for a more multileveled approach to life truth through other spiritual and philosophical traditions.

- At this stage, the individual is ready for significant encounters with other traditions in a quest for meaning and value in life. There is now an integration of the self that was previously unrecognized or suppressed. The end result is a reclaiming and reworking of one's identity and faith through understanding his or her life and how it relates to humanity.

- Neurophysiologically, this stage is associated with a decrease in overall brain metabolic activity. This decrease begins around the age of 40 and slowly progresses throughout the remainder of the individual's life.

- This decrease, while unknown to the person, may reflect or at least contribute to the notion of disillusionment because the brain no longer appears to be able to find the answers it was striving so hard to find with its full complement of functions.

- As neural connections are lost, there may be a sense that the answers are slipping away and that it is unlikely that they will be obtained on the present path. The self may also be perceived to be somewhat slipping away because the connections between the neurons subserving the self and the sensory and cognitive input become diminished. The result may be a concern that the self can no longer face the struggle to know and understand.

- The final stage of spiritual development, stage six in Fowler's model, is called the universalizing faith stage.

- The transition to this stage may be spontaneous or may require deep reflection and personal struggle. The ultimate goal is the notion of a more universal concept of religion and the universe.

- In universalizing faith, there is a sense of unity between the self and the tenets of the individual's religious tradition. This may represent a sense of union of the self with God or ultimate reality. This union may result from various spiritual practices or experiences.

- Looking at this stage from a neuroscientific perspective, we can make some very interesting observations. The experience of union with God likely arises from the deafferentation of sensory and cognitive inputs into the association areas that subserve the orientation abilities of the brain. The fact that there is already a concomitant decrease in overall neuronal function and interconnectedness may actually contribute to this type of experience, typically occurring in older individuals.

Suggested Reading

Fowler, *Stages of Faith.*

Heller, *The Children's God.*

Newberg and Newberg, "A Neuropsychological Perspective on Spiritual Development."

Questions to Consider

1. What are the different stages of spiritual development as people go through their lives?

2. How does spiritual development parallel brain development throughout the lifespan?

Spiritual Development
Lecture 6—Transcript

In our last lecture, we explored some possible neurological and genetic differences between believers and atheists. To me, this exploration raises a fascinating question: If people can become believers or atheists, how does this actually happen? When in each of our lives do we find our beliefs?

In his book *Stages of Faith*, Doctor James Fowler offered a template for spiritual development over the course of a human lifetime. He actually identified seven stages of development, beginning at stage zero—which was a pre-stage—and going through stage six. Each stage, he felt, corresponds to a particular period in a person's life from infancy through late adulthood that has to do with the development of a person's spiritual or religious beliefs.

Fowler's model is not meant to be taken too exactly; after all, not everyone goes through all seven stages, nor does everyone attain the same level of spiritual development at the same time or within the same context of their life. It's also not clear whether different traditions and cultures actually have different levels or types of spiritual development.

As I pondered some of these developmental questions, I started to turn towards my background in brain imaging. I've performed scans on people from infancy through adulthood and actually even at the point of death; and what I found fascinating in my studies of the human brain is how it changes and develops throughout a person's life. If that's the case, then perhaps we can learn something about spiritual development by looking at the brain's development. If we consider spirituality from a neurophysiological perspective, we might expect that spirituality develops along the same lines as the brain. In addition, we might expect that both spirituality and the brain develop in a similar way in almost every person; so there should be certain universal processes that we can understand in the context of a person's spiritual or brain development. With that in mind, I began to see how well Fowler's model of spiritual development matched what was going on in the brain during its development, and I came across a rather remarkable association.

In this lecture, let's look at Fowler's model of spiritual development and see what's happening in the brain at each of the seven stages. In order to accomplish this, we'll use what we know about the brain's development from a variety of brain imaging studies, including those that are both structural and functional, which have helped us delineate how the brain actually develops throughout our life. We'll eventually strive to develop a very integrated model that might be called a neurospiritual development model.

Let's begin and think about Fowler's model and the first stage that he talks about. In this case, it's stage zero, which as I mentioned a few moments ago is actually a pre-stage and corresponds to infancy. Fowler refers to this as the stage of undifferentiated faith.

From a neurological standpoint, there's little in the way of higher cognitive functions during infancy, especially with regard to integrating all the different sensory and cognitive information that exists out there in the world. As a result, there really can't be any identifiable or differentiated faith or belief system.

The infant operates almost exclusively in a stimulus/response mode without really thinking about anything in particular.

Even if the infant is raised in a highly-devoted religious family, he or she really can't absorb any of the cognitive information or the ideas that come about within the context of their particular religious or spiritual perspective.

This is still a very important stage even though there's no real religious ideology or concepts that are developing in the brain. This is the stage where the seeds of all of this occur; the seeds of trust, hope, love, and spirituality are developed.

Of course, it's imperative that the environment provides enough consistency and nurturance and isn't one in which there's a lot of deprivation.

When animals at least are raised in a very sensory- and love-deprived situation, the result is a brain that's very disconnected; there are very few neurons that connect to other neurons, and therefore they aren't able to develop in the same way that they would if they were brought up in a very enriched kind of environment. Such isolation is arguably associated with an overall lack of connections in the brain, and not only between the neurons themselves but between the individual person or animal and the rest of their entire environment. If such a lack of connection persists beyond this stage, then the individual's association areas that we talked about that help with all of that higher brain functioning may not form adequately, and this prevents the person from being able to explore their world and their spiritual sense and meaning in the first place.

This stage is critical to overall development, both psychologically and spiritually.

What actually is going on in the brain throughout that first year of life? The brain function patterns that are seen on brain scans basically show that all that's really working in the infants' brain are the sensory areas that receive all of the information from the outside world, the motor areas (because clearly infants can move), and a lot of the very core structures: the thalamus that we mentioned before, and the brain stem that connects the body and the brain to each other. There are no significant higher cortical functions, and subsequently there's no evidence for any kind of well-integrated cognitive functioning in this stage. Of course, anyone who's ever been around an infant can attest to this that they don't really think about anything. They really just function on a very stimulus response; they feel things, they can move, but that's really about it. At about eight to nine months, there's a beginning of increased activity in the frontal lobes and other brain association areas that correspond with the advent of some cognitive thought processes and social interactions. In fact, it's actually not until the infant is about one to two years old that the brain scan actually qualitatively looks like an adult brain. Interestingly, if we look at people's brains as they get much older—people who have very severe dementia from Alzheimer's disease, for example— it's amazing that their brain actually looks very similar to a child's brain. We might actually be able to infer a little bit about where spirituality may ultimately go as an individual develops all the way through life to the very end stages of their life. This brings us to the second of Fowler's stages. Remember, his first stage actually starts at zero, so this next stage is actually stage one. Fowler refers to stage one as the intuitive-projective stage; that's what he calls it.

For Fowler, stage one extends from about ages two to about six years old. During this stage, a child is able to gain some control over his world through the use of language and symbolic representation. The child is beginning to speak, they're beginning to think about things, but their thought processes are typically in a very magical kind of way; they're not constrained by the usual logical operations that we as adults tend to think along. Again, for anyone who's had any time to interact with a child in that two-to-three-year age range, we understand that. They're really just trying to understand their world and they put together things in very, very fun but also strange ways.

During this stage, a child has begun to integrate and conceptualize some spiritual ideas; they're beginning to understand what God is in the ways in which society has started to ingrain it within them. Typically this is done through stories, through fantasy, through different dramatic representation; and that's why we see oftentimes children taking part in church plays, or having fun at holidays, and hearing these religious and spiritual stories for the first time. They might be asked to engage in very simplistic prayers—the bedtime prayer, grace before a meal—and this is what a child basically can draw on in terms of their information about religious and spiritual ideas.

The neurophysiological development at this time is associated with a progressive increase in the brain's overall metabolism, particularly in the cortex; particularly in those higher areas of the brain. This initial increased metabolism is probably related to an overproduction of neurons and their connections. In fact, it's fascinating, but it's really during this kind of childhood time period that the brain actually has the highest metabolism that it will ever have throughout our lives.

What's going on during stage one? Basically, in the brain, the child's brain is establishing so many different kinds of connections all of the time, there's a great deal of expansion and really over-connectedness between the neurons. The result is that there are very few clearly-defined rules and there's a sense of blending many different kinds of experiences and ideas.

The child would therefore perceive the world as being comprised by many overlapping ideas, experiences, feelings; all different kinds of unusual and illogical ways that appear to be fantasy to older individuals but to the child they make a lot of sense.

Children in this stage therefore are likely to not see a whole lot of problem in blending all kinds of unusual ideas about God, especially with very mundane kinds of issues. For example, the child may think that God makes the toaster heat up the bread. One person I know used to believe that they could contact god by tying a letter to a helium balloon and letting it go from their backyard. Another person reported that when they were young, they believed that black and white animals like pandas and zebras were actually ones that God had forgotten to color in his coloring book.

We can see that there are some very unusual and funny ways in which children begin to think about their world, and particularly their sense of spirituality and about God. But they also have a developing sense of their self, and that comes along with increased activity in the brain, particularly in the frontal and the parietal lobes.

With this developing sense of self comes the beginning of experiencing concepts such as death, sex, different taboos of society (things that they shouldn't be doing), different moral ideas, and ultimate conditions of existence (what it means to be here on Earth).

However, children won't likely be able to make sense of all of these complex issues in the same way that a mature adult would; so they're starting to get a notion of what these ideas are all about, but they're not yet really able to engage them because they have so many different connections that there's no way for them to really create a very coherent idea about what the world is and how they should begin to understand it.

Fowler's next stage, stage two, occurs during the school age years from about 6–10 years of age. He refers to this stage as the mythic-literal stage, and it's during this stage that a child begins to internalize myths, different stories, beliefs, observances, and so forth that symbolize belonging to their community or their religious or spiritual group. As the child internalizes these ideas, it enables them to compose a worldview and an ideology that they can now begin to foster and create as they grow up. However, for the child at this stage,

beliefs still are relatively literal in terms of their interpretation; they think about religious ideas, doctrines in very concrete ways; and usually even the moral ideas, rules, and attitudes that they come across are thought of in very cut and dry ways.

What's going on there in the brain is very interesting, because I mentioned in the last stage they were over-connected, so what's starting to happen is the brain is starting to cut back different neural connections, and typically it starts with the inappropriate ones. By removing inappropriate neural connections, the brain allows for the appropriate connections to form, and this process likely involves very specific neural rules by which some connections are strengthened and others are actually cut.

In the neuroscientific world, we sometimes refer to this as being pruned back.

The rules are likely associated with the elaboration of different stories, myths, or ideas in order to provide information and understanding of the world around us to the child.

We'll be discussing myth in a later lecture, but for the purposes of what we're talking about right here, it's important to note that during this stage two, stories, drama, and myth are the primary venues in which these different ideas are experienced.

Again, what's going on here is that through these stories, the child's neuroconnections that are wrong—the wrong ways to think about God, the wrong ways to think about morality—those start to get cut away and the person begins to develop the kinds of neuroconnections that support the behaviors and the ideas that they're told to believe and that ultimately will work for them as they grow up into adolescence and adulthood.

Let's talk about the next stage, which is stage three and it's really the adolescent stage. For Fowler, he calls it the synthetic-conventional stage.

An adolescent's sense of spirituality is likely to be built upon notions of religion and spirituality that were established in the prior stages, in the childhood stages.

But during the synthetic-conventional stage, there's the elaboration of basic ideas of the person's overall world perspective.

This is really the period in which a person's basic approach to life, relationships, and their self and spirituality become galvanized; they become fully elaborated, or at least work towards being fully elaborated. Of course, many religions recognize how spirituality matures at this stage and actually incorporate specific religious ceremonies such as the Bar or Bat Mitzvah of the Jewish tradition when a child turns 13 or the Confirmation ceremonies in the Christian tradition. These ceremonies recognize that the individual has left his or her childhood belief system and is beginning to develop into the belief system of the adulthood.

From a brain perspective, this is a very complex stage, as almost every one of us knows as we've gone through it. But it's during this stage that many different factors—including our hormones, sexual maturation, peer groups; all of these different things—have an impact on t he brain's development. More and more of the inappropriate connections that were formed during childhood are being cut, but also the higher areas of the brain are forming and establishing the right connections for that person throughout the rest of their life; so they're beginning to think about things in a much more detailed way. The adolescent's world begins to extend beyond their family into their peer, into the other groups of people who are around them—their teachers and so forth—and all of these things are taking part in what's going on in the spiritual development and the brain development of the adolescent.

Neurophysiologically, this seems to be expressed by the continued development of different higher parts of the brain and corresponds to a time where the overall metabolism in the brain is actually beginning to decrease. In fact, it decreases most dramatically between the ages of about 11 and 20 years because it's cutting all of those connections to establish the connections that the brain wants so that we can go forward with the rest of our lives.

What we think is happening now is the person begins to have more formal operational thinking as they get to the end of adolescence; they're able to understand ideas from very complex perspectives; they have the ability to think about other perspectives, so we can actually understand a little bit more about what other people think, maybe people who don't agree with us or maybe people who disagree with the ways in which we were raised in the first place. Again, as many of us know, as we enter into adolescence and into early adulthood, these are the times that we really question the ideas and concepts that we were raised with.

The brain has the ability to continually change, but this ability to change—something called neuroplasticity; the ways in which the brain can continue to adapt and change to our environment—begins to decrease very notably as there's a decrease in the metabolism. Of course, there's still significant room for the continual development and expansion of all different kinds of new ideas and concepts, but these ideas aren't likely to be as foundational as the ones that were formed in childhood. If you think about it—and research has shown this—most people, when you ask them where their religious and spiritual beliefs are in adulthood, will tell you that they're very similar to the ones they developed in childhood and adolescence; so once those very foundational beliefs begin to form and are ingrained within the neural connections of the brain, that's something that stays with us—and continues to be with us—through the rest of our lives.Now we come to adulthood and Fowler's stage four, which he refers to as the individuative and reflective stage. This stage occurs when there's really a fuller break between the person's own belief system and whatever or whoever had been the authority figures in their life before.

There's a critical distancing of one's established value system.

This stage usually does occur during young adulthood, usually around the college age years, but it can happen as late as the ages of 30–40 years old. This stage is a time when one begins to take responsibility for their own choices, their own actions, irrespective of what other people feel.

Neurophysiologically, this stage is associated with the fullest development of our cognitive and emotional processes. These are now at the adult levels of brain functioning, and scans demonstrate very substantial activity going on and interacting between all the different parts of the brain—the higher parts of the brain, the emotional parts of the brain—that allow us to create a very stable and substantial view of the world, and certainly much more so than all the different changes that were going on in the previous stages. There are very few new neural connections that are established, and the pruning of connections is also limited in the brain; at least they're in some reasonable kind of balance.

This stage is where stability starts to kick in; this is the stage where a person's overall personality and the way they're going to be throughout their life really takes hold; and because there's such a balance between new connections and old connections, this is the stability portion of our stage of development and also our stage of spirituality.

As one moves into mid-adulthood, we begin to enter the fifth stage of Fowler's model that he calls the conjunctive faith stage.

The initiating factor that propels a person into this stage five is typically some kind of disillusionment with the person's compromises, issues that they faced in life, and a recognition that life is a lot more complex than one's ability to use the logic and abstract thought processes that had been developing since adolescence.

This leads to the search for a more multileveled approach to life, different ideas about truth and morality, and also different ideas about spiritual and philosophical issues and traditions. It's at this stage that the individual is ready for very significant encounters with other traditions in a quest—going back to our definition, a search—for meaning and value in life.

There's now an integration of the self that was previously unrecognized or even suppressed. As they went into adulthood, they were trying to find themselves; they found themselves, but now they're questioning that

. The end result is basically a reworking or even a reclaiming of one's own identity, and perhaps even a reclaiming of their faith, by an understanding of their life experiences and how it relates to them, and perhaps how it relates to all of humanity.

Neurophysiologically, this stage is associated with an overall decrease in the brain's metabolic activity. This decrease begins around the age of 40 and completely progresses very slowly throughout the remainder of the individual's life.

What's interesting is that the decrease in general is unknown to the person, even though it may ultimately reflect or at least contribute to the notion of disillusionment since the brain no longer appears to be able to find the answers that it was striving so hard to find with its full complement of its cognitive and emotional functions. Part of the reason why the person doesn't perceive this in a very dramatic way is because as this decrease begins to occur, it's in balance; all of the different parts of the brain continue to decrease very slowly, so we tend to not notice it even though it starts to creep into our various ideas and thought processes.

As we get into our final stages of development, we're getting into the older adulthood; and what's going on here is that as all these neural connections are continuing to get lost, there may be a sense that not only the answers but the questions are slipping away from us, and that it's unlikely that we're ever going to be able to get to what we were ultimately searching for from the beginning, at least on the present path.

The self may also be perceived to be somewhat slipping away since the connections between the neurons subserving the self and our sensory environment and our thought processes are decreasing. This is what we see on the scans, and this is what begins to happen within the person themselves. The result may be a concern that the self can no longer face the struggle to know and understand about our world.

The final stage is what's sometimes referred to as the universalizing faith stage, and this is stage six of Fowler's model.

The transition to this stage may be spontaneous; it may require deep reflection or some kind of personal struggle, maybe a struggle with a person, a spouse, or a health-related issue. The ultimate goal is the notion that the person needs to achieve a more universal conception of religion and the universe.

In universalizing faith, there's a sense of unity between the self and the tenets of that particular person's religious tradition. What I mean by that is that they begin to feel more deeply connected with their tradition—they return to that tradition; they want to take part in it—and they realize that the ideas and the beliefs of that particular tradition actually do have the meaning that they were looking for.

For some, this may actually represent a sense of a union of the self with God or even ultimate reality.

This universalizing stage really creates a sense of oneness, a sense of connectedness, between the self and something greater than the self. This may result from a variety of different practices or even experiences, and this relates back to some of the things that we talked about when we first discussed the brain scans: For example, the brain scans of the Franciscan nuns; that when we saw a decrease of activity in the parietal lobe of the brain—that part of the brain that helps us to establish our sense of self—maybe it's that decrease of activity in that area that's associated with this universalizing stage of faith. Looking in more detail at this stage of faith from a neuroscientific perspective, we can actually make some very interesting observations. Basically, the brain has had a progressive decrease of activity in all of the cortical areas and particularly in the parietal lobe; so not only do we see a decrease of activity in the parietal lobe when a person is actually in meditation or prayer and experiences the loss of the sense of self, but it can actually happen naturally as the person's brain gets older. Perhaps this is part of what's going on in this stage of development where we begin to experience a union with God, a union with our spiritual self, which arises from this overall decrease of activity in the cognitive and the sensory areas of the brain that help to support our overall sense of self.

Since there's already this decrease, and an overall decrease in the interconnectedness of different neurons and different connections in the brain, this may actually contribute to this type of experience typically occurring as people get older.

We'll return to the experience of spiritual union with God in later lectures; but for now, I want to pull together what we've learned from today.

Ultimately, the brain and spirituality appear to develop in parallel throughout the lifespan.

It's through this developmental process that we come to our religious and spiritual belief systems, first as children through stories, as adolescents where we begin to create our own belief systems, and finally into adulthood where we consolidate our beliefs.

As we grow and develop, our brain grows and develops along with us; and this appears to parallel our spiritual growth and our spiritual journey. It's interesting to reflect on how our beliefs have changed throughout our life and what parts of the brain might ultimately be involved in helping with that change.

After this lecture, spend some time reflecting on where your beliefs started, where they've gone, and where you are now in your belief systems. Are you more or less religious? Are you more or less spiritual? It will be an interesting reflective exercise that may give you some fascinating insights into your own life and your own spiritual development.

The Myth-Making Brain
Lecture 7

A fundamental part of religions is their elaboration in myths—the stories that form the basis of religions. In fact, there is evidence that our brain is a myth-making machine. Regardless of culture or belief system, myths often have similar components and content. Perhaps they are similar because the brains of all people are similar. In this lecture, you will learn why and how the human brain makes myths.

The Meaning and Purpose of Myths

- Human beings have always constructed myths, or stories, that become incorporated into burial rituals, temples, and civilizations.

- Contrary to popular belief, the term "myth" does not imply falsehood. The word actually comes from the Greek *mythos*, which translates as "word"—but one spoken with deep, unquestioned authority. *Mythos* is, in turn, anchored in another Greek term, *musteion*, which means "to close the eyes or the mouth."

- Myths are powerful stories, but apart from their expressive power and emotional impact, what are myths used for? Primarily, we develop myths to explain our world. Frequently, however, we use them to explain things we can't readily comprehend.

- Myths, therefore, help us to understand our universe and ourselves. Myths also show us what is most important and what, in terms of the inner life, is most deeply and profoundly true. The power of myth lies beneath its literal interpretations—in the ability of its universal symbols and themes to connect us with the most essential parts of ourselves in ways that logic and reason cannot.

- By this definition, religions must be based in myth if they are to have anything meaningful to say to us. In this sense, the story of Jesus would be a myth even if it were literally and historically true because the power of the story lies underneath the literal and historical facts.

In Judaism, the ritual of the Passover seder involves the retelling of the story of Moses, among other stories.

- Likewise, even if the extraordinary events that myths chronicle never happened and the beings they portray never existed, the lasting myths of past cultures all contain psychological and spiritual truths that resonate with the psyches and spirits of people today.

- However, myths are not just the great stories of the past. We actually create myths all the time to explain and understand the world. Our brain functions to generate stories about the world.

- Neuroscience tells us that the brain processes everything we think and perceive about the world. Brain scans show different areas lighting up in the brain when we see something, hear something, feel something, or think something. These processes then come together to provide a rendition of what is going on around us in the world.

- Given the brain's limitations, it seems that the brain does the best it can at creating a coherent story about what it is processing. This story helps the brain to respond to the world in effective and adaptive ways. On a fundamental level, we must always remember that the entire story our brain presents for us about the world is a second-hand rendition of what is actually out there.

- Our brain is simply trying to help us make sense of this bafflingly complex and uncertain world. Of course, that's what all the great myths from history do, too—they help us understand the world and our place in it.

The Structure of Myths
- Myths include language so that we can transmit them to others.

- Myths include ideas about spirituality, morality, and reality.

- Myths contain emotional content—both positive and negative.

- Myths provide examples or suggestions with regard to future behaviors we should implement.

- Essentially, all myths can be reduced to a simple framework.
  o Myths focus on a crucial existential concern—the creation of the world, for example, or how evil came to be.

  o They frame that concern as a pair of apparently irreconcilable opposites: heroes and monsters, gods and humans, life and death, heaven and hell.

  o Most importantly, myths reconcile those opposites, often through the actions of gods or other spiritual powers, in a way that relieves our existential concerns.

- The creation of these structured stories requires the creative, combined interaction of all the cognitive processes of the brain.

- The brain has four basic cognitive functions: the quantitative function, the binary function, the causal function, and the existential function. Two of these functions appear to play especially significant roles in the creation and understanding of myth.

- The first cognitive process that is crucial to the myth-making mind is the causal function; after all, myths are essentially about the causes of things. The second process is the binary function, which refers to the ability to frame the world in terms of basic polar opposites.

- The human brain's ability to reduce the most complicated relationships of space and time to simple pairs of opposites—above and below, in and out, left and right, before and after—gives the mind a powerful method of ordering external reality.

The Universal Myth-Making Process

- Each of us creates our own myths about the world, and in addition to the myths of our own creation, we also embrace and rely on myths that we have learned from others.

- Imagine a close-knit prehistoric clan. One of the members of this clan has just died. His body lies on a bearskin. Others approach and touch him gently. They sense immediately that the man who used to be no longer exists. What was once a warm and vital person has suddenly become a cold and lifeless thing.

- The clan's chieftain, an introspective man, slumps beside the campfire and broods over the lifeless form that was once his friend. He wonders what is missing, how it was lost, and where it has gone. As he watches the crackling fire, his stomach tightens with sadness and anxiety. His mind's need for cause will not rest until it finds resolution, but the longer he dwells upon the unnerving puzzle of life and death, the deeper he sinks into a kind of existential dread.

- In neurobiological terms, the grieving chief is in the grip of a strong arousal response that began in the chieftain's brain when the amygdala noticed frustration in the logical left hemisphere— the effect of the chief's intense, prolonged brooding over this existential problem.

- Interpreting this frustration as a sign of distress, the amygdala triggered a limbic fear response and sent off neural signals, activating the arousal system. As the chief continues to ruminate on his grief and fear, that arousal response intensifies. His pulse quickens, his breath grows shallow and rapid, and his forehead becomes beaded in sweat.

- The chief stares at the fire, turning his thoughts around and around in his head. Soon, the fire has burned down to embers: The fire was once bright and alive, but now it's gone, and soon there will be nothing but lifeless gray ashes. As the last wisps of smoke rise toward the sky, he turns to the body of his fallen friend. It occurs to him that his comrade's life and spirit have vanished as completely as the flames. Before he can consciously phrase the thought, he is struck by the deep conviction that the very essence of his friend has escaped to the heavens, like smoke, the rising spirit of the fire.

- This conviction begins as just one more possibility offered up by the intellectual pondering of the brain's abstract processes, most likely on the left side. However, as soon as it enters the chief's consciousness, it is embraced by the more holistic processes of the right side of his brain.

- Suddenly, the agreement of both sides of the brain causes a kind of neurological resonance that sends positive neural discharges racing through the limbic system to stimulate pleasure centers in the hypothalamus. Because the hypothalamus regulates the autonomic nervous system, these strong pleasure impulses trigger a response from the quiescent system, and the chief experiences this as a powerful surge of calmness and peace.

- All of this happens too quickly for the arousal response that triggered the chief's anxiety to subside. For a remarkable moment, both the quiescent and arousal systems are simultaneously active, immersing the chief in a blend of fear and rapture—a state of intensely pleasurable agitation that some neurologists call the eureka response—and the chief interprets this as a rush of ecstasy and awe.

- For him, he finally understands the meaning of death—and life. In this transforming flash of insight, the chief is suddenly freed from his grief and despair; in a deeper sense, he feels that he has been freed from the bonds of death.

- The insight strikes him with the force of revelation. The experience feels vividly, palpably real. In that moment, the opposites of life and death are no longer locked in conflict; they have been mythically, and perhaps mystically, resolved. He now sees clearly the absolute truth of things—that the spirits of the dead live on.

- However, he also feels that because of the intensity of his experience, he has discovered a primal truth. It is more than an idea; it is a sense that he has experienced some ultimate reality and meaning.

- Religious myths provide stories about how we as human beings relate to God. They teach us about being devoted to God and how and why to behave in certain ways.

- In this chieftain, many factors were involved, including strong emotions affecting the limbic system, visual stimuli (for example, the fire), the frustration of the brain seeking an elusive cause, the binary problem of life and death, and the holistic solution.

Science as a Form of Myth
- Science is a myth in the sense that it tells a story about how the world works. There are fundamental aspects of science that are similar to all myths.

- Science addresses fundamental questions such as: Where did the world come from? What makes the seasons change and the sun give heat and light? What causes earthquakes, hurricanes, and volcanic eruptions? Myths seek to answer questions like these—and so, of course, does science.

- The scientific method invokes opposites. The primary opposite is the difference between the measurer or observer (us) and what is measured (the universe). These come together in the form of the experiment, which unites them and creates an answer that pushes us closer to fundamental knowledge of the universe.

- Science differs from religious myths in that empirical data are the driver for new myth. However, there are certain fundamental concepts that underlie all science.

- The primary myth of science is that the universe will reveal itself to us, as the observer, if we follow certain rules of observation—the scientific method.

- Science, like other myths, has certain things that it cannot comment on—in particular, science has difficulty with telling us things about the human world, such as how to improve the economy or how to solve the conflicts among nations.

- However, just like the chieftain in the story, science tries to help us understand the world around us. Thus, the brain makes myth in order to understand the world and our relationship to it.

Suggested Reading

Campbell and Moyers, *The Power of Myth*.

d'Aquili, "The Myth-Ritual Complex."

———, "The Neurobiological Bases of Myth and Concepts of Deity."

Newberg, d'Aquili, and Rause, *Why God Won't Go Away*.

Questions to Consider

1. How does the brain help us make myths about our world?

2. What is the basic structure of myths, and how do they relate to religion and science?

The Myth-Making Brain
Lecture 7—Transcript

With our discussion of the brain and various aspects of belief and the nature of the spiritual brain, we've now laid the foundation for considering in more detail the important elements of religion and spirituality. A fundamental part of religions is their elaboration in myths, the stories that form the basis of religions. In fact, there's evidence that our brain is a mythmaking machine. But why and how does the brain make myths? That's the subject that we'll address today.

The noted anthropologist Joseph Campbell once stated (and I quote): "[Since] the earliest evidence of the emergence of our species, signs have been found which indicate that mythological aims and concerns were already shaping the arts and world of Homo sapiens." We've always constructed myths or stories that have become incorporated into our burial rituals, our temples, and our civilizations; so what are these stories and why are they so important?

One of the points that I want to start out making very strongly is that myth doesn't necessarily imply something that's false. So often in today's world, we tend to think about myth in that way—we might refer to the myths of dieting, or we'll talk about the myths of Ancient Greece and talk about how silly they sounded—but myth in and of itself is a very important kind of story; in fact, the word "myth" comes from the Greek "mythos," which translates as "word." But it isn't just a word; it's one that's spoken with deep and unquestioned authority. "Mythos" is in turn anchored in another Greek word called *musteion*, which means "to close the eyes or the mouth." Karen Armstrong, the author of the book *The History of God*, states that "to close the eyes or the mouth" roots myth "in an experience of darkness and silence."

What might that mean? If your sensory inputs are shut down—everything that you see and hear—then the myth can become the primary focus of your brain. In other words, all of our brain's processes are brought to bear on the myth itself, and that's ultimately what gives myths their incredible power. In a similar way, if you put someone in a sensory deprivation chamber, they're going to have much more intense sensory experiences and thought processes; and many spiritual practices such as meditation or prayer try to eliminate external stimuli, which appears to help create a more powerful experience for the person who's doing the practice. So myths aren't false things; they're powerful stories that have a deep impact on who we are as human beings.

Apart from their expressive power and their emotional impact, what are myths actually good for? What do we use them for? Primarily, we develop myths to explain our world, but frequently we use them to help explain things that we can't readily comprehend; questions like: Why were we born only eventually to die? What happens to us when we die? What's our place in the universe? Why is there suffering? How was the universe made in the first place; and how long will the universe last? Perhaps most pressingly: How can we live in this baffling, uncertain world and somehow not be afraid? Myths help us to understand our universe and ourselves. According to Campbell, myths show us how to be human. They show us what's most important, and what, in terms of our inner life, is most deeply and profoundly true. The power of myth lies beneath its literal interpretation in the ability of its universal symbols and themes to connect us with the most essential parts of ourselves in ways that to some degree logic and reason really can't reach.

By this definition, religions must be based in myth; after all, if they're to have anything meaningful to say to us, myth would be the most powerful way of trying to do that. In this sense, the story of Jesus would be a myth, even if it were literally and historically true, because the power of the story lies underneath the historical and literal facts. Likewise, even if the extraordinary events that myths chronicle never happened and the beings they portray never walked on the face of earth, the lasting myths of past cultures all contain psychological and spiritual truths that resonate with the psyches and spirits even of people today.

But myths aren't just the great stories of the past. We actually create myths all the time to explain and understand the world. Our brain functions to generate stories about the world. Think about this: When you get up in the morning, when you go to work, when you think about who to vote for on a political level; all of these approaches to life are ultimately stories that your brain puts together to tell us what to do, how to act, what to think about, and how to feel. Of course, neuroscience tells us that the brain processes everything that we think and feel about the world. One of the things that I always remark on to my students is that brain scans show different areas lighting up in the brain whenever anything happens to us. If we see something, hear something, feel something, or think something, something is always going on in the brain itself. In fact, these processes then come together to provide for us a rendition of what's going on in the world around us. I want to emphasize the word "rendition" because we don't really know for sure how accurate that rendition is; it's a second-order processing of whatever is out there in the world.

Therefore, if everything we think, feel, and perceive about the world is processed by the brain, how can we ever be certain that the world is represented in our brain accurately? In fact, we're going to see in a later lecture how problematic a time the brain really has at accurately determining what's going on in the world around us. The brain has a fair number of limitations, and given those brain limitations it seems that the brain has to do the best job it can at creating a coherent story about what it's processing; about what the world is all about. This story helps the brain to respond to the world in effective and adaptive ways. Again, this is the basis of what these stories are trying to do for us, which is to try to create for us a sense of what the world is all about and how to respond to the world. But we must always remember that on a fundamental level the entire story our brain presents for us about the world is just a secondhand rendition of what's actually out there.

Our brain is simply trying to help us make sense of this incredibly complex and uncertain world; and, of course, that's what all the great myths from history actually do: They help us understand the world; they help us to understand our own place within that world. This is what I mean when I say that our brains—all of our brains—make myths. We need to always make stories and construct ideas about the world because that's what our brain does: It does the best that it can to tell us what our world is about.

Let's return to Joseph Campbell. Remember that he said that myths are stories about things fundamental to human beings. Myths include language so that we can transmit them to others, and myths include ideas about spirituality, morality, and reality. Take the story of Jonah and the Whale; we all remember that famous story. Remember that he's asked to do what God wants him to do, but decides to flee instead. He goes onto this boat because he doesn't listen to God and, of course, this gets him into a lot trouble (in fact, it actually gets him into a great big fish). But the story tells us something about how to behave spiritually; how to behave morally. It tells us to follow our faith, and in this specific context to listen to what God asks us to do.

Myths contain emotional content, both positive and negative, and tell us something about the importance of what our behaviors and our beliefs are all about. The story of Jonah also contains a great amount of emotions. There's great fear and trembling in the men who are on the ship with Jonah because of the storm around them that they believe is caused by God's wrath, ultimately because God is angry at Jonah; and there's also the emotional component of Jonah's realization as to how he should behave and how he should come to follow whatever God is asking him to do.

The story about the destruction of Sodom and Gomorrah is another biblical story that has a great deal of emotional content. The immoral activities related to uncontrolled hedonism and pleasure are what ultimately create the whole story and create God's anger at the people who live in Sodom and Gomorrah. Of course, there's the compassionate side of God showing through as well at sparing Lot and his family in this story. These references to very strong emotions are an absolutely crucial aspect of what myths are all about because it's important to make sure that whatever we understand in the concept of a myth is something that we also feel emotionally; that's what makes us remember exactly what's going on and the point of that particular myth. Myths provide examples and even suggestions with regard to future behaviors that we should implement.

With those elements of myths in mind, let's talk a little bit about the actual structure of how myths form; and more specifically, let's see how those different elements of myth relate to the brain's functions and the different processes that the brain takes us through as we try to understand our world.

Essentially, all myths can be reduced to a very simple framework, I think: First, they focus upon a crucial existential problem; a concern that we have, perhaps the creation of the world or how evil came about in the world. Next, myths frame that concern typically as a pair of apparently irreconcilable opposites. It may be a hero versus a monster, god versus human beings, life versus death, or heaven versus hell. Finally, and perhaps most importantly, myths find a way of reconciling these opposites, often through the actions of gods or other spiritual powers; and somehow this bringing together of the opposites relieves our existential concerns.

The creation of these stories requires a very creative and combined interaction of a wide variety of cognitive processes in the brain. You'll remember from one of my earlier lectures that the brain has several basic cognitive functions: We talked about the quantitative function, the binary function, the causal function, and an existential function. Two of these functions tend to play a very important role in the creation and understanding of myth.

The first is the causal function, and this should be no surprise since myths are essentially about the causes of things. They're going to tell us something about what caused the world to come into existence; they're going to tell us what things that we do, what behaviors that we do, cause us to act in a faithful way or an unfaithful way, a moral way or an immoral way. Therefore, the causal area of the brain—this area that's probably located somewhere around here; somewhere in the region of your parietal lobe and temporal lobe—this is a part of the brain that's going to become very active when we engage in mythic stories because we want to understand causality in the world, we want to understand why the world works the way it does and if we do certain things what that will cause in the world. It gives us a feeling of understanding and a feeling of control, and this again is the power of what myths provide us.

The second cognitive process is also crucial to the mythmaking mind, and that's the binary process of the brain. Remember, this is a very important area that enables us to set things up in our world in terms of basic polar opposites. The human brain has this wonderful ability to reduce even the most complicated relationships of space and time into a simple pair of opposites. We might talk about above and below, in and out, left and right, or before and after; and interestingly, we apply the emotional processes of our brain to each of these kinds of concepts. Think about that for a moment: Is it better to be in, or better to be out? From a social perspective, we tend to want to be in; we want to be in with everyone else, not outside. Is it better to be up high, or down low? From a survival perspective, usually up high is better than down low. We start to understand a beneficial aspect to the mythmaking process that helps us to make these comparisons. We begin to understand the relationship of these opposites—why some are good or bad, better or worse—and we can begin to try to reconcile how those opposites can be brought together in a way that makes us understand our world more effectively.

Let's consider an example of a particular myth and see how the mythmaking process might actually occur. After all, each of us creates our own myths about the world—as I mentioned, we have myths about every aspect of our world—and in addition to the myths of our own creation, we also embrace and rely on myths that we've learned from others. Let's explore this universal mythmaking process by weaving a story of our own.

Let's imagine a very close-knit prehistoric clan, and perhaps one of the members of this clan has just died. His body lies on a bearskin in front of them, and as others approach him they touch him gently and they immediately sense that this person who used to exist no longer exists. What was once a very warm and vital person with personality, someone they could relate to, has suddenly become a very cold and a very lifeless thing. The clan's chieftain is perhaps a very introspective man, and he kind of slumps over by the campfire and he broods upon the lifeless form that was once his very good friend. "What is it that's missing" he thinks, "and how was it lost? Where has it gone?" As he watches the crackling fire, he's really overwrought by feelings of sadness and anxiety. His mind's striving for some way of understanding what's been going on. He needs to find a cause for what's happened to his friend, but the longer he dwells upon this unnerving puzzle of life and death, the deeper he sinks into this kind of feeling of existential dread.

From a neurobiological perspective, this grieving chieftain is really in the grip of a very strong arousal response of the autonomic nervous system. His heart is racing, his blood pressure is going up; he's upset, he's worried. His amygdala is firing; he's trying to think about what's going on and he's frustrated in the impossibility of his logical left hemisphere structures of the brain trying to figure out what's exactly happened here. The effect of the chief's intense, prolonged brooding over this existential problem is having a profound influence on how his brain is actually working. As his brain interprets this frustration as a sign of distress, the amygdala triggers a strong limbic fear response, and it sends off neural signals activating the arousal system so that he feels it, he thinks it, he feels it emotionally, he feels it throughout his body. As the chief continues to ruminate upon his grief and fear, his arousal response continues to grow and intensify. His pulse continues to go up, his breath grows shallow and rapid, he begins to swear, and he begins to worry more and more.

The chief stares at the fire, turning his thoughts around and around in his head; and as this happens, he notices that the fire has suddenly started to burn down, and it burns down to its embers. The fire that was once bright and alive is now all but gone; a little bit of smoke and then soon there'll be nothing but lifeless gray ashes that can never be resurrected again into flame. As the last wisps of smoke rise towards the sky, he turns to the body of his fallen friend and suddenly something starts to happen: It occurs to him that maybe his comrade's life and spirit have vanished as completely as the flames have vanished. In fact, before he can even consciously phrase the thoughts that he's having, he's struck by a very deep conviction, deep within himself, that the very essence of his friend has actually escaped—up to the heavens perhaps, like smoke—and that his spirit rises from the body much like a fire rises from the wood.

This conviction begins as just one more possibility offered up by his intellectually-pondering side of the brain's abstract thought processes, most likely on the left side of the brain. But as soon as it enters into the chieftain's consciousness, it's embraced by other parts of the brain, perhaps more on the right side, that are involved in the holistic functioning of the brain. You remember the holistic side is trying to find ways of bringing things together; so suddenly, there's an agreement of sorts between both sides of the brain, and this causes a kind of neurological resonance that sends very positive emotional discharges racing through the limbic system. It may stimulate pleasure centers of the brain, and particularly of the hypothalamus; and because the hypothalamus regulates that autonomic nervous system, these very strong pleasure impulses trigger a response all the way down into the body in the form of the quiescent system, and the chieftain experiences this as a very powerful surge of calmness and peacefulness.

All of this happens maybe in the wink of an eye, too fast for the arousal response that triggered the chief's anxiety in the first place; and for a very remarkable moment, both those quiescent and arousal systems maybe be simultaneously active. If you remember, we talked about this in an earlier lecture where we talked about the balance between the arousal and the calming sides of the autonomic nervous system, that normally they suppress the other but sometimes they both come on; and this very intense feeling of arousal and calmness can be a very strong kind of experience. Some neurologists refer to this as the "Eureka Response," or the "a-ha" kind of moment; and many of us have experienced that at one point or another in our lives when we're struggling with a problem and we finally get the answer. It's a tremendous feeling of an energy rush, a feeling of ecstasy, and perhaps even awe that this answer somehow came to us.

For the chieftain, he finally understands the meaning of death, and life and in this transforming flash of insight, the chief is suddenly freed from his grief and despair; in a deeper sense, he feels that he's been freed from the bonds of death. The insight strikes him with the force of revelation. The experience feels vividly and palpably real to him; and in that moment, the opposites of life and death that his brain presented to him are no longer locked in conflict. They've been mythically, and perhaps mystically, resolved; and now he sees clearly the absolute truth of things: He understands that the spirits of the dead live on. But because he feels this intensity of this experience, it actually translates as if he's discovered something that's primally true about our world. It's more than just an idea, a thought, or an explanation; it's a sense that he's experienced some ultimate reality and meaning about the world.

While this whole story might be a little oversimplistic in terms of the origin and nature of myths, it helps us to understand what myths are actually all about. Religious myths provide stories about how we as human beings relate to our world and how we are supposed to relate to God. They teach us about being devoted to God and why we should behave in certain ways. In that way, myths help to provide for us a sense of morality, a sense of how we're to interact with other people, a sense of what we're to do in our life and how we're to treat things in our world so that we can be successful, we can survive, and we can feel better about ourselves and the meaning that we bring to ourselves about our lives.

This little story about the chieftain shows the relevance of brain function in terms of helping us to create myth. In this chieftain, many brain processes were involved. We talked about his very strong emotions affecting the limbic system; the very strong fear and negative emotions about death, and the very positive and very warm feelings that he had when he understood the nature of the resolution of his problem; there was the visual stimulus of the fire and this example of how things actually work, and there was the frustration of the brain seeking some kind of elusive cause for life and death; there was the binary problem of life and death and how he could resolve this in some kind of holistic way. So while it's a simple tale, our story does give us insight into the brain functions and physiological processes that are involved in the creation of and in the response to myth.

Before we leave this entire subject of myth, I want to leave you with one other very interesting question: What about science? I'm a scientist, and I often wonder: Is science a form of myth? To some degree yes, and to some degree no. Science is a myth in the sense that it tells us a story about how the world works. There are fundamental aspects of science that are very similar to all myths. For example, science addresses fundamental questions such as: Where did the world come from? What makes the seasons change? What makes the sun give us heat and light? What causes earthquakes, hurricanes, or volcanic eruptions? Myths seek to answer questions like that, and so, of course, does science. The scientific method invokes opposites. The primary opposite is the difference between the measurer (the scientist, which is us) and that which is measured (the universe); and these come together in the form of the experiment, which unites them and creates an answer that pushes us closer to fundamental knowledge of the universe.

Science feels like a myth but also differs from religious myths in that there's empirical data that's the driver for new myths. In other words, the more we derive information and data, the more we begin to understand about our world, and the more we generate new ideas, new hypotheses, about how the world works. On some level, science does function as a myth; but there are also fundamental differences between what science does and what we typically think of in the context of myths that pertain to religious or spiritual ideas. The primary myth of science is that the universe will reveal itself to us as the observer if we follow certain rules of observation, which we often refer to as the scientific method. Science, like other myths, has certain things that it can't comment on; in particular, science has difficulty telling us about things that involve the human world: How do we improve the economy, for example? What's the best way to solve the Middle East conflict? But just like the chieftain in our story, science tries to help us understand the world around us.

Thus, the brain makes myths in order to understand the world around us and our relationship to it; and regardless of culture or belief system, myths often have very similar components and content. Perhaps they're similar because the brains of all people are fundamentally similar. But while the brain is good at understanding stories, it might be useful if there was a way to make our understanding even stronger and deeper. This is where rituals come in to play: to make myths not only a cognitive experience, but something that's felt deeply within us as well. It's this topic that we'll cover in the next lecture.

The Brain and Religious Rituals
Lecture 8

In the previous lecture, you learned that myths are powerful stories that affect multiple parts of the brain and tell people something meaningful about the world and about themselves. While these stories typically have a great impact on individuals and groups, religious rituals provide a way to make the impact of the myth even stronger. Rituals make myths not only cognitive, but also experiential. In this lecture, you will learn that rituals get the entire body into the act and help to create some of the most important experiences—spiritual or otherwise—that human beings can have.

Rituals and the Brain

- The brain is designed to act out thoughts. For example, we often use our hands while speaking in order to convey our thoughts to another person. We learn by combining movement with cognition. Therefore, we have the need to act out myths. This results in powerful understanding of the important points of myths.

- We have a visceral, emotional, and cognitive understanding. The cognitive process is probably what you think of when you hear the word "understanding."

- When you feel intense happiness or awe, that's an example of emotional understanding. When you think about an experience in which you have truly felt something throughout your body—maybe you felt great happiness or joy, but it wasn't just an emotion—that's an example of visceral understanding. Rituals involve these visceral and emotional levels of understanding.

- Many scholars have struggled with the definition of the term "ritual," but rituals generally appear to have several common elements.

Rituals are structured or patterned.

- Most rituals have a very specific structure in terms of what is done, how it is done, what objects are used, and how it connects to a particular idea or myth.

- For example, although there is some variation among churches, during the Christian practice of holy communion, a person typically walks to where the priest is standing, kneels or genuflects before the priest, receives the wafer, and drinks the wine. This is a very structured ritual and, of course, combines the actions of the ritual with the notion of incorporating Christ's body and blood as part of the practice, giving the concept a much more powerful emphasis.

Rituals are rhythmic and repetitive; they tend to recur in the same or nearly the same form with some regularity.

- This is one of the most important aspects of rituals. They are rhythmic in that the same music, phrases, dances, and ideas are repeated over and over. What makes rituals particularly powerful is how the repetition occurs on many different levels.

- Those who participate in the Jewish Passover seder sing songs, make certain movements, hear stories about Moses and how the Jews escaped slavery in Egypt through God's intervention, and pray about the importance of the Jewish covenant with God. During the ritual, there are many rhythmic elements that have a powerful impact on the brain and body.

- Another aspect of that rhythm is its repetition over your life. You first participate in the seder when you are a child and then continue to experience it through adolescence, adulthood, and into old age. Throughout your life, there is the rhythm of doing the seder ritual every year, which further binds your body and brain to the ritual and, importantly, to the ideas and stories associated with that ritual.

- Then, there is another rhythmic domain, which is that the ritual is performed across generations. You had the seder with your parents and grandparents and you now have it with your children or grandchildren. This generational rhythm binds the ritual and its associated ideas to an entire people and throughout history. It is not just your ritual; it is the ritual of an entire community and an entire people. All of these rhythmic, or repetitive, elements contribute to the effect of ritual on the brain.

Rituals act to synchronize emotional, perceptual-cognitive, and motor processes within the central nervous system of individual participants.

- The rhythms of ritual physically affect your body. Your body is always awash in rhythm, and your body is filled with rhythms. You have a heart rhythm, breathing rhythm, hormonal rhythms, and brain rhythms.

- When you experience an external rhythm such as a prayer or song, your body's rhythms can actually begin to synchronize with the prayer or song. Fast music can rev you up, and slow music can calm you down.

- Furthermore, as you engage in the rhythm, you will start to feel it within your body. As it drives your body and brain, the rhythmic activity drives your hypothalamus and, ultimately, your amygdala to generate emotional responses. Fast music makes you feel excited and happy; slow music makes you feel calm and content.

- Because our emotions are tied to our thoughts, we incorporate the feelings into our cognitions. Thus, if we have a thought about the importance of God in our life and then connect it with a ritual that generates a strong feeling of happiness or love, we begin to imbue our thoughts of God with positive emotions.

Rituals synchronize these processes among the various individual participants.

- This may be the most important part of rituals—the ability to not only connect an individual to a myth in a powerful way, but also to connect one individual to another. It does this by helping to break down the dichotomy between one person and another.

- Rituals certainly appear in humans, but they also appear in virtually every animal species as well. In animals, the primary type of ritual that exists is the mating ritual. Rituals perform two basic functions in this regard: the proper identification of a mate and the ability to join with that mate. Animals generally do not want to get too close to each other, but rituals help.

- The physiology of ritual is based on the rhythms synchronizing the brain so that it begins to actually diminish the usual flow of sensory information entering the brain. Normally, animals use their sensory information to identify the objects in their environment and to determine what is friend or foe. However, by stimulating the brain in a very specific rhythmic way, the normal sensory functioning begins to shift, and the animal looks at the world and others in a different way. Human beings are not immune to such processes.

- When mating, the mutual activation of the arousal and quiescent parts of the autonomic nervous system are associated with sexual orgasm—an ecstatic experience. A similar term—"ecstasy"—is also used to describe profound spiritual experiences.

- Both the arousal and quiescent parts of the autonomic nervous system might be mutually activated in moments of intense enlightenment. The activation of the autonomic nervous system activates the hypothalamus, which is the primary pleasure center in the brain.

- In terms of the brain, ritual joins the cognitive with the experiential in a unitary experience. You not only cognitively understand how you are connected to your spiritual group, but your entire body also participates, uniting your body and brain with a connection to something even greater—your spiritual group or even God.

- This unitary experience is critical because it helps to join the person with the ritual as well as with the others who are participating in the ritual. This connects the person to the myth, God, or the universe.

- As with animals, rhythmic activity causes interesting changes in the brain. Through the autonomic nervous system, the rhythm of ritual drives the brain and actually causes some important changes, including increased activity in the hypothalamus, thalamus, and limbic system.

- Some parts of the cortex, however, will experience a decrease in activity—particularly in the parietal lobe, which helps us form our sense of self and sense of space and time. If this area decreases in activity, it can no longer clearly distinguish the self from the rest of the world or determine spatial relationships in the world. The result is a loss of the sense of self and the loss of the sense of space and time.

- The loss of the sense of self is usually experienced as a blending of the self with something else—the ritual or the myth that is incorporated in the ritual. If this blending is intense enough, the person may feel as if they completely become one with the focus of the ritual. In most religious rituals, that focus is God.

Religious rituals make the impact of religious myths stronger than being just stories that are told repeatedly.

- Therefore, a person engaged in an intense religious ritual might ultimately feel that he or she becomes one with God, or a meditator might feel as if he or she becomes one with the universe. Thus, rituals can cause increasing feelings of oneness or connectedness as the rhythms of the ritual build and the person's brain becomes more and more affected.

- In addition to this sense of connectedness or oneness, the ritual also results in profound feelings of excitement or relaxation, depending on the nature of the ritual. If it is an intensely energetic and fast ritual, then they might feel great arousal. If it is an intensely calming and slow ritual, then they might feel overwhelming bliss. These experiences are mediated by the autonomic nervous system and its arousing or calming parts.

Individual versus Group Rituals

- Individual rituals, such as personal prayer and meditation, can create personal meaning and experiences and reinforce the person's belief system. However, rituals can also be done as a group. In fact, some rituals—including mass, services, and certain holiday gatherings—either require groups or are most effective when performed in groups.

- Group rituals help to synchronize many brains to the rhythm. Our brains have neurons that mirror what other people do and are called mirror neurons. When a group of people engages in a ritual, they all feel the rhythm and each other. In addition, because they all experience a sense of oneness or connectedness, they feel the rhythm with respect to each other. As a group, they become one. This is why rituals are frequently used within athletic teams and religious groups.

- Ultimately, rituals are all around us, and they help our brain guide us through our lives. We have waking up rituals, eating rituals, work rituals, and sleeping rituals.

- If rituals are all around us and are used for religious and nonreligious means, it would seem that they would generally be good for us. In general, this is true, but it turns out that rituals can also have a dark side.

- In fact, ritual is a morally neutral technology. Ritual can be used for positive or negative means. For example, rituals can decrease intragroup aggression but increase intergroup aggression.

- The negative behaviors that arise from religious rituals help us to understand ways in which religious beliefs can become destructive and detrimental.

- Terrorists and cults frequently utilize rituals as an important tool for inducing certain strong ideas about the nature of reality or how to behave.

- Rituals provide a powerful mechanism for reinforcing myths. Rituals help to make the story of the myth felt by people not just cognitively, but also emotionally and viscerally.

Suggested Reading

d'Aquili, "Human Ceremonial Ritual and the Modulation of Aggression."

———, "The Biopsychological Determinants of Religious Ritual Behavior."

d'Aquili, Lauglin, and McManus, *The Spectrum of Ritual.*

Newberg, d'Aquili, and Rause, *Why God Won't Go Away.*

Questions to Consider

1. How do rituals impact the brain and its functions?

2. Why are rituals so important to the brain, and are they always beneficial?

The Brain and Religious Rituals
Lecture 8—Transcript

In the previous lecture, we considered the origin of myths in the human brain. We learned that myths are powerful stories that affect multiple parts of the brain and tell us something meaningful about the world and about ourselves. But these are only stories, they're only words; and while they typically have a great impact on individuals and groups, what if there was a way to make the impact of the myth even stronger?

As we're going to discover today, religious rituals do exactly that. Consider, for example, the following account, which was given by one of the people who responded to our online survey of spiritual experiences that I described previously in Lecture Four. This was the description; she said: "Without any warning, I had an overwhelmingly enlightening experience during the Dwarf Spiritual Ritual of Taiwan's Saisiat people." This is an indigenous population with many ancient myths and rituals; and the Dwarf Spirit Ritual involves appeasing spirits of an ancient group of short-statured people who became embroiled with the Saisiat. The ritual includes all kinds of elaborate costumes, flags, and especially music. For this individual, she described the following; she said: "It was such a blissful experience that I was totally transformed overnight: I was never a 'religious' person before, but from that day on, the only thing that's meaningful in my life was to find a way back to that bliss." That's really a remarkable account. This individual is saying that a ritual that isn't even part of her tradition transformed her; it completely changed the core meaning of her life. How is that possible? What is it about rituals that give them such power over people?

The simplest example of this is the brain is designed to act out our thoughts. In fact, as I'm speaking to you right now, what am I doing? I'm moving my hands; so the movement of my body is part of my communication process. In fact, if you think about it, we really learn much better when we combine movement with cognition. Let's go back to the tennis analogy I brought up in a previous lecture: You could read all the books you want about how to hit a tennis ball, but until you put the racket in your hand and try it out yourself, you're never going to be able to do it well. But on the other hand, if you can combine what you read and learn with the actual act of doing, then that greatly enhances the way in which you understand the world and the way in which your brain works.

Ultimately, it's really wonderful if we can find a way to act out myth. Acting out myths would result in a very powerful understanding of the important points of myth; and, in fact, we wouldn't just have a cognitive understanding—a knowledge of the story—but we'd feel it deep inside; it would be a visceral feeling, something we'd feel throughout our body, and, of course, it would be emotional as well. The cognitive process is probably what we all think of whenever we hear the word "understanding," but when you feel intense happiness or awe, that's an example of emotional understanding. When you think about an experience in which you've truly felt something throughout your entire body—maybe you felt great happiness or great joy—it wasn't just an emotion anymore, it was something you felt throughout your body like a huge rush of energy; that's that visceral understanding that we all can have about our world. What ritual does is to involve these visceral and emotional levels of understanding and combine it with the cognitive understanding; and that, as we'll see, is why rituals can pack such a punch.

But first, let's back up a bit and ask a very basic question (the kinds of questions I like to ask): What exactly is a ritual? Many scholars have struggled with the definition of ritual, but rituals appear to have some very general common elements. One of the first ones is that rituals are structured or patterned. What do I mean by this? Most rituals seem to have a very specific set of things that need be done: What's done, how it's done, when it's done, maybe there are certain objects that are used; and all of these different elements are connected together as part of a particular idea or myth.

Take, for example, the common Christian practice of the Holy Communion. Although, of course, there's some variation among different churches and beliefs about how to do this ritual, there seems to be some very common elements; and certainly within any particular church, it's done almost the same way all the time. Typically a person is going to get up, they're going to walk to the front of the church where they kneel or genuflect before the priest, they receive a wafer, and then they drink wine. This is very structured and, of course, combines all of these physical actions of the ritual with the notion of literally incorporating Christ's body as part of the host (or the wafer) and the blood as part of the drinking of the wine, which is all part of the practice of the Holy Communion. This ritual gives the whole concept a much more powerful emphasis, since the person doesn't just understand the notion of receiving the blood and body of Christ, but actually does it; they actually experience it themselves.

Another essential element of rituals is that they're rhythmic and repetitive; they tend to recur in the same way or in the same form with some type of regularity. This rhythmicity to them is what gives rituals perhaps their greatest strength and is so important to the actual participation and practice of these rituals. The rhythmicity can be in many different forms including music, different phrases, movements or dance, or even that certain ideas are repeated over and over. What makes rituals particularly powerful are how this repetition occurs, and not only occurs but occurs on so many different levels. Take another example of a ritual: the Passover Seder in Judaism. For those people who participate in the Seder, they sing songs at specific times, they say certain prayers, they make certain movements such as washing the hands, or perhaps standing or sitting, and then they hear the stories repeated over and over about Moses and about how the Jews escaped slavery in Egypt through God's help, God's intervention; and then all of this comes together in terms of understanding the importance of the Jewish covenant with God.

During the Passover ritual itself—the Seder itself—there's a great deal of rhythmic elements that, as we'll describe in a few moments, has a very powerful impact on the brain and body. But another aspect of the rhythm is its repetition over the course of your entire life. You first participate in the Seder when you're a child, as an adolescent, and then into adulthood and even old age. Throughout your life, there's the rhythm of doing the Seder at the same time of year, with perhaps the same ideas and the same stories, and this further helps to bind your body and your brain to the ritual; and more importantly, it binds your body and brain to the ideas and the stories that are associated with that ritual. It's something that literally lasts your entire life. There's an even larger or global notion of this rhythmicity and repetition, because not only does it occur across your lifetime but it's actually performed across generations. For the people who particulate in the Seder, they have it with their parents and their grandparents when they're a child, and then as they grow older they have it with their children and their grandchildren. This generational rhythm binds the ritual and its ideas to an entire people and, in fact, throughout history; throughout centuries and millennia. It binds everyone who participates in this ritual into a singular community and a singular group of people.

All of these rhythmic and repetitive elements contribute the effect that ritual has on the brain; but how exactly does ritual actually work? What does ritual do to our bodies and our brains? One of the things that rituals do is to help to synchronize our emotional, our perceptual, and our cognitive brain processes, as well as bringing in our sensory and motor areas. What I mean by this is that the rhythms of the ritual that we were just talking about physically affect your body. In fact, your body in general is always awash in rhythms; your body is built on rhythms. You have a heart rhythm, a breathing rhythm, you have hormonal rhythms, and if you attach electrodes to your brain—electroencephalography—you can actually watch your brain rhythms as well. When you experience an external rhythm, such as a prayer or a song, your body's rhythms actually begin to synchronize with it. Think about it for a moment: What happens when you're listening to fast rock 'n' roll music? It revs you up, you feel it; you feel it deep down in your body, and you can feel your whole body turning on to that music. Of course, if you want to go to sleep, you put on slow music because that slow rhythm begins to calm you down and relax you as you get into that feeling of slowness.

Furthermore, as you engage the rhythm, you'll start to feel it within your body, and it drives your body and your brain; the rhythmicity activity actually drives your hypothalamus and ultimately your amygdala to generate a very powerful kind of emotional response. So return to that fast music: That rhythm stimulates the arousal system of your autonomic nervous system and therefore it activates your arousal system, activates your hypothalamus, and ultimately your amygdala; so you have a very profound emotional experience that you may never have had before. Since our emotions are tied to our thoughts, we incorporate the feelings into our thought processes, into our cognitions; thus, if we have a thought about the importance of God in our life, we connect it with a ritual that generates a strong feeling of happiness or love, and we begin to imbue our thoughts of God with all kinds of positive emotions. Many of the studies we've performed using brain scans to study prayer have shown that this type of ritualistic practice clearly causes all kinds of changes in the brain and in the limbic system.

Rituals clearly cause strong responses in the individual participants; but rituals go one better: Rituals synchronize these processes not only within the individual itself, but among other participants in the ritual. This may be an even more important part of how rituals actually work: They not only connect an individual to the myth in a very powerful way, but connect one individual to another. How does it do this? It does this, we think, by breaking down the dichotomy—the separation—between one person and another. How or why would this happen? To answer this question, let's look at the possible origin of rituals.

Rituals certainly appear in human beings, but they also appear in virtually every other animal species as well. In most animals, the primary type of ritual that exists is the mating ritual. These rituals perform two basic functions: On one hand, the ritual helps to properly identify a mate, another member of their species, so that they can join together in the mating process. After all, animals generally don't usually get too close to each other, but rituals help out; they bring them together in ways that they normally wouldn't come together. If you think about lions, for example, in the wilderness, they usually stay pretty separate; but then when it's time to mate, they need to figure out a way to come together, and this is where rituals begin to help out.

These rituals are enormously elaborate at times, even for some of the simplest creatures. Take, for example, the mating ritual of a butterfly called the Silver-washed Fritillary. When a male of the species spots a very nice-looking female, he closes in with amorous intent; the female actually takes right to the air and the male flies several looping circles around her with his wings almost brushing by her body. The two of them perform a rather spectacular joint flight with the male darting acrobatically above and below her as she glides—approvingly, hopefully—on a straight path. When the flight is completed, the butterflies land, posture, and exchange scents; and in all, it appears that the male actually performs about seven distinct acts and the female must respond appropriately to each one before the mating can begin. But this ritual, like all rituals, involves a rhythmic pattern of activity.

It includes smells and sights that enable the butterflies to form a union and come together for mating.

It turns out that the physiology of these kinds of rituals is based on the rhythms that synchronize the brain so that it begins to actually diminish the usual flow of sensory information entering the brain. Normally, the butterflies or other animals, even human beings, use our sensory information to identify objects that are in our environment; determine what's friend and foe, food or prey; and by stimulating the brain in a very specific, rhythmic way, these normal sensory processes begin to shift. The animal begins to look at the world in a very different way: They begin to recognize this other animal as something that it can join with; something that it can connect with in a very profound way.

Of course, human beings aren't immune to these processes either. Think about where and how we meet and select a mate: Usually the environment has all kinds of rhythmic stimulation; like going to a dance, for example. Even the act sex itself is highly rhythmic, as we all know; it's known absolutely to affect the autonomic nervous system in a very profound way. In fact, it actually requires an activation of both the arousal and the quiescent arms of the autonomic nervous system to be stimulated to be associated with sexual orgasm. That's fascinating, because we've talked about the importance of turning on both arms of the autonomic nervous system to create a tremendous sense of alertness, arousal, and energy, and at the same time a great sense of blissfulness and calmness. This is, in part, the experience of sexual orgasm; it's an ecstatic experience.

But we also find another place where we hear the term "ecstasy" used: It's actually used to describe profound spiritual experiences. Remember the story of our tribal chieftain from our last lecture? We mentioned that perhaps both the arousal and quiescent arms of his autonomic nervous system might've been mutually activated at the most intense moment of his enlightenment. The activation of the autonomic nervous system—as we've discussed—activates the hypothalamus, which is the primary pleasure center in the brain. So it's not too far a stretch to see how ritual can be a very useful kind of practice in creating a powerful, unifying experience, whether that experience is religious or otherwise.

On a brain level, as I mentioned earlier on in this lecture, ritual appears to be able to join the cognitive with the experiential, and to do so in a very unitary kind of experience. Remember our description earlier of rituals surrounding the Holy Communion or the Passover Seder. You not only cognitively understand how you're connected to your spiritual group, how you're connected to God, but your entire body participates and you unite your body and brain with a connection to something that's even greater: It's your religious group, your spiritual group, or even God. This unitary experience is critical since it helps to join the person with the ritual itself as well as with the others who are participating in that ritual. This connects the person who's engaged in the ritual to the myth that's part of that ritual, to God, and perhaps the universe.

How does ritual do this? As in animals, the rhythmic activity causes very interesting changes in the brain. Via the autonomic nervous system, the rhythm of rituals drives the brain and actually causes some very important changes. In fact, there's increased activity in the hypothalamus, thalamus, and limbic system in response to what's going on at the autonomic nervous system level; and, of course, there are very central parts of the brain that are involved in how we experience and how we feel about things going on around us in our world and contribute to the powerful experience that we get during rituals.

But some parts of the cortex, however, will also experience changes in activity. In particular, the parietal lobe, which generally helps us to form our sense of self and our sense of space and time, may actually experience a decrease of activity. If this area decreases in activity, it no longer is able to clearly distinguish between the self and the rest of the world; so we can't determine that spatial relationship between ourselves and what's going on outside of ourselves. The result would be a loss of the sense of self, and a loss of the sense of space and time; but the loss of the sense of self is usually experienced as a blending of the self with something else. The ritual, or the myth that's incorporated into the ritual, is what that person begins to feel connected to; and if this blending is intense enough, the person may feel that they completely become one with the focus or the stories involved in the ritual. In most religious rituals, its focus is God; so a person engaged in a very intense religious ritual might ultimately feel that they become one with

God. A meditator, for example, who may not necessarily believe in God per se, might feel that they become one with the universe instead. Thus rituals can cause increasing feelings of oneness or connectedness as the rhythms of the ritual build and as the person's brain becomes more and more affected by these rituals.

In addition to this sense of connectedness or oneness, the ritual also results in profound feelings of excitement or relaxation depending on the nature of the ritual; and this ties back into the autonomic nervous system. If there's this intense, energetic feeling it might be a very fast ritual, and that causes a great feeling of arousal as the arousal part of our autonomic nervous system kicks in and turns on. If it's a very intensely calming and slow ritual, then they might feel overcome by this overwhelming sense of blissfulness and calmness. But again, even this blissful feeling is mediated by the autonomic nervous system; that calming part, the quiescent side, of the autonomic nervous system that makes us feel calm, slow, and blissful.

Since we're talking about some of the differences regarding fast and slow rituals, you might begin to wonder what other elements and variations actually occur within rituals; and if there are other elements and variations, what types of experiences might result from them? In the study of rituals, there are actually many different forms. Rituals have an impact on multiple sensory systems. There are visual stimuli; things that we smell; things that we hear. There are the physical activities that we talked about, for example, with the Holy Communion. There are cognitive and emotional elements that are part of the ritual.

Think about the rituals that you know; maybe ones that are particularly important to you. Think about the beauty of the place of worship; where you do them. Maybe there's the burning of incense; the smells that you take in as you participate in that ritual. Maybe there's the sound of the organ, or a beautiful singing choir that regales us with songs of God or spirituality. There may be a variety of different musical patterns that are either fast or slow; and we've discussed this to some degree about how they activate the autonomic nervous system to engender a feeling of great energy or great calmness. If you put that together with a particular idea—perhaps the power of God—then you might want something that's very uplifting, so that you feel the power within you; and if you want to experience a sense of God's love for you, then perhaps you want a ritual that incorporates a very slow, calming feeling, rhythm, and music.

Up to now, we've generally been thinking about rituals performed by individuals, such as prayer or meditation; and we've even talked about the scans that we've done when people engage in these kinds of practices. These individual rituals create great personal meaning for people, and they create incredibly powerful experiences that reinforce the person's belief system. But rituals can also be done as a group; in fact, some rituals either require groups or are most effective when they're performed in a group setting. Think about going to a church or a synagogue service. When you do that, you take part with other people. Holiday gatherings, where you bring lots of people together. Of course, there are even great spiritual events, such as those that occur at Mecca or in the Yangtze River, bringing millions of believers together, which strengthens the entire experience not just for the individual but for the entire group.

Why do these group rituals work and what do they do? Group rituals help to synchronize many brains to the rhythm. Our brains have neurons that are actually called "mirror neurons"; and, not surprisingly, these mirror neurons mirror whatever it is that we see going on around us. If I lift up my arm, there's a neuron within you that to some degree lifts up your arm as well; and if I smile, then there's a neuron inside of you that makes you feel a smile coming on. When a group of people engage in a ritual, they all feel it and they all feel each other as part of that ritual. In addition, since they all experience a sense of oneness or connectedness, they feel it with respect to each other as well; they come together as a group, and that group forms a oneness that they all feel connected to. This is why rituals are frequently used when people are going to war, or on athletic teams, or even in religious groups, because it binds them all together in a common cause.

Think about one of my favorite rituals, which is going to a football game. It's a great example because it's also a nonreligious ritual; and we've been talking a lot about religious ones, but there are so many similarities between the nonreligious ritual of football and many religious rituals. For example, the football game is very repetitious; just like going to church, it happens on Sundays; and there are specific songs that you sing at certain times of the game; there are the smells, not of incense but of hotdogs and beer; and ultimately, there's a sense of thousands of people coming together to support a common cause.

Ultimately, rituals are all around us and they help the brain guide us through our lives. We have waking up rituals, eating rituals, work rituals, and sleeping rituals. Think for a moment about your own rituals: What are the things that you do every day in a similar way? How does that rhythm help you? What happens when you can't use your rituals? For example, I have a waking up ritual that I try to do almost every morning: I get up; I brush my teeth; I wash my face; then I go downstairs and I make and eat my breakfast; then I come back upstairs and I shave, brush my hair, and get dressed. If I have to cut all of that short or do it differently, it really kind of disrupts the rhythm of my day; it actually makes me feel a little uncomfortable, so it's actually disrupting my brain itself. I feel like I'm kind of getting off on the wrong foot.

If rituals are all around us and used for both religious and nonreligious means, it would seem that they're generally good for us, that's why we do them; and in general, this is true. But one of the things we do have to watch out for is that rituals actually do have a dark side. In fact, I always like to say that rituals are a morally neutral technology. They're something that human beings can use for great good, but unfortunately sometimes for great bad. Studies have shown that if you question people within a group, practicing rituals together decreases the aggression that people feel within the group; so they feel more connected to each other, they feel more loving and compassionate to each other. But rituals increase aggression across groups; so one of the most important questions that we have to think about in the context of the unitary experience that's felt during rituals is: What exactly does the person feel at one with? If they feel connected to just their group, it may actually foment hatred, anger, and violence towards other people. If, on the other hand, it's a sense of connection with the entire universe, then it may be a kind of experience that's very positive.

We have to be very cautious about what rituals do. They can turn someone into a terrorist or to follow a very destructive kind of cult that clearly uses rituals as an important tool for inducing very strong ideas about what people should believe and how they should behave; or we can turn rituals into something that are very, very positive and something that can contribute to the overall welfare of the individual as well as society as a whole.

Rituals provide a powerful mechanism for reinforcing myths. Rituals help to make the story of the myth felt not just cognitively, but emotionally and viscerally in your entire body. Rituals get that entire body into the act and help create some of the most important experiences, spiritual or otherwise, which human beings are capable of having.

The Biology of Spiritual Practices
Lecture 9

In this lecture, you are going to examine the biological underpinnings of two spiritual practices in particular: prayer and meditation. You will learn about how the tools of science can open new windows on the complex phenomena of prayer and meditation. Interestingly, you will also learn that the exploration of spirituality actually has the reciprocal effect of improving our knowledge of humans as biological creatures. Understanding the biology of prayer and meditation—the changes in our heart rate, hormones, and immune system—also leads us toward a greater understanding of the way these practices might affect our health and well-being.

Studying Prayer and Meditation

- The neurosciences allow us to relate the brain to the mind. Hence, we can now look at how the brain allows us to be spiritual. What has neuroscience been able to tell us about spirituality and, more specifically, about spiritual practices such as prayer and meditation?

- Interestingly, the knowledge we are gaining from studying prayer and meditation experimentally is not only teaching us something about the practices themselves, but it is also giving us some valuable insights about the way our brain regulates such basic physiological processes as heart rate and metabolism.

- There are many methodological questions that arise when considering a study of meditation or prayer. For example, it is important to ask questions like the following: What is the best way to study the biology of spirituality? What are the best types of practices or experiences to study? How do you measure the experience itself and correlate it with something biological?

- It is also important to define the practices and objects under study. When it comes to meditation, there are, of course, many different approaches and many different meanings associated with the various meditative practices, but we can identify some aspects of meditation that are common across the types.

- Meditation often involves focused attention, feelings of arousal versus bliss, diminishment of the sense of self, loss of the sense of space and time, eruption of ecstasy, and eventual experience of absolute unity.

- Similarly, there are many different types of prayer and many different meanings associated with the various ways that prayer is practiced, but again, there are some common elements.

- Prayer is similar to meditation in that it involves focused attention, feelings of arousal and bliss, loss of the sense of self, and loss of the sense of space and time. Prayer can also result in profound spiritual or mystical experiences of ecstasy or absolute unity.

- On the other hand, there are ways in which prayer differs from meditation. For example, some types of prayer are more conversational, such as saying grace at the beginning of a meal. In addition, prayer is typically more verbal and allows anyone to participate.

- However, prayer also more specifically is defined by particular religious traditions. Each religion has its own specific prayers and, frequently, specific ways of doing those prayers. In Judaism, individuals daven back and forth while repeating prayers. In Islam, individuals pray five times a day while facing Mecca. Prayer also usually has the particular goal of connecting with God.

- Data suggest that prayer is highly complex and involves many different brain structures and functions. Prayer practices and their associated experiences are so rich and diverse that it makes sense that many different parts of the brain would be involved.

- Recall the functions of the following essential areas of the brain in terms of what they normally do for us.

- The prefrontal cortex, or the attention area, activates during concentration tasks.

- The attention area inhibits brain activity through the hippocampus.

- The parietal lobe, or the orientation area, is involved in self-other as well as spatial-temporal orientation.

- The limbic system is involved in emotion.

- The hypothalamus is involved in sympathetic and parasympathetic activity.

- Scientists are able to study and learn about the parts of the brain involved in prayer by using a variety of neuroimaging techniques to evaluate different prayer practices.

© iStockphoto/Thinkstock.

Great spiritual events, such as those that occur at Mecca, bring millions of believers together, which strengthens the entire experience—not just for the individual, but for the entire group as well.

- In the study of the Franciscan nuns, the nuns that were studied had many years of experience doing centering prayer, a type of contemplative prayer. In the study, blood flow in the brain was measured.

- These initial studies utilized single-photon emission computed tomography (SPECT) scans. The advantage of using SPECT scans is that it is easier to capture the actual prayer state in an environment that is reasonably conducive to practicing prayer.

- One of the important elements about how a SPECT scan works is that a radioactive tracer is injected at the time that the person is doing the prayer practice. The tracer gets locked into the brain, and it can tell us exactly what's going on in the brain at the moment of prayer or meditation. Then, we can look at the brain scans and compare the resting state (when the person isn't doing anything in particular) to the activation state (the state when they're actually engaged in the practice of meditation or prayer) in order to see what areas of the brain are turned on or off.

- With SPECT scans, we also have the ability to apply a quantitative analysis; we can tell how much, in terms of percentages, a part of the brain is turned on or off.

- In this study of the Franciscan nuns, the SPECT scans showed that people engaged in prayer show increased activity in the prefrontal cortex, decreased activity in the parietal lobes, and increased activity in the thalamus.

- When people engage in a practice like prayer, even though they may feel calmer, it isn't really a calming practice. Instead, it's a highly active practice that activates many different parts of the brain. The increased activity in the thalamus is reflective of that; it is telling us that many things are going on in the brain during this particular prayer practice.

- In addition to SPECT studies, functional magnetic resonance imaging (fMRI) studies of spiritual experiences have now been used and offer certain advantages and disadvantages. The main advantages are that it uses no radiation, you can obtain multiple images to observe multiple states, and there is good temporal and spatial resolution. The main disadvantages are that it only measures blood flow—not neurotransmitters—and you have to be in the scanner while it operates.

- An fMRI study of 15 Carmelite nuns reflecting on their mystical experiences was reported from the University of Montreal. The nuns reflected on the most mystical experience they had ever had for five minutes while being scanned.

- The scans showed activation in the frontal cortex, right temporal cortex, right parietal lobules, right caudate, left insula, left caudate, and brainstem. These findings are somewhat similar to the study of the Franciscan nuns, with the exception of increased activity in the parietal lobes.

- Because the practice was so short, we might initially expect increased activity in the parietal lobes because they start out by orienting themselves to the experience or to God. In fact, this is a crucial point because many of the studies of meditation and prayer have had the person doing the practice for anywhere from a few minutes to an hour or more—and it would make sense that the practice of meditation or prayer is a dynamic process. Your brain is doing different things in the first minute, fifth minute, and 60th minute. Throughout the practice, you also progressively experience different things, such as deepening loss of self and increasing bliss.

- In another study, 12 experienced and 10 beginner meditators were scanned as they viewed negative, positive, and neutral pictures in a mindful state and a nonmindful state of awareness. In experienced meditators, there was decreased activity in the frontal lobe and cingulate cortex across all emotional categories.

- There were no changes in brain regions involved in emotional reactivity. On the other hand, beginners showed a decrease in the left amygdala during emotional processing. These findings suggest that the long-term practice of mindfulness leads to emotional stability rather than the elicitation of control over the limbic system.

- Another study showed that meditation can cultivate positive emotion, which alters the activation in brain areas linked to empathy and response to emotional stimuli.

- More recently, studies have been performed that are starting to look at neurotransmitters. For example, a positron emission tomography (PET) scan showed a release of central dopamine during yoga meditation. Another study using magnetic resonance (MR) spectroscopy showed increased gamma-aminobutyric acid (GABA) during yoga asana meditation practice.

The Effects of Prayer and Meditation

- Prayer and meditation result in decreased heart rate and blood pressure, increased heart rate oscillations, decreased body metabolism, and hormonal changes. In addition, they result in increased serotonin, dopamine, and GABA and decreased cortisol and norepinephrine.

- Spiritual practices such as meditation and prayer have an impact on the brain and body in multiple ways. Different practices typically have different patterns of brain activity, although there are also some similarities across practices.

- The changes in the brain associated with a given practice ultimately depend on the specific elements of the practice and its associated experiences. Thus, emotional components affect the emotional centers of the brain, behavior components affect the motor areas of the brain, and cognitive components affect the cognitive areas of the brain. However, as different as such practices and experiences may be, they are all considered spiritual.

Suggested Reading

Andresen and Forman, eds, *Cognitive Models and Spiritual Maps.*

Austin, *Zen and the Brain.*

Azari, Nickel, Wunderlich, Niedeggen, Hefter, Tellmann, Herzog, Stoerig, Birnbacher, and Seitz, "Neural Correlates of Religious Experience."

Beauregard and O'Leary, *The Spiritual Brain.*

Newberg and Iversen, "The Neural Basis of the Complex Mental Task of Meditation."

Questions to Consider

1. How are brain-imaging studies used to reveal changes in the brain during spiritual practices such as prayer, meditation, or speaking in tongues?

2. What parts of the brain are specifically responsible for the emotional, cognitive, or mystical content of spiritual practices?

The Biology of Spiritual Practices
Lecture 9—Transcript

In our previous lecture, we saw that rituals provide a powerful form of experience that involves the entire human body. We also began to explore some of the underlying neurological and biological processes that are involved in religious and even nonreligious rituals. In this lecture, we're going to take that exploration further: We're going to look at two spiritual practices in particular—meditation and prayer—and we're going to examine the biological underpinnings of these practices.

But as we explore the biology of prayer and meditation, we also have to reflect on what our newfound knowledge might tell us about the true nature and meaning of these practices and the experiences that they elicit. Can practices like meditation and prayer alter our physical wellbeing? Can they have an impact on physical circumstances and realities outside of ourselves? Are the effects of these practices only in our heads? These are the questions that will crop up at various points throughout this course; and one of my goals for this particular lecture is to give a solid foundation for addressing them. But more importantly, in this lecture I want to cover some of the specific biological effects of spiritual practices.

Perhaps the best way to begin our discussion is to reconsider our story of the monks arguing about the flag waving in the wind. If you remember that story and its conclusion, the idea was that it was actually the mind that was moving; it wasn't the flag, not the wind, not even reality itself. It's the mind that appears to make everything move for us. But in today's world, we now have the neurosciences, which allow us to relate the brain to the mind; and hence we can now look at how the brain actually allows us to be spiritual, which, of course, is the ultimate goal of this entire course.

What has neuroscience been able to tell us about spirituality and, more specifically, about spiritual practices such as prayer and meditation? Interestingly, the knowledge we're gaining from studying meditation and prayer experimentally isn't only teaching us something about these particular practices themselves, it's also giving us some valuable insights about the way our brain regulates a variety of basic physiological and neurophysiological processes; and these processes include not only what's going on in the brain itself changes to our heart, our heart rate, our respiration, and even metabolism throughout the entire body.

As we've learned, there are many methodological questions that arise when considering a study of meditation or prayer. For example, in our prior lecture on methods, we saw the importance of asking questions like the following: What's the best way to study the biology of spirituality? What are the best types of practices or experiences that we can study? How do you actually measure the experience itself and try to correlate it with something that's biological? We've also talked about the importance of defining the practices and objects under study; so toward that end, let's take a look at some of the defining aspects of meditation and prayer.

When it comes to meditation, there are, of course, many different approaches, perhaps thousands of different approaches, and many different meanings associated with these various practices. But we can begin to identify some specific aspects of meditation that are common perhaps across all types. One of the most common elements of many different meditation practices is that it involves the ability to focus a person's attention. In many ways, this is one of the key elements of all meditation practices: that we focus our mind on something. It could be a visual object, a sacred object that we have; it could be a word or a phrase, as we saw in our very first study that we talked about, the centering prayer study; but basically the person continues to focus their mind, to focus their attention, on this particular object throughout the entire practice itself.

While this is going on, it's always interesting to me that this is such a simplistic thing to do, just to focus on something; but as this happens, a person starts to notice many other feelings and experiences that start to crop up. One of them is a more emotional kind of feeling; so they may actually feel a sense of arousal, they might feel that their whole brain and body is turned on by this particular practice. Or perhaps just the opposite: Maybe they'll start to feel this incredible sense of calmness and blissfulness come over them; they may feel a more profound sense of blissfulness than they've ever felt before in their lives.

As they continue to do this practice, another thing starts to happen; and this one is a little harder to understand if you've never had this kind of experience before. They begin to feel a diminishment in their sense of self. What I mean by that is that they literally begin to lose the sense of who they are as an individual person. They no longer experience themselves as who they are, but they start to notice a blurring between the boundary of their self and the object that they're meditating upon or their self and the rest of the world. In fact, sometimes they even get to a complete .loss of a sense of space and time during this particular type of practice. If they continue to do this focus and continue to do the practice, they might actually experience something even more profound than all of these other experiences combined: It's a sense of almost an eruption of ecstasy, this incredibly powerful rush of all kinds of emotions coming over them; and eventually not only do they lose their sense of self, but they experience something that they may describe as a feeling of absolute unity, the notion that almost all things blur into one, everything becomes a gigantic oneness. We'll be talking more about this particular type of experience later on in the course; but for now, I wanted to give you at least a brief idea about what meditation is, what it does, and how it actually has an effect on what the person is experiencing.

Turning now to prayer, we can say again that there are many different types of prayer and many different meanings associated with the various ways that prayer is practiced. But, once more, there are some common elements of almost all types of prayer practices. For one, prayer is similar to meditation in that it frequently involves focusing attention. This focusing of attention is usually more specific in the context of a religious idea: They might be focusing on a particular prayer, on a particular phrase from the Bible, on the belief in God or some belief about their religion. But as they're doing this intense focusing, the person may also have a feeling of arousal and a feeling of calmness, depending on the circumstances; and just like meditation, in very intense practices of prayer they actually feel a complete loss of the sense of self, and a loss of the sense of space and time. Of course, prayer can result in some very profound spiritual or even mystical experiences of ecstasy or absolute unity, just like we see in practices of profound and deep meditation.

There are some ways in which prayer differs from meditation. For example, some types of prayer are actually more conversational. If you think about this in the context of saying grace at a meal: It's a way of talking it out; talking about what your beliefs are. Of course, many people pray to God simply as a form of talking to God; it's just a way that they can converse with God and try to communicate something back and forth with God. This is one of the ways in which prayer is very distinct from meditation, in which it has a very specific religious content to it. Of course, prayer typically involves a verbal kind of practice, so this is something that allows almost anyone to participate in prayer; and it's a way of engaging in the prayer process through language, which is often different than what we see in meditation practices, especially those that involve visualization.

Each religion has its own specific prayers and frequently specific ways of doing these particular prayers. In Judaism, we find individuals dovening back and forth; they move back and forth with their body, bending at the waist as they go through the prayer. In Islam, individuals are to pray five times a day while facing Mecca. Prayer also usually has the particular goal of connecting the individual with God.

With all of this prayer going on, what do we think is happening in the brain? It turns out that the data suggests that prayer is a highly complex process. It involves many different brain structures and functions; and, to me, this, of course, makes a great deal of sense because the prayer practices and their associated experiences are so rich and diverse that it seems that there has to many different parts of the brain that really get into the game as far as these spiritual practices are concerned.

Let's review for a few moments some of these essential areas of the brain in terms of what they normally do for us, and then focus on the brain scan studies that can detail for us exactly how these areas get involved in practices like meditation or prayer. If you remember, the frontal lobe—right behind the forehead—is a very important area of our brain that helps us to concentrate; to focus our attention on whatever task we have at hand. It might make sense, then, if we think about what's going on during prayer or meditation; if they're concentrating, would we see changes going on in this area of the brain that helps them to engage in that particular practice.

We also know that this attention-focusing area can block information from moving back and forth within other parts of the brain. In fact, one of the areas of the brain that we talked about a few lectures ago called the hippocampus—which is part of the brain's limbic system and also very involved in the ability to remember things—this is an area that starts to get blocked by the attention area. It can actually be the kind of thing where if a person is engaged in a deep practice such as prayer or meditation, that they become so intensely on the prayer that they start to screen out all of the other irrelevant sensory information that's trying to get into their brain; so they become intensely focused on this particular practice. Maybe we'll see changes in the brain in these areas that are involved in the practices of meditation or prayer.

I also talked about the parietal lobe, the orientation part of the brain, located back here in the back part of the brain. This tends to take all of our sensory information and helps to create for us a sense of our self as well as a sense of space and time for us. If a person is describing, as we just discussed, losing their sense of self, losing their sense of space and time, what could be going on in that parietal lobe during the practice? As far as the emotional elements of meditative and prayer practices, as we just discussed, they can be intensely emotional: intense feelings of arousal, bliss, other feelings of love, compassion, or maybe even fear or awe. We would expect some very substantial changes to be going on in the limbic system, that emotional center of the brain, when somebody is engaged in a prayer or meditation practice.

Finally, a very central structure: We talked about the master controller of the brain called the hypothalamus. This is a part of the brain that regulates the autonomic nervous system, that arousal and calming part of our body. If a person engages in a practice of prayer or meditation and they feel a deep sense of arousal or a very calming sense of bliss, what's going on in that autonomic nervous system and in that hypothalamus that might regulate that kind of experience?

How do we come to know what's going on in these different parts of the brain involved in prayer? My colleagues and I over the years have used a variety of different neuroimaging techniques to evaluate different prayer practices. As we spoke about in prior lectures, some of these include SPECT scans; the ability to inject a small amount of a radioactive tracer that follows blood flow or some other aspect of the brain's function that we can measure with the scan. Or we might do Magnetic Resonance Imaging to see what changes are going on in the blood flow of the brain that tells us something about the level or the changes of activity that are associated with these particular practices.

Let's look at some of the studies that I've performed with regard to prayer and meditation practices. We've already spent some time going over the study with Franciscan nuns. If you remember, in that study we studied nuns who had many years of experience doing a kind of prayer called centering prayer. It's a type of contemplative prayer, and we used SPECT scans to measure changes in blood flow in the brain. Again, if you remember, the brain works very nicely that the more active a particular part of the brain is, the more blood flow it gets; so we can actually see patterns of activity, changes in activity, on these SPECT scans while the person is actually in prayer. Also remember that one of the real important elements about how a SPECT scan works is that we inject a radioactive tracer at the time that the person is doing the prayer practice. Once that tracer gets into their body and up into their brain, it gets locked into the brain; so it can tell us exactly what's going on in the brain at the moment of prayer or meditation. What we can then do is compare the resting state (when the person isn't doing anything in particular) to the activation state (the state when they're actually engaged in the practice of meditation or prayer), and we can look at these brain scans and see what areas of the brain are turned on or what areas of the brain are turned off. We can also not just look at the scans themselves but we actually have the ability to apply a quantitative analysis; we can tell how much percentage-wise a part of the brain is turned on or how much of the brain is turned off.

When we looked at the results of the prayer study, we saw some very interesting changes that relate directly to what the person is doing subjectively and the kinds of functions that the different parts of the brain that we just talked about help us with. For example, we found substantially increased activity in the frontal lobe during the prayer practice. This makes so much sense because they're focusing their mind very deeply—focusing their brain deeply—on the prayer practice, and therefore we're seeing increases of activity in the part of the brain that helps us to focus attention. We also see a substantial decrease of activity in the parietal lobes. Remember, the parietal lobes help us with our orientation of our sense of self; so it makes sense, then, that as we lose our sense of self we see a concomitant decrease in the part of the brain that helps us to create that sense of self: the parietal lobes; that orientation part of the body. We also see an increase in the activity levels in a very central structure called the thalamus. If you recall, we talked about what the thalamus does in a prior lecture: The thalamus is a very key central structure in the brain that helps to connect different parts of the brain and helps us to interpret all of the sensory information that's coming up into our brain. The fact that the thalamus was substantially increased tells us how active of a practice this actually is.

I think that this is a very important point: When people engage in a practice like prayer, even though they may feel calmer, it isn't in and of itself a calming kind of practice. It's a highly active practice that activates many different parts of the brain, and the increased activity in the thalamus is reflective of that; it's telling us that lots of things are going on in the brain during this particular prayer practice.

How do the changes that we see in the brain during the prayer state compare to what we saw in a group of people who were doing a kind of Tibetan Buddhist meditation? The Tibetan Buddhist meditation practice was a visualization technique: They created a visual image in their mind that they brought their attention to; they focused on this particular visual image that was usually of a sacred object; and they concentrated on that for a period of up to an hour or more. What was interesting is that just like the practice is somewhat similar to what we see in centering prayer, we also saw certain similarities as well as some differences in the brain scans. For example, we found that there was very significantly increased activity in the Buddhist meditators in their frontal lobes. Again, this makes so much sense because they're also concentrating deeply on the particular practice; and hence we see increases of activity in the frontal lobes that signifies their intense concentration during the practice. We also see decreases in the parietal lobe, that orientation part of the brain. Again, this makes so much sense because they also lose their sense of self, lose their sense of space and time, just like the nuns and therefore see decreases of activity in the area of the brain that normally helps us to feel our sense of self and to feel our sense of space and time.

We also have begun to delve into doing Functional Magnetic Resonance Imaging studies of spiritual practices and experiences because there are certain advantages that these kinds of studies have over SPECT imaging. One of the main advantages that the fMRI studies have is that there's no radiation involved; we don't have to inject a radioactive tracer into the person, and that's obviously something that's very nice for the subject. The other bigger advantage is that the fMRI can actually obtain multiple images throughout an entire imaging session. We can take a picture of your brain now, and in a minute, and in 2 minutes, and in 5 minutes, and in 10 minutes, and all the way through the entire practice of the meditation. When we were talking about our SPECT studies a few moments ago, all that's able to do is capture that one point in time. When I do the injection of the tracer, once that gets into the brain that's the picture that I get; it doesn't give me any other information other than that one moment in time, whereas the fMRI can actually allow us to study multiple states of the brain over time. As we've been talking about, meditation isn't something that just occurs instantaneously; it's something that's a dynamic process that starts to occur over many minutes or even hours, and the fMRI allows us to do that.

One of the disadvantages of the fMRI is that all it can look at are changes in blood flow; it's not able to look at some of the more specific neurotransmitter or chemical changes that are going on in the brain, and that's something that really requires SPECT imaging or another related kind of imaging called Positron Emission Tomography (PET imaging), and we'll be talking about this more in our lecture on the neurotransmitters and how they relate specifically to spiritual experiences and practices.

But in returning to the fMRI studies, there are several very interesting studies that have been performed. One Functional Magnetic Resonance Imaging study was done with 15 Carmelite nuns and actually asked them to reflect on their most powerful mystical experiences that they'd ever had. The study was performed at the University of Montreal and basically brought in a group of very learned, very experienced nuns. When they came in on the imaging day, they were asked to simply think back on the mystical experiences that they'd had and to reflect on them for a period of time—typically very short, maybe about 5 or even 10 minutes at most—while their brain was being scanned by the fMRI.

What was interesting were the changes that were seen in terms of the brain activity. Again, like our studies of the nuns and the Buddhist meditators, there was increased activity in the frontal lobes. They were concentrating, they were focusing on the experiences that they'd had, and that was associated with a change of activity going on in the area of our brain that helps us with concentration and attention. The fMRI also allows us to get at some more subtle changes going on in the brain; for example, we see changes in the brain of these Carmelite nuns in the limbic areas that are involved in the emotional content of these experiences. We weren't able to observe that as well with our studies, but this particular study shows us that the limbic system is very involved in what these practices and what these experiences are all about. The other very interesting finding in this particular fMRI study was an increase of activity in the brainstem. The brainstem is the part of the brain that ultimately helps the brain to connect down through the autonomic nervous system to the rest of the body; so this speaks to the idea that not only are there changes going on up in the brain itself but these changes are being translated down into the rest of the body so that it's experienced not just cognitively and emotionally but viscerally as well, it's experienced all the way down throughout their entire being.

These findings are somewhat similar to the studies that we were just talking about with our Franciscan nuns and Buddhist meditators, but there had been some interesting differences across these groups. For example, when we looked at our Buddhist meditators relative to the nuns, one of the things that we saw in the Buddhist meditators was an increase of activity in the visual area of the brain. Remember back: The Buddhist meditators were doing a visualization technique, so it makes sense that the visual areas of the brain were what were turned on during this particular practice. On the other hand, the nuns actually activated the language areas of the brain, because they were doing a kind of verbal practice; they were doing prayer. If we look at the fMRI study of the Carmelite nuns, one of the things that they saw in this particular study was actually an increase of activity in the parietal lobes; in that orientation part of the brain. Remember, we tended to see decreases of activity in the parietal lobes.

Why was there a difference? Maybe it has to do with the experience itself during this study. With the Carmelite nuns, who had increases of activity in the parietal lobe, what was going on probably was that they were actually focusing their self—they're orienting their self—towards the experience; they were concentrating on how their self was related to the experience and hence because they were having an increase in what their self felt like we see an increase of activity in the part of the brain that helps them establish that sense of self. On the other hand, in our meditators and in our nuns doing prayer, they lost their sense of self and hence we see a decrease of activity in this particular area of the brain. In fact, this is a very crucial point since many studies of meditation and prayer have had the person doing these practices for anywhere from a few minutes to an hour or more, and it may take a while for the person to convert over from concentrating on the self and the relationship of the self to God or to the object of meditation to the point where they begin to feel this sense of oneness and sense of unity where they completely lose their sense of self. Again, this is why these kinds of studies will be so valuable because we can actually start to see what's going on not just at one moment in time, but we can look at things throughout the entire process; and therefore, throughout these practices, we'll expect to see progressively different experiences and progressively different things changing in the brain as the person undergoes these different kinds of experiences.

Other studies have actually tried to use Functional Magnetic Resonance Imaging to not evaluate the practice of prayer or meditation, but to see the changes of these practices that they cause in terms of our emotions or our cognitive processes. In fact, one fMRI study looked at 12 experienced as well as 10 beginner meditators and they scanned them not during the practice of meditation but they scanned them while they were looking at different types of pictures; pictures that had either a positive, a negative, or neutral emotional stance—some of them were very happy kinds of pictures, some of them were very angry and very scary kinds of pictures—and they asked the person to look at these pictures while they were either in a meditative state or a non-meditative state. It turned out that the experienced meditators had a decrease of activity in the frontal lobes when they were looking at all of the different emotional categories of pictures. There were no changes in the brain regions involved in emotional reactivity. On the other hand, the beginners actually showed a decrease in the left amygdala—that part of the limbic system that helps us to see fear and different emotions—there was a decrease in the amygdala during the emotional processing.

These findings suggest that the long-term practice of meditation leads to emotional stability rather than by eliciting control over the limbic system. Another study showed that meditation can cultivate positive emotions that actually alter the activation in the brain areas linked to empathy and our ability to respond to a variety of different emotional stimuli. More recently, studies have been performed that are starting to look at neurotransmitters and how these neurotransmitters are associated with different practices like meditation, prayer, and other types of religious experiences. We'll be discussing this in much more detail in an upcoming lecture, but a few studies are worth noting here briefly.

One PET study showed that there was a release of the brain's central dopamine during a yoga meditation practice. Dopamine, of course, is very involved in our emotional processing, and also how we perceive our reality. Another study used something called Magnetic Resonance Spectroscopy, which is a way of determining the chemical structure and the chemical milieu in the brain at a particular point in time and showed an increase in a particular neurotransmitter called GABA—which is an inhibitory neurotransmitter; it helps to calm things down—and they saw an increase of this GABA during a particular type of practice called yoga asana meditation. These studies are starting to show not just the changes of activity in the brain, but how there may be very specific chemical findings and chemical changes in the brain; and we'll be talking about these a little bit later.

Physiologically, in the body, we see that meditation and prayer practices result in an overall decrease in heart rate and blood pressure; a decrease in the body's metabolism; and a variety of hormonal changes as well. Also, we see increases throughout the body in a variety of different chemicals such as serotonin, dopamine, GABA (which we just mentioned); and a decrease in some of the stress hormones in our body such as cortisol or norepinephrine, which is kind of like adrenaline.

Spiritual practices such as meditation and prayer can have an impact on the brain and the body in multiple ways. Different practices typically have different patterns of brain activity and different changes that go on in the body, although there are also some similarities across all different kinds of practices. The changes in the brain associated with a given practice ultimately depend on the specific elements of the practice and the experiences that are associated with that particular practice. Thus, emotional components affect the emotional centers of the brain; if there are behavioral components, things that the person is supposed to do in terms of movement, this activates the motor areas of the brain; and if there are things that we're supposed to think about, cognitive components, then this affects the cognitive, the higher cortical, areas of our brain. Yet as different as all of these practices and experiences may be, what's also a fascinating issue is that they're all ultimately considered by the individual as something that's spiritual.

In this lecture, we've seen how the tools of science can open up new windows on the complex phenomena of prayer and meditation. Interestingly, what we've also begun to see is that the exploration of spirituality actually has the reciprocal effect of improving our knowledge of human beings as biological creatures. By understanding the biology of prayer and meditation—its effects on our heart rate, our hormones, our immune system, and our brain—this leads to a greater understanding of the ways in which these practices might be able to affect our overall health and wellbeing.

This will be the exciting topic that we'll consider in the next two lectures.

Religion and Health
Lecture 10

There are hundreds of scientific studies that show a relationship between religion and health. As a matter of fact, the interest in this topic is rapidly expanding. Before the 1990s, only about 25 to 50 research papers per year dealt with the relationship between religion and health, but since 2000, there have been over 400 papers published per year on this topic. These papers are consistently showing that religion has an effect on health—but what is this effect, and how and why does it occur? In this lecture, you will learn that religious belief has been shown to correlate with better overall health and well-being.

Linking Religion and Health

- Any attempt to link spirituality and health has to deal with a significant challenge: How do you develop a measurement for spirituality?

- For example, if you wanted to compare the overall health of a relatively spiritual person with the overall health of someone who is less so, you would need to find some way of measuring what makes one person relatively more spiritual, or religious than another person.

- You have to be able to place the people you're studying on some scale of spirituality or religiousness; otherwise, there's no way you can compare the health benefits or detriments of one group with another.

- Researchers make these kinds of measurements by relying on data on factors such as church attendance, religious attitudes, and frequency of private religious practices—all of which are currently available. These and other measures are generally underutilized. Many measures are unavailable because they were never published,

published in hard-to-find journals, or did not have the actual scales included. Furthermore, many measures rely on self-reporting.

- When you analyze data from different studies, for the most part, they relate to population-based analyses, which means that if a study shows that religion is correlated with a reduced risk of heart disease, then on average, being religious is associated with a reduced risk. However, there are plenty of religious people who get heart disease and plenty of atheists who do not, so you always have to be careful about how you interpret the information.

- There are ways of measuring the religious activities and commitments of individuals, and that allows researchers to look at groups of people with a high level of religious commitment, for example, and to compare their health outcomes with those of people who have a relatively low level of religious commitment.

The Effects of Religion on Health
- Studies have shown that church attendance is associated with decreased heart disease, blood pressure, emphysema, cirrhosis, and suicide. One of the earliest papers to report this association was published in 1972 by Johns Hopkins University and was based on an analysis of about 50,000 people in Washington County, Maryland.

- In this study, researchers divided people into groups of those who went to church once or more per week versus less than once weekly. The study found that those who went to church less often were twice as likely to die from heart disease, emphysema, or suicide. However, there was no association with deaths from cancer.

- A more recent study of almost 4,000 older individuals showed that those attending church more than once per week were 46 percent less likely to have died over the following six years.

Research shows that church attendence has a very beneficial effect on health.

- In a study of 40 patients who had heart transplants, strong religious beliefs predicted improved physical functioning, higher self-esteem, decreased anxiety, and enhanced compliance.

- It has been shown that increased worship and practice is inversely related to perception of disability among the elderly.

- In cancer patients, religious belief has been found to be associated with reduced perception of pain.

- Researchers have even found a relationship between religious activity and mortality. For example, multiple studies published in the 1980s and 1990s identified a correlation between frequent church attendance and a reduction in all-cause mortality.

- In a study of 232 patients undergoing cardiac surgery, patients receiving support from religion had reduced mortality.

- These results, and others like them, are extremely compelling and fascinating. It is remarkable that the medical establishment does not stand up and take notice of these studies as much as the data suggest that they should.

- On the other hand, there have been studies of patients in nursing homes that showed no clear relationship between death rates and religiousness.

- In addition to researching church attendance in general and its possible relationship to health, another fascinating line of research measures the comparative health outcomes of specific groups of believers, and what researchers seem to be finding is that the faith tradition you identify with may actually have an impact on your health.

- For example, studies have shown that Mormon males have decreased rates of cancer and all-cause mortality. In addition, it has been shown that Seventh-day Adventists live longer than the average population.

- There are many other potentially relevant factors involved in being religious that may have an impact on your health—for example, religious (or spiritual) preference or affiliation, history, social participation, private practices, support, and experiences.

- In 1992, a study was conducted of over 2,800 individuals who were over 65 years of age in the New Haven, Connecticut, region. The study found that elderly Christians and Jews were less likely to die in the 30 days before important holidays as compared to the 30 days after.

- Other studies have shown that chronically ill patients frequently use religious and spiritual practices.

- Spirituality among cancer survivors is associated with positive health habits and social and emotional support.

- Cardiac patients identify religion and prayer as a frequently used coping mechanism prior to surgery.

- Sometimes, religion can have a negative impact on overall well-being. For example, religion is sometimes viewed negatively; some people view the God they worship as a punishing God.

- Lack of spirituality may be blamed as the cause of a physical or psychological disorder, and even positive experiences may result in increased anxiety and depression.

- Cults are an interesting and problematic example because the participants in cults often feel that they benefit from being part of the cult group, even though they may not be functioning in society. Of course, cults can be associated with very poor outcomes, especially when they involve mass suicide.

How Religion Exerts Its Health Effects

- Despite some negative effects of spirituality, on the whole, it seems that spirituality and religious practices convey some health benefits to individuals—and that raises a very interesting question: Should patients and doctors discuss religion, and if so, how?

- In a study conducted by the Department of Pastoral Care and Education at the Hospital of the University of Pennsylvania, researchers interviewed patients and physicians to address this question.

- The results from evaluating about 200 patients showed that about 70 percent of patients wanted their physicians to ask questions about their spiritual or religious beliefs. This was highest among religious individuals, who also said that their religious beliefs were likely to have an impact on end-of-life health decisions. Even about half of nonreligious individuals thought that it was a good idea for physicians to ask them about their religious beliefs.

- Given all of these effects of religion on health, in scientific terminology, what is the mechanism of action by which religion exerts its health effects? How might this relate to the human brain?

- Religion has been associated with decreased participation in high-risk behaviors such as alcohol, smoking, drugs, and promiscuity. In addition, certain religious groups promote healthy dietary practices. Furthermore, church attendance is associated with increased social support.

- We can try to assess how the changes associated with religious practices can have an effect on health.

- Meditation and prayer can induce the relaxation response, which includes lower heart rate and blood pressure. This is mediated by activity in the anterior pituitary-adrenocortical axis.

- Changes are also found in the autonomic nervous system. In addition, relaxation training results in changes in immune system function.

- It is important to note that changes in heart rate and immune function do not necessarily translate into clinical effects. If white blood count increases, does this imply fewer infections? If blood pressure decreases, does this result in lower risk of heart disease or stroke? Are physiological or clinical findings more important? Are findings related specifically to religion or spirituality?

- Religion has been proven to generally have a positive health impact, reduce the risk of getting certain diseases, and even reduce the risk of dying prematurely. However, you can't pretend to be religious in order to get the health-related effects that are associated with being religious. You are religious because you believe in it, and if it has health benefits, then that is just an added bonus.

- Doctors and scientists are still trying to determine exactly how religion exerts its health effects, although they are starting to get a fairly good idea of the mechanisms by which it happens. Of course, one remaining question is whether there is something simply about being religious that causes a health benefit.

Suggested Reading

Duke University's Center for Spirituality, Theology, and Health, "Latest Religion and Health Research Outside Duke."

Hall, Meador, and Koenig, "Measuring Religiousness in Health Research."

Koenig, McCullough, and Larson, *Handbook of Religion and Health*.

Lee and Newberg, "Religion and Health."

Questions to Consider

1. What is the relationship between religion and physical health?

2. Does being a religious or spiritual person make you healthier?

Religion and Health
Lecture 10—Transcript

Suppose you picked up the newspaper and saw the following headline: "Elderly Christians Less Likely to Die in the 30 Days before Christmas than in the 30 Days After." Would this headline surprise you? What if I told you that there are actually hundreds of scientific studies that show a relationship between religion and health? It's true; and, as a matter of fact, the interest in this topic is rapidly expanding. For example, before the 1990s, only about 25–50 papers a year actually dealt with the relationship between religion and health; but since 2000, there have been over 400 papers published every year on this particular topic. What those papers are consistently showing is this: Religion really does have an effect on health.

But what is this effect, specifically? How and why does it occur, and is it always positive, or is it possible that sometimes it's negative? These are some of the questions that we're going to tackle in this lecture. We've already seen that religious practices cause measurable changes in the brain and the body, but today we're going to start examining the more practical side of these effects. Specifically, we'll look at how religion and spirituality relates to our health and wellbeing.

Of course, any attempt to link spirituality and health has to deal with a significant challenge right out of the gate: How do you even measure or attempt to develop a measurement for spirituality? Let's say, for example, you want to compare the overall health of a relatively spiritual person with the overall health of someone who is less so. To do that, you need to find some way of measuring what makes one person relatively more spiritual or more religious than another one, right? You have to be able to place the people you're studying on some scale of spirituality or religiousness; otherwise there's no way you can compare the health benefits or detriments of one group over another.

So how do researchers make these kinds of measurements? What data do they rely on? Some of the earliest work was actually done by asking some very basic questions. Usually they just asked a question like, "How often do you go to church?" Of course, people started to realize pretty quickly that, as I like to say "Just because you're in a garage doesn't make you a car," just because you're in a church doesn't necessarily make you a religious or spiritual person. We started to look at other ways of getting at this question: What are a person's religious attitudes? How often are they engaged in religious practices like meditation or prayer? These are the kinds of questions that we can try to get at to get a feel for how religious or spiritual somebody may actually be.

As a scientist, I've often tried to go to the medical literature, the psychological literature, to find questionnaires and scales like this so that I could use them in my studies, but unfortunately they're often very hard to find and a lot of times they're underutilized; in fact, many of the times these measures aren't even in the scientific literature but they've been published in these kind of back-end, hard-to-find journals and it makes it very difficult to be able to include these kinds of scales in research that's ongoing today. Fortunately, we're getting better and better at making these kinds of measurements, and more and more measurements are available.

But there are a couple of other problems that go on with these kinds of measurements, and one of the most pressing ones is that almost all of these measures of spirituality and religiousness rely on self-reporting. What I mean by that is that we have to ask the person, we have to say, "How do you feel?" Of course, if we do that, we don't always know if we're going to get an honest answer from that person; and it's also difficult to know how one person might answer in comparison to another. It's a little bit like trying to measure pain: Some people are very good at tolerating a lot of pain, and some people are panicking at the smallest sight of pain; so how do we know how to measure what pain is for that particular person, or one person versus another? The same question comes up with spirituality and religiousness.

I also want to raise one other very important point that pertains to this lecture and the next one on religion and health. When we discuss data from different studies, for the most part they relate to population-based analyses. By this I mean that if a study shows that religion or spirituality is correlated with a reduction in the risk of heart disease, then on average—the critical words "on average"—being religious is associated with a reduced risk. But there are plenty of religious people who get heart disease and certainly plenty of atheists who don't. So we always have to be careful about how we interpret this information, but at least it gives us a starting point to try to understand this overall relationship between spirituality and health.

As I mentioned, we do have ways of measuring the religious activities and commitments of individuals, and this allows us to look at groups of people with, let's say, a very high level of religious commitment and to compare their health outcomes with those of people who have a relatively low level of religious commitment. Let's take a look at church attendance.

As I mentioned, this is one of the easiest ways of asking the question, and while it's not perfect it's still pretty good; usually the more religious and spiritual you are, the more you're going to go to church. A large variety of studies have actually found that going to church—church attendance—is positively associated with improvements in heart disease, blood pressure, lung disease such as emphysema, liver disease such as cirrhosis, and even suicide. In fact, one of the earliest papers to report this association was published in 1972 by researchers at Johns Hopkins, and it was based upon an analysis of about 50,000 people in Washington County, Maryland. Researchers divided the people into either those who went to church once or more per week versus those who went to church less than once a week. The study found that those who went to church less were twice as likely to die from heart disease; they were also twice as likely to die from emphysema or suicide. However, there was no association with going to church and cancer deaths.

A more recent study of almost 4,000 older individuals showed that those attending church more than once per week were 46 percent less likely to have died over the next six years. In a study of 40 heart transplant patients—a very specific kind of population—strong religious beliefs predicted improved physical functioning, higher self-esteem, decreased anxiety in what was going on around them, and ultimately enhanced compliance with the medical treatments. If all of this is going on, it would seem that having a religious belief would correlate to an overall better health and wellbeing, whether it's for the general public or perhaps even for a specific population.

One interesting study that also is relevant is that increased worship and practice was inversely related with the perception of disability among the elderly. Again, simply by engaging in practice, having a religious belief, the person actually felt better; they felt less disabled. In cancer patients, religious beliefs have been found to be associated with the reduced perception of pain. In fact, there are a variety of studies now that are starting to get at and show that those people who turn to religion to cope with various problems and who are religious in and of themselves actually do regulate their pain responses better, they actually feel less pain than those people who aren't religious; and the more they engage in their religious beliefs—the more they focus on their religious beliefs at a particular moment in time—the less they respond to painful stimuli.

Researchers have even found a relationship between religious activity and overall mortality; the risk of actually dying. For example, multiple studies published in the 1980s and 1990s identified a correlation between frequent church attendance and a reduction in all-cause mortality. That means that the more people actually went to church, the less likely they were to die. Remember my caveat before: This is a population-based conclusion. It doesn't specify an individual effect; and therefore there are certainly plenty of people who go to church who die, and there are plenty of people who don't go to church who live long, healthy lives. But when we look at the population itself, we see a very significant relationship. Another interesting study of 232 patients undergoing cardiac surgery: For those individuals who received support from religion, they actually had reduced mortality.

Again, these results, and others like them, are extremely compelling and fascinating. It really shows us that being religious or spiritual seems to have some very powerful benefits in terms of your health and wellbeing. It's remarkable to me that the medical establishment doesn't actually stand up and take notice of these kinds of studies and really look at the data as something that's very important in terms of how we should actually help patients. In fact, for me personally as I've gone through my research and gone through the patients who I've talked to and interviewed for our studies and talked to in the hospital, I've always been so fascinated by how powerful religious and spiritual beliefs are for these individuals. It's so critical to their health and wellbeing; and when they're able to engage their religious and spiritual selves, they do tend to feel better, function better, and actually live better and live longer than those people who aren't religious and spiritual. Hence, I really feel so strongly that the medical establishment needs to look at this data, try to understand it better, and try to find ways of helping patients to better engage a side of themselves that might be very valuable for their overall health and wellbeing.

On the other hand, the picture isn't all rosy, and there have been some studies that have shown a potential negative relationship. In fact, in a very interesting study of nursing home patients, there was no clear relationship between death rates and religiousness. What did the authors conclude by this? One of the possibilities is that maybe when people are in a nursing home and very elderly, maybe they're very religious but because they're disabled, because they're in the nursing home, they can't engage their religious selves the way they normally would. They can't get to church, they can't get to the Mass or the different ceremonies that they want to, the holidays that they want celebrate, and that can be disturbing to them; it can upset them and actually cause them to live a shorter life. In fact, those individuals who struggle with their religious beliefs, it can really have a negative impact on their physical and ultimately their mental health.

Researchers have looked at church attendance in general and its possible relationship to health. Another fascinating line of research actually measures the comparative health outcomes of specific groups of believers. What we seem to be finding is that the faith tradition you identify with may actually have an impact on your health. For example, Mormon males have a decreased rate of cancer and all-cause mortality when you factor all other health-related factors out compared to non-Mormons. In fact, Seventh-Day Adventists also have been found to live longer on average than the general population.

But there are many potentially relevant factors involved in being religious that may have an impact on your health. For example, as we just heard, there may be something about your specific religious affiliation or preference. What's the group that you identify with, how do you identify with them, and how important is it a part of your life and your overall way of dealing with your health and wellbeing? Of course, it's also important to us to understand a person's religious or spiritual history. How have they gone down this path of their spiritual self? Did they go through periods of time where they really struggled with their religious or spiritual beliefs, or have they always been a very devout religious or spiritual person? It's important for us to understand the relationship between private and group practices and health and wellbeing. We know for sure that social interactions and social support are very powerful mediators for improving health and wellbeing, and maybe deriving support along those lines becomes very important for those individuals; that that group interaction and that ability to derive social support is something that's crucial to their overall health and wellbeing.

Of course, the beliefs that people have could be very, very relevant in the context of how they look at themselves and how they actually survive. If you remember the headline that we opened with, that really was a study that was conducted in 1992 where they looked at over 2,800 individuals over the age of 65 years in the New Haven, Connecticut region. They evaluated them and they looked at when they died; and what they found was that yes, in fact, that elderly Christians as well as Jewish individuals were less likely to die in the 30 days before important holidays compared to the 30 days after. What does this mean? There's this implication that the belief in trying to get to that holiday—the belief that this was something important to them; that this was something that would actually enable them to survive longer and get to that holiday and get to that very important event in their lives—that motivated them and that got them through; so we can see how powerful religious beliefs and ideas can actually be in helping an individual to stay healthy or to stay alive as long as they possibly can.

What about other patient populations? We also have a variety of studies that have shown that people who are chronically ill—people who are suffering from cancer, dementia, heart disease, liver disease—so often they use religious and spiritual practices as a way of helping them through. It's a way of helping them to cope; it's a way of helping them to make some sense out of what's going on in their lives; and because of this they derive a great deal of support and power from that so that they can deal with their particular situations. In fact, one of the reasons why I think the healthcare system needs to look at this is that many studies have shown that being a religious or spiritual person, because of all the different effects that it has, actually makes you more compliant with treatment; and if that's the case, people are going to do better. Spirituality among cancer survivors is also associated not only with better health habits but better social and emotional support.

Again, we're starting to see this entire structure or matrix of who we are as human beings that helps maintain our health and wellbeing; that religious and spiritual beliefs can be an extraordinarily important part of all of that. In fact, cardiac patients actually identify religion and prayer as one of the most frequent ways of trying to cope and deal with very, very stressful surgical procedures and medical procedures, and help to get them through those procedures; and because of that, they frequently feel that they do better through those procedures because they're less stressed, they're more relaxed, and have a more positive attitude and all of this together helps them to deal with those situations and deal with their health problems in a more effective way.

So far, we've been focusing on research that shows the health benefits of spirituality; but as I mentioned at the beginning, it's important to note that sometimes religion can have a negative impact on your overall health and wellbeing. What are the ways in which religion can be viewed negatively? One of the things that people frequently cite is the notion that they believe that God is punishing them and that's why they've gotten a particular disease. They've gotten cancer, they've had an addiction; this is an example in which God is punishing them for the things that they've done bad in their lives, maybe punishing them because they weren't spiritual enough. Again, this is a very important issue for us because even though we may find a beneficial relationship between being religious and health, we also need to think about the opposite of that and the possibility that if somebody looks at their religious or spiritual beliefs in a very negative way or looks at God as punishing them, then they're going to have an overall poor outcome. They may feel like, "Why should I go through treatment? Why should I try to beat this cancer if this is the punishment that God has for me?"

We also have to be very cautious that we don't want to get into this notion that a lack of religiousness or a lack of spirituality is actually blamed as the cause of a physical or psychological disorder. This can be a very destructive idea to get into; it's something that physicians and healthcare providers have to watch out for. Patients may feel that way, and sometimes their clergy or family may support that kind of a notion for them, but as a healthcare provider what I think we ultimately have to do is try to find ways of changing their religious and spiritual attitudes around into something that's more positive.

Another interesting problem is that spirituality and religiousness are there because they have intrinsic value. You're religious because you're religious, not because you think it's an intervention that may help with your health. In fact, I always remember this somewhat humorous moment where we were giving our very first research symposium on spirituality and health, and we were very proud of ourselves that we were kind of leading this field. After we presented all the data and some of our brain scans and the relationships with positive health there was a minister who stood up in the back and he said, "I think what you people are doing is terrible. Religion is not an intervention; it's not something that you do in order to stay healthy." Of course, I agree with that. It's not like we can tell people because they're sick to go home and take two prayers and call us in the morning; it's not like aspirin. Therefore we have to be very cautious about how religious and spiritual beliefs and practices are actually used in the context of healthcare. If it's something that's important for the person, then helping them to engage that is something that can be a very powerful mediator for their health and wellbeing; but it really doesn't make sense to ask an atheist or an agnostic to begin praying to God because it might help them with their heart surgery.

Even a positive experience that somebody may have can also lead to a potential negative health outcome. For example—as we'll hear later on in the course in a lecture on near-death experiences—sometimes a person may have a near-death experience that's so overwhelmingly positive; and after they've come back, they've been revived, and they want to tell people about this and they go and they tell their family, maybe they tell their clergy, and they get a lot of very odd looks, very condescending comments ("There, there, you were just a little crazy then" or "It's just the medication") but for the person it was a deeply meaningful experience. Therefore, all of a sudden, this incredibly overwhelmingly positive experience for them is now met with a great deal of frustration and anxiety and even causes depression because they feel that they can't share that with the people they care about and love, they may even feel ostracized; and therefore we have to be cautious about even when somebody has a positive experience, how it can ultimately turn negative.

Perhaps the final negative aspect of health in terms of religious or spiritual beliefs comes in the form of cults and very bizarre kinds of religious and spiritual beliefs. In fact, cults really represent a very interesting and problematic example because the participants often feel that they actually benefit from being part of that cult even though they may not be able to function well in society. Of course, as I often hear in terms of some kind of humorous response, cults ultimately create a very poor outcome especially when they end in mass suicide. This is the way a lot of cults actually do end; therefore, from a health-related perspective, it's a very, very bad thing.

We have to then think about the ideas about how religious and spiritual practices and beliefs can be beneficial, and watch out for the ways in which they can be very negative. This, of course, raises a very interesting question: Should patients and doctors discuss religion; and if so, how?

When I was at the University of Pennsylvania, I was part of a group of researchers including the pastoral care office who wanted to engage this question more actively. They actually interviewed patients and physicians to see what the answer to that question was. The results from evaluating about 200 patients in the pulmonology department showed that about 70 percent of patients wanted their physicians to ask questions about their spiritual and religious beliefs. Of course, this was highest among religious individuals who also said that their religious beliefs were likely to have an impact on decisions they made about their health, including end of life issues; but even about half of the nonreligious individuals thought that it was a good idea to talk with a physician or to have a physician ask them about their religious and spiritual ideas.

Why would they think that? What they said was that it showed that the physician cared about who they were as a person. The physician wanted to know who this person was and how all the different things that were going on were going to affect their lives and their health; and therefore even if the person wasn't religious, it was still reasonable for a physician to ask the question, "Are you a religious person and do your religious beliefs help you in some way, or is there something I need to know as your physician that your religious and spiritual beliefs may have an impact on your health or your decisions about health?"

Given all of these effects on religion on health, we might wonder how it happens. In scientific terminology, what is the mechanism of action by which religion exerts its health-related effects? Ultimately, as the overall topic of this course is, how is this related to what's going on in the human brain?

I like to break down the mechanisms of action into what I call the indirect and the direct mechanisms of action. The indirect mechanisms of action relate to how religions change a person's behaviors and what they do in life that ultimately has a health benefit. For example, we find out that people who are religious often have decreased participation in very high risk behaviors such as drinking alcohol, smoking, taking drugs, or even being promiscuous. For the most part, the reason is that these religious traditions tell people not to do these things; and, of course, if you have a religious tradition that's telling you, "Don't drink, don't smoke, don't be overly promiscuous," maybe even eat certain ways, this sounds a lot like what a very good doctor would tell you to do, and, of course, if it has the benefit and the strength of a religious tradition then people are going to more likely follow those particular edicts. Therefore, we happen to find that simply indirectly by religions telling you to do certain things, it could have a very powerful health benefit.

We've talked a lot about church attendance. Church attendance has a very beneficial effect on health, but what might the mechanism of action be? It turns out that when you go to church, one of the great things that you derive from that is social support. You're working with other people, you're talking to other people, and by interacting with all these other people that social support has a very profound impact on who we are as human beings. We are social beings, our brain functions in a social way, and the more social support we have clearly the better our brains function and the better our bodies function.

I want to spend a few moments talking about the direct mechanisms of action; and we discussed some of these mechanisms in the prior lecture because we can actually look at how religious practices, practices like meditation and prayer, can have a direct impact on health itself. For example, meditation and prayer can induce a kind of "relaxation response"; this is the term that Doctor Herbert Benson up at Harvard University coined back in the 1970s. This relaxation response lowers your heart rate, lowers your blood pressure; and if you think about a lot of the health-related issues in the world today, high blood pressure and high heart rate, these are things that are associated with an increased risk for heart disease and stroke; so if you're engaged in a daily practice of prayer or meditation, maybe it actually directly lowers your possibility of having a stroke or heart disease. This particular effect is believed to be mediated by the hypothalamus and the autonomic nervous system—the part of our body that regulates how our heart rate goes, how our different aspects of our body function—and therefore if a practice like meditation or prayer reduces the arousal side of that autonomic nervous system, brings up the calming side, then we'd expect to see improvements in our heart rate and our blood pressure that are physically and directly mediated by these practices.

If we have a lowering of stress as a direct result of doing these practices, then we see a decrease in our stress hormones, particularly the stress hormone cortisol. Cortisol, as many of you may know, is also something that you take to suppress the immune system. Think about this: If your stress levels lower by engaging in prayer and your cortisol level lowers, then its usual function of suppressing the immune system goes away and the immune system works better. It's possible that if people engage in their religious and spiritual practices that not only do they lower their heart rate and blood pressure but actually their immune system begins to work better. There are some studies that have shown that immune system function is actually improved when people engage in these kinds of practices; for example, patients' white blood cell counts increase and their actual functionality seems to improve.

Of course, we still have this larger question of if your white blood cells that help to mediate your immune system actually are working better and are greater in number, does this actually imply fewer infections or lower risk of cancer? These are the questions that research is now starting to get at. But there's certainly the implication that all of these direct mechanisms of action may be very important for reducing our risk of a variety of different disorders, including things like cancer, heart disease, and stroke.

One of the other questions that we also have to think about is whether or not these changes are specifically related to religion and spirituality; can you engage in any kind of meditation practice even if it doesn't have something to do with spirituality? Of course, to some degree the answer is that any of these practices can have benefit; but typically what we find is that the more an individual is engaged in that particular practice—the more they believe in it, the stronger their feelings are—then the more powerful those experiences actually are and the more powerful their health-related effects actually are.

One other thing that I'll just touch on is the possibility that prayer actually works; that there's a way of praying for somebody that could actually have some benefit to them. We know that prayer can be beneficial for the individual—we've seen the changes that go on in the brain—but is there a way that this kind of intercessory prayer actually works? There are some fascinating studies that have been done that help to show that maybe it does work sometimes, but at this point it's still a very controversial area, we don't really know if it works, and even if it did work we don't really understand exactly how it might actually happen.

We can begin to look at all of these direct effects; we can ask questions about whether we're rewarded for the good behaviors that we do; and at the top of this lecture, we looked at a very intriguing headline. Throughout this lecture, we've noticed that there seems to be a very strong correlation between good health and religious belief; and now that we've considered all of this additional evidence, I think we can say the following: Religion has been proven to generally have a positive impact on health; it reduces the risk of getting certain diseases; it may even reduce the risk of dying prematurely; but you can't pretend to be religious in order to get its health-related effects. You're religious because you believe in it, and if it has health benefits then that's just an added bonus.

Doctors and scientists like myself are still trying to determine exactly how religion exerts its health effects, both positive and negative. We're starting to get at a fairly good idea of the mechanisms by which this happens; but, of course, one remaining question is whether or not there's something simply about being religious that causes a health benefit.

Now that we've described some of the connections between religion and physical health in general, we're going to move on to the next lecture to an even more specific topic: How does religion affect our mental health? I'll see you next time.

Religion and Mental Health
Lecture 11

R esearch has repeatedly shown that many people with psychological problems also express some issues with their religious and spiritual beliefs. For this reason, there appears to be an important—yet often complex—relationship between religion and mental health. In this lecture, you are going to examine the relationship between religion and mental health from a scientific standpoint. You will consider a range of effects—both positive and negative—and you will learn what these effects can teach us about the nature of our spiritual brain.

How Does Religion Affect Mental Health?

- This simple question might have a complex—even an apparently contradictory—answer. There seem to be both positive and negative ways that religion can affect mental health.

- There are, in fact, positive effects of religion on mental health. For example, religiousness and spirituality have been shown to reduce anxiety and encourage impulse control. In research studies, many patients dealing with illnesses—especially chronic ones—cite religion as an important way of reducing their anxiety.

- Patients pray prior to surgery or other types of treatment in order to find comfort. From the medical perspective, this can help people respond better to treatment by enabling them to be more compliant.

- Another positive effect is that religiousness and spirituality foster intimacy and cohesiveness with others. This has been hypothesized to be one of the possible evolutionarily adaptive advantages of religion—to create more cohesive societies. In addition, religious rituals generate intense feelings of connectedness and oneness among participants.

- Religion and spirituality clearly create greater feelings of intimacy and cohesiveness, which can contribute positively to mental health. However, this positive effect is sometimes balanced by the increased antagonism toward those outside of the particular religious faith.

- Religiousness and spirituality also enhance one's sense of meaning and purpose in life. Most studies show a correlation between people's religious attitudes and their sense of having a purpose in life. Religion, of course, on a doctrinal level, provides meaning in the context of the human relationship with God and a sense of purpose, or what we are supposed to do in life. Having this sense of purpose is important to mental health.

- Of course, you don't have to be religious to have a strong sense of meaning in life, but the data suggest that religious faith is a very important source of meaning for many people. Keep in mind that these data pertain to populations and not necessarily to any given individual.

- Another positive effect of spirituality is that it fosters personal growth. By pursuing spiritual goals, people create a framework within which to grow personally.

- Phrases such as "personal growth," "social cohesion," and "sense of purpose" are rather broad ways of talking about mental health, but a large number of studies have also explored the relationship between religion and specific mental health problems, such as depression, anxiety, or substance abuse.

- These studies show mixed results. Some indicate that religion can improve these specific problems while others suggest that religion can worsen a problem.

- For example, anxiety can be improved when a person derives comfort and strength from his or her religion, but anxiety can actually be worsened if people feel that they struggle with their religious beliefs, don't fit into their religious community, or find themselves believing in a God that is punishing them.

- Social psychologist Erich Fromm proposed that humans have a strong need for a stable frame of reference and that religion apparently fills this need. In effect, humans crave answers to questions that no other source of knowledge has an answer to and that only religion may seem to answer.

- Chronically ill patients frequently use religious and spiritual practices to cope with their situations. Spirituality among cancer survivors is associated with positive health habits and social and emotional support. In addition, cardiac patients identify religion and prayer as a frequently used coping mechanism prior to surgery.

- Religious rituals can be very beneficial. In addition to the congregational support that is associated with rituals, a person also receives doctrinal support.

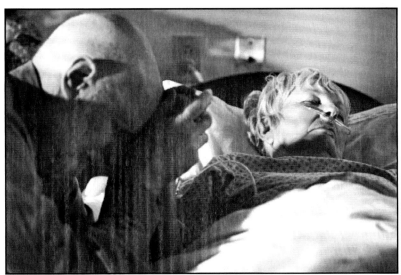

Whether an ill person is treated in a hospital or as an outpatient, spiritually-associated treatment programs can be very beneficial.

- The relationship between religion and mental health is complex; while in principle the relationship can be beneficial, it is not necessarily a cure-all, and may even, in certain cases, lead to worsening conditions.

- Perhaps the relationship between religion and substance abuse is the most complex and intriguing of all. Many researchers have studied the relationship between substance abuse and religion for several reasons.

- A primary hypothesis is that the addiction to drugs is similar to the strong belief (or addiction) to religion. What supports the notion of this link?

- Religious or spiritual involvement predicts less use of and problems with alcohol, tobacco, and drugs. However, there are denominational differences in terms of risk for substance abuse. In denominations that take a strict stand against the use of alcohol, the risk of alcohol problems is lower. Mormons tend to have among the lowest incidence of substance abuse because of the strict rules against it.

- In addition to alcohol, research has shown that spiritual or religious involvement is associated with higher success in smoking cessation.

- In general, religious involvement is low in patients that are undergoing treatment for substance abuse.

- Involvement in spiritually based interventions, such as Alcoholics Anonymous, is associated with better outcomes after inpatient and outpatient treatment. Patients in these kinds of programs do at least as well, if not better, than those treated with other approaches.

- Studies have shown that meditation-based interventions are associated with decreased alcohol and drug abuse.

- Alcoholics often report negative experiences with religion and hold punitive concepts of God. Following treatment for substance abuse, there is an increase in their sense of the meaning in life.

- There is also some evidence that there are common motivations for substance abuse and spiritual pursuits. Both might fill certain needs with regard to emotional support.

Combined Treatment Strategies

- Given the evidence for the relationship between spirituality and mental health, some researchers have tried to more explicitly develop treatment approaches that combine religious or spiritual content with more traditional psychotherapy techniques. They have then studied the use and effectiveness of these combined treatment strategies for different disorders, such as anxiety and depression.

- In general, the studies have shown that these combined interventions are as effective as standard psychotherapy, especially with religious clients. Interestingly, a therapist does not have to be specifically religious to do an integrated psychotherapy with a patient.

- If this type of intervention can be so effective, we might also wonder what other religious and spiritual practices might be useful in helping people with various types of mental illness.

- Forgiveness requires the sense of self (parietal lobe), the ability to compare the self to others (quantitative function), the ability to perceive injury (limbic system), and the ability to remember the causal events leading to the injury (hippocampus and memory areas).

- Eventually, people with various mental illnesses need to use their abstract and emotional processes to reconcile the injury and reframe their understanding of their relationship with the person who injured them.

- This might even apply to God. There are many examples in which a person becomes angry at God for the death of a spouse or because he or she has cancer.

- Furthermore, there is substantial evidence to show how psychologically powerful the forgiveness process can be, and this has now been incorporated with psychotherapy processes as well.

- There is a lot of research and data that support the positive relationship between religion and mental health, but it is not all positive. There are many circumstances in which being religious or spiritual can go wrong and can become detrimental to the individual or society.

- Indeed, there are some negative aspects of religion on mental health. For example, people suffer from their problems with spiritual or religious ideas. In addition, problems with psychological, physical, and sexual abuse have resulted in some people having very negative views about religions. Some people also have unusual views about religions, such as those who follow cults.

- Religion and spirituality may play an important role in psychology. In fact, integrating religion and spirituality into psychotherapy may be very successful in the appropriate setting because religious and spiritual beliefs can sometimes contribute to mental illness and can sometimes be useful in helping people recover from mental illness.

- Understanding the religious beliefs of an individual might be just as important as understanding his or her psyche. There can be so many reciprocal interactions that contribute to mental health and well-being, and ultimately, these interactions play out in the brain—in the emotional and cognitive centers that enable us to feel and think. By embracing the notion of the spiritual brain, we can help to make our approaches to mental illness and mental health as effective as possible.

Suggested Reading

Koenig, "Research on Religion, Spirituality, and Mental Health."

Koenig, ed, *Handbook of Religion and Mental Health*.

Lee and Newberg, "Religion and Health."

Paloutzian and Park, eds, *The Handbook of the Psychology of Religion*.

Questions to Consider

1. What is the relationship between religion and mental health?

2. How and why can religion or spirituality be beneficial or detrimental to mental health?

Religion and Mental Health
Lecture 11—Transcript

Monica was a 32 year old with an onset of depression. Although her therapist discussed a number of issues with her, Monica was still not responding well to therapy or the antidepressant medications that were prescribed for her. In one psychology session, her therapist asked her about her beliefs in God. This first surprised Monica, but then she reflected on her feelings for a few moments. She had a reasonably religious upbringing, especially because her mother was a very religious woman. But when her mother died from cancer, Monica lost all interest in religion. After all, God must not be very compassionate to have taken her mother, and particularly at such a young age. The therapist then asked Monica whether she thought God was on her side. "No," Monica said emphatically, although this bothered her since she felt that she should be better connected to God.

From that point on, the therapist and Monica explored the connection between her depression and her negative beliefs about God and religion. As Monica worked through this issue, she actually found a way to forgive God for her mother's cancer; and this ultimately started to make Monica feel better and less depressed. She eventually got over her depression and found new meaning in her life and in her relationship with God.

This example isn't universally applicable, but research has repeatedly shown that many people who have psychological problems also express some kind of issue with their religious and spiritual beliefs; and for this reason, there appears to be an important relationship between religion and mental health. The relationship is often complex; and it makes us consider: When is religion something beneficial for mental health, and when can it be something instead that's indicative of problems with mental health?

Perhaps these ideas raise an even larger question, one that isn't frequently addressed but may even be a little bit awkward for many of us to consider, let alone talk about; and that question is whether religious thinking is a sign of mental health, or if a well-balanced person who maintains a personal support system can actually engage in religious thinking, either as a sign of something or is it a sign of something normal or even delusional? In this lecture, we're going to look at the relationship between religion and mental health from a scientific perspective. We'll consider a range of effects, both positive and negative, and we'll see what these effects can teach us about the nature of our spiritual brain.

Let's begin by asking a fundamental question: How does religion affect mental health? As our opening story about Monica shows, this simple question might have a very complex and perhaps even contradictory answer. In Monica's case, religion seemed both to exacerbate her depression and ultimately to assist her on her path to recovery. In other words, there seem to be both positive and negative ways that religion can affect a person's mental health.

Why don't we start with some of the upbeat news—the positive effects of religion on mental health—and then later on we'll talk about the negative. For example, religiousness and spirituality have been shown in a large number of studies to reduce anxiety and to encourage a person's impulse control. In fact, even in dealing with patients who are faced with illnesses, especially chronic ones like cancer and heart disease, many individuals cite religion as an important way of reducing their overall anxiety. Patients will pray prior to surgery or perhaps other types of treatment like chemotherapy so that they can find some kind of comfort. From the medical perspective, this can help people respond better to the treatment and actually enables them to be more compliant; they can deal with it better and they can engage it better so that they ultimately have a better health outcome.

Another positive effect is that religiousness and spirituality can foster intimacy and cohesiveness with others. As we discussed in the second lecture of this course, this has been hypothesized to be one of the possible evolutionarily adaptive advantages of religion: It creates more cohesive societies. As we saw in the discussion of rituals, these rituals actually can generate very intense feelings of connectedness and even a feeling of oneness among the participants. So religion and spirituality clearly can create great feelings of intimacy and cohesiveness, and these can contribute to a person's overall mental health. Why? Because they can feel more deeply connected to the people around them: their spouse, their child, their people that they work with. All of these are very important elements in a person's overall mental health; and if religious and spiritual beliefs and practices can help create that feeling of intimacy, that feeling of connection, then that social support can be very beneficial for their mental health and can lower their feelings of anxiety and depression.

However, this positive effect can sometimes be balanced by the increased antagonism that people can feel towards those individuals who are outside of their particular faith; and we'll talk about this a little bit more in a few minutes.

Other studies have actually shown that religiousness and spirituality can actually enhance a person's sense of meaning and a sense of purpose in life. For example, most studies show a correlation between people's religious attitudes and their sense of having this purpose in life. This is something that can happen on a doctrinal level because the religion actually provides some kind of context for meaning in the human life. It tells us how we're to be human beings; it tells us why we're here; it talks about our relationship with God, for example; and all of that together helps create a sense of purpose and a sense of what we're supposed to do here in life. Of course, having this sense of purpose can be very beneficial to mental health because so oftentimes people get lost in terms of what their purpose is; and especially when people feel anxious or depressed, they wonder, they ponder, about why they're here, what's the meaning of all of this.

Religions can help to provide that; in fact, religions can provide a very strong sense of meaning and purpose, but you don't necessarily have to be totally religious or spiritual in order to get that. There are other ways in which people can derive meaning in life; in fact, if you remember from our definitions of religiousness, sometimes it can actually be a nonreligious goal that we strive for. Therefore it doesn't always have to be religious or spiritual, but the data certainly supports the notion that religious beliefs and religious faith is an extremely important source for meaning in people's lives. As we discussed in the last lecture, this data pertains to populations and not necessarily to any given individual; so you could be a religious person and still struggle with your sense of meaning and purpose in life, but on the whole religious and spiritual beliefs can be very beneficial with regard to this particular element of our mental health.

Yet another possible effect of spirituality is that it fosters personal growth. By pursuing spiritual goals, people actually create a framework within which they can grow personally. When we use phrases such as "personal growth" or "social cohesion" or even a "sense of purpose," these are rather broad ways of talking about mental health. On one hand, this is helpful because it tells us something about the global picture of how we can be healthy, how we can maintain our mental health, how we can maintain a positive attitude about our life and about what we're doing here. But a large number of studies have also explored the relationship between religion and specific mental health problems such as depression, anxiety, or even substance abuse.

These studies show something of a mixed bag in terms of their results. Some, for example, indicate that religion can improve these specific problems, while others suggest that religion can actually worsen a problem; and to some degree this may depend a lot on the setting within which the problem is occurring and how that person feels religiously or spiritually along with whatever psychological problems they're dealing with. For example, as we noted a few minutes ago, anxiety can be improved when a person derives comfort and strength from their religion. But anxiety can also be worsened if people feel that they struggle with their religious beliefs; if they feel like they don't fit into their religious community; or if they find themselves believing in a God that's punishing them. On one hand, we can find ways in which anxiety can be benefitted; but on the other hand, sometimes that anxiety can be augmented.

For example, one very interesting element of anxiety is actually thinking about it on a far more global scale, something that people have referred to as ontological anxiety. This ontological anxiety relates a little bit to what we were just talking about, that sense of meaning, that sense of why we're here; sometimes that creates anxiety for people as they struggle with that question. In fact, this was the basis of the work of the social psychologist Erich Fromm who proposed that human beings have a strong need for a stable frame of reference as they go through their life and that religion apparently fills this need. In effect, human beings crave answers to questions that no other source of knowledge truly has the answer to address; in some sense, it's only a way in which religion can somehow try to answer that question.

I'm often reminded of a very interesting story that was told to me when I was in medical school. It had to do with this notion of creating a framework within which we function, and it was talking about a doctor who was working in Africa and there was an individual who'd gotten malaria from a mosquito bite. The patient came to him to get the antibiotics to help to cure the malaria, but then a short time later the doctor saw him going into the tent of the local medicine man. After he came out, the doctor said, "Why are you doing that? If you believe in the effects of medicine, why are you going to talk to this other person who'll only deal with it in a spiritual context?" The patient just looked at him; he said, "I came to you because I got bitten by the mosquito, and I go to the medicine man to find out why." It's this ontological anxiety that we all have about why things happen to us and how we understand it that religious and spiritual beliefs can help us to make better sense of and to quell that ontological anxiety.

The social context within which different disorders occur also can influence anxiety, and therefore if we turn to religion and spirituality as a way of deriving social meaning, social support, and helping us to cope with various issues then that will help to improve our overall mental health and wellbeing. For example, chronically ill patients frequently use religious and spiritual practices as a way of helping them to deal with those particular problems. We talked about this a little bit in the physical health lecture, but it bears repeating in the sense that so often when you have a physical health problem, there's a psychological, mental health element that comes along with it— those fears, those anxieties about death, about pain, about what's going to happen—and those individuals who deal with these problems turn to religion and spirituality, whether they have cancer or heart disease, to try to help them get through these different issues that they face; and by providing a sense of cognitive support, emotional support, and social support, these religious traditions can actually help people as they deal with whatever problems that they face. Whether it's a cardiac patient or a cancer patient, each of these patients can benefit from the spiritual beliefs that they have. In fact, religious rituals themselves can be very beneficial. As an individual goes through different church ceremonies, as they go through meditation practices, prayer practices, as they develop support from their congregation, all of these different elements can come together to help to support a person and help them to resolve whatever psychological, mental health issues that they're facing.

By this point, we've been able to see that the relationship between religion and mental health is complex; and while in principle the relationship can be beneficial, it isn't necessarily a cure-all and it may even in certain circumstances lead to a worsening of conditions. Perhaps the relationship between religion and substance abuse is the most complex and intriguing of all. Many people have studied this relationship between substance abuse and religion for a variety of reasons. In general, there's the primary hypothesis that addiction to drugs is similar to a very strong belief in religion. It's this notion that you're addicted to something, and whether you're addicted to drugs or addicted to religion there may be a relationship; and perhaps if you can shift that addiction from drugs to religion, that could be a more beneficial avenue for an individual to take.

What supports the notion of this link? There's actual research; in fact, religious and spiritual involvement predicts less use of and less problems with alcohol, tobacco, and drugs. There are denominational differences as well: Denominations that have a very strict stance against the use of alcohol tend to have a much lower risk for having alcohol problems. Therefore, Mormons, for example, tend to have among the lowest incidence rates of substance abuse because it has a very strict rule against it. Spiritual and religious involvement is also associated with higher success in smoking cessation programs; so the more you're spiritually motivated, it tends to have a beneficial influence in improving a person's ability to overcome their smoking addiction.

Also, religious involvement is very low in patients who are treated for substance abuse; and therefore if there are interventions such as Alcoholics Anonymous that engage people in a spiritually-based intervention, then this is often associated with a much better outcome. Whether the person is treated in a hospital or as an outpatient, these kinds of spiritually-associated treatment programs can be very beneficial. In fact, when people have studied these kinds of spiritually-oriented programs in detail, they find that these kinds of programs do at least as well, if not better, than those who are treated with a variety of other approaches. When you incorporate other kinds of practices, like meditation- and prayer-based interventions, these also are associated with a decrease in drug and alcohol abuse.

It's also interesting that alcoholics report negative experiences with religion and often hold a very punitive concept of God; this goes back a little bit to even our first story of Monica: the notion that that negative view about God can actually lead people down the path towards a negative perception of their health and wellbeing, negative mental health, and even lead people into substance abuse. There's some evidence that following the treatment for substance abuse, there's an increase in a person's sense of meaning in life. There's also some evidence that there are common motivations for substance abuse as well as spiritual pursuits; they both seem to fill a certain emotional need, a certain support, which the person seems to require. By, again, trying to shift a person away from their addictions, away from these negative beliefs to something more positive we can actually get to a better, stronger mental health perspective and into a better relationship even in the context of spirituality.

Given the fact that there are these very positive relationships between spirituality and mental health, some researchers have actually tried to more explicitly develop treatment approaches that combine religious and spiritual content with more traditional psychotherapy techniques. When they've studied these kinds of combined interventions, they've actually looked at their effectiveness and how well they can be used and in what context to see how well they work, especially for specific disorders such as anxiety or depression. In general, these studies have shown that combined interventions are as effective, if not more effective, than standard psychotherapy. Of course, this especially is true with religious clients. If we go back to our story with Monica, she had these religious beliefs, and that was an important element of herself and her life; and by engaging that, the therapist was able to work through her spiritual issues as well as her psychological ones.

Interestingly, what the research also has shown is that a therapist themselves, they don't necessarily have to be a specifically religious person to do this kind of integrated psychotherapy that combines psychotherapy and religion with a patient; however, it's very important that the patient is open and willing to do this. Again, if it's a person who's a very staunch atheist, then this isn't the right kind of program for that individual; but if there's a person who does have some strong religious or spiritual beliefs, positive or negative, I think it's a very important area for a therapist to begin to explore to see where and how it may have contributed to whatever mental health issues the person faces; and are there ways of converting that into something that's more positive so that they can actually benefit and derive some psychological support as well?

In the following first-person account from a patient struggling with depression, we can sense this internal revolution, a spiritual transformation if you will, as the patient actually embraced their religious traditions; and when we see this, we can see how powerful of an experience this actually can be. The patient said this:

> It is easiest just to describe it, without too much detail here, as a force of energy that just came over me and was perceived by me as a peaceful force that had either come from an external source (maybe God?) or maybe it was physiologically triggered by my severe emotional state. ... But it was at that moment that I realized I would never be alone again and that some "thing" out there was there to help me and support me. It was an incredible shift in my life and brought whole new perspectives to me relative to my religious beliefs, the world, human dynamics, and to healing.

For this particular individual, this spiritual transformation that occurred in the context of them seeking therapy and treatment for their depression is what ultimately took them out of that mental health problem and took them in a whole new direction that was both beneficial from a spiritual as well as a psychological perspective.

If these kinds of interventions can be so effective, we might also wonder what other religious and spiritual practices might be useful in helping people with various types of mental illnesses. Some of these aren't specifically religious, but they're often part of the basis of what religions are about. For example: forgiveness. Forgiveness is something that actually is a very complex process; and if we think about what's going on in the brain when somebody undergoes this forgiveness process, it may actually be very complex. Think about a time when you forgave somebody; what was the whole process that went on there? Before you can forgive, it starts with some kind of injury to your self, it starts with some kind of insult to you; and therefore you have to start with a sense of your self.

If you think about the human brain, that sense of self may have something to do with our frontal lobes that help us to kind of organize our self and also our parietal lobe, which is that orienting part of the self; and it's that parietal lobe that may help to begin to compare how our self relates to others. In fact, this is a little bit of a quantitative function as well. We say are we doing ok; are we in some kind of equilibrium with somebody else? Are we at an advantage over them or a disadvantage? Therefore, we may ultimately be able to perceive some kind of injury. This is probably mediated by the limbic system, our emotional centers of the brain, that say, "Wow, something bad just happened to me." Of course, you have to have a causal function as well in the brain that remembers the event itself. I always think about if you have an Alzheimer's patient, for example, and you go in and you insult them and then you walk out of the room and come back and they don't remember the insult; there's no forgiveness process there.

But if you remember what's happened and you remember what were the causal events that led up to it, then you can start to think about what happened, how I was injured, who did it to me; and eventually you can use your abstract and emotional processes to try to reconcile that injury. You'll reframe your understanding of the relationship between you and that person who injured you. Of course, this may apply to you and another person, or it might even apply to you and God if you have a particular perception of a relationship with God. As we saw in our story with Monica, she was angry at God and part of the process was to forgive God for the death of her mother. The ability to forgive God or forgive others for whatever's going on in your life, whatever they caused in your life, this can have a tremendous benefit in terms of your overall psychological wellbeing; and there's substantial evidence to show how psychologically powerful the forgiveness process actually can be for people. For that reason, it's also been incorporated into the psychotherapy process just likes other aspects of religious and spiritual content.

Other practices like rituals, prayer, and meditation have also been shown to be very effective at helping to reduce stress and anxiety. There's a large literature base that shows that practices like mindfulness meditation, and I was even involved in a study looking at the effect of the Rosary, which showed that there was an overall reduction in anxiety levels for people and levels of depression; so simply engaging these practices can be very beneficial in helping people with their overall feelings of depression, anxiety, and other problems of mental health. To some degree, the more universal concept of suffering is something that people can acknowledge, can reflect on, and can decide whether or not that suffering can ultimately be converted into a very powerful, positive force in their life, or are they going to continue to wallow in whatever's gone on that makes them suffer?

As I mentioned at the beginning, there's a lot of research and data that support the positive relationship between religion and mental health; but it's not always good and it's not always beneficial. There are many circumstances where being a religious or spiritual person or just feeling these religious or spiritual feelings can go wrong and they can become detrimental to the individual or to the society at large. Let's take a look at some of these negative aspects of religion on mental health.

People suffer from their problems with spiritual or religious ideas. Often it can be in the form of being angry at God; struggling with what's true in life; trying to recollect problems that you have with your parents and maybe arguments that you have because of their religious tradition and it's different than what you believe. These kinds of problems with what a person actually believes can cause a great deal of internal struggle and strife, and that can lead to psychological anxiety and depression. Of course, there are problems with psychological, physical, and even sexual abuse that have resulted in people who have very negative views about religion. We even see examples today where this abuse has happened specifically in the context of religious and spiritual traditions; and therefore it can cause a great deal of problems and confusion for people when they think that religion is supposed to be there to support them and yet somehow it winds up creating a great deal of harm for them. As we mentioned in the last lecture, people can also follow some very bizarre kinds of beliefs that ultimately lead to cults; and, of course, in today's world, we have the whole issue of when religion leads to violence and hatred. How does this happen? What's the difference in a person's brain who's very religious and yet has a deep sense of anger and hatred for other people who don't believe in them; and how do we contrast that with a very deeply religious or spiritual person who's open and loving to all people?

At the top of our lecture, we considered the story of Monica, the young woman who was wrestling with psychological problems. As we said, she had been a very religious person who felt conflicted about her faith when her own mother passed away due to cancer. In the end, Monica was able to reconcile her faith with her mother's passing, and Monica remained a spiritual person, despite what had happened. Religion and spirituality may play a crucial role in our psychology; in fact, integrating religion and spirituality into psychotherapy may be very successful if done in the appropriate setting, since religious and spiritual beliefs can sometimes contribute to mental illness and sometimes can be useful in helping people find their way out of mental illness.

Understanding the religious beliefs of an individual might be just as important as understanding their psyche. There can be so many reciprocal interactions that contribute to mental health and wellbeing; and ultimately, these interactions play out in the brain, in the emotional and cognitive centers that enable us to feel and to think. By embracing the notion of the spiritual brain, we can help to make our approaches to mental illness and mental health as effective as possible.

Religion and Brain Dysfunction
Lecture 12

The phenomenon of speaking in tongues appears commonly in certain Pentecostal church services, but it is by no means limited to that setting. In this lecture, you are going to learn about phenomena such as speaking in tongues, and you are going to consider whether they are symptomatic of brain dysfunction—or whether, perhaps, there might be evidence suggesting that such phenomena may indicate a supernormal functioning of the human brain.

Speaking in Tongues

- People who speak in tongues sound like they are speaking some type of language, but linguistic analysis shows that it does not resemble typical language. Practitioners feel as if the spirit of God is taking over them. Some think it is the devil; others think it is a psychological abnormality—a psychotic episode.

- What are we to make of these types of intense spiritual states and practices? Are they normal or abnormal? Is the brain functioning appropriately or totally dysfunctionally?

- Schizophrenia and mania have long been associated with hyperreligiosity, which refers to a person becoming intensely religious, focusing on many spiritual or religious ideas to the exclusion of many other things in life. Temporal lobe epilepsy has been associated with hyperreligiosity and religious conversion.

- Care must be taken to avoid pathologizing spiritual experiences. In current psychiatric practice, we tend to label people with unusual experiences or thoughts as abnormal—but what is normal, and what is abnormal?

- Defining an experience as normal or abnormal is actually not that easy because it depends to some degree on the norm of society. If you live in a society that is proreligious, such as the United States, then being religious is normal. However, if you live in a society that is antireligious, then being religious might be abnormal and even bad for your health.

- When a person endures the death of a loved one, a very frequent experience is to see or hear the person who is deceased. The Diagnostic and Statistical Manual of Mental Disorders essentially defines such an experience as a normal hallucination.

- This is very interesting because we don't usually think of hallucinations as being normal. Usually, they are associated with severe derangements in brain function, such as schizophrenia. Why are these hallucinations normal? If these are normal, who is to say whether hearing God's voice is normal or abnormal?

- We might go a step further and question whether an otherwise psychologically normal person can have a normal or an abnormal religious experience.

- What about schizophrenic patients? Can they have normal religious experiences and ideas? At some point, it seems that we need to take a much closer look at how we define what is normal and abnormal in the context of psychology and spiritual experiences.

- Some scientists take a very reductionistic approach to this issue. In fact, one group of neuropsychologists from the Reed Neurologic Research Center at the University of California, Los Angeles, went so far as to evaluate a variety of leading religious figures throughout history and to "diagnose" the mental dysfunction they suffered from.

- For example, the group cited Saint Paul's conversion on the road to Damascus, in which he sees a sudden bright light, falls to the ground, hears the voice of Jesus, and experiences blindness for three days. Many of these elements of his experience have occasionally been described by people with seizures; they can hear voices and have unusual visual disturbances, including prolonged blindness.

Lessons from Professor Newberg's Research

When you study someone performing meditation, you see very little—the fireworks are on the inside. However, the act of speaking in tongues is entirely different. As I prepared to study the first Pentecostal subject in our lab, I had no idea what to expect. I had never seen someone speaking in tongues and did not know what it would look like.

I greeted our subject, who was a very sweet and intelligent-sounding middle-aged woman. She described the importance of speaking in tongues in her life.

I explained the experiment to her in detail. In particular, I described how we would have her do gospel singing during the first brain scan and then record her brain while she was speaking in tongues during a second scan.

We hooked up her IV and then began the gospel-singing part. She sang for about 10 minutes and really got into it. We injected her with the radioactive tracer that measures blood flow in the brain, allowed her to sing for another 10 minutes, and then scanned her.

We told her that she could speak in tongues whenever she wanted to. At first, she did more gospel singing in English, but then she slipped in something I had never heard before.

It was just for a few seconds, but it sounded like some weird language. Then, it occurred again and lasted a little longer. After a few minutes, the only sound coming out of her mouth was the speaking in tongues.

After about 10 minutes of speaking in tongues, I injected her and let her speak in tongues for about 10 more minutes before scanning her again.

The scans showed some very interesting findings. One of the most important findings was that the frontal lobes—the part of our brain that makes us feel in control of our actions and words—actually shut down. The scans also showed increased activity in the thalamus and basal ganglia.

Amazingly, when the subject was speaking in tongues, she had tears coming down her face and was oblivious to everything around her. Once she stopped, she returned quickly to the pleasant and intelligent-sounding woman I had met at the beginning of the study.

- Joan of Arc stated that she persistently "heard this voice accompanied also by a great light." Similar to Saint Paul, some of her symptoms have been reported in patients with temporal lobe epilepsy. Therefore, the group of neuropsychologists diagnosed Saint Joan as an epileptic. They also suggested that perhaps she had tuberculosis in her brain that contributed to this process.

- Saint Teresa of Avila, a medieval mystic, had many visions but also headaches, loss of consciousness, and tongue biting. Again, the neuropsychologists suggested that such experiences could be related to seizures.

- Joseph Smith, the founder of the Mormon church, had experiences in which he felt great fear, saw a "pillar of light," and

In modern times, a person who has a religious experience that is similar to that of Joan of Arc is usually regarded as having a psychological problem.

heard voices. He said that when the experience was over, he found himself lying on his back, looking up at heaven.

- On one hand, this is an exercise in futility because there is no way to go back in time and put eletroencephalography (EEG) electrodes on these individuals to study these experiences. The bigger issue, however, is that today, anyone who has experiences like those of Joan of Arc or Saint Teresa is usually regarded as having a brain pathology and is treated accordingly.

- Is our modern approach accurate and appropriate? Can mental disorders explain religion and mysticism? This is not a good argument for the nature of religious experiences for several reasons.
  - Mental illness is chronic.

  - Seizures are usually similar and repetitive.

  - Mental illness results in decreased function and poor social relationships.

  - Mental illness results in cognitive impairment.

  - Religion is typically beneficial.

  - Mystical experiences are usually described as being very positive.

Altered States of Consciousness
- A study on the language of altered states of consciousness assessed the different ways people describe three different types of experiences that are sometimes considered to be related: schizophrenic states, drug-induced states, and mystical states. Not surprisingly, when several investigators studied how people describe these three states, they found significant differences.

- Schizophrenic states were usually described in negative terms, as an abnormal process. One of the examples the investigators evaluated is as follows: "I do want to explain, if I can, the exaggerated state of awareness in which I lived before, during, and after my acute illness."

- Drug states were described with intense sensory perceptions: "I observed the myriad multiform ideas and images passing across and sensations and emotions flowing inward and outward. The light that illumined these images grew brighter and brighter until I was almost frightened by the intensity of the brilliance."

- Mystical states were described with words related to ultimate reality and meaning: "The experience took hold of me with such power that it seemed to go through my whole soul, so it seemed as if God was praying in, with, and for me." Mystical states truly represent a unique state of mind.

- Clearly, there is a relationship between brain disorders and unusual religious or spiritual experiences. This has led some to suggest that all religious beliefs are derived from some type of a pathological process.

- For example, some people have argued that all types of strong religious beliefs have their roots in temporal lobe seizure activity. They argue that such seizure activity is subclinical, so the person is not aware of it, but it has an impact on his or her experiences or beliefs.

- Such a hypothesis is theoretically testable, but it is very problematic to evaluate because it is difficult to know when such activity will arise and what type of effect it might actually have.

- Furthermore, only a small percentage of patients with temporal lobe seizures actually have unusual religious experiences. The simple truth is that it is a gross generalization to assume that religious beliefs are born from a pathological process. It is also, perhaps, unfair to classify them as born of "normal" brain experiences. Perhaps they are something in the middle of the two.

- How do we know what the true nature of these experiences actually is? In other words, what is the reality of such an experience?

- It appears that when the brain is suffering from some type of dysfunction, the result can be some of the most powerful and important experiences in a person's life. In these instances, perhaps the brain connects people to reality in ways that they normally cannot attain.

- Consider the possible conclusions we can draw from finding seizure activity in a person during an intense spiritual experience. One conclusion, which is perhaps the more scientifically biased conclusion, is that the seizure actually caused the experience. The experience, therefore, is purely a manifestation of the brain's dysfunction. In other words, the experience is not truly real—at least with regard to the attainment of an actual spiritual state.

- However, if we interpret the results from a spiritual perspective, we might conclude something different: The spiritual person might argue that the seizure activity represents an actual heightened activity state of the brain, which is certainly true scientifically. In this heightened state of activity, the brain is able to truly perceive an actual spiritual realm. In this way, the experience is truly real, and the seizure activity paves the way for such an experience.

- In a similar manner, the speaking-in-tongues study shows us what is happening in the brain of someone who is speaking in tongues. The scan does not tell us whether the act of speaking in tongues is generated by the brain or whether the brain is somehow responding to the spirit of God, who is creating the experience.

- This raises another intriguing question: Does brain dysfunction really represent dysfunction, or should we consider that it represents a kind of supernormal functioning?

Suggested Reading

Cardena, Lynn, and Krippner, eds, *Varieties of Anomalous Experience.*

Dewhurst and Beard, "Sudden Religious Conversions in Temporal Lobe Epilepsy."

Koenig, ed, *Handbook of Religion and Mental Health.*

Mohr and Huguelet, "The Relationship between Schizophrenia and Religion and Its Implications for Care."

1. How are specific psychological and neurological disorders associated with religious and spiritual phenomena?

2. Are religious or spiritual experiences normal or pathological?

Religion and Brain Dysfunction
Lecture 12—Transcript

It's 11:00 pm, January 1, 1901. In Topeka, Kansas, inside the Bethel Bible School, a group of students have spent the previous three days praying. Their goal? To contemplate the idea of the biblical verse that reads "to receive the gift of the Holy Spirit." Now, as midnight draws closer, one of the students, 30-year-old Agnes Ozman, asks her spiritual teacher, Charles Parham, to lay his hands upon her and pray. When he did, Agnes began to speak in a language no one had ever heard before. For three days, this continued. Some of the other students thought Agnes was just babbling, and others thought that she was speaking Chinese, but they all agreed that she had been touched by the Holy Spirit; that Agnes, in fact, had been given the gift of speaking in tongues.

The phenomenon of speaking in tongues appears commonly enough in certain Pentecostal church services, but it's by no means limited to that setting. For example, there was the case of a hospital patient found to be mumbling incoherently. This was believed to be psychotic episode, so the patient was seen by a psychiatrist, who actually recommended very strong antipsychotic medication. But as the medical team was getting ready to administer the medication, the family came in and told them that, "No, no, no, the patient's fine; she's just speaking in tongues."

There are certainly interesting stories about speaking in tongues; but what do they all have to do with a course on spirituality and the brain? Today we're going to look at phenomena like speaking in tongues and we're going to consider whether they're symptomatic of brain dysfunction, or if perhaps there might be evidence suggesting that spiritual phenomena like speaking in tongues may actually indicate a sort of "super-normal" functioning of the human brain.

What does speaking in tongues look like or sound like? People who speak in tongues sound like they're speaking some type of language, but when researchers have actually done a linguistic analysis it shows that it doesn't have any kind of resemblance to a typical language. The practitioners feel as if the spirit of God is taking over them. Interestingly, there are those religious individuals who say that this is the work of the Devil; and that it isn't the spirit of God, but it's the Devil that's causing this to happen. Of course, those in a more scientific mind think that it's a psychological abnormality; it may actually be some kind of psychotic episode or some problem with the brain.

Here's what I can tell you from our own study of people speaking in tongues. In our speaking in tongues study, it was fascinating because it was actually one of my favorite studies. After all, when you see someone perform meditation, it's kind of boring; you don't really see very much. All the fireworks—all the mental fireworks at least—are going on inside. But speaking in tongues is entirely different. In fact, as I prepared to study our very first Pentecostal subject, I had no idea what to expect. I had never seen it before; I didn't know what was going to happen. I didn't know if the subject was going to drop to the floor, start running around the room; I had visions of the exorcist in my mind with their head spinning around. I was really pretty uncomfortable as to what was going to happen.

In spite of that, I greeted our first subject as she came in through our laboratory doors and I talked to her. She was a very sweet, very intelligent-sounding middle-aged woman; and she described to me the importance of speaking in tongues in her life. She told me how important it was, how spiritual it was for her, and how it really had in many ways transformed who she was. After I talked to her for a little bit, I explained to her how the experiment was going to work, I described it in detail; and I described how we were going to create two states for her. One of them was when she was going to just be doing gospel singing, and this was going to be the first brain scan. We used our SPECT scanner—the same one that we had used for the Franciscan nuns doing prayer; the same one we had done with the Buddhist meditators—and I told her that we were going to do the first scan while she was just singing, doing religious singing, and then I told her that the second scan would be taken while she was speaking in tongues.

We got her IV hooked up and asked her to begin gospel singing. Part of the reason that we had her do gospel singing was that I realized right away that if I had her speaking in tongues in one scan and sitting there quietly in the other, of course I'd see all kinds of things going on; but I was really looking for something that would be spiritual and something that would be specific to speaking in tongues. I realized that if she's going to be moving around and dancing and singing something, then that should be the two states that I compare: one where she's just singing in English and the other where she's singing in tongues. First, she came in and did the gospel singing; she sang for about 10 minutes; she really got into it. I injected her with the radioactive tracer that measures the blood flow in her brain; I actually allowed her to finish singing, to continue for another 5 or 10 minutes; and then we scanned her.

Now came the moment of truth. We told her that that she could begin to speak in tongues whenever she wanted to. She started off listening to the same gospel music, she started to sing again, she started to sing in English; but after a few minutes, she slipped into something that I'd never heard before. It was just for a few seconds, but it sounded like some kind of weird language, and then it went back to English. Then the strange sound occurred again and lasted a little bit longer. After a few minutes, the only sound coming out of her mouth was the speaking in tongues.

After about 10 minutes of speaking in tongues, I injected her with the radioactive tracer, I let her speak in tongues for about 10 more minutes, and then we scanned her again. Remember, with these SPECT scans, at the moment of the injection, that's the picture I get; so the scans were going to show me something as to what was going on in her brain when she was engaged in the moment of speaking in tongues. What did the scans show? There were some very interesting differences. One of the most important differences, the most important changes, which we saw was in the frontal lobes. Remember that the frontal lobes, right behind your forehead, are what make us feel like we're in control of our actions. When I'm talking to you right now, my frontal lobes are turning on to generate the words, to generate the thoughts, and to tell you exactly what I'm thinking; and if I move, it's my frontal lobes that make me move.

What happened when the person was speaking in tongues? Instead of increasing in activity, the frontal lobes actually decreased in activity. Does this make sense? Let's think about what's going on: Remember, in meditation or prayer, the person is willfully concentrating on that particular prayer, on that particular phrase, or on that particular image. What was going on here? They weren't concentrating on anything; in fact, what they seemed to be doing was letting all of their conscious control of what was going on go away so that the experience for them was that their will was literally taken over—and what they believe was taken over by the spirit of God—to make this vocalization happen. When this happens, it looks like their frontal lobes literally shut down. The part of them that normally makes them feel in control actually decreases in activity, and it allows them to have this experience that they're not the ones who are actually in control of this process.

The scan also showed some very substantial increases of activity in the thalamus—remember, that very central structure that regulates all of our sensory information and connects all the different parts of the brain to each other—and also in the limbic and emotional centers of the brain, because this was a highly emotional practice. Amazingly, when the person was speaking in tongues she literally had tears coming down her face; she was oblivious to everything that was around her; she was in a completely different state of mind. But once she stopped, she returned quickly to being that pleasant, intelligent-sounding woman that I'd met at the very beginning.

What are we to make of these very intense types of spiritual states and practices? Are they normal, or are they abnormal? Is the brain functioning appropriately or totally dysfunctionally? Think about my subject, the Pentecostal woman I just described. Although the scan showed distinct changes in her brain when she was speaking in tongues, that in and of itself doesn't answer the larger question: Is this normal or not? This is the question that we now will wrestle with.

For example, many people—yourself included—may typically have in your mind the notion of that schizophrenic patient who ends up being in the inpatient hospital believing that they are Jesus Christ or the next Messiah. People who have mania, like people who are schizophrenic, often have had an experience of something called hyperreligiosity. Hyperreligiosity refers to a person who becomes intensely religious; in fact, they focus on many spiritual and religious ideas to the exclusion of all other things in life. Sometimes people with schizophrenia have hallucinations—that's certainly something that we know well—but when they hear voices, sometimes they take on a religious context; they think that God is speaking to them or angels are speaking to them. Therefore, this schizophrenic person has a problem in understanding where these different hallucinations are coming from, and they sometimes think that they have a religious origin and in that regard they become very hyperreligious; they focus very intensely on the religiousness of these ideas and these things that are swarming around in their brain.

As we'll see in a few moments, I'm going to talk a little bit about something called temporal lobe epilepsy: seizures in the temporal lobe, a part of the brain that's located along the side of the brain. This has been also been associated with people who are hyperreligious and may even contribute to people having religious conversions.

But I think that there's a significant caveat here that I want to talk about. We have to be very careful about overpathologizing spiritual experience; in fact, in current psychiatric practice, we tend to label people who have these very unusual experiences or unusual thoughts as "abnormal." But as I asked before, what exactly is normal and what exactly is abnormal? When I teach my classes on this topic, I actually challenge my students with this question. Maybe you should think about it for a moment. Have you ever had a profound religious or spiritual experience? If so, did you find it normal or abnormal? Have any of your friends ever told you about an experience like that; and when they did, what did you do, what did you think about that? Did you kind of acknowledge that they had it but in your own mind were thinking, "Boy, that person is really crazy? Maybe they had some kind of really bizarre experience, some kind of psychotic episode, but that certainly wasn't right; that certainly wasn't normal." How do you define normal and abnormal? This is actually not so easy since it depends to some degree on the norm of society. If you live in a society that's very pro-religious like the United States currently is, then being a religious person is relatively normal. But if you live in a society that's very antireligious, like some of the communist countries, then being religious may actually be abnormal; and, in fact, because of that, it can actually be bad for your health, both physical and mental.

Take another interesting example about this delicate problem of normalcy: When a person has a loved one who has died, a very frequent experience is to see or hear the person who is deceased. In fact, in the psychiatric profession, their primary manual called the *Diagnostic and Statistical Manual*—which essentially defines everything we need to know about mental illness— defines that experience as a normal hallucination. This is very interesting because we don't normally think of hallucinations as being normal; usually they're associated with very severe derangements in brain function such as schizophrenia. So why are these types of hallucinations considered to be normal? It's a bit of a slippery slope; if these kinds of hallucinations are normal, then who's to say if hearing God's voice is normal or not?

We might go a step further and question whether an otherwise psychologically normal person can have a normal or an abnormal religious experience. I was amazed at the subjects that we studied who were speaking in tongues because they seemed so normal; they were completely normal when they weren't speaking in tongues. As a group, they generally had good jobs, they were married, they raised children; they were completely normal human beings. But then you watch them speak in tongues, and see them doing something that looks and sounds so incredibly different from what we'd consider to be normal behavior, what do we make of that? Of course, for them, it's completely normal; not only is it normal, it's sacred.

But what about schizophrenic patients? Can they have a normal religious experience or a normal religious belief? Not all schizophrenic patients believe that they're Jesus Christ; maybe some of them are religious, and that's ok. At some point, it seems that we need to take a closer look at how we define what's normal and what's abnormal, and specifically in the context of psychology and spiritual experiences.

Some scientists have taken a very reductionistic approach to this entire issue. In fact, one group of neuropsychologists from the UCLA-Reed Neurologic Research Center went so far as to evaluate a variety of leading historical religious figures and actually attempted "diagnose" their mental dysfunction that they suffered from. For example, they cited Saint Paul's conversion on the road to Damascus in which he sees a sudden bright light, he falls to the ground, he hears the voice of Jesus, and the experience actually appears to result in blindness for him for about three days. These neuropsychologists looked at this description and they said many of the elements of this experience have occasionally been described in people who have seizures.

They can hear voices, they can have unusual visual disturbances, and sometimes they can even have prolonged blindness. Joan of Arc stated that she persistently "heard this Voice accompanied also by a great light"; and therefore, similar to Saint Paul, some of her symptoms have been reported in patients who have had seizures in their temporal lobes. So this group of neuropsychologists offered a possible diagnosis as epilepsy for Joan of Arc. They also suggested that perhaps she may have even had tuberculosis in her brain and that this contributed to the process; this may have been what caused some of the seizures.

Saint Teresa of Avila, a medieval mystic, had many visions, but she also had headaches, she had loss of consciousness, and tongue biting. Again, as our neuropsychologists looked at these descriptions and these different symptoms so to speak, they suggested as well that such experiences could have been related to seizures. The same may even go for Joseph Smith, the founder of the Mormon Church. Smith had experiences in which he felt great fear, he saw a "pillar of light," and he heard voices. He's quoted as saying that when the experience was over he found himself lying on his back looking up at heaven.

What are we to make of this entire exercise? On one hand, it's a little bit of an exercise in futility because there's no way to go back in time and put EEG electrodes on each of these individuals and see what was going on in their brain and try to find out whether or not they actually had seizures. The bigger issue, however, is this: Today, anyone who has experiences like those of Joan of Arc or Saint Teresa is usually regarded as having a brain pathology and therefore we just treat them accordingly; we treat them as if they have a psychological problem, they have brain dysfunction. But is our modern approach accurate and is it appropriate? Can mental disorders actually explain all that we think about when we think about religion and mysticism?

Here are some reasons why I think that this isn't always a good argument for the nature of religious experiences: First of all, mental illness is typically chronic. It's something that exists maybe from the time that they're a child, theoretically all the way out until a person dies. But when we see people who've had these very profound religious and spiritual experiences, mystical experiences, most of the time it's not something that occurs throughout their entire life; most of the time it's something that occurs on a very limited scale, sometimes they have only one or two of them. So it seems a little unusual that suddenly somebody would have a seizure or several seizures and then never have them again. In fact, seizures themselves are usually very repetitive and somewhat similar; so if you have a seizure disorder, you usually have very similar kinds of experiences time and time again. That doesn't totally explain the diversity of these very powerful religious experiences that some of these religious figures have described.

Another aspect of these types of brain dysfunctions is that they typically are associated with poor function—they have poor social relationships, they don't think clearly, their emotions are all over the place, they have cognitive impairment—but most of the time when we look at these religious figures, they perform cognitively, emotionally, extremely well; they're able to galvanize entire populations of people. It seems that when we think about these kinds of experiences, it doesn't seem appropriate to extend some kind of pathology to describing them; in fact, many mystical experiences are usually described in very positive ways. An earlier study from the 1980s that actually looked at the language of altered states of consciousness assessed the different ways that people describe three different types of experiences that are sometimes considered related, especially in the context of brain dysfunction. They evaluated descriptions of schizophrenic patients and the states that they were in, drug-induced states, and mystical states.

Not surprisingly, when these investigators actually looked at the descriptions of these different states—the drug-induced states, mystical states, and schizophrenic states—they found significant differences. The schizophrenic states were usually described in negative terms, as if it was, in fact, an abnormal process. One of the examples that they used was a quote from a patient who said: "I do want to explain, if I can, the exaggerated state of awareness in which I lived before, during, and after my acute illness." There was this recognition by this patient that it was, in fact, an illness; that it was abnormal; and that's not typically what we see when we are looking at people who've had spiritual experiences.

Drug-induced states were described primarily as having very intense sensory perceptions. One of the quotes was:

I observed the myriad multiform ideas and images passing across and sensations and emotions flowing inward and outward. The light that illumined these images grew brighter and brighter until I was almost frightened by the intensity of the brilliance.

Mystical states were typically described with words related to ultimate reality and meaning. Here's one of the quotes from one of these subjects: "The experience took hold of me with such power that it seemed to go through my whole soul, so it seemed as if God was praying in, with, and for me." As we'll see in later lectures, the mystical states truly represent a unique state of mind.

Clearly there's some kind of relationship between brain disorders, brain dysfunction, and unusual religious or spiritual experiences; but how far can we go? This has led some to suggest that all religious beliefs are derived from some type of a pathological process. As we saw with the neuropsychologists, they suggested that religious figures of history all may have had some kind of brain dysfunction. Some have argued that perhaps even all types of strong religious beliefs have their roots in a brain disorder such as temporal lobe seizure activity. They argue that such seizure activity may actually be subclinical, so that the person isn't really aware of it; they don't manifest as somebody who has seizures—we don't see them falling down to the ground all the time—but when they're having these little min-seizures, it actually has an impact on their experiences and beliefs, and induces very, very strong and intense spiritual feelings or religious experiences.

Such a hypothesis is theoretically testable, but it's very problematic to evaluate since it's difficult to know when such activity will occur and what type of an effect it might have on the individual. Furthermore, only a very small percentage of patients who have something like temporal lobe seizures actually have reported these unusual religious experiences. It may actually be less than five percent of these patients who've had unusual religious or spiritual experiences. The simple truth is that it's a gross generalization, I think, to assume that religious beliefs are born from a pathological process in all circumstances. It's also perhaps unfair to classify them as born of normal brain experiences as well. Perhaps there's something in the middle of these two dichotomous positions that will tell us something about the true nature of what these experiences are and what's going on in the brain of people when they actually have them.

In fact, this discussion also gives me an opportunity to raise an intriguing philosophical question that we're going to encounter in various forms throughout the rest of this course. This question is: How do we know what the true nature of these experiences actually is? Put another way, what's the reality of such an experience?

Some of you may have seen the movie called *Phenomenon*, in which the lead character played by John Travolta transforms from a regular everyday guy, a mechanic, into an absolute genius; in fact, he actually begins to develop certain powers of the brain such as telekinesis. In the end, they find that he has a brain tumor that somehow has enhanced his brain's function. Is there a real-life correlate of this kind of an experience? It turns out that there may be. A neuroscientist named Jill Bolte Taylor wrote a fascinating book called *My Stroke of Insight*. In this book, she book describes the mystical experiences that she had while suffering a stroke. It appears that when the brain is suffering from some type of dysfunction, the result can be some of the most powerful and important experiences in a person's life. If the movie *Phenomenon* holds any shred of truth, maybe somewhere in that dysfunction, the brain connects us to reality in ways that we normally can't attain.

If a person has an intense religious experience and we can document seizure activity, does that negate the experience or not? Consider the possible conclusions we can draw from finding seizure activity in a person during an intense spiritual experience. One conclusion, which is perhaps the more medically- or scientifically-based conclusion, is that the seizure actually caused the experience. The experience, therefore, is purely a manifestation of the brain's dysfunction. In other words, the experience isn't truly real, at least with regard to attaining an actual spiritual state or at least in terms of relating to something that's out there in the world.

But if we interpret the results from a spiritual perspective, we might conclude something very different. The spiritual person might argue that the seizure activity represents an actual heightened activity state of the brain. We know that this is certainly true scientifically; we know that we can see intense electrical activity going on in the brain when a person has a seizure. Is it possible that in that heightened state of activity the brain is able to truly perceive an actual spiritual realm? In this way, the experience is truly real and the seizure activity paves the way for such an experience. In a similar manner, the speaking in tongues study shows us what's happening in the brain of someone who's speaking in tongues. The scan doesn't tell us whether the tongues is generated by the brain, or the brain is somehow responding to the actual spirit of God creating the experience.

This also raises another intriguing question that challenges the title of this particular lecture: Does brain dysfunction really represent dysfunction, or should we consider that it represents a kind of supernormal functioning? Think back to the start of our lecture, where we considered Agnes Ozman and her three-day odyssey of speaking in tongues. Was she literally touched by the Holy Spirit? Or was Agnes just "crazy," in the crudest use of the term? Was this purely and simply a case of brain dysfunction, or something marvelously spiritual? Or yet a third possibility: Was she perhaps so filled with religious faith that her brain activity reached a new level of functioning; an unusual level, but one that's within the range of most "normal" humans? It's an intriguing possibility and, in my opinion, one that science really should explore.

Transmitters to God

Lecture 13

Neurotransmitters are a very important component of the underlying biology of religious or spiritual states and the practices that help bring them about. Science is only just beginning to understand the full importance of neurotransmitters, but it is likely that if our brain perceives itself to be able to communicate with God, the neurotransmitters are part of that process. Neurotransmitters may indeed be "spiritual molecules" that can enable us to have religious beliefs and spiritual experiences. In fact, they may truly be the brain's transmitters to God.

Neurotransmitters and Spiritual Experiences

- Dimethyltryptamine (DMT) is a naturally occurring neurotransmitter found in trace amounts in mammals, including humans. In large amounts, however, DMT can lead to hallucinations, visions, and euphoria. Its impact can be so profound that DMT has been called "the spirit molecule."

- Several scientists have been studying DMT, as well as other chemicals in the brain, to see what role neurotransmitters play in spiritual experiences. For example, could it be that those who are more religious may have larger amounts of certain brain chemicals? If so, how might that play into the act of speaking in tongues and other experiences that may involve supernormal brain functioning?

- There is growing evidence that many different neurotransmitters are involved in religious and spiritual practices and experiences.

- Neurotransmitters are the chemicals in the brain that allow for the transmission of information between nerve cells. They are particularly involved in the synapses, the spaces between one neuron and the next. There are a variety of different neurotransmitters with many different functions

- Ultimately, is there a spirit molecule? Is there one molecule that is necessary for creating the spiritual experience? Certainly, there are some molecules that play an important role, but given the richness and diversity of religious experiences, it seems unlikely that one molecule will help to explain it all. Some experiences make us happy while others make us sad. Some rev us up, and others calm us down. All of this is regulated by different neurotransmitters.

- Some neurotransmitters, such as glutamate, are stimulatory, or excitatory; they increase activity in the next neuron. Some neurotransmitters, such as gamma-aminobutyric acid (GABA), are inhibitory; they decrease activity in the next neuron.

- Some neurotransmitters are more involved in thought, some in perceptions, and some in emotions. A growing number of studies are pointing to their involvement in religious and spiritual experiences as well.

- How can this involvement be traced by researchers? One type of study involves measuring neurotransmitters in the blood. This is an easy approach, but it does not necessarily reflect what is happening in the brain.

- In general, there is increased serotonin, dopamine, and GABA and decreased cortisol and norepinephrine during spiritual practices such as meditation or prayer.

- Another approach to studying the effects of neurotransmitters is to use drugs that actually block them. One clever study used two drugs—naloxone and flumazenil—that block the opiate and benzodiezepine receptors, respectively. Would someone expect those receptors to be involved in meditation? Why?

- Researchers gave these drugs to an expert meditator to see if either would block the meditation experience. The drugs did not block the experience, and the eletroencephalography (EEG) findings suggested that these neurotransmitters were not specifically involved in meditation.

- In addition to measuring neurotransmitters in the blood and using drugs to block neurotransmitters, a third way to study the role of neurotransmitters in spirituality is to conduct a neurotransmitter imaging study. Unfortunately, only a few of these studies are currently available. In addition, due to the complexity of transmitter interactions, study design must proceed carefully.

- Because it appears that many neurotransmitter systems may be involved in spiritual practices and religious experiences, there are many opportunities for imaging studies.

- One study used positron emission tomography (PET) imaging to evaluate the dopamine system in meditators. A scan was performed using raclopride, a radioactive tracer that binds to the dopamine receptors in the brain. After meditation, there was less radioactive binding, reflecting more intrinsic dopamine release. In other words, meditation resulted in a release of dopamine, which is one of the most important neurotransmitters for positive emotions and the reward system.

- A different study used magnetic resonance (MR) spectroscopy, an elegant technique that can measure the amount of neurotransmitters in certain parts of the brain. This study showed that meditation practice resulted in a release of GABA, the main inhibitory neurotransmitter in the brain. This may be crucial to shutting down certain areas of the brain.

- Part of what may occur during meditation is that as you focus more and more on the object of meditation, sensory information is screened out from other areas of the brain, such as the orientation part. It may be that GABA helps to regulate or block the flow of sensory information into the orientation area, which may ultimately help contribute to the experience of no self and no space.

The Complexity of Neurotransmitters

- Glutamate is the main excitatory neurotransmitter and because spiritual practices and experiences involve many types of brain activity, glutamate is likely heavily involved. Interestingly, such practices also require the brain to regulate other areas—perhaps even shutting them down—and if calmness and relaxation are part of the experience, then GABA, the primary inhibitory neurotransmitter, also plays a prominent role.

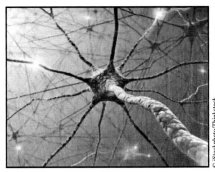

- GABA may be critical for helping to diminish sensory input to cortical structures such as the posterior superior parietal lobule (PSPL), which is associated with visual-spatial processing.

Many modern studies are pointing to the involvement of various neurotransmitters in religious and spiritual experiences.

- Glutamate from the prefrontal cortex also causes the release of ß-endorphins from the hypothalamus. ß-endorphins can enhance feelings of euphoria and have been suggested to be involved in spiritual experiences and near-death experiences. However, blocking the opiate system does not diminish the meditative experience, so the jury is still out on how the opiate system is involved.

- Increased glutamate can also result in an increase in neurotransmitters that have a similar effect as drugs such as ketamine, which can be used as an anesthetic. Ketamine is considered to be a dissociative hallucinogen, which means that taking this drug can cause you to hallucinate and specifically feel as if you are leaving your body behind.

- The fact that increased glutamate can have effects similar to the effects of Ketamine means that both can potentially lead to intense experiences in which people perceive that they are leaving their body. Interestingly, the neurotransmitters related to increased glutamate have been linked to near-death experiences and other spiritual experiences as well.

- A participant in the aforementioned online survey of spiritual experiences described a very interesting experience that actually occurred while the person was taking the drug ketamine. The individual described the experience as follows.
  - "I had a near-death experience from ketamine. I went up a rainbow into a place like a big womb—felt my physical pain, emotional pain, fears, and worries dissolve. I felt like I was being hugged by a million people who really loved and cared for me and were all holding me. I heard a voice say the words, 'You can breathe again now.' I opened my eyes, and I was back."

- This type of experience shows how drugs that affect specific neurotransmitter systems can result in very powerful experiences, including experiences that have a spiritual element to them.

- There are still other potential neurotransmitter effects during spiritual practices. During spiritual rituals, there is stimulation of the autonomic nervous system. Furthermore, activating the autonomic nervous system can activate the hypothalamus.

- The hypothalamus can stimulate the dorsal raphe in the brainstem to produce serotonin. Increased serotonin may have many potentially interesting effects on the brain as related to spiritual practices. For example, drugs that help increase serotonin slowly form many of the antidepressant drugs. A more rapid increase in serotonin can result from taking various hallucinogenic drugs such as LSD. Thus, serotonin is involved in affecting intense sensory experiences.

- Serotonin also may increase dopamine release, which has been observed in meditation practice. Dopamine is also known to be associated with feelings of euphoria.

- In Lecture 5, you learned about research that was performed by Dr. Dean Hamer, who was exploring the relationship between genes and religiousness. Recall that Hamer was looking at a particular gene that codes for the VMAT2 receptor. He found a significant correlation between this gene and people's feelings of self-transcendence.

- The VMAT2 receptor is particularly involved in regulating dopamine and serotonin. Because these two neurotransmitters are highly implicated in religious and spiritual experiences, it may be no surprise that the gene Hamer studied is sometimes called the God gene. In one study in Lecture 5, dopamine was used to alter a nonbeliever's perception of the world.

- The results from initial studies suggest many complex interactions. Individual practices and experiences may have different neurotransmitter effects. Dopamine and serotonin may work together or inhibit each other, depending on the practice or experience. The neurotransmitters also likely interact with the autonomic nervous system and, hence, other parts of the body.

- It appears that neurotransmitters play a fundamental role when it comes to the spiritual brain; they may be involved in helping to make people religious—or not.

Suggested Reading

Austin, *Zen and the Brain.*

Goodman, "The Serotonergic System and Mysticism."

Kjaer, Bertelsen, Piccini, Brooks, Alving, and Lou, "Increased Dopamine Tone during Meditation-Induced Change of Consciousness."

Newberg and Iversen, "The Neural Basis of the Complex Mental Task of Meditation."

Streeter, Jensen, Perlmutter, Cabral, Tian, Terhune, Ciraulo, and Renshaw, "Yoga Asana Sessions Increase Brain GABA Levels."

1. How do the different chemicals in the brain—such as dopamine and serotonin—play a role in religious and spiritual phenomena?

2. Does the effect of spiritual experiences on neurotransmitters result in good or bad experiences?

Transmitters to God
Lecture 13—Transcript

Dimethyltryptamine, or DMT as it's referred to, is a naturally-occurring neurotransmitter found in trace amounts in mammals, including human beings. In large amounts, however, DMT can lead to hallucinations, visions, and feelings of intense euphoria. Its impact can be so profound that DMT has even been called "the spirit molecule."

Several scientists have been studying DMT, as well as other chemicals in the brain, to see what role neurotransmitters play in spiritual experiences. For example, could it be that those who are more religious may have larger amounts of certain brain chemicals? If so, how might they play into the topics that we've explored in our last lecture where we looked at speaking in tongues and other kinds of experiences that may involve a "supernormal" brain functioning? There's growing evidence that many different neurotransmitters are involved in religious and spiritual practices and experiences; and in this lecture, we'll look at that evidence.

To begin with, let's review some basics. Neurotransmitters are the chemicals in the brain that allow for transmission of information to occur between the nerve cells. They're particularly involved in the space between the neurons, and that's something called the synapses; this is the space between one neuron ends and the next one begins. There are a variety of different kinds of neurotransmitters; each of them has many different kinds of functions.

Ultimately, we have to wonder if there really is a spirit molecule. Is there a spirit molecule, one that's necessary for creating the spiritual experience that so many human beings have? Certainly there are some molecules that play an important role, but given the richness and diversity of religious experiences, it seems very unlikely to me that one molecule will actually be able to explain it all. Of course, some experiences make us happy, other experiences make us sad; some rev us up, and others calm us down; and all of this is regulated by different kinds of neurotransmitters. As we've seen through some of our prior lectures, some of the neurotransmitters like dopamine or serotonin are these very chemicals that will make us feel revved up and feel very energetic throughout our body, while other ones will actually help to calm us down and to make us feel that feeling of blissfulness.

Let's talk about some of the specific neurotransmitters that may ultimately play a very vital role in a variety of religious states and experiences. For example, one of the neurotransmitters, glutamate, is actually considered to be stimulatory or excitatory. What glutamate does in the brain, then, is increase the activity in the next neuron. If one neuron fires and it wants to communicate with the next neuron, it can release glutamate in a little package that goes across that synapse, across that space, and it tells the next neuron it's time to fire, it's time to get excited; and for that reason glutamate is referred to as being excitatory. Some neurotransmitters, like something called gamma-aminobutyric acid, or GABA, are inhibitory neurotransmitters. They decrease the activity in the next neuron; so if one neuron wants to shut down another one, it'll release GABA so that it quiets the functioning in that next neuron. It's interesting to note that certain drugs—for example, antianxiety drugs—actually have a very big impact on the GABA system. Drugs that many of you may be familiar with such as Xanax or Valium affect the nervous system at the level of these GABA neurons and GABA receptions that help to calm us down and make us feel less anxious; they make us feel calmer.

A growing number of studies are pointing to the involvement of these different neurotransmitters in religious and spiritual experiences. How can this involvement be traced by the researchers? How can we actually get some information that tells us what's going on at the level of these different neurotransmitters? There are actually several different approaches that researchers have taken to try to explore what neurotransmitters are doing in the brain and in the body that help us when people have different religious and spiritual experiences.

One type of study involves measuring the neurotransmitters that are in the blood. On one hand, this is a very easy approach because you can just draw some blood out of somebody's arm and measure exactly how much of a particular neurotransmitter like glutamate or serotonin is actually circulating in their body. The downside of it is that it doesn't necessarily reflect what's actually happening in the brain at any given time. It's one way of getting at the information as to what's going on when people are engaged in different religious and spiritual practices, but it may not necessarily tell us the entire picture.

What have these actual studies shown that have looked at the blood levels of different neurotransmitters? In general, what these studies have shown is that there's an increase in serotonin and an increase in dopamine. If you remember back from our prior lectures, we did talk about the possibility that serotonin and dopamine may play a very important role in religious experiences; so it's not a surprise that these levels are increased when a person is engaged in a practice like prayer or meditation. GABA is also increased. This may be very important because, as we've talked about, sometimes certain areas of the brain are shut down during spiritual experiences and sometimes they're turned on; so maybe when these different areas are shut down, maybe it's related to a release of this GABA. We'll talk about this more in a few moments.

Two other neurotransmitters that are also affected during these experiences are cortisol and norepinephrine. Cortisol and norepinephrine are some of the main stress-related neurotransmitters and actually affect the brain and the body very strongly; so the fact that there's a decrease in cortisol and norepinephrine during spiritual practices such as meditation and prayer may tell us something about how those practices help to lower and reduce our stress levels. But how can we ultimately really study the more specific relationship between what's going on in the brain and the neurotransmitters in the brain and spirituality? Let's look in more detail as to how studies have been done to try to figure this out.

I mentioned the first approach was to just see what's going on in the blood; but how can we start to figure out what's happening in the brain itself? One clever approach is not so much to measure the neurotransmitters in the brain but to actually use a drug that blocks their activity. One group of researchers took two different drugs; one of them is called naloxone and the other one is called flumazenil. Naloxone blocks the opiate unclear in the body. Naloxone affects drugs like morphine—in fact, that's what it was primarily developed for, to help people out when they had an overdose of morphine by blocking its effects—but it can also block your brain's natural opiates that may or may not have an impact on spiritual experiences and practices. Flumazenil is another drug that helps to block the GABA receptors, so it's very important in affecting that particular system.

One of the questions that we can ask is would we expect these receptors to be involved in meditation, and can we figure out a way of blocking them to see if that actually happens? Basically, what happened was that these researchers gave these two different drugs to one particular expert meditator to see if it would actually block their meditative experience, and they also measured the electrical changes in the brain with EEG to see if that was affected by these drugs as well. The findings were very interesting: In general, it showed that both of these blocking drugs really had very little effect on the meditation practice. The person reported feeling exactly the same in terms of the depth of their meditation, the experiences that they typically had during their meditation; and it turned out that the EEG changes weren't any different either. The EEG that the person normally had during meditation was almost essentially the same.

Of course, one of the real downsides of this study was that it was a very small study; it was only done on one subject. It's a little hard to know exactly how to interpret this information; but it does tell us a little bit about how these different neurotransmitter systems may actually be involved in spiritual practices.

We've seen a couple ways that researchers can try to get at the relationship between neurotransmitters and spirituality. One way is measuring neurotransmitters in the blood; the other way involves using drugs that block different neurotransmitters. A third way is to conduct brain imaging studies that specifically look at what's going on in these neurotransmitter systems in the brain itself. This, of course, has been an area of great interest in my own research where we can inject small amounts of radioactive tracers that are similar to dopamine or serotonin; and even though we inject them into the bloodstream, they get up into the brain and they bind to the very receptor systems that we're interested in. These are wonderful and fascinating approaches to actually seeing what's going on in the brain itself; and, of course, as with some of the other brain scan studies that we talked about, we can see what's happening in the brain at rest, we can see what's happening when a person is engaged in prayer, meditation, or any other kind of spiritual practice.

But, of course, as with all studies there are some complexities in looking at neurotransmitters by doing brain imagine studies. One of the biggest problems is the complexity of how these different neurotransmitters interact with each other. That's something that we have to think about very carefully because it turns out that if you turn on serotonin, you might also affect dopamine; or if you turn on the opiates, you might also affect the GABA system. Since it appears that many different neurotransmitter systems could be involved, there are certainly many opportunities for developing brain imaging studies, and we're just beginning to see some of these studies coming about in the literature that tells us a little bit more about the nature of these practices and the nature of their experiences.

For example, one study used positron emission tomography (PET) imaging to evaluate the dopamine system in meditators. Again, remember that PET imaging is a way of looking at how the brain works by injecting a small amount of a radioactive tracer that the scanner picks up and shows where that tracer went. In this case, the scan was performed with a specific tracer, something called raclopride, which acts a lot like dopamine in the brain. It actually binds to the dopamine receptors in the brain, so when you put the person into the scanner you get a picture of what their brain looks like in terms of where dopamine goes in the brain. They scanned people while they were at rest, and then they asked the person to engage in a very intense practice of meditation; very similar to some of the other studies that we talked about that looked at blood flow in the brain, but now they were looking at dopamine.

What did these particular investigators find? After the meditation practice, they found that there was less radioactive binding in the dopamine system. You have to sort of think back a little bit about how this all works, because the radioactivity is actually attached to what look like dopamine molecules and they go to the receptors; so if there's less radioactive activity after meditation, that means that their own brain released more dopamine, and that means dopamine release is actually a part of the meditation process. When people engage in meditation, they increase the amount of dopamine in their brain.

As we've talked about a little bit already in previous lectures, dopamine is part of the neurotransmitters that are involved in our positive emotions and in our reward system; so when we feel good, when we feel excited, when we get a sense of happiness or euphoria, most research shows that there's a release of dopamine in the brain. One of the main ways that we know this is that the recreational drug cocaine actually causes a very intense release of dopamine in the brain; and that's part of what's involved in the euphoric feelings, the high, that people get with cocaine. If people are engaged in a meditation practice and they have a release and increase of dopamine in the brain, maybe that helps us to understand why it feels so good for people when they meditate; why it almost gives them a kind of high that makes it such a powerful experience for them.

What about other neurotransmitters and how they've been studied in the brain itself? A different study used a technique called magnetic resonance spectroscopy. This is a very elegant technique that can measure the amount of neurotransmitters in certain parts of the brain. It's a little bit like a MRI— in fact, it uses a MRI machine—and what it actually is doing is almost taking a chemical biopsy; it's going in, reaching into the brain, finding a piece of that brain, and telling you exactly how much of different molecules and chemicals there actually are.

This particular study decided to focus in on GABA; and remember we talked about GABA as being one of the main inhibitory neurotransmitters in the brain. What they did was have people engage in the meditation practice while they were in the scanner; and what they found based on this magnetic resonance spectroscopy is that there was an increase in GABA in the brain. This may be crucial because it could help to shut down certain areas of the brain during the meditation practice. Remember that one of the things that may occur during meditation is that as the individual focuses more and more on the object of their meditation practice, they begin to block out or screen out sensory information into other areas of the brain; and one of the most important areas that might be affected is the orientation part of the brain, that part of the brain that's located towards the back, top part of our head that helps us to feel our sense of self, to orient that self in the world, and to give us a sense of space and time. It may be that by having an increase of GABA that actually helps to regulate or block the flow of the sensory information into this orientation area and that this may actually help contribute to the experience of no self and no space that the person may subjectively experience during that particular practice.

We've seen that dopamine and GABA both appear to play an important role in the meditation practice and the experiences that people may have. But let's delve a little bit deeper into some of the other ways that neurotransmitters might get involved in religious and spiritual experiences. To some degree, this is based on how we know the different neurotransmitters work and the descriptions that people give us about how meditation and spiritual practices actually affect us. This provides us a beginning for us to continue to explore the relationship between these different neurotransmitters and how they're related to spirituality in general and practices like prayer and meditation in particular.

We've talked about glutamate already. Glutamate is the main excitatory neurotransmitter; and since these spiritual practices and experiences typically involve the activation of the brain, many different parts of the brain, it seems likely that glutamate would be a very important part of that. We might expect to see that when a person activates their frontal lobes to help them focus their attention on the prayer practice that they're actually releasing glutamate to tell the brain to focus its attention, and to activate other areas of the brain that help us to focus attention and actually turn on other parts of the brain including our emotional systems and the systems that connect to the rest of the body.

But interestingly, such practices also require the brain areas that regulate other areas to actually shut down; and as we were just talking about a few moments ago with regard to GABA, maybe GABA is a very important inhibitory neurotransmitter that plays a prominent role in these experiences because it helps to shut down the activity in areas like the orientation part of the brain so that part of the experience that the person gets is a very powerful sense of a loss of self and a loss of space and time. As far as what GABA can do for us, it also interacts with glutamate so that we can see these very complex kinds of interactions that help turn on and off all different kinds of parts of the brain.

What other kinds of changes might we except to be happening? Interestingly, studies have shown that a release of glutamate from your frontal lobe also causes a release of a neurotransmitter called ß-endorphin from the hypothalamus. ß-endorphins are the brain's natural opiates, so it's sort of like the structure of morphine; and it's been shown to be able to enhance or induce feelings of euphoria. We know that ß-endorphins are released when people experience pain because it's trying to help the person manage that pain, and that's part of why morphine has been found to be effective as a pain reliever, especially in people who have very severe pain problems.

But what about spiritual experiences? If a person has this kind of euphoric feeling during a spiritual experience, or perhaps some other kind of experience like a near-death experience, then maybe it's the ß-endorphin that gets involved. However, we also have to remember that other study that we talked about a little while ago that showed that blocking the opiate system at least didn't diminish the meditative experience. To some extent, the jury is still out in terms of how the opiate system may actually be involved. There's some evidence to suggest that it might be related, but there's other evidence to suggest that maybe it's not the primary neurotransmitter that's going to be involved in spiritual practices.

An increase of glutamate in the brain can also result in an increase in neurotransmitters that have similar effects to a drug called Ketamine. Ketamine is a drug that is frequently used as an anesthetic, but if given in high enough amounts it's also something that's called a dissociative hallucinogen. What this means is that if you take this drug it can cause you to hallucinate, and specifically that hallucination makes you feel as if you're kind of leaving your body behind; so you dissociate from your body, you go away from your body, and you have this very powerful kind of experience. So when I say that an increase of glutamate can have an effect similar to the effects of Ketamine, what I'm saying is that both can potentially lead to a very intense experience, and one in which people perceive that they're leaving their body.

Interestingly, these kinds of neurotransmitters, specifically those related to an increase in glutamate, have been linked to spiritual experiences and one in particular: the near-death experience. Consider this example that I want to share with you; this is one of the participants in our online survey of people's spiritual experiences where people were describing the different intense experiences that they had. This one was actually of a person who had an experience while taking the drug ketamine. The individual described the experience as follows; he said:

> I had a near death experience from ketamine. I went up a rainbow into a place that was like a big womb. I felt my physical pain, my emotional pain, and my fears and worries all dissolve, I felt like I was being hugged by a million people who really loved and cared for me and were all holding me. Eventually I heard a voice say the words "you can breathe again now." I opened my eyes and I was back.

This type of experience shows how drugs that affect specific neurotransmitter systems can result in very powerful experiences, including experiences that have this very strong spiritual element to them. We'll be talking about these kinds of drug-induced states in a future lecture; but it's important here to understand in the context of how these different neurotransmitter effects are related to spiritual practices.

We've talked previously about how during spiritual rituals there's the stimulation of the autonomic nervous system. Interestingly, when we talk about the stimulation of the autonomic nervous system, that stimulation can be either bottom up—from the body up; the body responding to different rhythms and so forth up into the brain—and also from the brain down; but in the context from the body going up, activating the autonomic nervous system can turn on the hypothalamus, that very key regulator in the center of the brain, and the hypothalamus can then stimulate a part of the brainstem at the very core of our brain to produce the neurotransmitter serotonin.

We've talked a little bit about serotonin; but why would a release or an increase of serotonin be relevant to these kinds of spiritual experiences? It turns out that an increase in serotonin may actually have some potentially interesting effects on the brain and particularly as it relates to spiritual practices and experiences. For example, drugs that actually help to increase the serotonin slowly form many of the antidepressant drugs, drugs like

Prozac and Zoloft; these are the drugs that help by activating the serotonin systems. On the other hand, if you get a very rapid increase in serotonin, this can result in all kinds of hallucinations; in fact, the famous drug that does this is LSD. If serotonin can be involved in these very intense sensory experiences and also perhaps in the overall practices themselves, then serotonin may actually be very involved in what spiritual experiences and practices do for us and may have some impact on the kinds of qualitative and subjective experiences—in terms of lowering our sense of depression, lowering anxiety—that's also a part of what these experiences do for us.

As I mentioned earlier, different neurotransmitters relate to each other; and an increase of serotonin actually causes a release of dopamine. As we've already seen, dopamine release has been observed in meditation practices and other types of spiritual practices as well. Remember that dopamine is known to be associated with feelings of euphoria; and since we're talking about dopamine and serotonin, it's a good time to even go back to a connection with what we were learning in Lecture Five.

In that lecture, we talked a little bit about the research from Dr. Dean Hamer; and in that particular study, what Dean Hamer found was that there was a relationship between a particular gene and feelings of self-transcendence, which he thought was related to a person's spirituality. Remember that that gene coded for something called the VMAT2 receptor, and he found a very significant correlation between this gene and the person's feelings of spirituality. As we noted in Lecture Five, the VMAT2 receptor is particularly involved in regulating dopamine and serotonin. Since these two neurotransmitters are highly implicated in religious and spiritual experience, it may be no surprise that the gene that Dr. Hamer studied is sometimes referred to as the "God gene." Also remember from that same lecture how in one study dopamine was used to actually alter a nonbeliever's perception of the world. Remember it changed their ability to see things in the world that they weren't able to see previously and sometimes even see things that weren't there; it actually turned their brain into functioning more along the lines of a believer than a nonbeliever.

The results from these initial studies suggest many complex interactions. Individual practices and experiences may have a variety of different neurotransmitter effects and we're only beginning to scratch the surface in trying to understand what those effects may be. Dopamine and serotonin may work together or they may inhibit each other at different times depending on the practice and the experience. The neurotransmitters also are likely to interact with the autonomic nervous system, and hence other parts of the body and the brain. It tells us a lot about this incredibly complex functioning of the neurotransmitters, the chemicals in the brain, and how they may be related to the practices such as meditation and prayer.

Finally, in thinking about the spiritual brain, it appears that the neurotransmitters really do play a fundamental role. They may be involved in helping to make people religious or not; and we can see that neurotransmitters are very important in the underlying biology of religious and spiritual states and the practices that help bring them about. Science is really only beginning to understand the full implications and importance of how neurotransmitters are related to our spiritual practices; but it's likely that if our brain perceives itself to be able to communicate with God, the neurotransmitters are a fundamental part of that process.

In fact, neurotransmitters may indeed be "spiritual molecules" that can enable us to have religious beliefs and spiritual experiences. They may truly be the brain's transmitters to God.

Stimulated States and Religious Experiences
Lecture 14

In this lecture, you will consider stimulated states from a neuroscientific perspective, and you will discover what these stimulated states teach us about spirituality and the human brain. You will learn that induced states help us gain a deeper understanding of the underlying biology of religious or spiritual states, but they raise even more interesting questions about the meaning and realness of these states—which lead to some fascinating issues that pertain to beliefs, reality, and the brain.

Stimulating Religious or Spiritual States

- There are several different ways to create stimulated religious or spiritual states, and each of these approaches provides another piece of the puzzle toward our understanding of the spiritual brain.

- After all, if we can understand the mechanism by which the stimulation occurs, it may tell us something about stimulated states in particular and religious and spiritual states more broadly. Stimulated states may also provide some interesting information regarding the realness of these experiences.

- Meditation and prayer are methods for naturally stimulating religious experiences. We can study what happens in the brain when people meditate or pray and how that affects their experiences.

- These practices might be thought of as a top-down approach. They start by activating the frontal lobes during the attention-focusing element and then end up affecting other parts of the brain, such as other cortical areas—including the parietal and temporal lobes, the thalamus, the limbic system, and eventually the autonomic nervous system. By modifying the activity in the higher parts of the brain, the lower parts and the body are affected. The end result can be very profound spiritual or mystical experiences.

- Similarly, we can study a practice such as speaking in tongues. In this practice, the brain is stimulated by the person engaging in intense prayer or worship. This affects the language areas of the brain, shutting down the normal language areas, and subsequently affects the limbic areas, thalamus, and basal ganglia. Again, the result is a very profound spiritual state.

- These might also be regarded as more natural methods of stimulation. They are stimulated from within the brain itself without any external factors playing a role.

- However, even most of these natural methods rely on some type of external stimuli. For example, if a person is praying in church, he or she might see the image of the cross, hear the sounds of the organ or people singing, or smell the incense burning. These are external stimuli that can include a variety of sensory systems.

- These stimuli form part of the ritual process. The stimuli trigger the amygdala to pay attention to the stimulus, and that marks it as being important or something we should pay attention to. When this is coupled with the rhythmic elements of the ritual, the person experiences profound shifts in his or her cognition and emotions that surround the important perceived stimuli.

- Natural practices—individual or in conjunction with practices such as meditation or prayer—can induce spiritual states. For example, states of starvation, sleep deprivation, or sensory deprivation can result in very profound experiences, especially when combined with meditation or prayer.

- Starvation can change the way the brain utilizes energy. Sleep deprivation causes all sorts of changes in brain function and may make it susceptible to unusual experiences. Sensory deprivation can result in profound sensory experiences as the underlying brain electrical activity is interpreted as actual sensory experience.

Lessons from Professor Newberg's Research

The primary visual cortex is an area in the back of the brain—the occipital lobe—that receives the initial input from the eyes. In the visual system, there are some neurons that fire only when they receive a stimulus that appears as a horizontal line, and there are other neurons that fire only when they receive a stimulus that appears as a vertical line.

Perhaps it is because of these two types of neurons that the cross is such a powerful symbol. Perhaps the cross is an effective symbol, at least in part, because it triggers a very strong response in the brain.

Based on this thinking, I constructed a study designed to look at the effect of symbols on the brain of religious and nonreligious people. I hypothesized that if there was something inherently powerful about certain symbols, then the variety of religious symbols would be limited.

I found several web pages that had hundreds of religious and spiritual symbols. There were lots of crosses used as religious symbols—and not just for Christianity. There were also a lot of stars and a fair amount of circles. However, there were no squares or triangles. What was it about stars and crosses, but not squares and triangles, that stimulated the brain in such a way that they made good religious symbols?

We decided to select some of the most powerful religious symbols and compared them to nonreligious symbols. We also selected symbols with very positive or very negative emotional content. We then scanned people's brains while they were looking at the symbols for only a few seconds.

Interestingly, the positive religious symbols activated the primary visual cortex. In fact, the religious symbols activated the primary visual cortex more than any other symbols. This seemed to support my hypothesis that these symbols stimulated the brain more. This would be a very exciting conclusion that supported the idea that certain types of symbols are more stimulating than others. It would also support the idea that the more powerful ones are more likely to become religious symbols because the effect on the primary visual system ultimately has a greater effect on the cortex.

However, there was another interesting possibility. Because the symbols were so well known, perhaps the cortex actually changed the way in which the primary visual system worked. This, too, would have some profound implications because it would mean that our beliefs literally affect the way we perceive the world. This study is a great start in understanding how religious and spiritual ideas and experiences can be stimulated simply by a visual object.

Researching Stimulated States

- Stimulated states are those that occur when the brain is affected by external stimulants, such as drugs. Some of the early work in this area involved patients undergoing brain surgery. Researchers found that when certain parts of the brain are touched with an electrode, the patient reports intense and vivid experiences that can sometimes have a spiritual quality.

- The parts of the brain that were particularly involved were the hippocampus and amygdala in the limbic system and also part of the temporal lobe. When these areas were stimulated, people reported very intense emotional states or intense visual experiences. Because these areas are involved in both emotions and memory, it was suggested that the direct electrical stimulation of them resulted in eliciting strong emotions or memories.

- This led a researcher at Laurentian University in Canada named Michael Persinger to try to stimulate the temporal lobes using weak electromagnetic fields. Persinger's work reveals that when people have their temporal lobes stimulated, they report different types of experiences—the most prominent of which is a "sensed presence." In other words, they become aware of the proximity of an unseen entity. This experience may feel like there is another person, usually a comforting entity, in the room.

- Persinger's apparatus has also been able to help induce other types of experiences that are spiritual or spiritual-like. Persinger's work further supports the importance of the temporal lobe limbic structures in religious or spiritual experiences.

Drugs and Other Stimulated Experiences

- Drugs can affect the physiology of the brain. LSD, cocaine, and amphetamines are all known to produce spiritual-like states.

- LSD affects the serotonin system, flooding the brain with increased serotonin. This increased serotonin may be partly or wholly responsible for triggering intense experiences via the amygdala or hippocampus because these structures are highly susceptible to stimulation by serotonin.

- Cocaine affects the dopamine systems, causing a substantial increase in dopamine levels in the basal

Cocaine causes a very intense release of dopamine in the brain, which is part of what causes the "high" that results.

ganglia. Brain-imaging studies show that this increase in dopamine is directly related to the euphoria obtained by taking cocaine.

- Another drug, peyote, is used in American Indian religious practices, and evidence suggests that it may have been used for almost 5,000 years. It is known to bind to the serotonin receptors. It works similarly to LSD, but it is not clear yet why stimulating these serotonin receptors would result in the powerful hallucinatory effects that are associated with peyote.

- Shamanic methods often use a variety of psychotropic agents that all appear to result in some type of altered state of consciousness. Given the reported experiences from different psychedelic experiences, scientists at Johns Hopkins University decided that it would be helpful to study the subjective nature of such experiences in a more systematic way. In particular, they studied the effects of the hallucinogenic drug psilocybin.

- Psilocybin, in the form of mushrooms, has been used for centuries—possibly millennia—within some cultures in structured manners for divinatory or religious purposes.

- In this study, subjects were given psilocybin or methylphenidate, the common attention deficit hyperactivity disorder (ADHD) medication, in a random order. Psilocybin is known to act on the serotonin nervous system, particularly in the limbic areas. Subjects were carefully monitored and described a variety of terrifying, peaceful, amazing, spiritual, and transforming experiences.

- Even two months later, the subjects rated the psilocybin experience as having substantial personal meaning and spiritual significance and attributed to the experience sustained positive changes in attitudes and behavior. Interestingly, however, a large number of the subjects stated that they would not want to do it again.

- This study is quite interesting, but it raises a variety of questions about the use of drugs and the study of drug-induced experiences.

- The advantages of drug-induced experiences include that drugs are easy to use, there is a rapid response, they induce strong experiences, and there is the control of timing. However, the use of drugs still requires appropriate context. The disadvantages of drug-induced experiences include uncontrollability, ease of integrating such experiences, misuse, and stabilizing gains.

- The biology of religious or spiritual states is very complex and involves many different brain regions and neurotransmitters. However, do these states tell us something about the causal nature of the experiences?

- In the Western-based approach, we might argue that if we give a drug and the person has an experience, then the drug caused the experience, but is this the correct conclusion?

- Stimulated states can be extremely intense and transformative experiences. They are not, however, experiences that can be verified intersubjectively. In other words, they really can't be verified by anyone other than the individual who experiences them. Does this make them any less valuable or valid?

- If you take the Western scientific view, these stimulated states are just that—stimulated. They do not reflect a real experience of the world but, rather, an experience colored by the effects of an external agent, such as an electric probe or a drug.

- However, a spiritual person, and particularly a Shaman, might argue that the use of such agents are a way of opening up a door into the spiritual realm. A Shaman might say, for example, that mushrooms allow the brain to see the spiritual realm as it really is, and even though the spiritual state is caused by the mushroom, it is not a false state.

Suggested Reading

Goodman, "The Serotonergic System and Mysticism."

Hill and Persinger, "Application of Transcerebral, Weak (1 microT) Complex Magnetic Fields and Mystical Experiences."

Hofmann and Tart, eds, *Psychoactive Sacramentals*.

Horgan, "The God Experiments."

Schultes, Hofmann, and Rätsch, *Plants of the Gods*.

1. What are the ways that spiritual states can be elicited by purposeful stimulation of the brain?

2. Are stimulated spiritual states real or fake, and do they tell us something about the nature of reality?

Stimulated States and Religious Experiences
Lecture 14—Transcript

A couple of times already in this course I've mentioned the online survey of spiritual experiences that my research team conducted. One of the individuals who participated in the survey reported an intense spiritual experience that he'd had while under the influence of a psychedelic drug. Here's how he described it:

> A high-dose experience led to a very important and spiritual feeling. Coming up to the peak, there was a strange sense of coming home and feeling that I was exactly where I was meant to be. As the peak approached, words stopped having any meaning and fell out of my mouth as abstract images that exploded and then faded away. When words lost all meaning, thought itself melted away and left only the transcendent nature of the experience. The rocks, trees, the whole universe all were permeated by a great energy that connected us all, and there was no sense of time.

When we hear about this kind of psychedelic experience, many of us probably think about the hippies from the 1960s or the fringe-thinkers like Timothy Leary. But, in fact, there's important information to be gleaned from studying these and other types of stimulated states from a scientific perspective. In this lecture, we'll look at stimulated states from a neuroscientific perspective, and we'll find out what these stimulated spiritual states have to tell us about spirituality and the human brain.

There are a variety of different ways to create stimulated religious or spiritual states. Each of these approaches provides another piece of the puzzle towards our overall understanding of the spiritual brain. After all, if we can understand the mechanism by which the stimulation occurs, and particularly in the brain, it may tell us something about stimulated states in particular and about religious and spiritual states more broadly. Stimulated states may also provide some interesting information regarding the realness of these experiences. Let's talk a little bit about the ways of stimulating religious and spiritual experiences and states.

Meditation and prayer are methods for "naturally" stimulating religious experiences. As we've described at various times in the course, we can study what happens in the brain when people meditate or pray, how that turns on different parts of the brain, and how that affects the experiences that they have. I sometimes like to think about these practices as a top-down approach because, as we've discussed, they start by activating the frontal lobes of the brain as the person focuses their attention on a particular spiritual object. From there, the frontal lobes affect other parts of the brain such as the orientation area; the temporal lobes, which help us with language and abstract thought; the thalamus, that very central structure that regulates a lot of our sensory information; the limbic system, which regulates our emotional responses; and eventually the autonomic nervous system that connects the brain all the way down to the body. By modifying the activity in the higher parts of the brain, the lower parts of the brain and the body itself are affected by these profound practices; and the end results are very intense spiritual or mystical experiences.

Similarly, we can study a practice like speaking in tongues; and remember that in that practice, the brain is stimulated by the person engaging in very intense prayer or worship. This affects the language areas of the brain, shutting down the normal language areas and subsequently affecting the limbic areas—the emotional areas of our brain—the thalamus, and even the basal ganglia, which are all part of our emotional responses to whatever's going on around us. Again, the result is a very profound spiritual state that affects many different parts of the brain.

Again, these might be regarded as more natural methods of stimulation; they're stimulated, but they're stimulated from within the brain itself without relying on any kind of external factors playing a role. However, even many of these natural methods rely on some other type of external stimuli as well as whatever the person is doing internally. For example, if a person is praying in church, they might see the image of the cross; they might hear the sounds of the organ or the people singing next to them; and they might smell the incense burning. These are external stimuli that can induce a variety of different sensory experiences; and as we learned in the lecture on rituals, these different sensory stimuli form an important part of the ritual process itself. The stimuli trigger the amygdala to pay attention to the stimulus and mark it as something that's very important; something that we need to pay attention to. When this stimulus is coupled with the rhythmic elements of the ritual, the person experiences a profound shift in their cognition and in their emotions that ultimately surround the importance of this entire practice and the entire event that they're now a part of.

In fact, this actually led me to one of my more recent studies. This was a study of how visual symbols stimulate different parts of the brain. The idea for this study actually originated way back when I was in medical school. I was listening to a lecture; one of the professors was talking to us about the primary visual cortex. This is the an area that's in the very back of the brain—a part of the brain called the occipital lobe—and this part of the brain receives initial input from the eyes, from the external world. Unfortunately, it was a rather long lecture and my mind started wandering and thinking about some of these age-old questions about religion and spirituality, questions I always go back to; and I was starting to think about how we might be able to look at them scientifically. I was even daydreaming a bit I'm sure when all of a sudden I heard the professor say something that set off a bit of a brief "aha" moment in my own brain. He said that in the visual system, there are some neurons that fire only when they receive a stimulus that appears as a horizontal line, and there are other neurons that fire only when they receive a stimulus that appears as a vertical line.

At that moment, the lecture on vision crossed circuits with my thoughts about religion. Maybe, I thought, it's because of these two types of neurons that the cross becomes such a powerful symbol. I wondered whether the cross was an effective symbol at least in part because it triggered a very strong and definitive response in the brain. After all, if you have some neurons that fire to a horizontal line and some that fire to a vertical line, when you put them together they form a cross. I returned to listening to the lecture with a little bit more interest hoping that I might learn something more that would be helpful; unfortunately, in this particular case it didn't happen. But it did plant the seeds; and I really didn't come back to it too much, although every once in a while I thought about it as an interesting issue over the next 15 years.

But about two years ago, I was approached by someone interested in funding a study on the effects of religious beliefs and the brain. We constructed a study that was designed to look at the effect of symbols on the brain of religious and nonreligious people. First, I needed to do a little more background research to make sure that my basic idea was correct. I hypothesized that if there was something inherently powerful about certain symbols, then the variety of religious symbols would be limited. I decided to go to the internet and I found several different web pages that listed pictures of hundreds of different religious and spiritual symbols from throughout the world. You'll never guess what I found: There were actually a lot of crosses that are used as religious symbols, and not just in Christianity. But there were a few other types of symbols that I found fairly universal, and that included stars and also a fair amount of circles. But I didn't see very many squares, and there weren't very many triangles either. I wondered: What was it about stars and crosses, but not squares and triangles, which stimulated the brain in such a way that they made good religious or spiritual symbols?

We decided to select some of the most powerful religious symbols and compare them to nonreligious symbols. We also selected symbols with very positive or very negative emotional content. For example, a positive religious symbol might be a cross, especially if somebody is Christian; and a negative religious symbol might be a picture of the devil, for example. A positive nonreligious symbol was something like a smiley face; and a negative nonreligious symbol was an image of a gun.

What we did was we scanned people's brains using Functional Magnetic Resonance Imaging (or fMRI) while they were looking at the symbols and, in fact, we only showed them the symbols for a couple of seconds because we just wanted to get their initial response; we wanted to see if there was something going on in the primary moment that they received this information that was going on in their brain. Interestingly, the positive religious symbols activated the primary visual cortex, the area my old professor was talking about, in a much more robust way than any other type of symbol. It seemed to support my hypothesis that these religious or spiritual symbols stimulated the brain more.

This would be a very exciting conclusion supporting the idea that certain types of symbols are more stimulating than others. It would also support the idea that the more powerful ones are more likely to become religious symbols because of their effect on the primary visual system. But there was one other very interesting possibility that crossed my mind as I was looking at this data. Maybe because the symbols are so well known, perhaps the brain's primary visual cortex actually changed the way that it worked. This would also have some very profound implications because it would mean that our beliefs literally affect the way in which our brains perceive the world. We'll talk about this a little bit more in another lecture, but this study is a great start in helping us understand how religious and spiritual ideas and experiences can be stimulated simply by a visual object. Of course, if we can stimulate them simply by a visual object, we can begin to wonder how many other ways that more powerful types of stimuli will actually have an impact on the brain and create very, very intense types of religious and spiritual experiences.

Other natural practices, whether individually or in conjunction with practices such as meditation or prayer, can also induce very profound spiritual states. For example, states of starvation, sleep deprivation, or sensory deprivation can result in very profound experiences, especially when they're combined with meditation or prayer. In fact, if you look at a variety of different traditions, they actually utilize these other aspects to help the person engage in the prayer process. We see so many times monks or nuns trying to limit the amount that they eat, limit the amount of sleep that they have, as they engage in a very intense meditation or prayer practice; and because of that, these are the kinds of states that ultimately are the most powerful for them.

Sleep deprivation itself causes all sorts of changes in the brain, which may make it very susceptible to unusual kinds of experiences. In fact, interestingly, after about 24 hours of sleep deprivation, some people's brains actually function relatively normally while other people's brains are completely out of whack; but usually by about 48–72 hours of sleep deprivation almost everybody's brain is working in a very bizarre and different way. Maybe by contributing sleep deprivation with prayer practices, we can find people who induce very powerful kinds of spiritual experiences.

Sensory deprivation can also result in profound sensory experiences, ironically enough, because of the underlying brain electrical activity; the brain's just working anyway, and even though there's nothing that's perceived from the outside world, the brain perceives this internal stimulation as something external. Therefore, in sensory deprivation, people can become immersed in very powerful kinds of what almost are hallucinatory types of experiences.

Of course, many of you might be wondering about what we normally think of when we talk about stimulated states; those that occur when the brain is affected by something external, an external stimulants such as a drug. Some of the early work in this area involved patients undergoing brain surgery. Researchers found that when certain parts of the brain are touched with an electrode, the patient reported intense and vivid experiences that actually could have a spiritual quality to them. You might be wondering: How did they even think about doing this? The amazing thing about the brain is that even though it's what receives all of our painful stimuli, the brain itself actually doesn't have pain senses in it. You can actually do open brain surgery with the person wide awake and as you go in there and manipulate certain parts of the brain, if you touch certain parts of the brain with an electrode, in that moment the person can describe for you what they're experiencing.

The parts of the brain that were particularly involved in these studies were the hippocampus and the amygdala, our old friends in the limbic system, which are very important parts of our emotional responses as well as our memories. When these areas were stimulated, people reported very intense emotional states or intense visual experiences. Again, this isn't a surprise since these areas are very involved in both emotions and memory, and it's suggested that the direct electrical stimulation of these areas of the brain could be involved in eliciting strong emotions and memories almost to the point where they actually felt that they were a spiritual kind of experience.

It was this open-brain surgery research that led a different researcher at Laurentian University in Canada by the name of Dr. Michael Persinger to try to stimulate the temporal lobes using a weak electromagnetic field. What he actually did was take a revamped motorcycle helmet that he'd put on the person's head, and within that motorcycle helmet he had certain electrodes that would induce a little bit of a magnetic field around the temporal lobes. He was very interested in the temporal lobes for a variety of the reasons that we've talked about in previous lectures: that the temporal lobes are part of the brain that may be involved with temporal lobe seizures, which may relate to different types of spiritual experiences; and as we were just talking about, when the brain is actually stimulated with electrodes during surgery, it's the hippocampus and the amygdala, which are in the temporal lobe, which may be involved in helping to elicit these kinds of states and these kinds of experiences.

Persinger's work actually revealed that when people had stimulation from this electromagnetic field of the temporal lobes, they would report a variety of different experiences. One of the most prominent ones was something that was referred to as a "sensed presence"; in other words, they became aware of the proximity of some kind of unseen entity. The experience may feel like there's another person in the room or sometimes perhaps even God, but usually it was some kind of comforting being, some kind of comforting entity, for that individual.

Persinger's apparatus has also apparently been able to help induce other types of experiences. In fact, in an article in *Wired* magazine, we see the description of a person who had an experience like this; the individual said that:

> During the 35-minute experiment, I feel a distinct sense of being withdrawn from the envelope of my body and set adrift in an infinite existential emptiness ... Occasionally, I surface to an alpha state where I sort of know where I am, but not quite. This feeling is ... like being reinserted into my body. Then there's a separation again, of body and soul, and ... I happily allow myself to drift back to ... oblivion.

Of course, we also have to consider whether this kind of experience is really spiritual or is only something that's spiritual-like. This may be a very important distinction since we need to know how these different types of experiences, especially those that are stimulated, are related to each other; and we also need to know how those kinds of stimulated experiences may be similar or different to those experienced during meditation or prayer, or perhaps things that just happen naturally to individuals that are part of their belief systems. But at a minimum, I think Persinger's work certainly supports the importance of the temporal lobes and particularly the limbic structures as being very involved in religious and spiritual experiences.

Let's now turn to see how different types of drugs can affect the physiology of the brain, and how they may or may not induce different kinds of experiences that may be considered to be spiritual or religious. We talked a little bit about this in the last lecture because one of the things to me that's very exciting about this kind of research is that it tells us a lot about the neurotransmitters, because we can look at where these drugs go in the brain to see how they affect the neurotransmitter system in the brain. Drugs, for example, like LSD, psilocybin, and even cocaine have been known to produce spiritual-like states.

As I said, we've known before that these compounds affect certain neurotransmitters. LSD is known to affect the serotonin system of the brain; it actually floods the brain with an increase in serotonin. This increased serotonin may partly or even wholly be responsible for triggering the intense experiences via its impact on the amygdala and the hippocampus; because, again, we know that if we stimulate these structures, and we know that they can be stimulated very intensely by serotonin, they may elicit the same kind of visual experiences that are spiritual-like that we talked about when people actually used an electrode to stimulate these parts of the brain.

We've also previously discussed how cocaine affects the dopamine system. Basically, it does this by causing a substantial increase in dopamine levels, particularly in the basal ganglia. I mentioned the basal ganglia a couple times; this is an area that's very closely linked to the limbic system and is very involved in strong emotions like euphoric feelings that are related to drugs like cocaine. Brain imaging studies have actually shown how an increase in dopamine is directly related to the euphoria obtained by taking cocaine.

Another drug, peyote, is used in American Indian religious practices and evidence suggests that it may have been used for almost 5,000 years. It's known to bind to the serotonin receptors, and because of that it actually works somewhat similarly to LSD; but, again, it isn't totally clear why stimulating these serotonin receptors would result in such a powerful hallucinatory effect.

Shamanic traditions often use a variety of different psychotropic agents that all appear to result in some type of altered state of consciousness. In fact, one description of being on these kinds of mushrooms is the following:

> I felt as if death was very close and I started seeing the world and universe how it truly was. I felt tremendous love for my lover and every living thing that I had ever seen. Everything seemed to have a connected force of energy.

Given all of these anecdotes of the powerful experiences that people have when they ingest or take in these different drugs, this led to a very interesting study by some scientists at Johns Hopkins University. They wanted to try to study the subjective nature of the experiences from this kind of drug in a much more systematic way; and in particular, they focused on the hallucinogenic drug psilocybin. Psilocybin, in the form of mushrooms, has been used for centuries, possibly even millennial; and it's typically been used in cultures in a very structured manner for creating some kind of spiritual or religious state and therefore for a religious or spiritual purpose.

In the research study at Johns Hopkins—and, of course, we can even start by the issue of it's amazing that they even got this study done in the first place, given all of the ethical and regulatory issues that they had to face—they were able to do it, they were able to set it up in such a way where subjects were given one of two drugs. One of them was psilocybin, the other one was methylphenidate, which is a very common drug that's used for Attention Deficit Disorder. They gave these drugs in a random order and asked these individuals to tell them what they felt.

Again, psilocybin is known to act on the serotonin nervous system, particularly in the limbic areas; so these researchers were very interested in trying to see what kinds of emotions were actually perceived and felt by these subjects. The subjects were carefully monitored, and they described a variety of different kinds of experiences. Some of them were terrifying; some of them were incredibly peaceful; some of them were amazing; some people said they were incredible spiritual experiences; and almost all of them had some kind of transformation as the result of the experiences. Even two months later, the subjects tended to rate the psilocybin experience as having substantial personal meaning and spiritual significance and attributed to the experience a sustained positive change in attitudes and behaviors for that individual.

It was also interesting that a fair number of the subjects who were involved in this study and had very amazing experiences said they really didn't want to do this again. They said that because as powerful as the experience was, they felt like it was almost too strong and they were concerned of what would happen to them if they underwent this kind of experience again.

This study is certainly very interesting, but raises a variety of questions about the use of and the study of these kinds of drug-induced experiences. For example, one of the benefits of these kinds of studies is that these drugs are easy to use. Of course, a lot of times they're illegal to use, so there are a lot of regulatory and ethical questions that have to be addressed; but if you look at their effect, you can see that they have a relatively rapid response, you can control the timing of it—you know when it's going to turn on, you know when it's going to happen—and you can very clearly evaluate the effect of that drug. Of course, one of the other things that's also important is the context within which the drug is given; and that may have a lot to do with the kind of experience that the person has. The big disadvantages of using drugs are, of course, their uncontrollability—you don't know exactly what kind of experience they're going to have; it could be very positive, it could be very negative—and the bigger issue, of course, is how it could be misused, how people could wind up becoming addicted to these drugs; and therefore, even though the research is fascinating, we have to be very cautious about saying that this is a common kind of study that should be done or something that should be explored by all people.

What do all these different stimulated states tell us? The biology of religious and spiritual states is very complex, and as we've seen it seems to involve many different brain regions and many different neurotransmitters; so trying to get at how these different states can be stimulated could be very important for telling us exactly how the brain is involved in these spiritual states. But do these simulated states also tell us something about the causal nature of these experiences? In the Western scientific paradigm, we might argue that if we give a drug and the person has an experience, then the drug caused the experience. But is this the fully correct conclusion? In 1815, the Romantic poet William Wordsworth cautioned against "the tyranny of the eye"; an unwillingness to believe that which can't be seen. Other senses, Wordsworth suggested, are just as valid.

As we close this lecture on stimulated religious or spiritual states, I'd like us to consider the concept of what's real and what isn't. Is a religious or spiritual vision something real if you're the only person who perceives it? More importantly in the context of this lecture, should we consider these stimulated experiences to be real if they're produced by something external to the brain, even though the experience is only going on inside? Perhaps this raises a larger question: What's real and what's not? How do we define reality? By what we can see, can we verify what we see as being real? How do we assess something that's, in fact, real? Is it something that we imagine, something that we comprehend, or is it emotional? I'll be addressing this later in this lecture and also throughout the rest of this course since it's perhaps one of the most important philosophical questions that this field of study confronts.

But let's return to our discussion of stimulated states, which can be extremely intense and transformative. They aren't, however, experiences that can be verified intersubjectively. In other words, they really can't be verified by anyone other than the individual who experiences them. Does this make them any less valuable or valid? It would seem that it depends on your point of view. Again, if you take the Western scientific view, these stimulated states are just that: they're stimulated. They don't reflect a real experience of the world, but rather an experience colored by the effects of some kind of external agent such as an electric probe or a drug. But what would a spiritual person say? A spiritual person, maybe a Shaman, would maybe argue something very different. They might say that the use of such agents is actually a way of opening up a door into the spiritual realm. He might say, for example, that mushroom allows the brain to see the world or see the spiritual realm as it actually is. If a Shaman takes a mushroom to induce a spiritual state, he doesn't feel that even though it's caused by the mushroom it's, in fact, a false state.

The analogy I sometimes like to talk about is wearing glasses; this is something that I do, many of you might. When I wake up in the morning, it's a very blurry world, and I put my glasses on and I can see the world clearly. That changes the way in which my brain responds to the world; but does that mean that now that I have my glasses on that my brain is seeing the world in a false way, or merely in a more accurate way? Can we apply this analogy to different drugs or other types of induced states that may actually allow the brain to see reality in a different way but not necessarily an inaccurate one?

Induced states help us gain a deeper understanding of the underlying biology of religious and spiritual states. But they may raise even more interesting questions about the meaning and the realness of these states, and this leads us to some fascinating issues that pertain to beliefs—beliefs about reality, and even the brain—topics that we'll consider in future lectures.

Near-Death Experiences and the Brain
Lecture 15

O n a biological, psychological, and even cultural basis, researchers know that near-death experiences frequently share a set of core components; appear to be related to a variety of specific brain processes, including vision, emotions, and memory; and often have life-changing consequences. In addition, near-death experiences can radically change a person's beliefs. However, researchers do not know if these newfound beliefs are truly new or if they were somehow always there and the near-death experience simply helped the person access them. These uncertainties require a thorough evaluation of near-death experiences from a neuroscientific perspective—in spite of the challenges that lie ahead.

Core Components of Near-Death Experiences

- To a researcher, there are many fascinating aspects to a near-death experience. Most remarkably, many near-death experiences simply transform the people who experience them. People come away from a near-death experience with a radically altered set of beliefs about themselves, the meaning in life, relationships—everything. How does this happen in an instant?

- Basically, the common components of near-death experiences can be broken into three categories: what is seen, what is heard, and what is experienced.

- What is seen includes a being of light or entering into the light (only about 10 percent of near-death experiences involve this), a dark tunnel, and an out-of-body experience.

- What is heard includes the noise surrounding the experience.

- What is experienced involves a few stages. The beginning of the near-death experience involves hearing the news of one's own death, the review of life events, meeting people that the person did not know had died, the knowledge of one's death, clarity of thought, anomalous experiences, out-of-body experiences, and seeing other events.

- Midway through the near-death experience, the person senses a border, meets others, and starts to feel that it is time to come back to reality. Toward the end of the experience, there is a sense of ineffability, which is accompanied by feelings of peace and quiet.

Some of the earliest reports of near-death experiences were made by survivors of avalanches.

- Near-death experiences typically occur when one is near death. They are described in states of cardiac arrest, drowning, car accidents, and suicide. Interestingly, however, near-death experiences have even been reported in times of life-threatening situations, such as avalanches, even though the person was not actually near death.

- Researchers have not found any correlation between the type of death and the likelihood of having a near-death experience. However, some studies suggest that the administration of drugs—either by the person in a suicide attempt or by doctors trying to save the patient—may lessen the chance of having a near-death experience.

- Some hallucinogenic drugs produce experiences that have many characteristics of near-death experiences. However, drug experiences tend to be more heavily based upon sensory experiences, such as intense visions, beautiful colors, and seeing other beings. These are certainly part of near-death experiences, but near-death experiences also appear to have some other elements that are not typically found with drug states—such as the life review or the notion that it is time to go back. Furthermore, most near-death experiences result in powerful consequences for the individual in terms of how he or she thinks about death and life, which are not common with drug-induced states.

- Although the majority of modern reports of near-death experiences are about very positive experiences, there are many examples of negative experiences.

- For example, in her book *Otherworld Journeys*, Carol Zaleski writes about the horrific accounts given by medieval men and women who had near-death experiences. These accounts include fiendish tortures, dismemberments, tearing and burning of flesh, and other assorted horrors before the individual had a glimpse of heavenly glory.

Studying Near-Death Experiences

- How can we study near-death experiences in a way that we can actually learn something about how they relate to the brain? Because the person is unresponsive, there is no way of knowing what the person is feeling or when it is happening.

- In fact, it is even difficult to document that a person was, in fact, clinically dead during the experience. Even if you find some interesting brain activity, how do you know what it might be related to?

- Of course, one of the biggest problems in studying near-death experiences is that you never know when they are going to happen. You always hear about it after the fact.

- There is no way to do brain scans on people at the moment of a car accident. However, you could try to study near-death experiences in environments in which they are more likely to occur. Environments such as emergency rooms or operating suites in which patients undergo life-threatening operations are possibilities.

- However, even though a near-death experience is more likely to occur in one of these locations, because the person is near death, you can't ask him or her what he or she is feeling or experiencing in the moment.

- Even if we took a brain scan at the moment a person's heart stopped, we don't know which patterns of activity we should correlate with the experience itself. We can only make guesses and inferences. Some of these guesses might be educated guesses based on a variety of data—from the physiology of the dying process to drug-induced states to the experiences people describe.

- With this in mind, there are many theories about the origin of the near-death experience, including that it involves the effect of drugs, hypoxia (an oxygen deficiency), or strong autonomic activity. In addition, perhaps a near-death experience occurs as a result of the soul actually leaving the body.

- No explanation answers all aspects of near-death experiences, and there is no explanation for the long-term effects of near-death experiences.

- Perhaps the most interesting aspect of near-death experiences from a brain perspective is how they can be so life changing and transformative. People no longer fear death, and they have a new way of looking at life and relationships. People are more spiritual and less religious.

- The brain normally changes slowly over time, but in a flash of an instant during a near-death experience, people frequently change all the ways they think about themselves and the world.

- Many people who have near-death experiences say things like: "I don't think there is a God; I know there is a God." However, one individual described the experience as being "bigger" than religion. It made her feel as if religion was not sufficient to help encapsulate the near-death experience.

- Furthermore, there are people who have had a near-death experience but have not been moved to a religious or spiritual conclusion. In fact, an atheist described an experience that was very similar to a positive near-death experience but then said, "It was an amazing experience to feel while my brain was dying." For her, it was a purely material experience.

- One of the most amazing aspects of near-death experiences is the anomalous experience. People describe out-of-body states in which they not only feel like they float outside of their body and up to the ceiling, but they also actually see and hear what is going on around them. Some have reported going into different rooms in the hospital and seeing what is going on there.

- Another frequent anomalous occurrence is when people describe a meeting with others who have died—sometimes when they don't know that the other person is actually dead. There are many researchers who have received such stories from people who have had a near-death experience.

Studying Anomalous Experiences

- A group of researchers have started a study attempting to confirm or refute anomalous experiences. The approach is to put pictures up in emergency rooms in hospitals that are too high for people to see unless they float out of their body and up to the ceiling. There are no results yet, but either way, the results could be very important.

- In fact, such a study truly fascinates scientists—especially those who study the spiritual realm—because it has paradigm-shifting implications. If we can find some kind of decisive evidence that a person's awareness can somehow leave his or her body, that implies that something about us is more than simply the material body. Somehow, our consciousness, mind, soul, or spirit would be able to leave the material body and experience the world in a different way than science currently believes is possible.

- Of course, the study would potentially raise more questions than it answers. For example, how is such a process possible? How do the material and nonmaterial relate to each other? Is there really a soul, or is this effect related to the nature of consciousness? This would imply that consciousness is able to extend beyond the brain and that maybe it even exists independently in the world alongside matter. These are fascinating possibilities, but we have to wait for the data.

- Human beings have a lingering fascination with near-death experiences; we are interested in trying to understand if something exists beyond this life.

- Perhaps, if we discover that there is some truth to anomalous experiences, we might find ourselves facing a radical shift in our understanding of the material world, science, consciousness, and even the soul.

Suggested Reading

Beauregard, Courtemanche, and Paquette, "Brain Activity in Near-Death Experiencers during a Meditative State."

Blackmore, *Dying to Live*.

Greyson and Bush, "Distressing Near-Death Experiences."

Holden, Greyson, and James, eds, *The Handbook of Near-Death Experiences*.

Moody, *Life after Life*.

1. What are the potential brain processes associated with near-death experiences?

2. Can we use science to explore the anomalous aspects of near-death experiences?

Near-Death Experiences and the Brain
Lecture 15—Transcript

A patient is rushed into an emergency room. An oxygen mask is placed over his mouth, and he's given an IV. Surgery begins immediately; the patient's appendix has ruptured. At some point during the procedure, however, the patient goes into full cardiac arrest. His vital signs disappear; he has no pulse, no heartbeat, no breathing. The patient is clinically dead. However, the team of doctors and nurses continue trying desperately to resuscitate the man; and by a medical miracle, the patient's heart finally begins to beat. The patient has, from a medical standpoint, been brought back to life.

After this ordeal, when the patient finally wakes up a couple days later, he's asked if he had any memory of the entire experience. This is what he says; he says:

> At first, I had the sense of hovering over my body. I was watching the doctors working frantically around me. Amazingly, I felt quite calm. And then I experienced a sense of moving down a dark void and arriving at what appeared as a gate made of brilliant light. Beside the gate was a tall column of light and it had a consciousness in it. I assumed it to be an angel at the gates of heaven. But he refused to let me go through to the other side and I was very angry. Telepathically he said that I had to return to life, but I didn't want to. Then it felt like I was being dragged back and as I got closer to being conscious I began to hear the people talking and feel the pain coming back into my body.

What this patient has described is a near-death experience, or what we sometimes refer using the abbreviation NDE. To a researcher like myself, there are many fascinating aspects to the NDE; and personally, the one that I find most remarkable is the fact that so many NDEs simply transform the people who experience them. People come away from an NDE with a radically altered set of beliefs about themselves, about meaning in life, about their relationships, about everything. As a brain scientist, I have to wonder: How does this happen in an instant?

I'm going to come back to the transformative nature of the near death experience later in the lecture, but let's start by examining a little bit of the core components of the NDE. Basically we can probably break these NDEs down to about three different categories of common components: what the person sees, what they hear, and what they experience.

When people have an NDE, what do they typically describe as what they see? Typically, people talk about light, a being of light, or entering into some kind of realm of light, although typically the realm of light is entered into by only about 10–15 percent of people. Another thing they talk about seeing is a dark tunnel, just like our patient talked about; this dark void that he traveled through. Interestingly, a lot of people also describe, like our patient, a kind of out of body experience where they see the things that are going on around their dead body. They can see the doctors and the nurses, or whoever's trying to help them out and resuscitate them, doing all kinds of things around them; they may even see their actual body lying there on the table.

People also can hear things. Sometimes they hear an annoying noise that's kind of like a buzzing sound, and occasionally people say that they hear the most beautiful music that they've ever heard.

They also experience a lot of different things that go through a relatively defined progression throughout the entire process of the NDE. At the start of the NDE, frequently people actually hear the news of their death; they hear somebody say, "My gosh, this person's heart stopped." The other thing they may experience right away is a kind of very quick review of their life's events. That's the classic notion of your life flashing before you; that really does happen. Sometimes people, when they're in a NDE, actually meet other people who've died; in fact, sometimes the person who's having the NDE didn't even know that that person died. To some degree, they have a clarity of thought; they feel that they're seeing things clearly, things are slowing down, they feel calm, so it's a very powerful but very clear kind of experience for them. One of the more interesting elements, which we'll talk about a little bit later, are what are sometimes referred to as anomalous experiences; and this can happen, often at the beginning but perhaps at any time during a near death experience, where things that don't seem to go along with the way we normally think about science actually happen.

About halfway through a near death experience, sometimes people will reach some kind of border. This is a very important border for them because it tends to be the border between going forward to full death and coming back into life. Sometimes they meet others. I mentioned already that sometimes they meet people who've died, but sometimes they just meet other beings, so to speak; they're not even sure what they are, or even if they're other human beings, but this sense of some kind of presence that's there and they meet this other presence.

Towards the end of the experience, there's this sense of coming back. They actually often have this decision point that occurs; either something or someone telling them to go back, or they have this notion that "It's time for me to go back." Then finally, they have great feelings of peace, calmness, and sense of indescribability of the entire experience.

When do near death experiences occur? Obviously, as the name states, near death. They're typically described in states of cardiac arrest when the heart stops, drowning, car accidents, or suicide attempts, as a variety of different examples. But interestingly, near death experiences have also been reported at times of life-threatening situations. In fact, some of the earliest reports were of survivors of avalanches; and they actually hadn't died, but they had these kinds of very unusual experiences that were eventually called near death experiences.

Researchers have thought, "Gee, there are lots of different ways that a person can die; is there a relationship between the type of death and the likelihood of the person having a near death experience?" There have been a few studies that have suggested that when people are administered certain drugs, either by the person who maybe is trying to kill themselves in a suicide attempt or perhaps by doctors who are trying to save their life, this may actually lessen the likelihood or the chance of them having a near death experience. On the other hand, as we talked about in the last lecture, there are a variety of different hallucinogenic drugs that can produce experiences that have characteristics of near death experiences; however, these drug experiences tend to be more heavily based upon the sensory elements: the intense visions, beautiful colors, seeing other beings. These are certainly part of the near death experience, but the near death experience also appears to have some other elements that aren't typically found with the drug-induced states, such as the life review or the notion that it's time to go back. Furthermore, most of the near death experiences result in very powerful consequences for the individual in terms of how they think about death and life, and these aren't quite as common when you think about drug induced states.

The description I've given so far makes it sound like most of these near death experiences are actually pretty positive, and a lot of the literature actually supports that. But there are some examples of negative experiences. In fact, if we go back in time, we find that some of the medieval accounts actually describe some horrific kinds of experiences. A scholar named Carol Zalesky wrote in a book called *Otherworld Journeys* about these fiendish tortures, dismemberments, the tearing and burning of flesh, and a whole bunch of other assorted horrors that occurred in people who underwent these near death experiences before they ultimately moved on to some kind of beautiful light, some type of heavenly glory. For example, in a story called the *Vision of Barontus*, there's a description of a near death experience of a seventh-century monk. This monk was in the grip of a very severe illness, and Barontus, the monk, envisions these terrifying demons who try to grab him; and they try to grab him by the throat in order to take him towards Hell. What's very interesting at least about the story is that other monks who were caring for him at the time actually saw him trying to move his hands towards his throat almost as if he was trying to protect himself.

There's a lot of information about the subjective experience of the experiences that people have when they have a NDE. Oftentimes they're positive, but they can be negative. Of course, all of this brings us to the question that lies at the heart of this entire course: But what about their biology? What's going on in the person's body and brain during the near death experience, and does that tell us something about the nature of these experiences?

The first issue, of course, is how do we study the near death experience in some kind of way that we can actually learn something about what's going on in the brain? Obviously there are a lot of problems with studying a person's brain when they're in a near death state. First of all, the person's unresponsive, so there's no way of even knowing what the person's feeling or when it's happening. If somebody has their heart stopped for 20 minutes, we don't know if they had the near death experience at the beginning of that or at the end of that. Of course, even if you find something interesting going in the brain, how can you even ask the person what it might be related to? There's no way to do that.

Of course, one of the biggest problems in studying near death experiences is that you never know when they're going to happen; typically you hear about them after the fact. There's also no real good way to do a brain scan on somebody who's near death. If you think back to some of the studies that we've talked about in terms of SPECT imaging and PET imaging, it requires us to inject a radioactive tracer into their bloodstream that gets up into the brain and if they don't have any blood flow, then that tracer isn't going to get there; there's going to be no way of actually measuring what's happening in the brain itself.

Can we envision some other way of trying to get at that actual near death state? Some of you may remember back, a movie called *Flatliners* explored an interesting premise about trying to actually induce death in people; and, in fact, in the movie, a group of medical students used different medications to literally kill their colleagues—at least temporarily—in order to see what kind of experiences they might have. As the movie goes on, they allow their friends to stay dead for longer and longer periods of time. This rather eerie idea is certainly something that would be fascinating to try, but most likely would have a great deal of difficulty flying past any kind of institutional review board's ethics committee.

Is there another way to do this? Researchers are always pretty resourceful, and maybe we could think about situations, environments, in which a near death experience is more likely to occur; maybe environments such as an emergency room—a trauma bay, for example—or an operating suite in which people are going to undergo life-threatening operations. These might be good possibilities, good targets for us to think about to try to find when people have near death experiences and what goes on in their brain.

But even though a near death experience may be more likely to occur in one of these locations, again since the person is near death and is unresponsive to you, you never really know what they're doing, when they're doing it. Even if there was some way to get at some aspect of the brain's function—maybe some kind of brain scan or maybe an electrical study of the brain, an EEG study—you don't really know which patterns of activity would correlate with the experience itself. We can only make some guesses and inferences based on how we know what the brain does, what we know is happening during a near death state, and what people have described for us after the fact. These guesses, even though they're guesses, might be actually pretty educated guesses, and they may give us some fairly good information about what might be going on during this near death state.

With this in mind, there are many theories about the origin of the NDE. For example, some people have thought that it really is the effect of some kind of drug or at least some unclear , some type of neurotransmitter, occurring in the brain itself. But the problem with that hypothesis is that a lot of people aren't taking drugs or aren't given drugs, and it seems a little unlikely that the internal neurotransmitter releases would be so strong to be able to create such an experience. Other people have suggested that hypoxia, a loss of oxygen in the brain, may be responsible for this kind of experience. Basically, the idea is that as oxygen is gone away from the brain, as the brain is deprived of oxygen, it begins to shut down; and in shutting down, much like your computer shuts down in a very specific way, your brain shuts down and shuts down along the lines where you generate this kind of an experience. In fact, one of the thoughts that I always had was when we think about this one element of the experience, the tunnel, maybe this has something to do with how their visual system shuts down; that it's the periphery of the visual system that shuts down first, leaving only the central aspects of our visual system, and that can create a sense of tunnel vision that may be related to the experience.

Others have suggested that very strong autonomic nervous system activity lies at the heart of the near death experience. It makes some sense; after all, if you're near death, your autonomic nervous system is going to be going pretty crazy at that moment. It's an extraordinarily stressful moment for the body, and your arousal system is going to be turned on to its maximum. As we've talked about before with regard to rituals, we may actually see that type of autonomic activity creating all kinds of changes going on in the brain. But, again, unfortunately not everybody is in that kind of a state.

If you're a religious person, you might say, "I know the answer, it's very obvious. The near death experience is literally the soul leaving the body."

It's the experience of the soul migrating out of the body down some pathway towards Heaven or Hell (depending on the circumstance), and that that is actually the experience that the person has.

Unfortunately, no explanation appears to answer all of the aspects of the near death experience; and also no explanation has actually been able to describe the long-term effects of the near death experience. Let's return to that. This, to me again, is one of the more interesting aspects of the near death experience from a brain perspective. How is it that this moment in a person's life can be so life-changing and so transformative? If you go to a large number of near death experience accounts, which can be found on the website, we can see some incredible descriptions of how near death experiences have occurred, the experiences they've had, and the transformation that's resulted in a person's life as a result of that experience. A large number of NDE accounts can be found on the website of the International Association for Near Death Studies. It's an excellent resource if you're interested in getting more information about near death experiences.

One person, in reflecting back on her NDE, said this:

> Looking back over the years, the experience has changed me tremendously. I usually feel a wonderful inner peace almost all the time, and I lack a fear of death. I enjoy life and feel life gets better with each passing year, I feel a longing to go home and not infrequently I am jealous of those people who pass on.

Another person who'd been in a serious car accident said this:

> I only remember light and darkness and strong feelings while I was unconscious. What is really significant about the experience is that I became a markedly changed person immediately afterward. I became profoundly concerned about other people and humanity as a whole and that change has directed my whole life. I lost my fear of death, and pretty much all fear whatsoever.

We can see by these two descriptions that people no longer fear death, they have a new way of looking at life and relationships, and it truly transforms who they are. When people are asked about their religious or spiritual attitudes, we also get some interesting answers. People sometimes say that they're more spiritual, but sometimes they actually feel less religious. When asked to explain this in a little bit more detail, what they sometimes say is that the experience was really too powerful or too big to be fit into any particular religious tradition.

How do we understand all of this from a neuroscientific perspective? Normally when we think about how the brain changes, and if we think back to our lecture on spiritual development, the brain changes slowly over time; it changes over the course of an entire lifespan as we go from childhood, to adolescence, to adulthood. But somehow in a flash of an instant during the near death experience, the person changes everything about themselves. How does this happen? How can we think about this happening from a brain perspective?

I think one of the things that we have to look at is how we understand the brain's ability to change; and maybe we're not always so correct in thinking that it takes time. But, of course, how we actually understand this kind of change occurring is something that may have a profound impact on the nature of the near death experience as well as the ability of our brain and how it works.

Many people who've had near death experiences will say things like, "I don't think there's a God, I know there's a God. " But one individual that we know actually described the experience as being "bigger" than religion, and it made her feel as if religion wasn't sufficient to help encapsulate the near death experience in its entirety. Of course, there are some interesting people who haven't been moved to a religious or spiritual conclusion as a result of their near death experience. In fact, my research team spoke to an atheist who described the experience as being very positive and in many similar ways as those people who do feel spiritual afterwards, but the atheist said to us, "It was an amazing experience to feel while my brain was dying." For her, it was a purely material experience. Again, what do we make of this? What's going on? Was it really the same kind of experience, or was the atheist's brain not primed for that kind of interpretation? These are questions that we have to think about going forward in terms of how we try to understand the nature of spirituality and how these kinds of powerful experiences like the near death experience actually have an impact on spirituality.

But in the end, one of the most amazing aspects of the near death experience is the anomalous experiences. People have described out of body states in which they not only feel like they float outside their body, but actually can see what's going on around them. In fact, the common report is that they're up in the corner of the room looking down on everything that's going on around them. Some people have actually reported going into different rooms in the hospital and seeing what's going on in there. You'll hear some interesting anecdotes about an individual who could see what another patient looked like or what was going on with another patient.

One person from our online survey of people's spiritual experiences described a near death experience during a poisoning. She said:

> The first thing I remembered was being above my body on the table and "seeing" everything that happened in the room. I could see the doctors talking with the nurses and see them using the resuscitation equipment. Then I sort of drifted up to the ceiling and went through it. I was then in a tunnel of light. As I moved through this tunnel of light, there were two robed beings with faces that seemed etched in light who came toward me. They somehow communicated to me that it was not my time and I was returned to my body. I thought Noooooo, I don't want to go back. They communicated that I must as it was the best thing that I needed to do.

Other anomalous experiences occur when people describe a meeting with others who've died. What's interesting is that sometimes when they see this person who's died, they don't actually know that the person was dead. Take this very interesting example that I found on the internet. It describes a four year old boy who'd almost drowned, and he'd been revived after about 15 minutes of not breathing. The four year old boy apparently spoke about going to the other side in a similar way as other people who've had near death experiences. At first no one really thought much about it until he made a comment that in this experience he met his brother. This was a very odd kind of statement because this child was an only child; and only later was it found out that the child's mother had had an abortion when she was much younger, one that she'd never told anyone about.

As a scientist, my first thought about such a story is that this has got to be fictional; this can't be a real thing. But there are many researchers who've received similar types of stories in which the person who's having the near death experience meets a deceased individual, especially one that they don't know is actually dead.

As a researcher, what should we do with these kinds of stories, with these kinds of anecdotes? Do we just laugh them off? Do we try to confirm them in some way? Again, even if we went to the person and said, "Did you really have this experience?" Take this boy for a minute: How do we know that that really meant that he was seeing this deceased brother? Maybe it was just some strange coincidence that he hallucinated that he had a brother? Maybe he always wanted to have a brother, and in this state he hallucinated that he had one. In short: How can we test anomalous experiences?

A group of researchers has started a study that's an attempt to confirm or refute at least some of these kinds of anomalous experiences. It goes back a little bit to what we talked about earlier in the lecture about where would be a good place to do these studies? They started with emergency rooms, and they went to emergency room hospital beds and what they'd do is they'd put pictures up, usually on some kind of shelf that was above where the beds were so that if somebody was wheeled into the room and they were in a near death state they'd never be able to see this picture; it would be up too high, it would be facing the ceiling. But theoretically, if somebody described the experience of floating out of their body and going up to the ceiling, would they potentially see this picture? They made these pictures kind of unusual pictures—maybe a picture of the Eiffel Tower, for example; something that would be out of place—with the hope that if they go back and talk to individuals who've been in a near death state, if they find somebody who's had a near death experience, they could say, "Did you see anything?" If they say, "Yes, I happened to see a picture of the Eiffel Tower, I don't understand why," that could be pretty interesting.

There are no results from this study yet, but they could be extraordinarily important. In fact, such a study truly fascinates me as a scientist and someone who studies the spiritual realm since it has paradigm-shifting implications. If we could find some kind of decisive evidence that a person's awareness or consciousness can somehow leave their body that implies that something about us is more than simply material. Somehow our consciousness, our mind, soul, or spirit—whatever we want to call it—is able to leave the material body, leave the brain, and experience the world in a different way than science currently believes to be possible.

Of course, it would probably raise far more questions than it answers; after all, even if it turns out to be the case that people can see these pictures, how is such a process possible? How does the material and the non-material relate to each other in some kind of functional way? Is there really a soul or is this effect related to the nature of human consciousness? This might imply that consciousness itself is able to extend beyond the brain and maybe even exist independently in the world alongside matter. Certainly these are fascinating possibilities, but we're going to have to wait for the data.

We do have a lingering fascination with near death experiences, though. We're interested in understanding what happens next; we're interested in trying to understand if something exists beyond this life. What do we know about NDEs from a biological, psychological, or cultural basis? We know that they frequently share a set of core components, and that these appear to be related to very specific brain types of processes—processes like vision, emotions, and memory—and they often have life-changing consequences. We've also seen that the near death experience can radically change a person's beliefs. But what we don't know is whether these newfound beliefs are truly new, or if they were somehow always in their brain, somehow always within them, and that the near death experience simply helped the person find a new way to access them.

In other words, are the new beliefs merely revisions and refinements of the beliefs that they already held, or has the brain literally been rewired by the experience and hence changed the person's belief system permanently? These questions require a thorough evaluation of the near death experience from a neuroscientific perspective in spite of the challenges that lie ahead. Maybe, if we discover some truth to the anomalous experiences that people describe, we might find ourselves facing a radical shift in our understanding of the material world, of science, consciousness, and maybe even the soul.

The Believing Brain
Lecture 16

eliefs are important because they affect every part of our lives, and every part of our lives affects our beliefs. In other words, we must be very careful about our beliefs, constantly challenging them and questioning them. In addition, perhaps we should be more compassionate about other people's beliefs, which are simply expressions of their brains' best attempt at understanding the world. In this lecture, you will learn that our beliefs are shaped by the way the brain perceives, thinks, remembers, and experiences emotion. You will also learn that social consensus is another important factor that influences our beliefs.

Beliefs Have Tremendous Power

- The placebo effect is the phenomenon whereby a placebo pill, which does not contain any active medication, improves a patient's condition simply because the patient has the belief that it will be effective.

- Modern medicine has a generally negative view about the placebo effect. Doctors tend to look at the placebo effect as unreal, but if it is very powerful, maybe we should try to understand it more. In fact, if the placebo effect works, why don't we use it more often?

- Most research studies have shown that the placebo effect works, on average, in about one-third of situations, and in some studies, the placebo effect is effective in as many as two-thirds of patients. This is particularly true in studies of psychiatric disorders such as depression or anxiety, in which the placebo works as well if not better than some antidepressant and antianxiety medications.

- Given these fascinating statistics, some scientists have tried to unravel the mystery of the placebo effect. For example, brain-scan studies have shown that the beliefs that we engage as part of the placebo effect can have a powerful effect on our mind and body.

- Beliefs have an impact on many aspects of our lives and, thus, we find them in advertising, culture, politics, morality, and religion. Even though beliefs are all around us, we might wonder why we need them so much. Why does our brain create beliefs? In fact, why do we believe anything at all?

- If the universe is everything that is out there, our brain only has access to a very small percentage of that everything. On top of that, the brain filters out much of what it receives so that what you are consciously aware of is a very small amount of the world. Therefore, we are left with trying to derive our entire understanding of the universe by working with a very tiny amount of information.

- We need to establish beliefs to help us to navigate through the world effectively. The brain is a believing machine.

What Are Beliefs?

- A belief may be defined as a feeling that something exists or is true, especially one without proof. In other words, a belief draws a distinction between things that can and cannot be proven. However, what constitutes "proof" is different for science, religion, theology, and philosophy.

- Belief can be defined biologically and psychologically as any perception, cognition, emotion, or memory that a person consciously or unconsciously assumes to be true.

- The brain exists in an almost infinite world. The brain takes in millions of pieces of information, but only a limited amount reaches consciousness. Many pieces remain in the subconscious.

- The brain likes to fill in perceptual gaps, and sometimes the brain makes mistakes. We can be made to see lines and shapes even though they are not really there. For example, there is an illusion that causes people to see a square when one does not really exist.

- Another illusion uses a fancy checkerboard pattern to make it look like there is a curvature to the lines of the board, even though each one of them is completely straight. In addition, the dragon illusion involves a statue that looks like a dragon that follows you with its eyes, but it actually remains perfectly still.

- On one level, the brain sometimes makes us believe that we see things that aren't really there. It sometimes constructs a reality that, upon closer examination, turns out to be nothing more than an illusion.

- Beyond the question of illusions, the brain is always constructing perceptions of the external world—but what does our brain do with those perceptions?

- Basically, it begins to think about them. These cognitive processes then help us interpret the perceptions by providing us beliefs about those perceptions.

- Beliefs have a certain logic that makes sense to us, and cognition helps us find the "proof." We use cognition to help create beliefs and also to maintain them.

© Hemera/Thinkstock.com

The most interesting optical illusions are the ones that involve complex patterns that are difficult for the eye to decipher.

- One of the tools that cognition uses to build and maintain beliefs is memory. For example, the memory that someone once snubbed us at a party serves as "proof" for our belief that this individual is hostile to us and should therefore be avoided.

How Reliable Is Memory?
- In the 1980 presidential campaign, Ronald Reagan would sometimes cite the story of a World War II pilot whose plane had

been hit by enemy fire. He was going to jump from the plane, but one member of the crew was too injured to jump. The pilot said, "Never mind, we'll ride it down together."

- Reagan would sometimes have tears in his eyes while telling this story. However, it turns out this never happened in real life; instead, it was a scene from the movie *Wing and a Prayer*. Interestingly, Reagan's brain made him think that it was something that really happened—and this happens to all of us.

- Just as our brains lead us to fill in gaps in our visual perception so that we sometimes see things that aren't really there, our brains also fill in the gaps in our experiences. Cognition can actually grab bits and pieces of experiences and piece together a false story that nevertheless feels true to us—a story that we believe because we think we're accurately remembering the way things happened.

- Indeed, one of the reasons that memories—even false ones—can be so powerful is because they often have such strong emotions attached to them. Think of the Reagan example. Those tears in his eyes were real. The emotion was real, even if the memory was inaccurate.

- Emotions are important for placing value on beliefs. Strong emotions elicit strong beliefs because our brain wants us to remember important things and forget unimportant things.

- Our brain assesses what is important—and, therefore, what is remembered and believed—based on the emotional content, which can be positive or negative. Emotions also help us defend beliefs.

- Perceptions and thoughts that do not have strong emotional content may never even reach consciousness.

How Are Beliefs Strengthened?
- Beliefs are strongly influenced by the other individuals we interact with throughout life. Our parents help us form our initial beliefs, and our peers lead us to new beliefs in adolescence.

- Society leads to beliefs of whole populations—whether they are political, cultural, or religious—and group consensus heavily influences beliefs.

- Given the influences of our perceptions, emotions, thoughts, and social interactions, how do beliefs actually form and work in the brain?

- Interneurons and neurotransmitters strengthen connections when we use them, and connections that are not used ultimately weaken. When we have an emotion or a thought that we focus on, the neural connections that support that belief strengthen.

- In fact, if it is true that the simultaneous firing of neurons leads to increased connections between those neurons, then the more we get a few neurons to fire together, the stronger the belief becomes. Repetition is, therefore, an essential element for forming and strengthening beliefs.

- However, are there religious or spiritual activities that are repetitive? In fact, almost all religious rituals and practices are repetitive. This is why meditation and rituals work so well; they are very repetitious.

- To strengthen beliefs, it is important to tie beliefs to useful information and behaviors, emotionally support the beliefs that we hold, and reject beliefs that contradict those that we hold.

- These processes are true for all beliefs—including religious, social, political, and scientific beliefs—so the brain is a believing machine.

- Beliefs are constructed out of our perceptions, emotions, thoughts, and interpersonal interactions as each of these factors affect the very neural connections that form our beliefs.

- However, while the brain does a great job of formulating beliefs that work well for us and help us understand the world, beliefs are also fraught with many potential flaws. The brain can make mistakes at many different levels while constructing its beliefs.

Suggested Reading

Harris, Kaplan, Curiel, Bookheimer, Iacoboni, and Cohen, "The Neural Correlates of Religious and Nonreligious Belief."

Newberg and Waldman, *Why We Believe What We Believe*.

Shermer, *The Believing Brain*.

Questions to Consider

1. How does the brain make beliefs about religion, politics, morals, and every aspect of the world?

2. What are the flaws the brain has in making beliefs, and can we become better believers?

The Believing Brain
Lecture 16—Transcript

Mr. Wright wasn't expected to make it through the night. He had cancer throughout his entire body, and in 1957 there was not much that could be done for him. But Mr. Wright had heard that there was a Dr. Klopfer who was doing an experiment with a new drug called Krebiozen. Dr. Klopfer agreed to put him on the study, admitted him into the hospital to give him the drug on a Friday, and left for the weekend. Dr. Klopfer really wasn't too confident that this was really going to be helpful, but basically the patient felt that he was in such desperate straits that this was his last chance and Dr. Klopfer agreed. On Monday, when Dr. Klopfer came back to the hospital, he really didn't even think that Mr. Wright would be alive; but not only was he alive, his tumors had actually shrunk to about half their size. Dr. Klopfer gave him that medicine for 10 more days and all the signs of his disease disappeared. Ultimately, Mr. Wright was discharged home with no evidence of cancer.

Two months later, the Food and Drug Administration reported that the studies with Krebiozen were ineffective. When Mr. Wright heard about the reports, he immediately became ill again and his tumors returned. Dr. Klopfer was a good scientist and he thought that maybe the response had something to do with the patient's belief that the drug worked even though the drug in and of itself wasn't working; so Dr. Klopfer readmitted Mr. Wright and gave him injections of just sterile water, even though he told the patient that it was a "new, super-refined, double strength product." Once again, Mr. Wright had a dramatic response and remained well for some time, until the newspaper published the headline "Nationwide Tests Show that Krebiozen is a Worthless Drug in the Treatment of Cancer." After reading this, again Mr. Wright fell ill, returned to the hospital, and died two days later. It seems on one hand that his belief in the drug was such a powerful mediator for the effect; and that once his belief in the drug disappeared, his resistance to the disease expired as well

What does this story tell us? Mr. Wright's case certainly is very dramatic; and it's probably even unique insofar as we don't typically think of cancer as being able to respond to a placebo like those injections of sterile water.

But in other ways, Mr. Wright's case is really just one of a remarkable many studies and examples of what scientists often call the "placebo effect." The placebo effect is the phenomenon whereby a placebo improves a patient's condition simply because the patient has the belief that it will be effective.

I'm sure that many of you have heard about the placebo effect, but modern medicine has a generally negative view about it. Doctors tend to look at the placebo effect as kind of being unreal or maybe even being the power of nothing. But if the power of nothing is very powerful, maybe we should try to understand it a little bit more. In my role as director of research at the Myrna Brind Center of Integrative Medicine at Thomas Jefferson University in Philadelphia, I've often felt that doctors need to give more consideration to the placebo effect. In fact, if the placebo effect works, why don't doctors use it more often? Most research studies have shown that the placebo effect works on average in about a third of the situations; and in some studies, the placebo effect is actually seen in as many as two-thirds of patients. This is particularly true in studies of psychiatric disorders such as depression or anxiety; in fact, in those conditions, the placebo sometimes works as well if not better than traditional antidepressant and anti-anxiety medications.

Given these fascinating statistics, some scientists have tried to unravel the mystery of the placebo effect. I actually found three brain scan studies that were particularly enlightening regarding the mechanism of the placebo effect. One of the studies looked at people with depression; and in that study they looked at the effect of the placebo on the brain's serotonin receptors. What they found was that the brain released serotonin when the patient responded to the placebo. Another study looked at pain; and what they found is that when people responded to the placebo when they had pain, they actually had a release of the brain's own opiate molecules, the endorphins, in the brain. The final study that I found was a study of patients with Parkinson's disease; and in these patients, who actually have a complete deterioration of their dopamine system, when they responded to the placebo and their symptoms got better their brain found a way to release dopamine.

To me, these studies are very compelling and tell us something about how the beliefs that we have that help us to engage the placebo effect can have such a powerful and very specific effect on the human brain and ultimately our body.

But beliefs have an impact on many other aspects of our lives, and therefore we find them in advertising; in our cultural interactions with other people; certainly in our politics and what we think is right and wrong in politics, and who should be our president and who should represent us; we have moral beliefs; and, of course, the traditional way we think of beliefs is that we have religious and spiritual beliefs. Even though beliefs are all around us, we might wonder a little bit about why do we need them so much? Why does our brain create beliefs? In fact, we might ask the question: Why do we believe anything at all?

This is one of the questions that has perplexed me since I was a child and propelled me down his entire path of exploring the topic of the spiritual brain; because to some degree in my mind I realized that if we exist in the universe—the universe is everything that's out there—somewhere our brain is moving through this universe and only has access to a very small percentage of that everything. Think about it: You're listening to my lecture right now and your brain is taking in that information. But it doesn't know what's going on in the next house, or the next city, or the next country; your brain only has the information upon which it receives right at that moment. On top of that, the brain filters out a lot of the information that it receives so that you're actually only consciously aware of a very small amount of what's out there in the world. Our brain is ultimately left with trying to derive our entire understanding of the universe by working with a very tiny amount of information.

I would argue that we need to establish beliefs—the brain needs to establish beliefs—so that we can work at all effectively in the world; that we can navigate ourselves through the world and survive. I would argue that the brain is and has to be a believing machine; it needs to create those beliefs so that we can survive.

But what exactly are beliefs? According to the *Oxford English Dictionary*, a belief can be defined as the following: A belief is "a feeling that something exists or is true, especially one without proof." This is an interesting definition because one of the things that it does is it draws a distinction between things that can and can't be proven. But what constitutes a "proof?" There are very different approaches to what constitutes a truth; it's very different for science, for religion, for philosophy. In the scientific model that I tend to live in as a researcher, for me a proof is a "randomized double blind placebo-controlled trial." But that doesn't necessarily follow for someone who's trying to make a philosophical argument and trying to find a philosophical proof of something, or somebody who's religious and who wants to have some kind of proof that there religion is the right way to think.

I actually would think about beliefs a little bit differently; and again, I'm looking at this a little bit from a brain perspective. We talked about in a much earlier lecture the importance of operationalizing some of our definitions, and I want to do that for the definition of belief right now. I'd say that a belief can be defined biologically and psychologically as "any perception, cognition, emotion, or memory that a person consciously or unconsciously assumes to be true."

Why did I choose this definition? There are a couple of important points to it: One is that it speaks to the importance of our perception, our thoughts, and our emotions as helping us to generate our beliefs. A little later in this lecture, we're going to see exactly how all those different components come together to help us form our beliefs. But the definition also includes another important aspect: that beliefs can be conscious or unconscious. Why is this important?

There are some interesting studies that have shown how important the unconscious mind is for the things that we do and the ways that we think; and it turns out that so often it's the case that when we're making our decisions about life that these unconscious beliefs keep cropping up and affecting the decisions that we make. Our beliefs can be conscious, they may be unconscious, but either way they have a very powerful effect on the ways in which we deal and go about our lives. Ultimately within the brain, these different elements are all swirling about; our perceptions, our thoughts, our emotions, and even the ways in which our brain interacts with other people. That's a very important piece to the beliefs that we hold as well, which we'll explore in a few moments. Let's think about these different elements of beliefs and how they work; how well they work, and how well they may not work.

We've already talked a little bit about the fact that the brain exists in a huge, infinite world; and the brain, even though it takes in a very small amount of the overall information, is still taking in millions of pieces of information and only a very limited amount of that actually even reaches our consciousness. There are many pieces that remain in our subconscious mind, and unfortunately the brain tries to fix all of these things that are missing; it fills in perceptual gaps, it even makes mistakes (as we'll see in just a few moments). But one of the things that, to me, is sometimes the most amusing but also the most problematic is that the brain never bothers to tell us when it's made a mistake. We all go through our lives believing the things that we do, thinking that we believe them and thinking that we understand them, even though our brain may be fooling us all the time. Let's see how this may happen.

Let's talk about the perceptions that come into our brain. We may be having all of our beliefs sit on a mountain of misperceptions. In fact, studies have shown that there are so many ways of tricking the brain from a perceptual point of view; illusions can be generated in so many different ways that will fool the brain. For example, one type of illusion is where we actually may see a shape in a picture that isn't really there. Maybe we'd see the corners of a square, for example, but we don't actually see the square; and yet somehow our mind fills in the lines, and we can actually see the lines and the shading around the lines that's important for creating the shape even though it actually isn't there. Other illusions rely on more complex patterns: Maybe a checkerboard kind of pattern that typically has its lines all very horizontal and parallel and perpendicular, and yet there can be a way to make a checkerboard look as if all of the lines have a curvature in them; even though you know that the lines are straight, you can't help but see the curvature.

These are just static illusions. One of the most interesting illusions I came across on the internet was a little dragon statue that's just sitting there on a table and it has a little face that looks at you, and as you walk around this statue it looks like that little dragon keeps following you with its eyes; and whether you look up or down or left or right, it keeps following you and looks like it's moving around with you to follow you, even though it obviously is remaining perfectly still.

At one level, the brain sometimes makes us believe that we see things that aren't really there. It sometimes constructs a reality that, on closer examination, turns out to be nothing more than an illusion. But even beyond the question of illusions, the brain is always constructing perceptions of the external world. Now the question becomes: What does our brain do with those perceptions?

Basically, it begins to think about them. The perceptions come in through the brain—through the eyes, ears, and so forth—and now you start to apply your cognitive processes to help interpret those perceptions and to try to create for us a sense of what that world is. Interestingly, our cognitive processes actually do a lot with those perceptions. They tell us how things work; they find causality in the world; they try to establish connections between objects in the world; and therefore these cognitions help us to make sense out of those perceptions. In fact, to some degree the cognitions help us to find those "proofs" that we were talking about earlier in our definition of beliefs. We see something happen, and we now use our cognitive processes to compare that to what we have in our memory. Does it make sense to us? If we hear a story on the street, if we read something in the newspaper or watch something on television, are we applying that information in a way that makes sense to us; and can we use that to create our beliefs and also to defend and maintain them? After all, if you confront somebody who has a different kind of belief than you, you'll use your cognitive processes to try to convince them otherwise.

One of the tools that cognition also uses to help to build and maintain our beliefs is our memory. For example, the memory that someone once snubbed us at a party serves as a "proof" for our belief that this individual is hostile to us and therefore is a person that should be avoided. But how reliable is memory? In the 1980 presidential campaign, Ronald Reagan would sometimes cite the story of a World War II pilot whose plane had been hit by enemy fire. He was going to jump from the plane, but one of the crewmen was too injured to jump; and the pilot said, "Never mind, we'll ride it down together." Reagan would even sometimes have tears in his eyes while telling this story. It turns out that this actually never happened in real life but was a scene from a movie called *A Wing and a Prayer*. But in Ronald Reagan's brain, it made him think that this was something that really happened.

This, of course, happens to all of us. Just as our brains fill in the gaps of our visual perceptions so that we sometimes see things that aren't really there, our cognition can kind of grab these different bits and pieces of information and put together an entire story, which often may be false, and nevertheless feels as if it represents a true reality; a story that we believe because we think that we're accurately remembering the way things really happened. You can even reflect back in your own life the ways in which you've tried to remember things or used your memory; how often have you said something only to have a spouse or a friend say, "No, no, no, that's not the way it happened at all." Indeed, one of the reasons that memories—even the false ones—can be so powerful is that they often contain such strong emotions that are attached to them. Again, think about the example from Ronald Reagan: Those tears in his eyes were real; that emotion was very real for him, even though the memory wasn't inaccurate.

Emotions are also very important for placing value on our beliefs. In fact, strong emotions elicit strong beliefs Again, remember: Why does this happen? Because your brain wants to remember important things and forget the unimportant ones. It assesses what's going on around it, and it uses its emotional powers to decide what things are important and what things aren't important. Of course, this pertains to both positive and negative emotions; in fact, negative emotions actually typically have an even more powerful effect on what we remember. If we think back again to what happened in 9/11/2001, it was that negative emotion that made those memories so powerful for us. But, of course, positive emotions can also create very powerful memories for us and ultimately very powerful beliefs.

We also use our emotions to help us to defend our beliefs. I mentioned a few moments ago that the first thing that we do to confront somebody who has a different belief system from us is that we start to logically, rationally try to convince them otherwise. But what happens when that doesn't work? Things get heated; our emotions kick in and we use our emotions to try to support and defend our beliefs. Perceptions and thoughts that don't have a strong emotional content may actually never become a part of our belief system, but those that do wind up becoming a very essential element of what our beliefs are all about.

In fact, there's one other important element to our belief system as it pertains to emotions, and that has to do with what happens when we wind up confronting evidence that goes against our emotions? In that case, we see how our brain responds to that in such a way that we have a decision to make: We have to decide whether our existing belief system is correct or the other belief system is correct. When we're confronted with this paradox, our emotions are triggered; we don't like the fact that we might be wrong and our emotions take over to try to reestablish our beliefs and to argue very strongly against an alternative belief system. This actually spills over into how we interact with other people, and how that has an important role in shaping our beliefs.

We've seen that our beliefs are shaped by the way the brain perceives the world, by how the brain thinks and remembers our world, and how we feel emotionally about those experiences; but social beliefs are also very important in influencing the beliefs that we hold. Beliefs are actually incredibly strongly influenced by other individuals that we interact with throughout our life. Think about your own life and think about your own beliefs. Where did your beliefs come from? For most of us, our initial beliefs come from our parents. They help to form our initial beliefs about everything: about how to be a good person, what we should do when we're working, what political party to believe in, and what religious ideas and beliefs we should hold. As we get older, we begin to have interactions with society at large; we begin to interact with our peers, our teachers; and all of them contribute to and affect our belief systems. Society can actually be set up in such a way that it leads to beliefs of an entire population, which can be cultural, political, or religious; and we see large groups that come together that help the individuals form their beliefs.

In fact, studies have shown that group consensus heavily influences our beliefs. Some very simple studies have been done where they put a test subject into a room with one, two, or even more other people who try to convince the test subject of a particular answer. What's interesting is that the more people you put into the room that try to convince them of a specific answer, the more that test subject is likely to accept that answer even though it's so obvious that the answer is wrong.

Given the influences of our perceptions, emotions, thoughts, and social interactions, how do beliefs actually form and work in the brain? If you remember from one of our earlier lectures, we talked about the fact that neurons that fire together wire together. The neurotransmitters that we've talked about, the nerve cells as they interact with each other, literally strengthen the connections when we use them. If we have a particular belief, the more we bring our mind to that belief, the stronger those connections become. Of course, the brain also works in the context of "use it or lose it"; so as those beliefs that you hold you begin to kind of let certain beliefs go, those connections literally become weakened.

When we do have an emotion or a thought that we focus on, those neural connections actually support that particular belief; it strengthens that belief. If it's true that neurons that fire together wire together, then the more that we get neurons to fire together, the stronger that belief becomes. Repetition is therefore an essential element for forming and strengthening beliefs. But are there religious and spiritual activities that are repetitive? Almost all of religious rituals and practices are repetitive. Remember, that was one of the essential elements as to why they've created such powerful experiences for us, and that's part of why those kinds of practices also have such a powerful impact on our belief system. This is why practices like meditation, prayer, and other types of religious rituals work so well: because they're very repetitious.

In fact, the more we continue to focus on a particular religious or spiritual idea through a practice like meditation or prayer, the more that becomes the belief that's ingrained within the neural connections of our brain. As we also have found, it's very important to tie our beliefs to other useful information and to our behaviors. We use our emotions to support the beliefs that we hold, and we reject beliefs, ideas, and data that contradict those that we hold. Of course, these processes are true for all beliefs; not just religious and spiritual ones, but social ones, political ones, and scientific ones.

I want to return to my earlier statement that the brain really is a believing machine. Our beliefs are constructed out of our perceptions, our emotions, our thoughts, and the personal interactions that we have with other people. As each of these different factors affects the very neural connections of our brain, they also affect our beliefs. But while the brain does a great job formulating beliefs that work well for us and help us to understand our world, beliefs are also fraught with many potential flaws. We've seen that the brain can make many mistakes at all different levels while constructing its beliefs. It can make mistakes in its perceptions; it can make mistakes in terms of how it remembers things; it can use emotion in ways that may be too strong or too weak to support a particular belief; and, of course, all of our beliefs ultimately can be heavily influenced by those individuals who are around us, the people that we rely on the most.

So while we often think that our beliefs are so much a part of who we are . . .

The Brain's Influence on Religious Ideas
Lecture 17

In this lecture, you will explore how specific religious and theological ideas might arise in the brain and why they might be compelling to thinking creatures. You will also learn how religious ideas can derive from a variety of brain processes. These ideas can range from the practical or mundane to the very esoteric or even mystical. It may be that this entire range—all of the religious ideas that human beings are capable of having—are not only related to brain functions, but are also structured and limited by what our brain can do.

Definitions and the Brain
- Let's return to some of the definitions from an earlier lecture and see how they may be related to specific brain functions. First, you have to realize that these definitions are conceived via the processes of the human brain.

- The terminology that has defined and described religion and spirituality uses cognitions, emotions, and perceptions. Can this be tied to neuropsychology? What room is there for a soul?

- Definitions can come from many different points of view. The brain of a scientist may use the previously described operational definitions.

- For example, in Lecture 2, spirituality was defined as the subjective feelings, thoughts, experiences, and behaviors that arise from a search or quest for the sacred. In this definition, "search" refers to attempts to identify, articulate, maintain, or transform, and "sacred" refers to what the individual perceives as a divine being, ultimate reality, or ultimate truth.

- This definition includes the criteria for spirituality and/or a search for nonsacred goals (such as identity, belonging, meaning, health, or wellness) in the context of spiritual criteria. In addition, the means and methods of the search receive general validation and support from within an identifiable group of people.

- Would the brain of a sociologist, philosopher, or theologian come to the same definition? Would it rely on the same abstract concepts, such as search and sacred, binary comparisons of sacred and nonsacred, or even the notion of differentiating spirituality from religiousness and both positive and negative emotions?

- Given how the brain might look at definitions, how might the brain look at more specific religious and spiritual concepts?

How the Brain Turns Spiritual Experiences into Religious Ideas

- The previously mentioned definitions and descriptions provide a way to begin to understand spirituality and religion, and the following are some of the basic ways in which our brain processes information that also bears directly on religious and theological ideas.

- The causal function is located in the region of the inferior parietal lobe, and it enables us to determine cause and effect. When the causal function is applied to the physical world, the result is the scientific method. When the causal function is applied to the human world, the result is social science. When the causal function is applied to the spiritual realm, the results are concepts related to God or ultimate reality.

- What would happen if our brain did not have a causality mechanism? How would we perceive God then? God could be perceived as being loving—but not as the cause of all things. Of course, what our brain thinks has no real bearing on what reality actually is. If we don't believe in gravity, we still will fall down if we jump off a ladder.

- The abstract function is located in the region of the superior temporal lobe and is closely associated with language. The abstract function allows for the categorization of things. When applied to the spiritual realm, the abstract function enables a discussion of various religious concepts related to religious practices, meaning, and morals and ethics. This function also provides the basis for rational thought by holding various representations of objects for analysis.

- The brain's causal and abstract functions lead to specific kinds of concepts and ideas when they are applied to the nonphysical, or spiritual, realm. What about the other brain mechanisms? How do they shape and influence our religious ideas?

- The binary function is located at the junction of the superior temporal and inferior parietal lobes. The binary function helps us to create a comparison of opposites. For example, it establishes our concept of good and evil, right and wrong, and heaven and hell.

- In religion, the basic opposite is God versus man. In fact, this is the fundamental problem in all religions. The mythic structure of religions attempts to resolve these opposites—by holistic functioning, for example.

- Scientifically, the holistic function allows us to look at the whole rather than the parts. Doctors in integrative medicine advocate the need to look at the whole person in terms of their biological, psychological, spiritual, and social domains. To truly heal someone, the holistic function of these doctors tells them to look at everything working as a whole.

- The holistic function appears to be partly related to right-brain function and may be related to the blocking of sensory information that occurs during practices such as meditation or prayer. This leads to an experience of things being considered as a whole.

- Of course, the sense of wholeness or oneness can vary. In fact, there may be a unitary continuum of human experience and thought, including the emergence of the sense of oneness as a property of smaller processes, a oneness of God, and a oneness of all things.

- The concept of God as a unifying force is important to the sense of wholeness or oneness. In addition, there is a need to consider the individual characteristics of God as a part of the whole. This sense of oneness is also an important element in the creation of social cohesion.

- The opposite of the holistic function is the reductionist function, which is related to left-brain function and is located in the temporoparietal junction. This function attempts to break down things into their parts.

- Theological development based on foundational myth is the basic reductionist function associated with religious thought. It starts with a basic story and breaks it down into many individual parts and interpretations.

- We see this as the basis of theology—including books such as the Talmud in Jewish thought—which takes the primary sacred text and stories and breaks them down into concrete ways so that we can understand them. When something cannot be reduced, it is possible to miss the big picture.

© Stockbyte/Thinkstock.

- The causal, abstract, binary, holistic, and reductionistic functions of the human brain all help us to process the enormous amount of data coming into our brains from the external world.

Sacred texts, such as the Talmud, attempt to break down stories into their individual parts so our brain can understand them.

Relying on these functions, the brain is able to construct a reality that works for us as humans.

- The important thing to remember is that these same functions that we apply to the physical world must also be applied to the spiritual realm. These functions allow us to form concepts about such notions as God, the soul, and the afterlife.

- Two other brain functions that are crucial to the way we develop religious ideas are the quantitative function and the emotional function. The quantitative function is obviously used in mathematics and science, but it also relates to special numbers in religion—specifically, to the assignment of meaning to numbers.

- With all of these cognitive processes that our brain can use, perhaps the most important aspect of brain function that leads to religious and spiritual ideas is our emotional system.

- We have a need to organize all of our thoughts based on some emotional value, which helps us establish a hierarchical ordering of thoughts and concepts. Our emotional system is theologically associated with emotions such as love, agape, joy, and awe.

- The Judeo-Christian idea of redemption emerges out of several brain processes, including the binary—being saved versus not being saved—and the abstract—understanding what redemption is in the first place.

- The impact of redemption on the believer is more potent and durable because it involves an emotional component—not just the idea that God saves, in the abstract, but that concretely God redeems us (a people) or you (a person) from some form of oppression and bondage. Often, it's the emotion aroused by an idea that gives it significance and staying power among generations of believers. This makes sense from a neuroscientific perspective because the brain isn't designed to be purely rational.

- Let's revisit how the brain may help us to understand and respond to myths and rituals. Myth involves binary function and holistic function. Rituals enable an acting out of myth, which involves multiple sensory systems—including sight, sound, smell, and physical activity. In addition, there are both cognitive and emotional components.

- All of these elements affect the development of our own spiritual beliefs. The myths and rituals help the brain create all kinds of religious ideas, but if all of these different things—myths, rituals, and doctrines—have an impact on our various religious beliefs, then how can we begin to think about and define the ideas that arise from some of the most powerful spiritual experiences?

Describing Mystical Experiences

- There are several ways in which people have described powerful spiritual, or mystical, experiences.

- A scholar named Walter Stace talked about extrovertive unitary experiences, and he defined them as having a unifying vision in which the person sees all things as one. This is related to the notion of the brain's holistic process, which includes the concrete apprehension of the "one" as being something that is internal to us—something that we feel.

- There's also the sense of an objective reality of the experience; it feels real to us. In addition, there are feelings of peace and of something that's sacred.

- Some of these powerful experiences feel very paradoxical. They wreak havoc with our binary processes because suddenly things that seemed to be completely oppositional of each other are being brought together and are making sense to us. Ultimately, many people who have these experiences say they're ineffable, or indescribable by language. If this is true, then maybe those areas that help with abstract thought and language are just not able to interact with these particular experiences.

- What happens when we're not able to process these experiences in the same way? Obviously, they're going to lead to very different kinds of experiences and very different kinds of ideas than the ones that we normally have.

- Stace also talked about other types of mystical experiences that include a unitary consciousness—a sense of pure consciousness or awareness in which all the person experiences is the experience itself.

- Stace also talks about mystical experiences as being nonspatial and nontemporal. This relates to the orientation part of the brain—the part of the brain that helps us feel spatial and temporal relations and how we relate to the world.

- All of these different processes of the brain come about in these very intense experiences. Then, they come together, and the person has to extract from them meaning and understanding.

- Religion is associated with many different characteristics—not just mystical ones. Religious experiences can include practices such as forgiveness, worship, prayer, Bible studies, and group ritual. Religion is also associated with feelings and behaviors related to awe, charity, love, and altruism and theological principles of morality, causality, numerology, ontology, and epistemology.

Suggested Reading

Gay, ed, *Neuroscience and Religion*.

Mecklenburger, *Our Religious Brains*.

Newberg, *Principles of Neurotheology*.

Newberg and Waldman, *How God Changes Your Brain*.

1. How do specific brain processes, such as causality, influence our religious and spiritual beliefs?

2. Can we use brain studies to address questions such as whether we have free will?

The Brain's Influence on Religious Ideas
Lecture 17—Transcript

Where does a religious idea come from? What gives birth to theological concepts? For example, we may hear a philosopher say that "God is the unmoved mover," or a theologian might argue that "God cannot be the author of evil in the world"; but how does the brain arrive at these conclusions? Even more important, why do assertions like these seem so compelling to us human beings? Why do they make sense to so many of us and even take their place as doctrines to which millions of people willingly subscribe?

These are the sort of questions that we'll be addressing today. Now that we have a better understanding overall of how our thoughts and beliefs are related to the brain's functions, we're going to look at specific religious and theological ideas and explore both how they might arise in the brain and also why they might be so compelling to thinking creatures like us.

The first thing that we should do is return to some of the definitions that we considered in an earlier lecture and see how they may be related to specific brain functions. First, we have to realize that these definitions are, in fact, conceived via the processes of the human brain. We can ask questions such as: How has religion and spirituality been defined and described by the human brain? To some degree, whatever definitions we come to, we have to use terminology that includes cognitive elements, things that we think abstractly; different emotions that have to do with how we feel about our religious and spiritual ideas and beliefs; as well as the perceptions that we have about the world. We can also tie all of this into our neuropsychology, because when we start to talk about our cognitions, we can talk about the areas of our brain that help us to think things through, to think abstractly, and so forth. We can talk about the limbic system and its effect on emotions and how those emotions play out in our definitions and our ideas about religion and spirituality. Of course, if we keep all of our focus on the human brain, one other question that often comes up is: Where's the room for the soul? Where's the room for that part of us that's spiritual that may have nothing to do specifically with our biology?

So let's return to some of our earlier definitions. Again, definitions can come from many different points of view, and hence many different kinds of brains. For example, the brain of a scientist like myself may use the previously described operational definitions; so we may talk about spirituality as being the subjective feelings, thoughts, experiences, and behaviors that arise from a search or quest for the sacred. You probably remember this definition, but it speaks very specifically to some of these brain processes; and therefore the brain of a scientist likes this definition because it can help us grab hold of it in a more effective way and actually apply our scientific techniques to try to learn more about what spirituality is. Religiousness, on the other hand, includes the criteria for spirituality and/or it includes the search for non-sacred goals. If you remember, the non-sacred goals include things like identity and belonging, which are also feelings and ideas that are manifested through the functions of the human brain.

Ultimately, part of what's also important in the context of religiousness is that the means and methods are defined by a population of people. What does that mean to define these ideas by a population of people? That means you need an entire group of brains basically that are coming together to think about how they define themselves, the ideas that they hold to be sacred, and how they understand that in the context of their lives.

Again, I mentioned this is a series of definitions from the brains of scientists; but what would the brain of a sociologist, a philosopher, or even a theologian come to in thinking about the definitions for spirituality or religiousness? Would they rely on the same kinds of abstract concepts such as the concept of a search or the concept of something sacred? Of course, the binary comparisons; remember we have this binary processing in our brain that allows us to make a distinction between that which is sacred and that which is non-sacred, or even the notion of trying to differentiate spirituality from religiousness. In addition, when we talk about religiousness and spirituality, we talk about emotions; and our binary processes help us to define the difference between the positive and negative emotions.

Given how the brain might look at definitions, now we can start to explore a little bit more deeply as to how the brain may look at more specific religious and spiritual concepts. Let's look at some of these specific concepts and think about the different cognitive functions that we've talked about in previous lectures and how they would relate to these different religious ideas. As we've seen, it's the very nature of the brain to try to make some kind of sense both of the external world as well as whatever we're feeling on the inside. What I'd like to do next is to describe the tools and processes by which the brain makes sense of all of our thoughts, feelings, and experiences. In other words, I'd like to explore the mechanisms by which the brain turns spiritual experiences into religious ideas.

The above definitions and descriptions provide a way to begin to understand spirituality and religion, but can we be more specific about how the brain actually helps us to understand them? The following are some of the basic ways that we've touched on throughout the course in which our brain processes information and that bears directly on specific religious and theological ideas. Let's start with that causal function. You may remember that the causal function is probably located in the region of the junction between the parietal lobe, which is located towards the back part of the brain, and the temporal lobe, which is located along the side of the brain. This is an area that helps us with a lot of abstract ideas and concepts and seems to be fundamentally involved in our experience of causality.

Causality, this causal function, actually enables us to determine causes and effects in the world. If we apply the causal function to the physical world, the result is the scientific method; it's our ability to try to understand all the things that are going on in the material world that we can apply science to and try to understand how different things affect other things, how they work, and so forth. If we apply the causal function to the human world, the result may be social sciences. How do we as human beings function with each other? How do we talk to each other? How do we resolve conflicts among different populations of people? All of these very intriguing issues and questions come up when we apply causality to that domain of existence.

When the causal function is applied to the spiritual realm, the results are probably religious concepts related to God or ultimate reality. For those of you who go back to remembering some of what you learned back in your college days in terms of philosophy, Aristotle talked about causality in a very explicit way. In fact, he actually talked about four different kinds of causality—efficient causality, material causality, formal causality, and final causality—and if you apply these different ideas about the nature of causality, how things work, and apply this to God you get some very important religious and spiritual concepts.

What would happen if the brain didn't have a causal mechanism? How would it begin to think about God? Could it perceive God as being able to cause the universe to come into existence or to cause the universe to perpetually be in existence? Again, if you didn't have this causal function in the brain—if that part was somehow magically removed from your brain—you couldn't think about God that way; you'd have to think about God in some other way. Perhaps your limbic system would take over and maybe you'd think about God in a more emotional way; maybe you'd think about God as being an ultimate loving thing or being in the universe. But God would never be able to be perceived as the cause of all things because that's not what your brain has the capability of doing. Of course, there's one other big problem with all of this: Whatever our brain thinks has no true bearing on what the reality actually is. For example, if we don't happen believe in gravity and we jump off of a ladder, we still will fall down. So irrespective of what we believe about God, whether God exists and if God does exist what God's like, the idea about how our causal function—or any of the functions that we'll be talking about in this lecture—actually have an impact on what God is, that's something that's still open for debate.

The next function I'd like to look at is the abstract function. This is the function of the brain that actually allows us to think about things in an abstract way. To some degree, this is probably in the region of that temporal lobe and parietal lobe junction that we've been talking about; probably a little bit more in the temporal lobe because it's also very associated with language. The abstract function allows us to categorize things. For example, it's the abstract function that allows us to look at an elm, a spruce, and a maple and say, "These are all trees." It can apply a categorization to things, and it can allow us to manipulate these different ideas.

What will happen if we apply the abstract function of the brain into the spiritual realm? This really enables for a discussion of a large variety of different religious concepts. These concepts may relate to different religious practices, aspects about religious and spiritual meaning, morals, and ethics. It's our abstract process of the brain that allows us to bring some kind of rational thought to whatever ideas that we have before us, whether they're religious or otherwise; and therefore it provides a basis for how we begin to think about all of these different religious and spiritual concepts.

To some degree, this abstract process may even be responsible for our sense of "thingness"; how we decide that something actually is a thing. The reason that I say that is that by categorizing "thing," it tells us how things are and how things relate to each other, so we start to think about the religious things— God, morality, maybe even things like angels, Heaven and Hell— our abstract abilities of the brain allow us to begin to understand what these things actually are, try to apply some overall understanding to them, and make them something that we as human beings can grasp and make a part of our belief systems.

So the brain's causal and abstract functions lead to a very specific kind of concept, very specific kinds of ideas, when they're applied to this non-physical or spiritual realm. But what about the brain's other mechanisms, the brain's other processes? How do they shape and influence our religious ideas?

In the past, we've talked a lot about the binary functioning of the brain. This function is also located in the region between the temporal and the parietal lobes; there's a lot that goes on right here. As we've seen in previous lectures, the binary function probably helps us to create a comparison of opposites. Growing up it helped us to determine synonyms and antonyms of words, and in a religious or spiritual context the binary process is really fundamental to developing so many of the ideas that we hold as part of religious and spiritual traditions. The binary process helps us to establish the concepts of good and evil, right and wrong, or Heaven and Hell. Therefore, when we address these particular ideas in a religious or spiritual way, that binary process is what holds them up for us to evaluate; to determine what we think is good and bad, what we think is right and wrong.

Of course, in religion, perhaps the most fundamental opposite is God versus human beings. This is, after all, the most fundamental issue that all religions have to face: If there is a God and God is this infinite, omniscient being that floats around in the universe, how do we as very finite mortal human beings have any kind of connection with God? This is what the mythic structure actually helps us to do, which is to take these opposites and somehow reconcile them, somehow bring them together; and therefore it uses another aspect of the brain's functions: the holistic function.

Scientifically, the holistic function allows us to look at the whole rather than the parts. I've mentioned a few times before that my current position is a doctor of integrative medicine; and in that role, I always talk about the need to look at the whole person in terms of their biological, psychological, spiritual, and social domains. For me to truly heal someone, my holistic function tells me that I have to look at all of these different domains; I need to look at everything working together as a whole. As we previously discussed, the holistic function appears to be partly related to the right brain's functioning, and it may also be particularly related to the ability of our brain to preferentially block sensory information as it's going into the parietal lobe—that orientation part of the brain—because as that area's deprived of information, it begins to give us a sense where we lose our sense of self; a sense of oneness, a sense of interconnectedness of all things. We've also found that this is a kind of experience and a kind of brain state that's frequently found in practices like meditation and prayer; so it makes sense that these practices will lead to ideas in which we experience God or the universe as a whole. Therefore, our holistic process of the brain becomes very relevant in trying to understand a holistic view of God or religion.

Of course, the sense of wholeness or oneness can vary from individual to individual; and, in fact, I've actually argued that there may actually be a unitary continuum of human experience and thought. What I mean by this is that we can experience anywhere from a very distinct and separate sense of our self, to a feeling of some connectedness maybe with our family or with a spouse, to these very powerful mystical experiences where a person feels at one with everything. But we'll consider these kinds of experiences a little bit more later on in the course.

The holistic function also is related to the notion of the oneness of God. Certainly in the monotheistic traditions this was the primary concept that led to their coming into existence; this is the fundamental idea that separates the monotheistic traditions from the religious and spiritual ideas that came before: the notion that there aren't lots of different gods, there's just one God; and within this oneness of God there's a oneness of all things. The holistic function of the brain is perhaps one of the most crucial in terms of the monotheistic traditions and their idea about God as a unifying force of the entire universe.

Of course, there are some problems that arise when you bring in this holistic process of the brain because we also sometimes think about God as having different parts or different characteristics. In fact, in Christianity when we talk about the Father, the Son, and the Holy Spirit, these are three different parts of God that somehow the holistic function has to bring together into one; and therefore this sense of oneness is very fundamental to the notion of a doctrine about what God is and how we understand that concept that's so crucial to that religious tradition.

One final aspect that I think is relevant in the context of the holistic process of the brain is the adaptability of religions that we talked about in one of our early lectures and how that relates to social cohesion; the notion that by having a singular belief, all the people that are part of that belief become connected and become one. This holistic function is very important not only in terms of the doctrinal elements of religions, but also in terms of the practical nature of what they do for the group of people.

The opposite of the holistic function is a reductionist function in the brain. This is probably a little bit more on the left side of the brain and is in the region of the temporal lobes and a little bit of the parietal lobe. This reductionist process is where our brain tries to break down things into their individual parts. Again, if we applied this to the physical world, we'd get back to another element of science; and interestingly, science can go both holistically—trying to understand the whole world—and also trying to break it down into an individual part, individual components. If we think about the medical paradigm, we can think about the whole person but sometimes we need to just focus on what the heart is doing, or what different neurotransmitters are doing in the brain and how they work.

Theological development is also based on this reductionist process of the brain by taking the overarching doctrine, the overarching goal—what some people refer to as the foundational myth of the religion—and try to understand all of the things that derive from it. The reductionist process of the brain starts with a very basic story and breaks it down into many individual parts and interpretations. For example, we see this as the basis of theology including books such as the Talmud in Jewish thought. Again, here we see taking the primary sacred text of the Bible and breaking down each of these stories in very concrete ways so that we can understand them. For example, they may take a specific phrase out of the Bible and from that deduce all of the different rules of being kosher, or all the rules about how we're supposed to dress; and therefore this reductionist process allows us to deduce all of these different elements of what a religion is about and how people engage that religion on a very practical level.

Sometimes we run into problems because sometimes we can't reduce things; and that's where our reductionist function starts to get a little frustrated and it may even evoke an emotional response as well. We might wind up having to bring in other brain processes to try to rectify the problem. We might bring in the holistic function, or the binary function; and therefore we can use all of our different processes together. Of course, one of the other problems with the reductionist function is that sometimes we can miss the big picture.

So far we've looked at the causal, the abstract, the binary, the holistic, and the reductionist processes of the brain. All of these processes help us to sort through enormous amounts of data that come into our brain from the external world and try to make some sense out of it. We rely on these functions to be able to construct a reality that works for us as human beings. The important thing to remember is that these same functions that we apply to the physical world and to the human world are also applied to the religious and the spiritual realm. These functions allow us to form concepts about God, about the soul, about the afterlife, and so on.

Let's now turn to two other brain functions that I also think are very crucial in the ways in which we develop religious and spiritual ideas: the quantitative function and the emotional function of the brain. The quantitative function is something that ultimately helps us with developing mathematics, science, and statistics; that so much we understand. But because our brain feels that numbers play a very important role in how it understands the world, numbers also wind up playing a very special role in our religious and spiritual beliefs. For example, we assign meaning to certain numbers. If you go back into the Bible, for example, we find certain numbers over and over again: We find that it rained for 40 days and 40 nights; we find that Moses wandered through the desert with the Jews for 40 years. We're able to think about numbers in very powerful ways that we utilize to make our religious and spiritual beliefs more important to us. These numbers identify something that makes these ideas and concepts important to us; that make our brains take notice of them; and because of that, that's part of how we help to ingrain different religious and spiritual ideas and concepts into our ways of thinking about ourselves and about the world.

Finally, with all of these cognitive processes that our brain can use, perhaps the most important aspect of our brain's function that leads to religious and spiritual ideas is the emotional system. Remember, the emotional system is deeply tied into the limbic areas of the brain: the amygdala, the hippocampus, the hypothalamus; these are very central structures that enable us to feel all the different emotions that we have throughout our day and apply these emotions to the various ideas and concepts that we develop throughout our lives.

We need to organize all of our thoughts to some degree based on emotional value. These emotions help us to establish a hierarchical ordering of thoughts and concepts; the emotions tell us what ideas are the most important. Think about a religious or spiritual idea: Every religion has not just one but often many; and therefore we have to decide which of those ideas are the most crucial, the most important, for that religious tradition. How do we make that decision? Ultimately it seems to come down to a large extent to the emotions that we have. In fact, some people have even argued that emotions are necessary for rational thought because the rational thought just gives us the ideas—it allows us to think about them, to manipulate them—but it's the emotions that actually tell us which of these are important.

You might think, for example, of the Judeo-Christian idea of redemption. Here's an idea that emerges out of several different brain processes including the binary process (the idea of being saved or not being saved), the abstract process (understanding what redemption is in the first place); but ultimately the impact of this idea on the believer is more potent and durable because it involves an emotional component. It's not just the idea that God saves us in the abstract form, but that somehow concretely God actually redeems human beings; redeems them in terms of helping them to break out of oppression, bondage, and create a sense of freedom. Often it's the emotions that are aroused by this particular idea that give it its significance and staying power among generations of believers.

Of course, this all makes perfect sense from a neuroscientific perspective because as we've seen, the brain isn't designed to be purely rational. We need to turn to our emotions to help us understand all the things that are going around us; and even when we look at the myths and the rituals that people have developed that we've talked about in prior lectures, we understand that it involves all of these different processes put together. Myths involve the binary function, the holistic function, brings them all together; uses rituals to help act out the mystic elements; brings in all different kinds of sensory systems that affect our hearing, sight, and the smells. All of this comes together to create a sense of how we understand something. It has an impact on our cognitive processes, and more importantly the emotional processes that make it so important to who we are.

But remember that all of these elements affect the development of our spiritual beliefs. The myths, the rituals, help the brain create all kinds of religious ideas. But if all of these different things—these myths, rituals, and the doctrines that are part of these religious traditions—have an impact on all of the various religious beliefs, how can we begin to think about and define the ideas that arise from some of the most powerful spiritual experiences?

There are several ways in which people have described some of these truly powerful—maybe we'd even describe them as "mystical"—experiences; and while we'll consider them in more detail in a later lecture, I want to spend a few minutes introducing how these experiences relate to brain processes and more specifically religious and spiritual ideas, the kinds that we've been talking about in this particular lecture.

A scholar named Walter Stace talked about extrovertive unitary experiences, and he defined them as having a unifying vision, where the person sees all things as one. That should trigger in our mind the notion of the holistic process of the brain. It also includes the concrete apprehension of the One as being something that's internal to us; something that we feel. Think again about the parts of our brain that help us to feel things and to feel that connectedness with things. There's the sense of an objective reality of the experience; it feels real to us. We'll be talking about how the brain processes a sense of reality in a future lecture. There's a feeling of peace, feelings of something that's sacred; all of these are playing out on our emotional systems in the limbic areas of the brain. Some of these powerful experiences are very paradoxical feeling; they really wreak havoc with our binary processes because suddenly things that seemed to be completely oppositional of each other are being brought together and make sense to us. Ultimately, many people who have these experiences say they're ineffable, indescribable by language; and if they're indescribable by language then maybe those areas that help with abstract thought and language are just not able to interact with these particular experiences.

What happens when we're not able to processes these experiences in the same way? Obviously they're going to lead to very different kinds of experiences and very different kinds of ideas than the ones that we normally think about. In fact, Stace also talked about other types of mystical experiences that include a unitary consciousness, a sense of pure consciousness or pure awareness where all the person experiences is experience itself. While I understand that might sound a little strange to some of you, it's something that nonetheless has been an important element of many of these different kinds of experiences.

Stace also talks about them as being non-spatial and non-temporal. Remember, this goes back to that orientation part of the brain; that part of the brain that helps us feel spatial and temporal relations and how we relate to the world. All of these different processes of the brain actually come about in these very intense experiences, and then come together where the person then has to extract from them meaning and understanding. In fact, if we go back to this concept of neurotheology—the notion of how we bring together the religious and spiritual ideas with what's going on in the brain itself—we can find that we can address not only these very powerful mystical experiences, but all the different aspects that make up religious and spiritual ideas.

A lot of the ideas that we already have talked about and some that we'll talk about—ideas about worship, prayer, ritual, feelings like love, charity, altruism—all of these things ultimately have some correlate with what's going on in the human brain, and the more that we can learn about what's happening in the human brain, the better we'll understand how all of these different religious and spiritual beliefs come about.

In this lecture, we've seen very broadly how religious and spiritual ideas can derive from a variety of brain processes. These ideas can range from the very practical or mundane things that we make a part of our everyday life to the very esoteric or even mystical; and it may be that this entire range—all of the religious ideas human beings are capable of having—aren't only related to brain functions, but are structured and limited by what our brain can do.

In the next lecture, we'll look at how the brain may affect our understanding of two very specific religious concepts: revelation and salvation.

Revelation, Salvation, and the Brain
Lecture 18

In this lecture, you will examine the way that the brain is involved in helping people understand two important religious concepts: revelation and salvation. These two concepts are fundamental to the teachings of a wide range of religious traditions—both ancient and modern, Eastern and Western—and the brain appears to be an essential element in these two religious experiences. Through our newfound abilities to study the brain, it is possible for us to ask and answer a lot of fascinating questions about how and why human beings experience revelation and salvation.

Defining Revelation and Salvation

- Revelation is the experience of receiving important information through active or passive communication with a supernatural or divine entity.

- Salvation is the deliverance of the soul from sin and its consequences. It may also be called deliverance or redemption from sin, which implies that—like revelation—salvation is experienced as being given by God.

- How might science approach the experience and claims of revelation? If revelation is a way of receiving information from God, then we can start by asking how we receive information from anything—such as another person.

- The part of the brain that helps us comprehend what another person is saying to us is the verbal-conceptual area. When someone is talking to us, we hear the words, connect the words to our memory system, and ultimately use our abstract brain processes to make sense of what is said.

- We can apply a similar scientific approach to revelation experiences. What do people hear when they receive a revelation, and how do they comprehend it?

Experiencing Revelation

- One pathway of revelation is a verbal experience: God is perceived to communicate with human beings in a direct way that provides specific verbal content. Orthodox Judaism and traditional Christianity generally hold that the first five books of Moses were dictated by God in such a fashion.

- Recall that our brain has the verbal abilities in its temporal lobe, and thus, language is one of the most effective ways for human beings to come to understand something. It would certainly make sense that our brain would be built in such a way to receive religious or spiritual information in a verbal manner.

- Another path is nonverbal revelation, in which the person perceives something about God, but it is not based in language. It is based on the brain's perceptions and abstract thought processes, but it is not specifically perceived in language. From the brain perspective, this is an interesting way that revelation occurs because we know that human beings can derive meaning and understanding from nonverbal communication.

- In fact, much of how we communicate with other people is through nonverbal cues. We look at someone's face or posture and glean a lot of information about them. The brain is designed to pick up on this type of information. In fact, nonverbal forms of communication might be much more important at times than verbal forms.

- The rhythms, music, and actions of ritual are a crucial part of making meaning, so the brain can certainly derive knowledge in nonverbal ways, and revelation would theoretically be no exception.

- The Aristotelian scholars of the medieval period espoused another way of receiving divine information. They held that revelation was the discovery of absolute truths about God through logical philosophical inquiry. In this way, the brain's rational thought processes were considered to be the means toward revelation.

- Where do our rational thought processes come from? We know that there are parts of the brain that think about causality, abstraction, and comparison in such a way that we can deduce new ideas, so this overall mechanism could be another possible way in which revelation occurs.

- Others, such as the philosopher Baruch Spinoza, suggest that God reveals himself through creation, and therefore, we can learn about religion and God by observing nature. Thus, the use of our brain in scientific inquiry—through physics, cosmology, and other fields— is the basis of revelation. In other words, the ability to see causality in the world, explore the world through questioning, and use the reductionistic processes of the brain may not merely be the way we perform science; for the religious individual, this may also be the way we receive information from and about God.

© Getty Images/Photos.com/Thinkstock.

Dutch Jewish philosopher Baruch Spinoza (1632–1677) believed that God reveals himself through creation.

- Ultimately, regardless of how a person might think revelation occurs, if we consider revelation in the context of the brain, we would likely conclude that revelation is the ability of the human brain to receive and be changed by a spiritual message. However, when we take a neuroscientific perspective on revelation, we also uncover some interesting questions. For example, what limitations might the brain place on the kind of information human beings can receive? How is the brain altered both during the revelation experience and in the transforming aftermath of that experience?

- Several scholars have stressed that revelation occurs all the time by various mechanisms. If this is the case from a religious perspective, then the brain must be involved. Of course, revelation is more religiously, rather than neurologically, oriented.

- However, the brain must interpret whatever information it perceives about God's active presence in the world, and the neuroscientific perspective provides insights into issues pertaining to revelation that were previously only the domain of religion and theology.

- For example, Christian theology has sometimes described a difference between communicable and incommunicable attributes of God. If human beings can only have access to communicable aspects of God, then there are specific limitations that are placed on the ability to perceive and understand God.

- Communicable attributes are usually related to those things that human beings can potentially perceive for themselves, such as mercy, justice, wrath, and love. From the neuroscientific perspective, we can understand and study the biological underpinnings of these attributes. We can look at the emotional system of the brain and see how it interacts with our abstract thought processes as we engage in feelings of mercy, justice, wrath, or love.

- Incommunicable attributes of God usually include those related to being omnipotent, eternal, infinite, omniscient, and omnipresent— things that human beings simply are not.

- The neurotheology perspective offers an explanation, though, as to why we can have some notion of the incommunicable concepts as well—even though we cannot truly understand them. After all, the brain does have some knowledge (omniscience), some idea of time (eternal), and some control over the universe (omnipotent). Thus, while the human brain cannot truly grasp the extent of these attributes, neurotheology would argue that they must be partially communicable at least insofar as the brain can provide a hint of these attributes, or at least abstractly conceptualize them.

- The brain can use its processes such as the holistic, binary, or causal processes to interpret the world around us, but then God or religious information can only be considered in certain ways—such as through our senses, emotions, and cognitions. If that is the case, then there theoretically should be a limited number of neurological avenues by which the human brain can experience revelation.

- It is likely that revelation is different for each individual's brain and, hence, each individual. The brain plays a fundamental role in revelation experiences, and its capabilities and limitations may have an impact on the nature and type of experiences.

Experiencing Salvation

- Depending on the religious tradition, salvation is considered to be caused either by the free will and grace of a deity (in theistic religions) or by personal responsibility and self-effort (in the yogic traditions of India, for example). Religions often emphasize the necessity of both personal effort—through repentance and asceticism—and divine action, such as grace.

- The concept of salvation as the phenomenon of being saved by divine agency belongs mostly to Christianity, Judaism, and Islam— the major monotheistic religions. Analogous concepts within Indian religions, such as nirvana, are not exact equivalents to the concept of salvation in that they do not depend upon divine agency per se. However, almost all religions speak of a way of saving the person or saving the person's soul.

- Author Ernest Valea suggested three aspects that are important to consider in assessing the experience of salvation: the resources needed for attaining salvation, the actual way of getting saved, and the meaning of being saved.

- These aspects are quite similar to scientific approaches to a variety of mechanistic questions. We often need to understand what is needed for a given physical phenomena, the mechanism by which it happens, and how we can understand the meaning of it.

- First, what are the resources necessary for attaining salvation? The brain is probably one of those resources. For salvation to occur, the brain has to comprehend what is needed and go about helping the person obtain the necessary resources. Furthermore, the resources might refer to a certain emotional attitude—such as feeling sorrow for sin—or to certain doctrines to be followed. Access to these resources is also supported by the brain processes.

- Second, what are the ways of getting saved? The brain helps us to understand what practices we must do, what beliefs we must hold, and what experiences we must have in order to be saved. If we have to do something such as behave in a particular way or do a practice such as prayer or meditation, it is the brain that helps us do it.

- Third, what is the meaning of being saved? The brain uses its cognitive processes to derive meaning from all of our thoughts, feelings, and experiences. To do this, we utilize our causal, abstract, and emotional processes. In the context of salvation, the meaning is compared to the overall understanding of the spiritual tradition and its doctrines and goals. Importantly, the brain must somehow be able to identify salvation as something truly remarkable and beyond the normal part of our experiences.

- In addition to applying the neuroscientific perspective to a general model of salvation like Valea's, we can also apply this perspective to the teachings of specific faith traditions.

- In Eastern traditions such as Buddhism or Sikhism, salvation appears to come from ending the cycle of suffering, death, and rebirth by attaining liberation and enlightenment. This occurs through intense contemplation and meditation and by moving one's life toward a detachment from the body and physical world.

- Meditation and related contemplative practices appear to have a dramatic impact on the brain's functioning both during meditation and after. These data support the notion that meditation practices result in a unique pattern of brain function and create an enduring response in the brain. It certainly seems conceivable that meditation can lead to a transformation of the person—one that is probably mediated in some way by the brain.

- Neurotheology can be of great help in understanding these different approaches toward salvation and determine which methods appear to be most conducive from an integrated physiological and theological perspective.

Suggested Reading

Arzy, Idel, Landis, and Blanke, "Why Revelations Have Occurred on Mountains."

Mecklenburger, *Our Religious Brains*.

Newberg, *Principles of Neurotheology*.

Questions to Consider

1. How does the brain enable us to exhibit behaviors that are frequently associated with religion, such as altruism or giving charity?

2. What is the brain process by which forgiveness occurs?

Revelation, Salvation, and the Brain
Lecture 18—Transcript

In our last lecture, we saw that the various functions of the human brain, such as the causal function and the holistic function, shape our ideas about the spiritual realm. We're now prepared to look at two very specific religious ideas: that of revelation and salvation. Our goal today is to examine the way that the brain is involved in helping us to understand these two very important religious concepts.

I've chosen to focus on revelation and salvation because these two concepts are fundamental to the teachings of a wide range of religious traditions; both ancient and modern, Eastern and Western. Let's start, as we often do, with some definitions. "Revelation" is the experience of receiving important information through either active or passive communication with a supernatural or divine entity. Salvation is the deliverance of the soul from sin and its consequences. It may also be called "deliverance" or "redemption" from sin, which implies that, like revelation, salvation is experienced as being given by God.

We'll return to salvation later in the lecture, but first let's focus on revelation. How might science approach the experience and claims of revelation? This seems like a rather big question, so maybe we can try to simplify it into some constituent parts. If revelation is a way of receiving information from God, we can start by asking: How does the brain receive information from anything, maybe like another person? We know that there are parts of the brain that help us to comprehend what another person is saying to us; this is that verbal conceptual area that we've spoken about in earlier lectures, probably located in the region between the temporal lobe and the parietal lobe along the side of the brain. So when someone is talking to us, we hear the words, connect the words to our memory system, and ultimately use our abstract brain processes to make sense of what is actually being said.

But we can apply a similar scientific approach to revelation experiences. What do people hear when they receive a revelation, and how do they actually comprehend it? One of the most impressive biblical descriptions of a revelation occurs in the book of Ezekiel, where we read:

A whirlwind came out of the north, a great cloud, and a fire infolding itself, and a brightness was about it, and out of the midst thereof as the colour of amber, out of the midst of the fire.

Also out of the midst thereof came the likeness of four living creatures. And this was their appearance; they had the likeness of a man.

And every one had four faces, and every one had four wings

And the spirit entered into me when he spoke unto me, and set me upon my feet, that I heard him that speak unto me.

Assuming that the experience actually happened to Ezekiel, how might we think about Ezekiel's experience from a brain perspective? First, it appears that the sensory system, particularly vision, factors in very prominently. Note how unusual the visual imagery is, however. Apparently, this strangeness denotes to Ezekiel that something important or even supernatural is occurring. He also seems to have a very visceral feeling of God entering his body; entering him himself. The areas of the brain that are involved with our body's sensations—such as vibration, heat, and even the position of our body—may have been involved as well so that the body actually felt different. Finally, there's language and comprehension going on. The parts of the brain involved in the understanding of abstract concepts and language appear to play a role.

You can see how we might begin to understand this experience from a totally new perspective. Please remember, it doesn't diminish the potential religious import of this event. But it gives us something very new to think about; and this possible neurobiological understanding may be useful for comparing this experience to others, including even those in the present day.

Let's actually talk a little bit about the different ways in which revelation is experienced. One pathway is revelation through verbal experience: The notion that God is perceived to communicate directly with the human being by exchanging verbal content. Orthodox Judaism and traditional Christianity generally hold that the first five books of Moses were dictated by God in such a fashion. But remember that our brain has the verbal abilities in its temporal lobe, and thus language is one of the most effective ways for human beings to come to understand anything. It would make sense, then, that our brain would be built in such a way so that it could receive religious or spiritual information in a verbal manner. That's the way that we understand things and receive information so effectively; wouldn't it also happen in a religious or spiritual context?

Another path would be nonverbal revelation in which the person perceives something about God but it isn't based in language. Maybe it's based more upon the brain's perceptions and abstract thought processes, but it isn't specifically perceived in any kind of language. This is an interesting way that revelation can occur from the brain perspective since we know that human beings can also derive meaning and understanding from nonverbal communication. In fact, studies show that much of how we communicate with other people is through nonverbal cues. We look at someone's face or body posture and glean a lot of information about them. Are they being honest with us? Are they telling us something that they really believe in? The brain is designed to pick up on all this kind of information. In fact, it might be that nonverbal forms of communication are even more important at times than the verbal forms. Think back to our discussion about rituals. The rhythms, music, and actions of rituals are a crucial part of creating meaning for us. So the brain can certainly derive knowledge in nonverbal ways, and revelation would theoretically be no exception to that process.

What about other ways of revelation? Aristotelian scholars of the medieval period espoused another way of receiving divine information. They held that revelation was the discovery of absolute truths about God through logical philosophical inquiry. In this way, the brain's rational thought processes were considered to be the means towards revelation. It was through our rational self that we could actually obtain knowledge and ideas about God. Where do our rational thought processes come from? We know that there are the parts of the brain that think about causality, abstraction; how we compare different objects and different ideas to each other in such a way that we can deduce new ideas. This overall mechanism could be another possible way in which revelation can occur.

Others, such as the philosopher Baruch Spinoza, suggested that God reveals himself through creation; and thus we can learn about religion and God by observing nature itself. To some degree, the use of our brain through scientific inquiry—through the study of physics, cosmology, and other fields of science—would be the basis of revelation. In other words, the ability to see causality in the world, to explore the world through questioning, and to use the reductionistic processes of the brain may not merely be the way in which we perform science, but for the religious individual may also be the way in which receive information from and about God.

Ultimately, regardless of how a person might think revelation occurs, if we consider revelation in the context of the brain, we'd likely conclude that revelation is the ability of the human brain to receive and be changed by a spiritual message. But when we take a scientific—and particularly a neuroscientific—perspective on revelation, we also uncover some very interesting questions. For example, what limitations might the brain actually place on the kind of information human beings can receive? How is the brain altered both through the revelation experience itself and then in the transforming aftermath of that experience?

Several scholars have stressed that revelation occurs all the time by various mechanisms. One scholar, Avery Dulles, put it: "A comprehensive doctrine of revelation … cannot limit itself to God's self-disclosure in biblical times; it must deal with God's active presence to the world today." If this is the case from a religious perspective, then the brain must also be involved because it's something that happens today as well.

Of course, revelation really is something that's supposedly more of a religious event than something that's neurologically-oriented; but still, the brain must interpret whatever information it perceives about "God's active presence" in the world and somehow make sense of that. The neuroscientific perspective provides insights into issues pertaining to revelation that may have been previously only the domain of religion and theology. For example, Christian theology has sometimes described a difference between communicable and incommunicable attributes of God. If human beings can only have access to communicable attributes of God, then are there certain specific limitations that our brain places on us in terms of what we can actually perceive and understand?

Communicable attributes are usually related to those things that human beings really do have the ability to perceive themselves. These include things like mercy, justice, wrath and anger, and love. From the neuroscientific perspective, we can understand and study the biological underpinnings of these attributes. We can look at the emotional system of the brain and see how it interacts with our abstract thought processes as we engage in our own feelings of mercy, justice, anger, or love. But what about the incommunicable attributes of God? Usually these include concepts such as omnipotence; the sense that God is eternal, infinite; God is all-knowing or omniscient; and God is everywhere, omnipresent. These are certainly things that human beings simply are not.

But if we begin to apply this combination of neuroscience and religion in the topic of neurotheology, we can take a very different kind of perspective. Neurotheology may actually offer an explanation as to how we can even have a notion not only of the communicable, but the incommunicable concepts and attributes of God. Of course, we can't fully understand them because we aren't omniscient and omnipresent; but the brain does have some elements of these characteristics. We have some knowledge, so we can kind of understand what omniscience is all about; we have some idea of time, and hence we can understand a little bit about what eternalness is about; and we have some power, we have some control over the universe, and therefore we have some notion of what omnipotence is about. But while the human brain can't truly grasp the extent of these attributes, a neurotheological perspective would argue that we must be partially able to understand them, at least insofar as the brain can provide a taste of what these attributes are so that we can at least abstractly conceptualize what they mean.

We've already considered in previous lectures how the brain can use its processes such as the holistic, binary, and causal processes to help us interpret the world around us. But then God or religious information can only be considered in these particular ways, such as through our senses, emotions, and those thought processes. But if that's the case, then there theoretically should be a limited number of neurological avenues by which the human brain can experience revelation. It's likely that revelation is different for each individual's brain and hence each individual, but how they engage it is probably limited by what their brain can do.

Scholar Monika Hellwig stated that:

> What God reveals is received or seen according to our present capacity. That capacity is shaped by our individual human maturity, [and] by the maturity of our society and its culture and language.

The important point here is that revelation should be considered an individual experience that's perceived by the individual brain and that it depends on our capabilities; it depends on what that brain can do that enables that revelation to occur. Another scholar stated quite clearly that: "The medium of revelation, therefore, is human experience. The revelation of God to man takes place in human experience." Together, these two quotes imply that the brain must play a fundamental role in revelation experiences and that its capabilities and limitations have an impact on the nature and type of these revelation experiences.

Let us consider a few theoretical examples. If an individual has a revelation that God is the cause of all things, we'd expect that the causal process of the brain is what's involved in enabling that experience. But the causal process may also restrict the experience. For example, we typically apply causality to physical objects—for example, we understand how one object causes a different object to start to move, or we understand it in the context of science—but we don't tend to observe causality in a nonphysical way. This might create an actual problematic duality in which we can't really understand how a nonmaterial thing such as God can affect a material thing. But is this really a real problem or just our brain doing the best that it can in interpreting a revelation kind of experience?

What about our emotions? Many experiences of revelation contain strong emotional content, feelings of awe or absolute joy. Are these the typical emotional processes of the human brain? In fact, perhaps the importance of these experiences are recognized because they're labeled by these very,

very strong emotions. It's those emotions that tell us this is something that's different than our everyday reality. It's something that we must pay attention to; maybe it's something that has some kind of origin beyond the material world, it's supernatural.

Others have also commented on the importance of emotions and the limitations of rational thought processes when it comes to revelation. For example, the Sufi mystic Ibn al-'Arabi stated:

> God deposited within man knowledge of all things, then prevented him from perceiving what He had deposited within him. … This is one of the divine mysteries which reason denies and considers totally impossible.

In this example, it's suggested that reason isn't something that we can use to fully understand religion and God. Reason can help us to understand the problem, but it can't help us fully resolve it. Of course, this frustration can cause strong emotional experiences as well; emotions that contribute to the overall experience of what revelation is all about.

Once revelation has occurred, the individual must then determine how to respond to that revelation. In fact, according to the Catholic Church, the appropriate response to revelation is faith in which "man completely submits his intellect and his will to God." But how does this happen? One can consider a theological mechanism, but there also has to be a biological one. If the intellect and the will arise from the many brain functions that we've talked about, then surrendering them should entail a manner by which these functions are shut off, or at least to some degree reconfigured.

There's actually some evidence about several studies which show how the brain can shut down certain functions, particularly in a religious or spiritual context. Remember our discussion of the speaking in tongues study where we did brain scans that showed that the frontal lobes actually decreased in activity because they felt that they'd surrendered their will during the process of speaking in tongues. By surrendering their will, they actually reduced the willful areas of the brain in the frontal lobe.

What's particularly interesting about the experience of speaking in tongues in this context is that those people who do the practice actually seem to derive some new meaning about different problems in their life. It's to some degree a form of revelation in which knowledge, either spiritual or sometimes practical, is obtained by the individual. Of course, the bigger question is still whether this knowledge comes from God or is derived from the unusual functioning of the brain in which new ways of thinking about things are created; maybe there are different ways in which the brain starts to connect with itself that allows people to think about things in very creative ways.

Revelation experiences are clearly important in terms of how the person derives knowledge about their religious or spiritual beliefs; but does receiving this knowledge help the individual or even humanity as a whole gain salvation of some type? Does it change us, does it transform us, in a very different kind of way? With that question in mind, let's turn to the second of our two fundamental religious concepts in this lecture: that of salvation.

Depending on the religious tradition, salvation is considered to be caused either by the free will and grace of a deity (specifically in the theistic traditions God) or by personal responsibility and self-effort (sometimes in the monotheistic traditions but more particularly in the yogic traditions of India). Religions also emphasize the necessity to some degree of both personal effort through repentance and asceticism as well as divine action through God's grace. The concept of salvation as the phenomenon of being saved by divine agency belongs mostly to Christianity, Judaism, and Islam, the major monotheistic traditions. But there are analogous concepts within the Indian religions, such as nirvana; they're not exact equivalents to the concept of salvation in that they don't specifically depend upon a divine agency per se, however almost all religions speak of a way of saving the person or saving the person's soul.

Here's a very interesting salvation story from one of the participants of our online survey of spiritual experiences:

> I was kneeling, praying, and not knowing how to pray, but trying nonetheless. I felt like I was talking to a stranger. Suddenly my extended arms began to feel heavy, like pins and

needles crawling up my arm. I felt myself beginning to cry, my heart was very heavy as if a Hero of Heroes were wielding a sword inside of me and fighting His way to my soul. That's exactly what was happening; I was baptized in the Spirit that night. I was ready to learn what this power was, and who this power was from. Somehow even then, I knew this was going to be the most exciting journey of my life.

In this story, the person has an experience in which they feel that their entire life has been changed. They now understand God and their own spirituality in a much deeper way than ever before. But how do we assess this experience from a neuroscientific perspective?

The author Ernest Valea suggested three aspects that are important to consider in assessing the experience of salvation. These three aspects are: Number one, the resources needed for attaining salvation; number two, the actual way of getting saved; and three, the meaning of being saved. These aspects are actually quite similar to scientific approaches to a variety of mechanistic questions. We often need to understand what is needed for a given physical phenomena, the mechanism by which it happens, and how we can understand the meaning of it. Let's see what happens when we apply neuroscience to these three aspects. What are the resources necessary for attaining salvation?

I would think that the brain has to be one of those resources. For salvation to occur, the brain has to comprehend what's needed; it has to understand how to go about helping the person obtain the necessary resources, the behaviors, the emotional attitude. Whatever they need to feel, it's the brain that allows them to do this. It allows them to feel sorrow for the sins they've committed; it allows them to understand certain doctrines that need to be followed. Access to these resources is also supported, then, by the brain processes themselves.

What are the ways of getting saved? The brain helps us to understand what practices we must do, what beliefs we must hold, and what experiences we must have in order to be saved. If we're to have to do something such as behave in a particular way or to do a practice such as prayer or meditation, it's the brain that helps us do it as we've described in detail in previous lectures. It engages our body and our brain in a certain process that results in a powerful experience.

Finally, what's the meaning of being saved? Here the brain again is crucial since it's the brain that helps us to derive meaning from all of our thoughts, feelings, and experiences; so the brain has to use its cognitive processes to establish meaning. How do we do this? Again, we go back to our causal, abstract, and emotional processes; and in the context of salvation, the meaning is compared to the overall understanding of the spiritual tradition and its doctrines and goals. But importantly, the brain must somehow be able to identify salvation as something truly remarkable and beyond the normal part of our experiences.

In addition to applying the neuroscientific perspective to a general model of salvation like Valea's, we can also apply our perspective to the teachings of some specific faith traditions. For example, the Churches of Christ generally teach that the process of salvation involves four key steps, which we can also consider from a brain perspective: First, one must be properly taught, and hear; but hearing and learning require the brain to make meaning of what we hear. Our verbal conceptual areas help us to do that. But we've also seen how problematic our perceptions are and how problematic our understanding of language can be; so can we use this information to help more clearly determine what we're perceiving and how accurately we're perceiving it?

Second, one must believe or have faith. Faith is interesting in terms of the brain: Clearly the brain is a mythmaking machine, and I've also argued that it's a belief-making machine. So the brain certainly appears up for the job to create beliefs via its various brain functions.

Third, one must repent, which means turning from one's former lifestyle and choosing to embrace God's ways. Here's a behavioral change that needs to be made: The brain is being asked to change the way it functions and to adopt a more spiritual path. This sounds related to the topic of spiritual development that we heard earlier in the course and neural plasticity in terms of how the brain can change itself. If we're going to go down a new path, how does the brain do it? Are there new connections that are formed or are existing ones changed? We're actually in the process of developing studies to evaluate the changes in brain function that relate to transformative experiences because such research may actually shed light on the biological correlates of this kind of a process.

Fourth, one must remain faithful until death. Again, the topic of spiritual development arises in terms of how the brain creates a stable system of beliefs about the world and about God as its neural connections become solidified. Learning more about how neurological connections remain stable or change could be valuable in better understanding how transformations lead to a new state of being for the individual. We might even begin to wonder how often a person can have a transformation. We can ask the question: Can you be saved more than once? Can you be saved three times?

But what about the part of salvation that comes from the outside of our brain? The Catechism of the Catholic Church specifies that "salvation comes from God alone." But it also states that we receive this salvation and must have faith in God and Jesus Christ in order to obtain salvation. Again, I'd argue that the brain still must help us to develop an abstract notion of what salvation is, why it's important, and how we're to obtain it. Even if it originates outside of the brain, it's the brain that helps us to process what we're receiving; what we're understanding and trying to incorporate that salvation process into who we are.

Maybe we could conceive of a research study in which we actually evaluate some subjects who believe that they've been saved and compare them to those people who say they haven't been saved or have no such belief. While such a study would certainly not address the religious issues per se, it would be fascinating to know if there's something biologically distinctive going on in the people who believe they've been saved; and if so, what does it look like?

In Eastern traditions such as Buddhism or Sikhism, salvation appears to come from ending the cycle of suffering, ending the cycle of death and rebirth, by attaining liberation and enlightenment. This occurs through intense contemplation and meditation and by moving one's life towards a detachment from the body and the physical world. As we've seen throughout this course, though, neuroscience can provide fascinating data and insights into the mechanism of meditation. Meditation and related contemplative practices appear to have a dramatic impact on the brain's functioning both during meditation and after. This data supports the notion that meditation practices result in a unique pattern of brain function and create an enduring response in the brain itself. It certainly seems conceivable that meditation can lead to a transformation of the person and one that's probably mediated in some way by the brain itself.

The study of neurotheology can be of great help in understanding these different approaches toward salvation and determine which methods appear to be most conducive from an integrated physiological and theological perspective.

Finally, we might consider the ways in which the brain limits what types of revelation and salvation experiences human beings can have. What I mean here is that if we have certain types of senses, then we're limited by those senses. We can't pick up a revelation that's transmitted in radio waves because our brain doesn't perceive radio waves. If we're supposed to meditate or pray as part of our process for achieving salvation, then we have to do this in a way that's consistent with the functions of the brain and the body. The brain can't go without sleep for too long, so salvation can't require a process in which people have to go without sleep for weeks on end. Whatever revelation or salvation a person experiences, some part of it has to be comprehensible to the brain, perhaps in language or emotions but comprehensible nonetheless.

The brain appears to be an essential element in the religious experiences of revelation and salvation. In addition, their religious and spiritual meanings are important to us such that the experiences are not just experiences but require our senses, our thoughts, and our emotions; essentially what our brain provides us. Through our newfound abilities to study the brain, it would seem that we could ask and answer a lot of fascinating questions about how and why human beings experience revelation and salvation.

Ultimately, the brain must combine these experiences into a belief and then into behaviors; behaviors that are related to a whole different way of thinking. But the brain also may limit what elements and types of spiritual experiences we can actually have. Knowledge of the brain and its functions can lead us to an important new perspective on these very powerful spiritual experiences.

The Brain's Influence on Religious Behavior
Lecture 19

T his lecture focuses on three behaviors that are crucial to almost every religious tradition: altruism, empathy, and forgiveness. As you will learn from the scientific research that is presented in this lecture, neuroscience seems to make a real contribution to religious and theological discourse. In addition to showing the neurophysiological conditions that make such behaviors as altruism, empathy, and forgiveness possible, the research also offers evidence that religion can play an important role in shaping a more empathic and less antagonistic world.

The Behavior Debate
- Even before the emergence of neuroscience, people were grappling with the relationship between our moral aspirations and our physical, or animalistic, nature.

- In *Summa Theologica*, Thomas Aquinas engages the issue of human biology and the mind by distinguishing between the *actus hominis* and the *actus humanus*.

- Similarly, the Jewish mystical perspective of the Kabbala posits the nefesh (animal part), the ruach (the spirit that helps distinguish good and evil), and the neshamah (higher soul but is related to intellect).

- In the 16th century, Desiderius Erasmus argued that the human being is the center of creation and that the measure of God's goodness is that God created a world in which human beings were allowed to develop naturally. Thus, Erasmus insisted on a role for the human will and personal responsibility, as well as God's grace, in achieving salvation.

- Martin Luther, who was considerably less optimistic about the human potential for good, argued that grace alone provides salvation for human beings.

- This debate centered on the ability of the human will to choose good behavior over bad and, ultimately, to steer the individual toward salvation.

- It would be most interesting to consider how Luther and Erasmus might have responded to current neuroscience research regarding the nature of moral reasoning and the identification of parts of the brain that appear to function as the "seat of the will."

German theologian Martin Luther (1483–1546) believed that grace provides salvation for humans.

Neuroscience and Altruism

- In a very interesting study, an fMRI scan was performed on 20 students while they looked at different pictures that were designed to elicit feelings of compassion or feelings of pride. Compassion induction was associated with activation of the midbrain—in a region that is activated during pain and the perception of others' pain—and that has been implicated in parental nurturance behaviors. This type of compassionate feeling might be part of the altruism response.

- Another study involved 22 students who were asked to imagine helping someone by easing their pain. The fMRI data showed that easing the pain of another was associated with increased activity in the basal ganglia, which is involved in reward pathways and is also strongly stimulated by dopamine.

- These two studies combined show that the basis of altruism may have a lot to do with the pain areas of the brain and the emotional areas of the brain that help us to perceive another's suffering. Activity in these areas may ultimately motivate altruistic behavior.

- Another study showed that giving oxytocin to subjects drives a response that promotes in-group trust and cooperation and defensive, but not offensive, aggression toward competing out-groups.

- Oxytocin is a hormone that is released naturally in our body at very interesting times. It appears to be very important in helping us to establish an intense, loving relationship with another. It is released in women during birth and through the processes of nursing infants. It is believed to contribute greatly to the bond formed between the mother and infant. It is also released in both men and women during sexual orgasm—another moment of intense bonding.

- The role of oxytocin is also noted in other animal species. Interestingly, there are two species of small rodent creatures called prairie voles. One species is monogamous, mating for life, while the other seems to never settle down and bond with another. The species that forms intense monogamous relationships has more oxytocin.

- Oxytocin is important to creating loving bonds that support behaviors leading to intimate relationships and, ultimately, to altruism—which seems to be a fundamental part of human thought and behavior.

- Altruism may be expressed differently, depending on the physiological processes of our brain, but it is very important in helping us to establish bonds with others.

Neuroscience and Empathy

- An fMRI study conducted in 2010 by researchers at Northwestern University showed that empathy for in-group members is neurally distinct from empathy for humankind in general. This study involved 28 individuals: Half of them were African American, and the other half were Caucasian.

- Participants in the study showed a greater response in the anterior cingulate cortex and bilateral insula (emotion areas) when observing the suffering of others—which clearly indicates that empathy for humankind activated the emotional areas of the participants' brains.

- However, in this study, African American individuals additionally recruited the medial prefrontal cortex when observing the suffering of members of their own social group.

- Moreover, neural activity within the frontal lobe in response to pain expressed by in-group relative to out-group members predicted greater empathy and altruistic motivation for one's in-group.

- The results suggest that the brain processes associated with creating our sense of self underlie extraordinary empathy and altruistic motivation for members of one's own social group.

- Another study found that inferring the emotional state of someone who is not similar to us relies upon the same neural structures as having empathy for someone who is similar to us. In particular, the parts of our brain that are responsible for perceiving emotions in ourselves are important for developing empathy for those who are similar to us and those who are different from us. Empathy for those who are dissimilar to us requires added frontal lobe function in order to make these empathic inferences.

- In other words, this study suggests that it is easier to have empathy for those you know and feel similar to, but you can do it for others. This is a very interesting finding. In fact, it gives us a new neuroscientific basis for understanding a moral precept that is crucial to many religious traditions—namely, that you should love your enemies as well as your friends.

- Research also shows that while empathy is to some degree an inherent human trait, it can also be affected by the frontal lobe and other cognitive processes. In other words, at least theoretically, empathy can be learned. This has implications for religious concepts because we can promote altruism and empathy via religious belief systems and practices.

Neuroscience and Forgiveness

- Forgiveness is a behavior that is even more fundamental than altruism and empathy to the great religious traditions of the world. Various cognitive processes are involved in this highly complex—and distinctly human—behavior.

- Forgiveness is complex because it includes many intellectual and behavioral elements—including altruism, love, cognition, and empathy. However, if we look at the entire process of forgiveness from a neuroscientific perspective, we can identify certain core components that make the complexity a bit more intelligible.

- The first thing that has to happen in the forgiveness process is that you have to have something happen to you that requires forgiveness—which can be referred to as the injury to the self.

- Perceiving an injury to the self appears to require four elements: a sense of self, an expanded sense of self, an ability to evaluate the behavior of others as being injurious or beneficial, and memory of the event in order to link that injury to the offending person.

- Ultimately, the forgiveness process involves the causal, binary, abstract, quantitative, and holistic processes of the brain in order to rework the equilibrium in a way that reestablishes the sense of self in the context of the injury.

- The causal process identifies the causative agent of the injury—who did it to us and what the injury caused.

- The binary function provides information about good and bad, helping us to identify the injury and also the moral basis for it.

- The quantitative function provides a relative notion of greater than or lesser than and, thus, is important in evaluating the extent of the injury and ensuring that a balance is ultimately restored.

- The abstract function helps us to manipulate religious, spiritual, moral, and legal concepts so that we can restructure in our mind how the injury occurred and how it is ultimately resolved.

- The holistic function provides a reunification of the balance that exists so that we can feel better about the new equilibrium that we are connected to.

- While it is not a surprise that empathy, altruism, and forgiveness are associated with brain function, the results from various studies provide some insight on the specific emotional and cognitive processes involved. Significantly, these studies support the notion that we can change our brain and our thoughts and behaviors. If religions promote such positive behavior, the behavior can become integrated in the brain's functions more effectively.

Suggested Reading

Hood, Hill, and Williamson, *The Psychology of Religious Fundamentalism.*

McCullough, Pargament, and Thoresen, eds, *Forgiveness.*

Mecklenburger, *Our Religious Brains.*

Newberg and Waldman, *How God Changes Your Brain.*

Questions to Consider

1. If a person has a revelatory experience, how does the brain help that person experience and interpret it?

2. If a person is saved, is his or her brain also saved?

The Brain's Influence on Religious Behavior
Lecture 19—Transcript

Every major religious tradition prescribes a set of behaviors. In the Qur'an, for example, the covenant is kept by: one, remembering one's obligations towards others; two, abstaining from yielding to the desires of the lower self; and three, maintaining a constant remembrance of the Divine and seeking to reflect His attributes. In the Hebrew Bible, we have the Ten Commandments, which provide a remarkably compact and enduring foundation for human conduct, both in relation to God and also in relation to our fellow human beings. And Christians look to the teachings of Jesus, and especially to his Sermon on the Mount, for the principles that guide their actions.

As a scientist, I'm fascinated by these and other great systems of behavior; and in particular I'm intrigued by the possibility that neuroscience might shed some light on the reasons why these systems have proved to be so durable throughout human history. In the preceding lectures, we explored the ways that various structures and functions of the brain relate to the creation and the maintenance of religious ideas. Today, I'd like turn from ideas to behavior itself. Is there something about the way that the brain works that actually predisposes us to acknowledge the rightness and wrongness of various behaviors, especially of those behaviors that are either prescribed or prohibited by religious authority?

Of course, even before the emergence of neuroscience, people were grappling with the relationship between our moral aspirations and our physical or animal nature. As we talked about in an earlier lecture, Saint Aquinas, in his *Summa Theologica*, where he engages the issue of the human biology and the mind, he distinguishes between the *actus hominis* and the *actus humanus*, and he talks a lot about how those two pieces of our selves— that higher part, that spiritual self, perhaps the nonmaterial self—relates to the biology of who we are and how those two interact with regard to our thoughts and our behaviors. Similarly, the Jewish mystical perspective of the Kabbalah posits the *nefesh* (the animal part), the *ruach* (the spirit that helps distinguish between good and evil), and the *Neshamah* (which is the higher soul but is related to our intellect). How might cognitive neuroscience deal with these concepts as they relate to the brain?

I'm intrigued by a lot of the recent studies that have been done that have tried to understand that nonmaterial part of who we are. When we talk about our ideas, our thoughts, our moral reasoning; all of these are part of that spiritual part of our selves, that intellectual part, and that ultimately has an impact on the biological part and our behavioral part.

We might actually ponder not just what goes on scientifically, but let's take a historical perspective for a moment. In the 16th century, Desiderius Erasmus argued that the human being is the center of creation and that the measure of God's goodness in the world is that God created a world in which to allow human beings to develop naturally. For Erasmus, he insisted on a role for the human will and personal responsibility, our personal behaviors, as well as God's grace in achieving salvation. Martin Luther, on the other hand, was considerably less optimistic about the human potential for good in terms of our behavior. Martin Luther argued that grace alone provided salvation for human beings. Fundamentally, this debate centered around the ability of the human person to choose between behaviors that are good or bad and try to steer us in a direction as to how we achieve salvation.

It would be very interesting, I think, to consider how these two scholars, these two people arguing in this debate, Luther and Erasmus, might've responded to the current neuroscience research regarding the nature of moral reasoning and the identification of parts of the brain that appear to function as the "seat of the will." These studies have actually had a very dramatic impact on philosophical ideas because it tells us something about how we engage these concepts and how we turn them into our behaviors. How will we actually behave based on these ideas? It'd be very interesting to see whether they'd take this information in some way and use it to either support or refute the other's ideas about human moral behavior and its ultimate importance in attaining salvation.

Clearly it's too late for neuroscience to have an impact on their particular debate, but what about us? Can scientific research tell us anything at all about human behaviors, and particularly those that might actually have an impact on religious and theological discourse? That's a pretty big question. It'll be helpful to perhaps narrow the range of our discussion somewhat; so I'm going to focus on several behaviors that are very crucial to almost every religious tradition. The three behaviors that I'm going to focus on are altruism, empathy, and forgiveness.

Let's find out a little bit about what scientific research has had to tell us about these different behaviors. First, let's take a look at altruism. In one very interesting study using Functional Magnetic Resonance Imaging (or fMRI), they did scans of 20 different students that were performed while they were looking at different pictures that were designed to either elicit feelings of compassion or feelings of pride in the test subjects. What these researchers found was that the compassion induction was associated with the activation of the midbrain, that very central part of the brain that actually is a region that's activated when we feel pain and particularly when we perceive pain in others. This area has also been implicated in parental nurturance behaviors; how parents take care of their children. It may be that this type of compassionate feeling is an important part of the altruistic response; that we'll behave altruistically because the parts of our brain that perceive someone else as struggling and needing help elicits this internal response that essentially compels us to act in an altruistic way.

Another study involved 22 students who were asked to imagine helping someone by easing their pain; and the fMRI data showed that easing the pain of another was associated with an increase of activity in a very central structure called the basal ganglia. You may remember that this is a part of the brain that's connected to the limbic system and is very involved in the reward pathways of the brain. It also happens to be strongly stimulated by dopamine.

When you combine these two studies, what they seem to be showing is that the basis of altruism may have a lot to do with areas of the brain that perceive pain and the emotional areas of the brain that help us to perceive another's suffering. In fact, it's interesting to note that research studies with brain scans have actually shown that the perception of physical pain activates the same areas of the brain as emotional pain. It makes sense then that these areas of the brain may ultimately motivate us towards altruistic behavior.

Another study showed that giving a particular molecule called oxytocin drives what they called a "tend and defend" response. Specifically what that does is it promotes trust and cooperation within a group of people. It also, though, may create a sense of cohesion but may sometimes create somewhat of a feeling of aggression towards other competing groups. This is a very interesting study because oxytocin is a hormone that's released naturally in our body, and it's released at very interesting times. It appears to be very important in helping us to establish intense, loving relationships with another. For example, it happens to be released in very high quantities in a woman at the moment of birth and throughout the processes of nursing infants. In fact, it's believed to contribute greatly to the bond formed between the mother and her infant. It's also released in both men and women during sexual orgasm; again, this is a moment of very intense bonding.

The role of oxytocin has also been studied in other animal species, and there's a fascinating set of studies that have been done that have looked at two very related species; they're these little rodent creatures called prairie voles. What's interesting is that one of these species is incredibly monogamous; they find their mate and they mate for life. The other species—a very similar kind of prairie vole, looks the same—they actually never settle down; they're very promiscuous, they never bond with each other. Which one do you think has more oxytocin receptors in their brain? If you said it was the species that forms intense monogamous relationships, you would be right. We can see that oxytocin, this chemical that's actually a kind of neurotransmitter, is important in creating loving bonds that support behaviors that ultimately lead to very intimate relationships and eventually to altruistic behaviors. The notion that a woman will give her life for her child; this notion of altruism is something that's perhaps fundamental to human thought and behavior, and these studies are starting to tell us about the biological processes, the physiological processes, which are going on in our brain. We're starting to better understand the nature of how we establish our bonds with others and how we create these different kinds of altruistic behaviors.

In addition to what we're learning about altruism, brain science is also turning up some very interesting results relating to the feeling of empathy. For example, an fMRI study that was conducted in 2010 by researchers at Northwestern University showed that empathy for members of your group (the ingroup) is actually neurally distinct from the feeling of empathy for humankind in general. In this interesting study, it involved 28 individuals, half of whom were African American, the other half were Caucasian. The participants in the study showed a greater response in two areas of the brain—one called the anterior cingulate cortex and the other the insula— when they were observing the suffering of others.

What do these areas do? The anterior cingulate is located between the frontal lobes and the limbic system. One way to think about what it does is that it functions to some degree as a fulcrum between our cognitive control of our emotions and our emotions. As we've talked about in the past, the emotions may respond—somebody insults us and our emotions want to punch them in the mouth—but our frontal lobe says, "No, no, no; let's try to find a better way of doing this." That interaction occurs via the functioning of the anterior cingulate, that area that balances between the frontal lobe and the limbic system.

The insula is also a very interesting structure that's located between the limbic system and other parts of the cortex, the higher parts of the brain. The insula is believed to be a very important structure in how we perceive emotions; how we feel the actual emotions and how we think about them. This clearly indicates that empathy for humankind in general activates these emotional areas of the brain, and particularly those areas that help us to regulate our emotional responses and to feel our emotional responses.

But in the study of the African American individuals, they found that they actually had an increase of activity in the larger parts of the frontal lobe when they were observing the suffering of members of their own social group. It suggests that the frontal lobe—another structure—becomes part of this sense of empathy for their own group, which is a little bit different than when people are looking at humanity in general. Moreover, neuronal activity within the frontal lobe in response to pain expressed by either members of the person's group or members of another group was actually part of the experience of empathy and altruistic motivation for the person's ingroup, for their own group. The results of this particular study suggested that the brain processes associated with creating our sense of self actually underlie an extraordinary empathy and altruistic motivation for members of our own social group. Again, what we're seeing is this very profound sense of connectedness, empathy, and understanding that motivates behaviors that are deeply tied into the religious concepts that are often taught as part of religious traditions.

Yet another study suggested that inferring the emotional state of someone who isn't like us relies upon the same neural structures as having empathy for someone who's similar to us. In particular, the parts of our brain that are responsible for perceiving the emotions in our self are important for developing empathy for those who are similar to us and those who are different from us. It's just that empathy for those who are dissimilar to us requires additional frontal lobe function in order to make those kinds of empathic inferences. Ultimately, what the brain research shows is that it's easier to have empathy for those who you know and feel similar to, but you can have empathy for others. This is a very interesting finding; in fact, it gives us a new neuroscientific basis for understanding a moral precept that's crucial to many religious traditions: Namely, that you should love your enemies as well as your friends.

Here's something else that we're learning from the research: While empathy to some degree is an inherent human trait, it can also affected by the frontal lobes and other cognitive processes. In other words, at least theoretically, empathy can be learned. This, of course, has very important implications for religious concepts since religions ask us to be altruistic and try to promote feelings of altruism, empathy, and behaviors that are related to them as part of their doctrine. That means that we actually can change our brain—we can actually alter the functions of our frontal lobes and our emotional systems— so that we can feel more empathy and ultimately more compassion for others.

So far we've been talking about altruism and empathy; but there's a third behavior that in many ways is even more fundamental to some of the great religious traditions of the world, and that behavior is one of forgiveness. Let's turn to forgiveness now and look at how various cognitive processes play out in this very complex, and very human, kind of behavior.

We talked a little bit in a prior lecture about the rudiments of forgiveness, but I want to spend a lot more time right now because forgiveness is a very complex kind of human behavior; and I call it "complex" because it includes so many intellectual, emotional, and behavioral elements. It includes altruism, love, cognition, and feelings of empathy; but if we look at the entire process of forgiveness from a neuroscientific perspective, we can identify certain core components that make this complexity a bit more intelligible.

Let's think about the forgiveness process and what happens. The first thing that has to happen in the forgiveness process is that you have to have something that happens to you that requires forgiveness to be given. We might refer to this as the "injury to the self." Perceiving an injury to the self appears to require four distinct elements that all are rooted in neurobiological functioning. You need to have a sense of self. The idea here is that if you don't have a sense of your self, than you don't have any way of relating what exactly is going on that might injure that self. To some degree, you also have an expanded sense of self; the idea that you feel things to you stronger than how you understand what other people feel. You have to have the ability to evaluate the behavior of others as being injurious or beneficial, and you have to have a memory of this event in order to link that injury to the offending person so that you can actually go ahead and forgive them.

Let's look at each of these elements in more detail and how they relate to very specific brain processes. The sense of the self derives from the brain's ability to perceive the self. Remember that our brain takes in sensory perceptions about the world. Some of them come in from the outside world and they tell us where our self is in relation to that world. That's that parietal lobe; that area in the back of our brain that gives us our orientation of our self. But other parts of the parietal lobe and other parts of our body give us an awareness of our self; of our body itself. We can feel our emotions, we can reflect on who we are as a person—we have a self that reflects on the self—and we have emotional values that we apply to the sense of self. We feel who we are, we know who we are, and we have an emotional attachment to who we are.

All of that also contributes to an expanded sense of our self; and this is where we sometimes run into problems. The issue is that we feel everything that we feel, and we feel it stronger than how we can ever empathize with somebody else's feelings. Our limbic system, our parietal lobe, our sensory awareness of the things that are going on in our own body help us to make us feel our self; and to some degree, we necessarily protect our self above all other things. To some degree, this is what our brain is designed to do: We must protect our selves, and therefore we must be extra careful about the things that are going on around us. We have within our brain the ability to perceive our self; but when we actually experience some kind of injury or hurt, the brain has the ability to not only feel it but to some degree to feel it very strongly because we need to know how to respond to it.

How does the brain actually perceive this injury or self? Where does that come from? In the brain, we also have the ability to perceive relationships between our self and other things in the world; between a given individual and the people who are in their group. There's actually a type of balance that's maintained in this group; and if we think about the areas of our brain that might be involved in this, we might think about our binary system that distinguishes our self from other and tells us a little bit about how they relate to each other. We have the abstract ability to bring that together to understand what that relationship is. The ordering, the balance that we have, the equilibrium that we have with other people can actually be both vertical as well as horizontal.

What do I mean by that? If you work for somebody, you have a vertical kind of relationship. You have a boss that's working with you, you're working for them; and therefore they're allowed to do certain things to you that perhaps somebody who works underneath you or perhaps a friend isn't allowed to do. But we understand that; our abstract processes of our brain understand what that relationship is and understands that there's a limit to what other people can do to us irrespective of that vertical ordering. We understand the sense of equilibrium across all people as well as people who are theoretically above us or below us in the overall social order. To some degree, we're all at least at one level equal, at least in the sense that we're all human beings; and therefore we're not allowed to abuse other people irrespective of our station in life.

This equilibrium, which our abstract processes and our emotional processes hold for us so that we understand, can then be changed in either a positive or negative way. If there's a positive change, the change is in favor of our overall sense of wellbeing. Usually it happens because the person compliments us, does something kind to us, and ultimately we feel that we've actually been taken out of that balance, out of that equilibrium, and sometimes it's being placed higher than the other person. Sometimes we actually respond by trying to do something nice for them; the old "if you scratch my back I'll scratch yours."

A negative change is an injury or an insult that ultimately makes us feel badly about ourselves because we recognize that that equilibrium has now shifted so we're now lower than we were; and now we have to decide ultimately how to respond to that particular injury. The notion of injury can apply to both the individuals and how we relate to each other as well as the group as a whole and perhaps even other things. For example, this actually can apply to a kind of self/world equilibrium, a self/world balance, or a relationship between our self and God as one other example. Once this balance or equilibrium has been negatively altered, the processes of forgiveness or sometimes revenge can begin to occur.

Revenge itself is actually a little bit easier to understand than forgiveness. It's in the Bible, the Lex Talionis: An eye for an eye. This idea exists in virtually all cultures and all religious and spiritual traditions; in fact, it's sometimes used to justify violence and hatred in a religious context because if somebody does something wrong to us, then we can go and do something wrong to them. But an individual who begins to feel this way still has to decide as to whether there may be another alternative; is there something that they can do other than revenge? Can they actually turn to some aspect of forgiveness? We'll talk about how that happens in just a moment.

But one of the other important elements of what forgiveness is all about is that you have to be able to use your memory processes and your causal processes of the brain to be able to establish the sequence of events that led to the injury so that you know who to get revenge on, or ultimately who to forgive. Because, after all, if you can't remember who did the injury to you, then you don't know who to seek revenge on or you don't know who ultimately to forgive in terms of the perpetrator of that injury.

Forgiveness is ultimately the foreswearing of resentment and revenge. Ultimately, the forgiveness process involves a lot of different brain processes. It involves causal reasoning because you've established what the causal problem was, the injury was, and now you have to reestablish how you'll now relate to that individual. You have the binary function, which sets you up with that other individual and now has to rectify the problem, the situation. Your quantitative functions get involved because they're telling you what's better than or worse than other ways of thinking, or trying to resolve that problem in terms of "Are you better than or have you been injured by the other person?" You have the holistic processes that ultimately are going to be brought in to try to rework that sense of equilibrium in a way that helps to establish the overall sense of self in the context of that injury.

Again, you can utilize the causal process, you can look at the binary function, as all of these different ways of trying to understand what the injury was, the nature of it, perhaps the moral basis of whether you need to forgive or not, and how you can try to reestablish that balance that's so important in the forgiveness process. In fact, the abstract function itself helps us to kind of bring that to a conclusion by manipulating all of the different religious, spiritual, moral, and even legal concepts in a way that we can restructure in our mind the nature of the injury that occurred and how it's finally resolved. I mentioned that the holistic function is probably a crucial part of finally reunifying that balance, reunifying you with the other individual, so that you can feel better about this new equilibrium and feel better about the forgiveness process. This ultimately leads to very powerful emotional responses that are part of the forgiveness process that make the forgiveness process one of the most important ones in most of our religious traditions.

It's not a surprise, then, that empathy, altruism, and forgiveness are associated with brain functions. The results from different brain scan studies that we've been looking at provide some insight into the specific emotional and cognitive processes that are involved. Significantly, the studies support the notion that we can change our brain and our thoughts and behaviors; and if religions promote such positive behaviors, it can become integrated in the brain's functions more effectively, it can change the neural connections in our brain. Thus neuroscience does seem to be able to make a very real contribution to religious and theological discourse. In addition to showing the neurophysiological conditions that make behaviors like altruism and forgiveness possible, the research also offers evidence that religion can play an important role in shaping a more empathic and less antagonistic world.

How the Brain Changes God
Lecture 20

In this lecture, you will learn about how our brain shapes our beliefs about religion and God. You will learn that the different cognitive and emotional processes of the brain dramatically affect our beliefs of God. In addition, you will learn that there are fascinating ways of trying to understand what people actually think about when they think about God. Furthermore, you will learn how people's thoughts about God relate to the brain processes that support those thoughts.

What Is God Like?

- In 2006, Baylor University's Institute for Studies of Religion published the results from their extensive study on religion and spirituality. More than 1,700 people participated in Baylor's study, and each of them answered nearly 400 questions about religion and spirituality.

- According to the results of the survey, the American public described four primary types of God: an authoritarian God, a critical God, a distant God, and a benevolent God.

- Baylor's research team noted the complexity of American religious beliefs. Among other things, the study concluded that gender and income affect the way we perceive God. For example, women in the study tended to select an "engaged" God, such as one who was either authoritarian or benevolent. In addition, the higher the income, the less likely the participant was to describe God as angry.

- In short, when it comes to the question of what God is like, people have different answers, and these answers seem to be influenced by a variety of factors—both physiological and social.

- From a neuroscience perspective, this is not surprising. When we think about how our brain processes religious and spiritual information, we must also realize that its capabilities and limitations have a profound impact on how we understand religion and God.

- Of course, the way our brain represents the outside world to us has no necessary correspondence with the world as it actually is. The same is true for any spiritual reality, and in particular, the same is true for God.

- Whether or not there is a God, and regardless of what attributes God might have, each of our brains interprets this information for us, and our interpretations are constrained by the structure and function of the brain. In other words, we make of God what our brains allow us to make of God.

- Moreover, even though people do share a number of similar perspectives, their experiences differ. As a result, each person's interpretation of reality—and of God—is bound to be, to some degree, unique.

- How does the brain think about God? What is going on in our brain when we try to imagine or articulate what God is like? Can neuroscience help us understand how our brain shapes our personal image of who God is?

- Much of the research in this area is subjective because people who are studied are often asked what they personally think or feel, but it also helps us get at the underlying neurophysiology.

- Ultimately, there are many ways of approaching the concept of God, including religious, theological, anthropological, sociological, artistic, cultural, and—of course—neuroscientific ways.

- The different cognitive functions of the brain that help us to perceive the world are also important not only in understanding basic religious ideas and behaviors, but also in understanding the more specific ideas about God.

Shaping Our Notions of God

- We can turn to our brain processes to try to understand the tremendous variety of beliefs about God. The cognitive functions that we have considered include the holistic function and its counterpart, the reductionistic function. We have also dealt repeatedly with the causal, abstractive, and binary functions, among others.

- The holistic function of the brain involves the parietal lobes and is responsible for the sense of the oneness of God and the oneness of all things. The concept of God as a unifying force is important. There is a need for us to consider the individual characteristics of God as part of the whole.

- Many people, no matter how holistically they think about God, still envision God in a humanized manner. They think of God as a super person—the old man with a beard in the clouds, much like Michelangelo's vision on the Sistine Chapel—because our brain has specialized areas for seeing and interpreting faces. Thus, it is no surprise that we treat God, to some extent, like another person.

- By involving the brain's visual areas in the way we think about God, we're able to make God more accessible—easier for us to understand—but this process of visualization also limits what God can be for us. When we give God a human face, it makes it easier for us to understand the concept of God.

- Brain-scan studies show that conversational prayer treats God like we treat another person, activating our social areas of the brain in the parietal lobe.

- Our emotions tell us what is important and what is not. They allow us to communicate properly, and ultimately, they shape our beliefs. How do we think about God emotionally?

- In the Baylor study, emotions play an important role because some view God in a negative emotional way, and others view God in a positive emotional way.

- Emotions are also important for how we express and understand language. In fact, we need emotions to interpret what people are saying, and we have specific brain areas that help with the emotional inflections in language.

- Language helps us understand religious concepts, and of course, language is a part of rituals, myths, and prayer. We must use language to understand sacred texts and to explain religion, spirituality, and God. How do we use language, and how does our language limit our understanding of God?

- For many, God is indescribable. This is an interesting description because it implies that a particular thought—God—cannot be relegated to any clear language. Language is crucial for our understanding of God, but it also presents specific problems because it is so difficult to fully describe God.

- Another fascinating element of different religious traditions, specifically with regard to how we act and think about God, has to do with willfulness or surrender. How do we understand God's will?

- The feeling of willfulness comes from the frontal lobes. Do we have free will? Do we control our thinking about God? What do we think God wants us to do in terms of our behaviors and thoughts?

- Is God something we should surrender ourselves to? By surrendering themselves, some individuals find a new understanding of God and a new relationship with God. Thus, the act of surrendering becomes an important way for some people to change their beliefs about God.

Our Brain and the Existence of God
- The brain believes that the things it perceives are real. We assign reality based on the degree to which something seems real. In conjunction with the binary operator, we can establish existence from nonexistence.

- Why do some believe God exists and others do not? Regardless of your beliefs, it is the brain that draws the line between a belief that God does or does not exist. For example, research has shown that there are differences in the brain scans of atheists contemplating God. For them, the brain is not able to activate in the same way as a religious person's brain—largely because they do not have a clear sense of God's existence.

- It remains unclear why we think anything exists or does not exist, but through research, we can explore questions such as: What does God look like? What does God feel like? What is God's personality? How are these attributes related to our own?

- For example, when researchers asked participants about what they think God looks like, 60 percent drew abstract or nature scenes, 20 percent drew faces, and 15 percent were blank. However, a blank response did not always mean "no answer." Of atheists, 50 percent left it blank.

- The Baylor study found that Americans believe in four principle types of God: an authoritarian God, a critical God, a distant

© iStockphoto/Thinkstock.

Many research studies have brought up the important idea of whether the way in which our brain thinks about God has something—or even anything—to do with what the actual nature of God is.

God, and a benevolent God. These four types proceed along two dimensions: spatial and emotional. Could there be a fifth type of God—a mystical God?

Suggested Reading

Baylor Institute for Studies of Religion, "American Piety in the 21st Century."

Deacon, *The Symbolic Species.*

Lauglin, McManus, and d'Aquili, *Brain, Symbol, and Experience.*

Murphy, Ellis, and O'Connor, eds, *Downward Causation and the Neurobiology of Free Will.*

Newberg and Waldman, *How God Changes Your Brain.*

Questions to Consider

1. Do specific brain processes influence our perception of God?

2. What limitations does the brain place on our ability to conceive of and relate to God?

How the Brain Changes God
Lecture 20—Transcript

In 2006, Baylor University's Institute for Studies of Religion released a report on what *Time* magazine called "the most extensive and sensitive study of religion ever conducted." More than 1,700 people participated in Baylor's study, and each of them answered nearly 400 questions on religion and spirituality. According to the results of the survey, the American public described four primary concepts or types of God: an authoritarian God, a critical God, a distant God, and a benevolent God.

Baylor's research team noted the complexity of American religious beliefs. Among other things, the study concluded that gender and income actually affect the way we perceive God. For example, women in the study tended to select an engaged God, such as one who was either authoritarian or benevolent; and the higher the income, the less likely the participant was to describe God as an angry God. In short, when it comes to the question "What is God like," people have very different answers; and these answers seem to be influenced by a variety of factors, both physiological and social.

From a brain perspective, this isn't really that surprising. When we think about how our brain processes religious and spiritual information, we also must realize that its capabilities and limitations have a profound impact on how we understand religion and God. Of course, as we've also said all along, the way our brain represents the outside world to us doesn't necessary correspond with what's going on in the world itself. The same may be said for any kind of sense of spiritual reality; and in particular, I'd say the same is true for the concept of God. Whether or not there actually is a God and regardless of what attributes God might have, each of our brains interprets this information for us; and our interpretations are constrained by the structure and function of the brain. In other words, we make of God what our brains allow us to make of God. Moreover, even though people do share a number of similar perspectives, their experiences differ; and as a result, each person's interpretation of reality and of God is bound to be, to some degree, unique.

My favorite analogy is the famous story about a whole bunch of flies buzzing around an elephant; and if you could ask each of the flies what an elephant was, they'd describe something very different. One might describe an elephant as a trunk; one would describe it as a tail or as a tusk; and to some degree each of them would be right, but each of them would also be limited. This also take us back to the original Zen story I shared with you in Lecture One, that it is the mind that moves us through reality and interprets that reality. The minds of these little flies buzzing around the elephant, they all interpret the reality of the elephant in their own way; and, again, to some degree they're all correct and it works for each of them. But ultimately, they're limited in what they actually know about that reality.

But what's going on in our brain when we try to imagine or articulate what God is like? Can neuroscience help us understand how our brain shapes our personal image of what and who God is? Interestingly, there's a reasonable amount of research in this area. A lot of the research is much more subjective since we've had to ask people about what they think or feel about God; but remember, as we've been talking about all along throughout the course, those different ideas—the thoughts, the feelings, and experiences—have some kind of underlying neurophysiology; so trying to understand them better helps us to better understand that physiological process that establishes that expiree for us.

Ultimately, there are many ways of approaching the concept of God. There's obviously the religious and theological way. Religions define God in certain ways, understand God in certain ways; theology helps us to make sense of all the different attributes of what God is. But there are other ways of thinking about God: There are anthropological ways, and sociological ways; how do groups of people come together to think about God? Artists have long found ways of trying to create images of what God is and what God may look like, feel like, and how God may interact in our world. Of course, there's the neuroscientific approach—the approach that we're taking in this course—about how the brain actually thinks about God.

Remember the different cognitive functions of the brain that we've been talking about all along that help us to perceive the world. These are also important not only in understanding basic religious ideas and behaviors as we discussed in the last couple of lectures, but also the more specific ideas about what God actually is. Let's pause for a moment: Think about your beliefs regarding God; are you religious or not? Whether you are or not, whether you believe in God or not, you have some notion in your mind about what God is. Do you think about God in terms of a traditional religious view? Are you Christian, Jewish, or Muslim and look at God in that particular context? Do you think of God as some kind of super-person, or is God an abstract spirit that exists somewhere in the universe?

We can turn to our brain processes to try to understand the tremendous variety of beliefs about God. The cognitive functions we've considered in our previous lectures include the holistic function and its counterpart, the reductionistic function; and we've also dealt repeatedly with the causal, abstract, binary, all these different functions of the brain. What I'd like to do now is to look at some of these brain functions and processes that play an especially important role in shaping our notions specifically about God.

Let's take, for example, the holistic function. As we've talked about, the holistic function is very involved with our parietal lobe; how we begin to think about our self and the relation of the self to the rest of the world. We've also talked a lot about the concept of a oneness of God; the notion of God being a unifying force in the universe. We might consider an individual who actually has a very strong functioning holistic process; and if we consider such an individual, maybe they'd really very strongly think about God as the whole, and they may even consider themselves to be part of God in that respect.

Many people no matter how holistically they think about God still envision God in a humanized form. They may think about God as a super-person; this is the famous old man with a beard in the clouds, a lot like Michelangelo's vision of God on the ceiling of the Sistine Chapel. Why is this? It turns out that our brain has very specialized areas for seeing and interpreting faces. In fact, we tend to see faces in lots of different things. Think about your car, for example; if you look at it from the front, the headlights and the grill kind of look like a face. It's no surprise that we would treat God to some extent like another person and try to create some notion of a face of God that we can somehow interact with. By involving the brain's visual areas in the ways in which we think about God, we're actually able to make God more accessible to us; it's easier for us to understand and interact with. But this process of visualization also limits what God can be for us.

When we give God a human face, it makes it easier to understand the concept of God; and brain scan studies actually can show us how our brain works with regard to making those visualizations. In addition, brain scan studies have shown that we can have a conversation with God. In fact, it's very interesting that when people have been scanned while they're engaged in a conversational type of prayer, they find the same brain areas activating as when they're simply speaking with another individual; so the areas of our brain that support social interactions with other people also become involved when we interact with God in a social, personal kind of way.

Frequently in this course, we've seen the importance of the emotional-value function that our brain has. Our emotions tell us what's important, and they also tell us what's not. In fact, they allow us to communicate properly and they ultimately shape our beliefs. As we've said all along, the stronger a particular emotion is for us, the stronger whatever that emotion applies to becomes a part of our brain; it becomes a part of our belief system. The emotions are critical in shaping our ideas and our concepts, and therefore also our concepts about God.

How do we think about God from an emotional perspective? In the Baylor study, emotions play a very important role since some view God in a very negative emotional way and others view God in a positive emotional way. When we think about it in this context, that notion of God as being punishing, as being angry, as being disappointed in us, these are the negative emotional feelings that many people have about God that the Baylor study showed us. In fact, God was divided along two different dimensions of emotions with regard to God being either critical or God being benevolent; and that's an emotional way of thinking about God. Are emotions necessary for rational thought? Again, we've spoken about how the emotions are critical for helping us to make sense of language; helping us to determine what ideas, what concepts that we have are important to us; and therefore we need these emotions to help us not only understand things but to interpret how people are saying it. If you go to a church, or a synagogue, or a mosque and you listen to what somebody's saying in a sermon, the emotions are a very important part that tell you what's going on that shape and affect specific brain areas that are involved in the emotional inflections of language; and because of that, that tells us a lot about how we understand these religious concepts.

We've really understood the importance of emotions and subsequently the importance of language in helping us understand our concepts about God; and that occurs through different myths, prayers, and rituals, all of which activate these language areas of the brain, the emotional areas of the brain, and give us our ideas about God. In fact, we have to use language to understand the sacred texts, and we use the language to explain religion, to explain spirituality, and ultimately our ideas about God.

But how do we use language and how does our language limit our understanding of God? Interestingly, while we spend a lot of time trying to describe God using language, for many God is indescribable. This is an interesting description since it implies that a particular thought (God) can't actually be relegated to any clear language; there's no way to actually try to describe language. In some traditions such as Judaism, "God" isn't a word that can be spelled; you can't actually access it through language.

An example from one of the participants in our online survey talked about this issue of the indescribability of God. They said:

This churning pillar of force, I understood, must be the same experienced for ages by the prophets and saints of old. This was the pillar of fire described in the Old Testament. This was the ancient of days. This was the Holy Spirit. This was primordial Shakti. By the magnificence of its sheer force and undeniable presence, I suddenly understood what God is. This was what man calls God. It was, it was. There's little more to say in an attempt to describe it. But I now understood why the ancient Hebrews adhered to the deepest reverence for this force by declaring its name as unpronounceable.

Language is crucial for our understanding of God, but also creates problems because God is almost impossible to describe. We can try to get at it in some way or another as a concept, but our words fall short.

Another fascinating element of different religious traditions, specifically with regard to how we act and think about God, has to do with how our relationship is formed with God; and this relates to some degree to our frontal lobes and the notion of human will. Our frontal lobes allow us to feel a sense of willfulness, and we sometimes apply that understanding of having a will to God. We talk about "It's God's will," but what does that mean exactly? How do we understand that God has a will to do certain things in the world?

As I mentioned, willfulness actually comes from the frontal lobes—we activate our frontal lobes whenever we do something of willful intent—but it also raises a kind of more fundamental question, at least about how we as human beings can behave, because we have to wonder whether we have free will and how we direct our will into thinking about God. Do we control the ways in which we understand God, or not? What do we think about God in terms of what does God want us to do with regards to our behaviors and thoughts? Fundamentally, we also have to ask the question as whether God is something that we need to surrender our wills to. In fact, the ability to surrender our will to God may actually change the way we understand God. That may sound a little strange, but let me give you another example from a participant of our survey. They said this was part of their experience; they said:

> I prayed longer, another couple of days of the anguish continued. Finally, I decided I could not withhold my assent. I surrendered everything, including my faith and my salvation, and only for one reason. I loved God, I gave up everything because I loved God. I assented to His request. In an instant, God returned everything to me, transformed. God liberated me. From that day forward, a new relationship existed between God and me. It is ever present, no distance, no separation. It just is!

By surrendering herself, this individual found a new understanding of God and a new relationship to God; so thus this act of surrendering became an important way for this individual to change her beliefs about God. Remember back to our study of speaking in tongues; what happened to the frontal lobes? In contrast to the meditation and prayer practices where the frontal lobes turned on, their frontal lobes shut down; and we might imagine that when anyone surrenders themself to this experience of God, that frontal lobe shuts down and when that happens it allows other areas of the brain to turn on. When that happens, we develop new ideas, new ways of thinking about things; so it's not a surprise, then, that this notion of surrender may be a critical piece to how we begin to understand the concept of God.

We've now reviewed several different cognitive and emotional ways in which we come to understand the concept of God, but we still haven't addressed the even more fundamental question: Does God exist? How does our brain approach this question? How does your brain approach this question? It's very interesting to me, because the one thing that we all seem to take for granted is the notion that we feel that things exist; the brain perceives and believes that there are things that are real out there in the world. We assign reality based upon the degree to some extent to which that thing feels real to us. We also have a binary operator that sets that opposition apart. There are things that exist that are real and there are things that don't exist that aren't real.

Why do some believe that God exists and others don't? We covered some of this in the earlier lecture on believers and nonbelievers; but regardless of your own beliefs, it's the brain that draws the line between a belief that God does or doesn't exist. We even found differences in the brain scans of atheists contemplating God. For them, the brain wasn't able to activate, especially the frontal lobes, in the same way as a religious person; in large part because they didn't have a clear sense of God's existence. But it remains unclear why we think anything exists at all, and this will be a topic that we'll cover in one of our concluding lectures; it's an actually fundamentally important topic that engages religion, philosophy, and all the aspects of how we understand who we are.

We've considered a variety of cognitive and emotional processes that directly relate to how we perceive and experience God. We can now turn to some specific experimental approaches to help us explore how people understand God and the beliefs and ideas that actually arise from the brain's functions. We can therefore ask a very specific question; we can ask a question like: What does God look like? What does God feel like? What is God's personality? We may even ask how these attributes are related to our own; and we can explore such questions through experimental research.

We decided to ask the question: "What does God look like?" We went to about 300 or 400 people and we handed them a piece of paper and a pencil and we said, "Draw God. Draw your image of what God is." You may even want to try that right now. What would you draw? When we analyze the different figures and the different pictures that people have drawn, we realize that we could start to categorize them into several specific groups, and they were very interesting and very relevant in telling us what people think God is. Only about 20 percent drew a face, drew an anthropormic version of God; the God on the roof of the Sistine Chapel. About 60 percent drew either some kind of abstract image—which may have been swirls, hearts, different shapes—or some kind of nature scene, and that 60 percent was divided pretty evenly. The people who drew nature scenes usually talked about God being nature, and they drew mountains, and the sun, and so forth.

About 15 percent left the picture blank, and we realized that as part of this entire study we didn't want to just impose our own interpretation onto these pictures; we wanted to hear from the people drawing them what they thought their picture represented. In fact, it was very interesting, when we got the information back for the people who left it blank; because for the people who left it blank, some of them were incredibly religious and some of them were incredibly nonreligious. For the incredibly religious, they said, "We left it blank because God is undrawable." Of course, for the atheists, about half of them left it blank; they simply said, "There is no God, there's nothing to draw."

We can ask another question: What does God feel like to us? At the beginning of this lecture we talked about the Baylor study and found that Americans believe in four principle types of God; and they were very clear to say that this isn't the only way people believe in God, but there are these four notable points. They talked about God as authoritarian, as critical, as distant, and as benevolent. I actually found these four types to be very exciting from a brain perspective because they seem to proceed along two very specific dimensions: a spatial dimension and an emotional dimension. For the spatial dimension, we're talking about God as being right here around us or being very distant; and therefore we can think about how the parietal lobe— that orientation part of the brain that helps us with our sense of space—is involved in that experience; so that for some people, they perceive God as being far away, and other people feel that God is right around them. The other dimension is the emotional dimension, our limbic system, asking us "Is God loving or is God hating?" Do we look at God positively or negatively; the critical God that's always looking down on us or the very benevolent, compassionate God that's always there to support us?

If we think about these emotional responses, we might also begin to ask the next question, which is: How do these emotions ultimately affect us going forward? Do these emotions, positive or negative, actually change our brain? This is something that we'll be covering a little bit more in our next lecture.

But I also want to bring up one other idea; because our research suggests that there may even be a fifth type, a fifth way of thinking about God, and this would be a mystical sense of God. If you remember, when people try to understand God, they think about God in terms of this oneness, this sense of connectedness; and if that's the case, it may seem to expand beyond these other four dimensions of the Baylor survey, because it may or may not have the same kind of emotional way or spatial way of relating to God when you think about God in some kind of mystical or deeply spiritual sense.

These studies also bring up one other important idea, which is whether or not the way in which our brain thinks about God has something or even anything to do with what the actual nature of God is. Just because we happen to think about God as existing or not existing, or being benevolent or being very negative towards us, being very critical; that doesn't necessarily tell us anything about the actual nature of what God is. Even though we can think about …

How God Changes the Brain
Lecture 21

In this lecture, you will learn how God and religion change your brain. Change might come about through spiritual practices, as a result of long-held beliefs, or even from a religious experience. Scientific research is helping us understand how certain beliefs and practices lead to positive changes in the brain while others lead to negative changes. Based on that research, perhaps we can find ways to create more positive experiences—which arguably are beneficial not only for the individual, but also for society as a whole.

How Do Spiritual Practices Change the Brain?

- Perhaps the most effective way of assessing the way religion shapes the brain is to study specific spiritual practices. One way is to combine imaging and other scientific measures with subjective and phenomenological evaluation. For example, longitudinal findings compare meditators with nonmeditators over a long period of time.

- In a study of Kirtan Kriya and memory, researchers recruited older individuals with memory problems but no history of prior meditation. They were taught Kirtan Kriya meditation, which derives from the Kundalini yoga tradition. It is considered to be one of the fundamental meditation practices. In fact, one yoga master suggested that if you have to learn only one meditation practice, this is the one to learn.

- The practice involves two different elements: chanting the sa-ta-na-ma mantra, which incorporates primal sounds into the meditation, and making finger movements called mudras.

- Researchers scanned the brains of participants before and after eight weeks of training and tested their memory using a variety of neuropsychological tests, including tests of verbal memory, visual attention and task switching (referred to as the trails test), psychological state, and spirituality.

- In addition, they compared the Kirtan Kriya group to a group listening to music. The results were fascinating on a number of levels.

- Cognitively, people in the Kirtan Kriya group performed, on average, about 10 percent better on the verbal memory task and the trails test after the eight weeks of training. This suggests that the meditation program improved memory. Furthermore, the improvements in memory were correlated with changes in activity in the frontal lobes and thalamus.

- Perhaps the most important changes were in their emotional state. People practicing Kirtan Kriya were found to have significant reductions of 10 to 20 percent in stress, anxiety, depression, and fatigue. These changes correlated with changes in activity in the limbic and emotional control centers of the brain.

- If a secular version of a meditation practice that people did for 12 minutes per day for eight weeks causes these kinds of changes, imagine what kind of changes occur when people engage in a religious or spiritual tradition for many years. The effects should be profound.

- On the scans, researchers discovered some fascinating changes. They found an overall increase in the frontal lobes—not just during the practice, but even at rest. They also noticed a change in the thalamus.

- A small study of five people doing Iyengar yoga meditation was conducted to evaluate the effects of a three-month yoga program on brain function. Researchers found similar increased frontal lobe activity after the program.

- These are not the only studies that show the impact of spiritual practices on brain function. Several studies of people who have had intense religious or spiritual experiences show that those experiences have a direct impact on the brain.

- For example, a study from the University of Montreal asked 15 patients who had near-death experiences to meditate on their experience of the light while in the fMRI scanner. The results showed increased activity in the brainstem, prefrontal cortex, right superior parietal lobule, and insula.

- The University of Montreal group also did a study involving 15 Carmelite nuns, who were asked to mentally relive the most intense mystical experience of their lives. When they did, fMRI scans showed increased activation in the orbitofrontal cortex, temporal cortex, parietal lobules, caudate, prefrontal cortex, anterior cingulated, and brainstem.

- However, while these studies are fascinating, an important question remains: Were the states studied the same as the actual experiences?

What Happens When God Gets Angry?
- Thus far, the studies that we have evaluated appear to be generally positive effects of spiritual experiences. However, as wonderful and positive as religion and religious experiences can be, there are a great many examples of negative experiences.

- People can struggle with their religious beliefs, or they may have a positive experience but struggle to incorporate it into their spiritual belief system.

- Negative perspectives on God can be very detrimental. In the individual, negative views of God can cause stress, anxiety, and depression.

- Negative thoughts activate the brain structures that are associated with negative emotions and create a stress response. The more the brain thinks negative thoughts, the stronger those neuronal connections become. In other words, hatred leads to more hatred.

- Many ancient sacred texts are full of violent conflicts. For example, the Inquisition was rooted in religious beliefs. While religion may not always be the root cause of a conflict, those fighting frequently turn to their religious beliefs to support them. They feel that God is on their side.

- What is the difference in the brain between those who are violent and hateful and those who are not? There is some evidence in the study of violent criminals, for example. When these individuals have their brains scanned, usually one of two results are seen: Either they have reduced frontal lobe function or increased limbic system function.

- The hypothalamus regulates our rage response, and while it is difficult to image the hypothalamus, this structure is also likely involved when people feel fear or hatred. In addition, the more a person focuses on hateful or violent ideas, the more they become a part of the brain's connections. Rituals designed to enhance such feelings also augment these negative emotions.

Can We Foster the Compassionate Side of God?
- Religion can foster great compassion. History abounds with examples of individuals whose religious beliefs moved them to perform acts of great charity and kindness.

- What is the difference between someone who is religious and enormously compassionate and someone who is religious and very hateful? Can neuroscience help to clarify which practices and beliefs foster more compassion and social cohesion?

- Positive emotions activate brain areas that are involved with happiness and reward. Positive emotions lower the stress response and improve memory and behavior.

- A number of research projects have attempted to improve compassion among people through meditation and related practices. For example, the Institute of Noetic Sciences and a group of researchers affiliated with the Transcendental Meditation Program have led some controversial studies.

- Several thousand meditators have been brought into cities such as Washington, DC, and crime rates dropped by about 25 percent. In a particular study, weekly violent crime was measured by the Uniform Crime Reporting Program of the Federal Bureau of Investigation. Violent crimes include homicide, rape, aggravated assault, and robbery. These data were obtained from the District of Columbia Metropolitan Police Department for 1993 as well as for the preceding five years (1988–1992).

- The results showed a decrease in violent crime associated with the weeks that they brought together about 4,000 meditators in the region. Of course,

The way in which religion shapes the brain can be studied by analyzing the brains of meditators and nonmeditators.

there have been a variety of critiques of this study. For example, were the crime measurements appropriate? Could there have been other factors that affected the results, such as weather or more police?

- What if such an experiment could be confirmed? What would it tell us about how our brain can be utilized in a compassionate way to not only affect itself, but also to affect the world around us?

- Research can also help us to determine the most effective practices to help foster compassion. We can learn whether meditation, prayer, or other practices have the same or greater effects on the brain and emotions.

- We might even conceive of creating specific practices that take advantage of the data available to create a healthier, more positive experience of religion or spirituality. For example, we might create a practice that helps to enhance communication between two people. A brief meditation that involves dialogue between two individuals fosters intimacy and is shown to be useful in group and individual settings.

Suggested Reading

Ashbrook and Albright, *The Humanizing Brain.*

Beauregard and Paquette, "Neural Correlates of a Mystical Experience in Carmelite Nuns."

Newberg and Waldman, *How God Changes Your Brain.*

Newberg, Wintering, Khalsa, Roggenkamp, and Waldman, "Meditation Effects on Cognitive Function and Cerebral Blood Flow in Subjects with Memory Loss."

Newberg, Wintering, Waldman, Amen, Khalsa, and Alavi, "Cerebral Blood Flow Differences between Long-Term Meditators and Non-Meditators."

Questions to Consider

1. How do religious and spiritual ideas have an impact on the brain?

2. Why do some people develop compassion while others develop hatred as part of their religious beliefs?

How God Changes the Brain
Lecture 21—Transcript

When I was a medical student, one of the most intriguing articles that I came across was in the *Journal of the American Medical Association*. It was a theoretical piece written by a neuroscientist who'd gone to Rome and seen the Sistine Chapel. When he looked up at the central part of the painting where we see God reaching his hand out to Adam, he noticed some fascinating things. Being a neuroscientist, his brain tended to look at everything from a brain point of view. He actually thought that the image of God that he saw in the painting—and God was surrounded by these flowing clouds and angels—actually looked a lot like the outline of the brain. Interestingly, the outstretched hand of God as it appears to be coming out towards Adam looks like it's coming out of part of the frontal lobes if we see the brain in that image the way this neuroscientist did.

The author of this article actually argued several points. One of his points was that it may not be completely farfetched to think that Michelangelo would know something about the structure of the human brain. Apparently, at the time, a lot of artists did do dissections so that they could better understand the form of the human body; and therefore it wouldn't be a complete surprise that Michelangelo would have some notion of what the brain actually looked like. But the more relevant point from the perspective of the article and this lecture is that the neuroscientist was arguing that the painting might actually suggest a slightly different interpretation of the creation of man. Thee argued that it may not have been so much the actual physical creation of human beings that was important, but it was that we were subsequently endowed by God with the brain, the thought processes that make us human. In this way God changed our brain. We were given the ability to think, plan, feel—and most importantly for the purposes of this course, we were given the ability to think about God.

So what DO we think about when we hear the word "God"?

Is there any word that:

Stirs up more emotion?

Creates more confusion?

Causes more controversy?

Causes more love and hatred?

But what does this word mean and how does it have such a huge impact?

In our last lecture we looked at how the structures and processes of the brain influence the way we think about God. Put differently, we looked at the way our brain "shapes" God.

In this lecture we're going to turn that formula around. Today we're going to look at the way God and religion shape the brain.

How Do Spiritual Practices Change Your Brain?

Perhaps the most effective way of assessing the way religion shapes the brain is to study specific spiritual practices.

Combine imaging and other scientific measures with subjective and phenomenological evaluation

Longitudinal findings

Comparison of long-term meditators with non-meditators

Do spiritual practices affect the brain over time?

Kirtan Kriya and memory study

Recruited older individuals with memory problems

No history of prior meditation

Taught them Kirtan Kriya meditation. This meditation derives from the Kundalini yoga tradition. It is considered to be one of the fundamental meditation practices. One yoga master suggested that if you have to learn only one meditation practice, this is the one.

The practice involves two different elements.

SA, TA, NA, MA

Finger movements (mudras)

Scanned their brain before and after 8 weeks of training

Tested their memory using a variety of neuropsychological tests.

These included verbal memory (how many fruits or animals you can name in a minute); and the Trails test as well as measure of psychological state and spirituality.

In addition, we compared the KK group to a group listening to music.

The results were fascinating on a number of levels.

Imaging results. Baseline to baseline. Meditation to meditation.

Frontal lobe and anterior cingulate increase.

Asymmetric thalamus.

Cognitively, people performed on average about 10% better on the verbal memory task and the trails test. This suggests that the meditation program improved memory. Further, the improvements in memory were correlated with changes in activity in the frontal lobes and thalamus.

But perhaps the most important changes were in their emotional state.

People practicing KK were found to have significant reductions of 10-20% in stress, anxiety, depression, and fatigue.

These changes correlated with changes in activity in the limbic and emotional control centers of the brain.

So if a secular version of a meditation practice that people did for 12 minutes a day for 8 weeks causes these kinds of changes, can you imagine what kind of changes occur when people engage a religious or spiritual tradition for years and years? The effects should be profound.

What did we find on the scans? We saw some fascinating changes. We saw in overall increase in the frontal lobes, not just during the practice, but even at rest. We also saw a change in the thalamus.

We even did a small study of five people doing Iyengar yoga meditation. This study evaluated the effects of a 3 month yoga program on brain function. We found similar increased frontal lobe activity after the program.

But these are not the only studies that shows the impact of spiritual practices on brain function. Several studies of people who have had intense religious or spiritual experiences show that those experiences have a direct impact on the brain

For example, a study from the University of Montreal asked 15 NDE patients to meditate on their experience of the light while in the fMRI scanner. The results showed increased activity in the brainstem, prefrontal cortex, right superior parietal lobule, and insula

And you'll remember from an earlier lecture that the University of Montreal group also did a study involving 15 carmelite nuns. The nuns were asked them to mentally relive the most intense mystical experience of their life, and when they did so fMRI scans showed increased activatyin the orbitofrontal cortex, temporal cortex, parietal lobules, caudate, PFC, anterior cingulate and brainstem.

But while I am fascinated by the findings from these studies, I do have one very important question. Were the states studied the same as the actual experience?

What happens when God gets angry?

So far, the studies we have reviewed have evaluated what appear to be generally positive effects of spiritual experiences.

But as wonderful and positive as religion and religious experiences can be, there are a great many examples of negative experiences.

In the lecture on NDEs, we related negative NDE experiences. And in another lecture we talked about Monica, whose anger at God had a negative impact on her mental health. People can struggle with their religious beliefs. Or they may have a positive experience but struggle to incorporate it into their spiritual belief system.

Negative perspectives on God can be very detrimental

In the individual, negative views of God cause stress, anxiety, and depression.

Activates those brain structures that are associated with negative emotions and create stress response

The more the brain thinks negative thoughts, the stronger those neuronal connections become. Hatred leads to more hatred.

Causes outward destructive behaviors

Terrorism and rituals

Violence

Many ancient sacred texts are full of violent conflicts. The Inquisition was rooted in religious beliefs. And while religion may not always be the root cause of a conflict, those fighting frequently turn to their religious beliefs to support them. They feel that God is on their side.

Hatred

What is the difference in the brain Between those who are violent and hateful and those who are not? There is some evidence in the study of violent criminals for example. When these individuals have their brain scanned, usually one of two results are seen. Either they have reduced frontal lobe function or increased limbic system function. It is also known that the hypothalamus regulates our rage response and while it is difficult to image the hypothalamus, this structure is also likely involved when people feel fear or hatred. Also, remember that neurons that fire together wire together. The more a person focuses on hateful or violent ideas, the more they become a part of their brain's connections. Rituals designed to enhance such feelings also augment these negative emotions.

Can we foster the compassionate side of God?

But religion can also foster great compassion. History abounds with examples of individuals whose religious beliefs moved them to perform acts of great charity and kindness. So what is the difference between someone who is religious and enormously compassionate and someone who is religious and very hateful? Can neuroscience help to clarify which practices and beliefs foster more compassion and social cohesion?

Positive emotions activate brain areas involved with happiness and reward

Positive emotions lower stress response, improve memory and behavior

Tale of two wolves

A number of research projects have attempted to improve compassion among people through meditation and related practices.

Institute of noetic sciences and a group of researchers affiliated with Transcendental Meditation have led some controversial studies

Several thousand meditators have been brought into cities such as Washington DC and crime rates dropped by about 25%. In this study, weekly violent crime, was measured by the Uniform Crime Report program of the Federal Bureau of Investigation; violent crimes include homicide, rape, aggravated assault, and robbery. This data was obtained from the District of Columbia Metropolitan Police Department for 1993 as well as for the preceding five years (1988–1992). The results showed a decrease associated with the weeks that they brought together about 4000 meditators in the region. Of course, there have been a variety of critiques of this study—were the crime measurements appropriate? Could there have been other factors related to weather, more police, etc.? But what if such an experiment can be confirmed? What would it tell us about how our brain can be utilized in a compassionate way to not only affect itself, but the world around us?

But research can also help us to determine the most effective practices to help foster compassion. We can learn whether meditation, prayer, or other practices have the same or greater effects on the brain and emotions.

We might even conceive of creating specific practices that take advantage of the data available to create a healthier more positive experience of religion or spirituality.

For example, we might create a practice that helps to enhance communication between two people.

A brief meditation that involves dialogue between two individuals

Fosters intimacy

Shown to be useful in group and individual settings

God and religion clearly can change our brain. That change might come about through spiritual practices or as a result of long-held beliefs or even from a religious experience.

We might even ponder whether God actually affects our brain's functions (i.e. if God exists it makes sense that we would have a brain that can receive and be changed by God like in the Sistine Chapel story)

Scientific research is helping us understand how certain beliefs and practices lead to positive changes in the brain while others lead to negative changes. Based on that research, perhaps we can find ways to create more positive experiences—which arguably are beneficial not only for the individual but for society as a whole.

Why God Won't Go Away
Lecture 22

The brain functions in specific ways toward self-maintenance and self-transcendence, and religion provides powerful mechanisms to accomplish these goals. Thus, the functions of religion map very well onto the functions of the brain. Because of this, the brain is likely to hold onto religious beliefs and ideas very strongly—regardless of whether they are accurate or right. Unless the brain undergoes some fundamental change in the way it works and what it does for us, it would seem that religion and God are not going to go away for a very long time.

The Dialogue between Science and Religion

- Despite the supposed end of religion at the end of the 19th century, religion is experiencing a resurgence in many different arenas, including in the context of integrating science with traditional belief systems.

- Many traditional religions are maintaining their strength. The numbers show that about 80 to 85 percent of people in the world identify with some religion.

- In the United States, large percentages of people believe in heaven and hell, angels, and God. In fact, recent polls indicate that about 81 percent of Americans believe in heaven while approximately 75 percent believe in angels.

- Religions are adaptive and continue to bring in new people. In addition, there is a growing interest in the relationship between science and religion.

- Traditional religions are generally intrigued by science—specifically if it supports religious practices—but they are careful about how science handles religion.

- Various religious groups are generally supportive of the dialogue between science and religion, but they may want to utilize scientific information to prove their views.

- Religious groups might also be interested to see if brain information can be used to improve spirituality and liturgy. In the past, liturgy and ritual was probably based on doctrine—but also trial and error. For example, clergy members tried different songs or prayers in certain ways and observed the reaction of the participants.

- This is not a very systematic approach, but we may find ways using science that can determine practices that do work better, depending on the goal. For example, if an entire liturgy is comprised of music, prayers, and stories, could we consider a study that might show how effective each element is?

- In today's world, we often find people stating that they are spiritual but not religious, and there are a number of groups and movements that support this approach. Some of these are referred to as new-age ideologies, but there is tremendous variability in their beliefs.

- Many of these ideologies have some common elements, such as they generally like everything to work out, so they usually put a positive spin on things—including the intersection between science and religion. They are interested in proving some of their ideological concepts, which include ideas about consciousness and even psychic types of phenomena.

- In addition to these more spiritually oriented interests in science and religion, science itself is taking a renewed interest in the topic. While science has a strong cadre of materialists, there is increasing interest in how science may be used to help better understand religion. This has led to a wealth of research studies.

- The overall perspective is that science is interested in studying humanity and because religion (or spirituality) is such an important part of humanity, it would make sense for science to actively pursue this topic.

- Some scientists are merely interested in seeing how far science can go and what happens when it bumps up against religion. Scientists exploring boundary issues such as quantum mechanics, cosmology, or neuroscience recognize the possible importance of spiritual concepts.

- In the field of medicine, there is also growing interest in spirituality. This interest in religion is reflected in the biomedical literature, where the number of research articles on the interplay between faith and human physiology has increased dramatically over the past 25 years.

- Among nurses and doctors, there is a growing realization that we need to incorporate spirituality into patient care, but others are concerned about the appropriate use of religion in relation to health care.

Self-Maintenance and Self-Transcendence

- From a neuroscientific perspective, religion affects the brain and mind. There are many structures and functions of the brain, but generally, it seems that the brain has two basic functions or goals: self-maintenance and self-transcendence.

- The self-maintenance function of the brain is very broad. It incorporates all of the things that our brain does to help us survive, including eating, drinking, mating, and simply navigating the complex and sometimes threatening world in which we live.

- The self-maintenance function is also the function that helps us avoid dangers—by enabling the fight or flight response, for example. To some degree, the abilities of this function are similar to the adaptive advantages of religion. Ultimately, a spiritual brain appears to help us survive.

- Research on the relationship between religion and health have generally shown that religion is beneficial to our physical and mental health. In this way, religion supports the primary brain function of self-maintenance.

- However, self-maintenance is only part of the story because an organism doesn't merely maintain one steady, unalterable state or condition throughout life. People change, and as a result, the brain must have the ability to change and adapt as well.

- To some extent, self-transcendence is part of self-maintenance because, presumably, an adaptable brain will handle the many vagaries of the world more effectively. The brain needs to be able to change and adapt, and self-transcendence refers to the brain's ability to do this.

- As we grow up and go through our lives, we learn new ideas and behaviors, meet new people, and continue to develop as a person. From a physiological perspective, the brain maintains a sense of self-identity even as it processes and adapts to all the changes in a human life.

- The brain has the ability to change itself by rewiring the connections between neurons and possibly even changing the function of the neurons in a process referred to as neuroplasticity.

- Recall that the brain can strengthen or weaken connections. Thus, there is a certain degree of stability within the brain and its connections. This allows us to be who we are throughout our entire lives. However, the brain also has flexibility, variability, and changeability. This allows us to transcend ourselves from one moment of life to the next.

- Evolutionarily, we should theoretically be transcending toward something that is even more adaptive—if not actually better—but the issue is that we don't always know what is adaptive. The brain keeps trying new ideas, new beliefs, and new behaviors. Through learning and trial and error, the brain begins to figure out the best ways to manage itself through life. However, it is important to realize that the brain is more interested in adaptability and surviving than accuracy.

- It seems that religion may be a powerful source of self-transcendent activity. The primary tenet of most religions is to better ourselves. Religions generally provide a system of morals, set of practices, and set of beliefs that we are to strive toward. This means that religion is providing a framework for change.

- As the brain ponders how and why to change in the future, religions tell human beings to try to be more kind, to be more charitable, and to strive to do good.

- Religions often provide specific rites of passage, including birth rituals, childhood rituals, marriage rituals, adult rituals, and death rituals. Religions appear to realize the process of change that human beings experience throughout their lives. Religions help to put this change into context.

In the Christian faith, when babies are baptized, they become official members of the Christian church.

- There are certain religious and spiritual experiences that might be the pinnacle of self-transcendence. These mystical experiences—sometimes called salvation or enlightenment—are a powerful source of self-transcendence. The experience is frequently perceived as the person changing into an entirely new state of being.

- These experiences are also associated with neurophysiological processes. However, much of the neurophysiological description is somewhat speculative because it is almost impossible to know when someone is going to have a transcendent experience, and when they are having it, we can't interrupt them because that would disrupt the entire experience. However, we can infer a lot based on the studies of practices such as meditation and prayer because these practices are known to induce mystical states.

- Mystical states appear to be associated with profound changes in the autonomic nervous system. Recall that one of the areas that is involved in meditation and prayer practices is the parietal lobe, or the orientation area. There is evidence that during such practices, neuronal information may be blocked from reaching this orientation area, resulting in a decrease in activity in this structure.

- If the structure normally provides us with our sense of self, then decreased activity may be associated with a loss of the sense of self. However, we might also expect that the greater the decrease in activity, the greater the loss of the sense of self and the greater the person begins to feel connected to, or at one with, God or some ultimate reality.

- If this is the case, there may actually be a continuum—a unitary continuum—along which different transcendent states occur. There may even be an absolute unitary state in which the individual completely loses his or her sense of self and feels that everything is incorporated into a total oneness. In fact, such a mystical state may reflect the ultimate self-transcendence.

Suggested Reading

Beauregard and O'Leary, *The Spiritual Brain.*

d'Aquili, "Senses of Reality in Science and Religion."

———, "The Neurobiological Bases of Myth and Concepts of Deity."

d'Aquili, Lauglin, and McManus, *The Spectrum of Ritual.*

McNamara, ed, *Where God and Science Meet.*

Newberg, d'Aquili, and Rause, *Why God Won't Go Away.*

Questions to Consider

1. What is it about the relationship between religion and the brain that results in religion not going away?

2. How is religion or spirituality fundamentally linked with the human brain?

Why God Won't Go Away
Lecture 22—Transcript

By the end of the 19th century, religion and God were supposedly dead, or going to be very soon. There was the education of the masses with the notion that as people learned more, they wouldn't need this archaic concept of God. There was also the higher criticism of the Judeo-Christian scriptures; and ultimately, with the scientific method, many people thought that we were going to learn so much about how the world works that we simply weren't going to need God and religion anymore.

But despite the supposed end of religion more than 100 years ago, religion in many ways is experiencing a resurgence in so many different arenas, including in the context of integrating science with traditional belief systems. Of course, many traditional religions are still maintaining their strength. The numbers show that about 80–85% of people in the world identify with some type of religious belief system. In the United States, large percentages of people believe in heaven and hell, angels, and God. In fact, a recent poll indicated that about 81% of Americans believe in heaven, while approximately 75% believe in angels.

Religions are clearly doing fairly well; they're very adaptive, they find ways to continue to bring in new people into their ranks; and it's also interesting because religion has tried to adapt to the developments of technology in society. There's a growing interest in the relationship between science and religion. In fact, traditional religions are generally very intrigued by what science has to say about our world; and specifically, when science actually supports religious practices, that can be very beneficial from a religious or spiritual perspective. But, of course, traditional religions are also a bit careful about how science handles religion and what the ultimate conclusions of science may be and whether they'll be in contradistinction to what religious and spiritual beliefs actually say about our world.

I would say that in generally most religious traditions are supportive of the dialogue between science and religion. They may want to utilize the information to help to prove their views. For example, I've actually been asked at various times by different groups to help to do a brain scan to prove that their belief system is really the best or most true. I try to explain to them how our brain scans work and the types of implications that we can obtain from those scans; but nonetheless, they're still interested in trying to prove one belief system or another as being more right.

Religious groups might also be interested to see if the brain information can help to improve spirituality or the liturgy that has developed around their religion. For example, in the past, liturgy and ritual was probably based upon doctrine to some degree, but also to some extent trial and error. A clergyman might try a different song or a different prayer in some kind of way and observe the reaction of the participants. I always have in my mind the notion that they may have tried a new song and then afterwards waited to see what the response was. Did people come up them and say, "That was an amazing song, that made me feel really spiritual," or did the people come up and say, "Boy, I don't understand why you did that song, I didn't get that at all"; and then from there, they began to develop a new liturgy, either dependent on that song or not, based on how people responded to it.

But, of course, this isn't a very systematic approach, the kind of systematic approach that we're trying to develop throughout this course. We may find ways of using science, some way of investigating these questions, which can help to determine practices that do work better depending on the goal. For example, if an entire liturgy is comprised of music, prayers, and stories, we might consider a study that could show us how effective each element actually is. What if some of the music turns out to be not very helpful, maybe it even interferes with the liturgy? By doing a research study that asks that kind of a question of the participants, we might be able to do a better job than simply relying on the few people who come up afterward. Maybe we can find out truly what are the "active ingredients" of that particular ritual or that particular liturgy.

In today's world, we often find people stating that they're spiritual but not religious; and, of course, there are a number of groups and movements that support this overall approach. Some of these are referred to as New Age ideologies; but there's tremendous variability in their beliefs, and some of them actually go back thousands of years. Many of these ideologies have some common elements. For example, they generally like things to work out well; they usually put a positive spin on things including the intersection between science and religion. Just like traditional religions, they might be interested in proving that some of their ideological concepts—maybe some of their practices and the various ideas they have about consciousness or even psychic types of phenomena—are real and accurate.

In addition to these spiritually-oriented interests in science and religion, science itself is taking a renewed interest in the topic. Of course, that's what we're here for in this course, to see how science can take a new look at spirituality and religion. While science has had a strong cadre of materialists, there's increasing interest in how science may be used to help better understand religion. This has led to much of the research studies we've discussed throughout this course. The overall perspective is that science is interested in studying humanity, and since religion and spirituality is such an important part of humanity, it would certainly make sense for science to actively pursue this topic.

Some scientists are merely interested in seeing how far science can actually go and what happens when it bumps up against some of the doctrines and ideas of religion. Scientists exploring these so-called boundary issues include scientists looking at fields such as quantum mechanics, cosmology, or even neuroscience; and they recognize the possible importance of spiritual concepts. For example, a cosmologist who's interested in understanding the origins of the universe may actually want to think a little bit about what religious and spiritual traditions have told us about that. It might tell us something about where the universe comes from and how we can understand it, perhaps in a very holistic way that can ultimately be incorporated back into how we think about things scientifically.

In fact, a leading cosmologist at NASA named Robert Jastrow for many years quipped regarding the scientific theories about the origin of the universe; he said that:

> For the scientist who has lived by his faith in the power of reason, the cosmological story ends like a bad dream. He has scaled the mountains of ignorance; he is about to conquer the highest peak; [and] as he pulls himself over the final rock, he

is greeted by a band of theologians who have been sitting there for centuries.

What he means by this is that as the cosmologist keeps trying to understand the origins of the universe, he may come across theological and philosophical ideas about the origin of the universe that go back thousands of years.

Of course, in my field of medicine, there's also a growing interest in the study of spirituality and religion. Take, for example, Francis Collins, who's the current director of the National Institutes of Health. He was the head of the Human Genome Project, but wrote in his book, *The Language of God*, how he came to realize that the human genome and the human person are simply too amazing not to have been created by a God.

This same interest in religion is reflected in the biomedical literature where a growing number of research articles on the interplay between faith and human physiology have continued to increase; in fact, it's increased dramatically over the past 25 years. Among nurses and doctors and other healthcare providers, I certainly see a growing realization that we need to incorporate in some way spirituality into patient care. We've come to understand that spirituality is such an important part of so many people's lives that to ignore that part of them we really aren't going to do the best job that we can of helping to heal them. But how do we do that? How do we engage this part of a person in appropriate ways to help them benefit their health?

Of course, others are concerned about this very issue about how the appropriate use of religion actually occurs in healthcare. Is it appropriate for doctors to pray with patients, or to pray for patients? One of the things that I always tell the medical students who I teach is that almost every one of them is going to be asked by one of their patients at some point to pray with them. What do they do? How should they respond? Science hasn't really answered this question yet; and therefore science needs to be able to look at these questions, look at these issues, and try to figure out the best way to understand how we incorporate religious and spiritual ideas into our sense of healthcare.

In all these divergent areas, there's a persistent and intense interest in religion, and also the intersection between science and religion. This needs to be handled very carefully, but it's also very intriguing. After all, this leads, at least in my mind, to a very important conclusion: Religion is made of some pretty tenacious stuff. It still holds on in spite of all these other swirling issues all around it; in spite of the idea that religion was going to go away, it hangs on. But how do we make sense of the tenacity of religion? What is it about religion that affects us so profoundly? As a neuroscientist, I have to come back to the brain. I think it must affect the brain and the mind in some kind of very powerful, very profound way that helps us to understand the tenacity of religion.

As we've noted before, to some degree as we start to think about the brain and its relationship to religion and spirituality, we also have to think about the relationship between the brain and the mind. In general, what I've tried to do is define the brain as the organ that's inside of our head. It's comprised of the different lobes, the frontal lobe, the temporal lobe; the limbic system, our emotional system; the different neurons that are all connected to each other; and those chemicals, the neurotransmitters, which help all the different parts of the brain communicate with each other.

The mind is the more ethereal part; the thoughts, the feelings, and perceptions. We typically regard them, at least from a neuroscientific perspective, as arising from the function of the brain. As we've described in prior lectures, many of the specific structures and functions of the brain help us to create all of these different functions; but when we get down to it, it seems that the brain ultimately has two very basic functions or goals. We've talked about all these different ways in which the brain works, but it seems to come together into these two very fundamental things that the brain does for us. Those two things I would refer to as a mechanism of self-maintenance and a mechanism of self-transcendence. Let's talk about what these two very basic functions of the brain are all about.

The self-maintenance function of the brain is very broad. It incorporates all of the things that our brain does to help us survive. This includes some very basic functions like eating, drinking, mating, and simply navigating through this very complex and sometimes threatening world in which we live. The brain helps us to develop morals, a sense of family, community, and society that are all part of how we're able to survive. The brain also helps us to avoid dangers. Remember our autonomic nervous system—that arousal part of that autonomic nervous system that helps us with what we call the fight or flight response—it tells us when we need to run, when we need to avoid things; and as we learn about our environment, the cognitive aspects of our brain tell us what things to eat, what things not to eat, to avoid going too close to the edge of a cliff, so it helps us to survive. To some degree, these are also very similar to the adaptive advantages that we've spoken about in a prior lecture; about how religion may actually be helpful from an adaptive perspective and how that may relate to the brain's ability to be adaptive. But ultimately, the spiritual brain may actually help us to survive by helping the brain to engage this self-maintenance aspect of itself.

We've actually explored this in even more detail when we considered the relationship between religion and both physical health and mental health. In general, the results have shown that religion is beneficial to both our physical and mental health. In this way, religion helps to support this very primary brain function of self-maintenance. Remember when we talked about the various physiological benefits of religious practices; the idea that it helps to lower stress levels, improve our feelings of anxiety, and teach us ways of dealing with the world, help us with ways of coping with the world; and if all of that comes together to help improve our mental wellbeing, to help increase our overall lifespan, and reduce the risk of different disorders or different diseases as we talked about, then we can see how potentially important religion could be as a way of helping the brain in its goal of self-maintenance.

If we think about the brain, it's certainly wired to favor behaviors and beliefs that help the human organism to maintain itself; and, again, religion seems to offer a range of benefits that mesh very well with this overall self-maintenance function. But as I mentioned, self-maintenance is only part of the story, because clearly an organism that doesn't merely maintain a steady state but can adapt is extremely important. In fact, an organism that remains only in some kind of unalterable state or condition is probably not going to survive in a very changing environment. People change; people change all the time, and as a result the brain must have the ability to change and adapt as well.

This brings us to the second function that I mentioned a moment ago: that of self-transcendence. To some extent, I'd argue that this is actually part of self-maintenance, since presumably an adaptable brain will help be able to handle the many vagaries of the world much more effectively. The brain needs to be able to change; it needs to be able to adapt and adjust to whatever's happening in our environment so that we function as effectively as possible.

Of course, self-transcendence refers to the brain's ability to actually do this. Think about how the adaptability of the brain is prevalent throughout your life. You're still the same person you were when you were 3 years old, when you were 15 years old, when you were 27 years old; and as much as we're still the same person, we're clearly different. As we grow up and go through our lives, we have to learn new ideas and new behaviors. Otherwise, we'd always act like 3-year-olds—and, of course, some of us like to do that from time to time—but we have to think about ways of developing and adapting so that we're constantly changing to our environment. Of course, as we go through our lives, we meet new people and we continue to develop as a person. We hear new ideas, we come up with new thoughts, and all of this is very important.

From a physiological perspective, how does the brain maintain this sense of self-identity even as it processes and adapts to all the changes in a human life? This is the self-transcendence part of the brain that we're talking about. The brain has the ability to change itself by rewiring the connections enough between the neurons and possibly even changing the functions of the neurons in a process that's frequently referred to as neuroplasticity. If you think back to our lecture on beliefs, when we talked about this we talked about how the brain can actually strengthen or weaken different connections based on what we're doing. The more we use a certain pathway, the more we come back to a particular belief, the stronger those connections become; and the less we use a particular idea or the less we think about something, the weaker those connections become.

This is very important because we have a certain degree of stability; within the connections of the brain, there's a certain degree to which they maintain themselves so that we're always ourselves. This allows us to be who we are throughout our entire lives; but the brain also has the flexibility, the variability, and changeability so that we can transcend ourselves from one moment of life to the next. Of course, if evolution has anything to say about this overall process, we should theoretically transcend towards something that's even more adaptive than next time, if not actually better. The issue is, of course, that we don't always know what's adaptive. The brain keeps trying new things, new ideas, new beliefs, and new behaviors hoping to always come up with something that works a little bit better. Through learning, by talking to others as to what works, and through our own personal trial and error, the brain begins to figure out the best ways to manage itself throughout our lives. But it's important to realize that based on all of this, the brain is more interested in adaptability and surviving rather than actual accuracy. This will be a very crucial point for us to come back to when we expand on this in the last lecture.

The brain has the goal of helping us to transcend ourselves from one moment of life to the next. But are there certain aspects of human life that support this function? Are there certain human beliefs and practices that can help the brain change in an effective manner? It seems that religion may be a very powerful source for this self-transcendent activity. Think about how religion might aid the brain in its self-transcendent promoting function. The primary tenet of most religions is to better ourselves. Religions generally provide a system of morals, a set of practices and behaviors, and a set of beliefs that we're supposed to strive towards.

This means, of course, that religion is providing a framework for change. This is a little different than what sometimes people think about when they think about religion. They often think about religion as being this very static thing; you have to believe one kind of way. But what most evidence shows is religion is all about change; it's all about how we become better and continue to adapt within ourselves and within our brain. As the brain ponders how and why to change in the future, these religious traditions tell human beings to try to be more kind, to be more charitable, and to strive to be good. Religions also provide specific rites of passage including birth rituals, childhood rituals (growing-up rituals, for example), marriage rituals, adult rituals, and ultimately death rituals. Religions appear to realize the process of change that human beings experience throughout their lives. To some degree, religions help to put this change into context; they give it a certain degree of meaning so that we can understand what the change is all about, not fear the change, and in many ways embrace that change.

Finally, there are certain religious and spiritual experiences that might be the pinnacle of self-transcendence. These mystical experiences, which we'll discuss in detail in the next lecture, are a powerful source of the self-transcending itself. The experience is frequently perceived as the person changing into an entirely new state of being. In the Judeo-Christian traditions, we might call it a feeling of salvation. In Buddhism and Hinduism, we might call it enlightenment.

But as we've discussed throughout this course, these experiences are also associated with neurophysiological processes; so let's reflect on the potential neurophysiological processes that might be involved. To some degree, we have to keep in mind that much of this neurophysiological description is somewhat speculative since it's almost impossible to know when someone is actually going to have this kind of transcendent or mystical experience; when they're going to have it and how they're going to have it, we simply don't know. Of course, part of the problem from a scientific perspective is that even if somebody was having it, I can't tap them on the shoulder and ask them how they're doing; "Where are you right now in your transcendent experience?" That would completely disrupt their entire experience.

But based on the information that we've talked about so far in our course, we can infer a lot based upon the studies of practices such as meditation and prayer that are known to be able to help to induce these kinds of mystical states. From the bottom up, we might start with the autonomic nervous system. Mystical states appear to be associated with very profound changes in the autonomic nervous system. They're experienced as having either a tremendous sense of calmness and blissfulness, which would be part of that quiescent side of the autonomic nervous system, or they might be associated with an intense feeling of arousal; and, of course, the sympathetic or arousal part of our autonomic nervous system may be an important part in mediating that kind of response. In fact, sometimes people have a little bit of both, as we'll talk about later on, and it may have something to do with both arms of the autonomic nervous system being involved.

These experiences are also incredibly powerful emotionally; and we've talked a lot throughout this course about the limbic system and how it generates different kinds of emotions. If somebody has this incredible powerful feeling of love or immense joy, what's going on in the amygdala? Maybe it's lighting up like crazy because it's such a powerful emotion. Maybe they have an incredible feeling of fear and awe, which also lights up the amygdala and tells our brain to pay attention to this unbelievable experience that we're having.

Remember that one of the other areas that seems to be very importantly involved in practices such as meditation and prayer is the parietal lobe, that part of our brain that helps us to orient our self and to create a sense for our self. We know that in these practices there sometimes is a decrease of activity in this area that we think is associated with the progressive sense of losing the sense of self, a sense of oneness. There's a lot of evidence that during these practices, as this neuronal information is blocked from reaching that orientation part of the brain, the person begins to engage a kind of unitary experience. In fact, this structure, which normally helps us to create our sense of self, if it's truly blocked from having all of this sensory information coming into it, we may completely lose our sense of self during the experience.

We might actually think about how this loss of the sense of self actually affects the way the person feels connected to or at one with God or some ultimate reality for them. If this is the case, there may actually be some kind of continuum—maybe we would refer to it as a unitary continuum— along which different transcendent states occur. There may be an increasing feeling of oneness, connectedness, and unity that the person feels as there are progressive changes going on in this orientation part of the brain; and there may even be a state that we might refer to as absolute unitary state in which the individual completely loses their sense of self and feels that everything is incorporated into a total sense of oneness. In fact, such a mystical state may reflect the ultimate in self-transcendence

With this overall discussion in mind, we can begin to understand why God won't go away. The answer may lie in the functions of the brain itself. After all, the brain functions in specific ways towards self-maintenance and self-transcendence; and religion seems to provide a very powerful mechanism to accomplish these goals. As we've discussed, through the idea of how religion and spirituality provide ways of helping us to survive and adapt, and helping the brain change and go through its entire life, it's helping with these goals. Thus the functions of religion map very well onto the functions of the brain; and because of this, the brain is likely to hold onto religious beliefs and ideas very strongly, irrespective of whether they're actually accurate or right.

We must come to the conclusion, then, that unless the brain undergoes some fundamental change in the way it works and what it does for us and what its goals are, it would seem that religion and God aren't going to go away for a very, very long time

The Mystical Mind
Lecture 23

In this lecture, you will learn about how brain processes such as abstract process, perceptual processes, and holistic processes are involved in mystical experiences. You will try to better understand the subjective nature of the experience itself—what the person feels, thinks, and perceives—and you will learn how these experiences relate to some of the universal processes of the human brain. In addition, you will perhaps come to understand the universality of mystical experiences—both in terms of different spiritual traditions and the brain itself.

Oneness, Unity, and the Brain

- The spiritual brain is capable of a wide range of perceptions and experiences, but of all these experiences, the mystical experience is surely the most intense. Mystics describe an experience in which the distinctions between self and other—the barriers between inside and outside—are completely broken down. These distinctions and barriers are replaced by a perception of the oneness and unity of all things. Moreover, the perception itself tends to be associated with a sense of tranquility or peace.

- The most important aspect of the experience is oneness—the holistic process—but there is also the notion of peace, which is likely associated with the calming part of the autonomic nervous system.

- How does neuroscience approach this perception, or experience, of the absolute unity of all things? What is it about the spiritual brain that makes it capable of even conceptualizing a notion like the oneness of the cosmos?

- The first question is actually about love, which is usually regarded as an emotion. Brain-scan studies show that love appears to be experienced in several areas of the brain—including the reward system, which includes areas involved with dopamine; the insula, which helps us perceive our emotions; and the social areas. In addition, some studies have suggested that the parietal lobe is decreased, which may go back to the original notion of connecting the self with another.

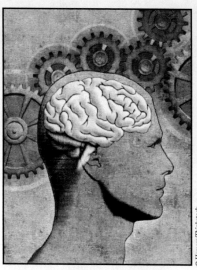

In addition to basic brain functions, other brain processes play a role in very profound spiritual experiences.

- The brain may not only be spiritual in so far as it can have spiritual experiences, but it may actually be mystical. First, there are good reasons for calling the brain mystical just by looking at the physical structure of the brain. The brain works by integrating biological, psychological, social, and spiritual elements. All of these things together make up who we are. Thus, the brain is intensely integrated. It is a oneness made up of billions of neurons and molecules to provide a generally unified view of reality.

- The brain is also intensely integrated with the world around us. In fact, we have trouble truly knowing where the brain ends and the world begins.

- Consciousness and subjective experience are intimately tied to the biological workings of the brain, but we have no clear way of describing how this happens. This indescribability of how a physical brain relates to a spiritual mind is very similar to the kinds of paradoxical and ineffable descriptions we see arising from mystical experiences.

- In addition, because we are forever trapped within our own consciousness, we may never figure out how this relationship occurs. It remains a fundamental mystery—just like the nature and elements of mystical experiences.

- Finally, and perhaps most obviously, we can call the brain mystical because the brain is clearly capable of having mystical experiences. Indeed, people have been having mystical experiences throughout time and across a wide range of cultures.

Mystical Experiences and the Brain

- If it is possible to apply science as a way of gaining new insights into the nature of religion, spirituality, and mysticism, then the scientific study of the spiritual brain could have tremendous implications for how religious ideas and even theology arise from or are associated with profound spiritual experiences such as mystical ones. This is one area in which the exciting new field known as neurotheology may contribute.

- As we explore the potential links between mystical experience and the brain, we might be able to better understand the nature of these experiences and also how the brain interprets and incorporates such experiences into belief systems. In addition, such an analysis may provide a unique perspective on philosophical and theological concepts such as morality, causality, ontology, and epistemology.

- A variety of different cognitive processes are involved in much of how religious and spiritual experiences are perceived and interpreted subjectively. These experiences are then converted—along with our memories, sensations, emotions, and social interactions—into a set of beliefs.

- The causal function of the brain is responsible for the notion that the oneness is somehow causing the material universe to come into existence, and if the experience is perceived as God, then the mystical understanding of God is such that God causes the universe.

- With the holistic function, not only is the universe experienced as a oneness, but this notion also can become the prevailing tenet of a spiritual tradition such as Buddhism or Hinduism.

- The binary function of the brain differentiates the mystical reality from the everyday reality we experience. This requires some way to address how these two perspectives on reality are related.

- The emotional value of the brain might allow you to experience the mystical as a mixture of awe or joy.

Mystics and God

- The conclusion of the mystics is that God is by nature unknowable. God is not an objective fact or an actual being; God is, in fact, the absolute, undifferentiated oneness that is perceived to be the ground of all existence.

- When we understand this concept that the mystics claim regarding God, then we conceive of God using the extremes of our brain's functions. However, the mystical experience, although indescribable, is for some reason experienced as deeply connecting the individual with his or her notion of God. It makes the experience completely and wholly tangible.

- If we turn to the comforting images of a personal, knowable God—a God who exists apart from the rest of creation as a distinct, individual being—then we tend to conceive of God via the standard brain mechanisms that include emotions, thought, and behaviors. However, mystics feel that they can form an intimate union with God, which is the notion that God is not around us but within us.

- There is another fundamentally important aspect of these mystical experiences. For people having them, the mystical experience of reality is extremely real. Because of this, it changes the way they look at reality in general, and it changes their life in particular. Mystical experiences are known to result in a feeling of enlightenment, which changes the entire way a person thinks.

- The following is a quote of a woman's transformative spiritual experience.
    - "I was lost; I had no sense of God's direction. Everything was dark. I cried out—nothing. Finally, God asked me if I would do anything he asked. I surrendered everything, including my faith and my salvation. In an instant, God returned everything to me, transformed. He liberated me. From that day forward, a new relationship existed between God and me—but I am not attached to doctrine, dogmas, rituals. I see God's action all around me. I cry easier at the joy of what I see, I sing spontaneously, and I have found myself and my beliefs continually expanding, becoming more inclusive, more universal."

- The realness and intensity of this experience, combined with the emotions and the sense of connectedness, brought this individual to a very different and new way of conceiving of herself, her relationship with God, and her relationship with the rest of the world. In this way, her beliefs have changed dramatically.

- One can get a sense about how different religious or spiritual beliefs might actually come about as the result of such an experience. Her initial religious beliefs were of a distant, and to some degree critical, God. Everything was negative and dark. However, as the result of the experience, God is seen as a liberator and one that connects with the person without religious doctrine or ritual.

- Theologically, this would lead to a notion of God as directly interacting with a person's personal life in a loving manner rather than being distant. This reflects an overall shift in the function of the orientation part of the brain from a sense of distance to closeness.

- God is also not viewed as critical, but as related to joy, and thus, the limbic system has changed its overall perspective. The experience leads to a new set of beliefs that are related to changes in personal orientation, surrender, and emotions.

- Thus, understanding the brain provides new insights into how a person's beliefs—and perhaps a religion's beliefs or doctrines—may be related to profound spiritual experiences. Such insights may lead to a new understanding of fundamental questions related to theology, philosophy, and epistemology, but they also tell us about the brain—a brain that apparently is far more changeable than perhaps we ever imagined.

- However, no matter how much the brain changes, the one fascinating constant is that the brain keeps telling us that it is seeing reality clearly. For this individual, her initial reality was that of a distant God, and now it is of a close and intimate God—but the brain treated both of these ideas as if they were reality.

Suggested Reading

Beauregard and O'Leary, *The Spiritual Brain*.

d'Aquili and Newberg, *The Mystical Mind*.

Newberg, *Principles of Neurotheology*.

Questions to Consider

1. How is the brain associated with mystical experiences?

2. Can mystical experiences tell us something about how our brains perceive reality?

The Mystical Mind
Lecture 23—Transcript

In describing a cosmic religious feeling, one scholar said the following:

> It is very difficult to explain this feeling to anyone who is entirely without it. … The individual feels the nothingness of human desires and aims and the sublimity and marvelous order which reveal themselves both in Nature and in the world of thought. He looks upon individual existence as a sort of prison and wants to experience the universe as a single significant whole.

That scholar was Albert Einstein; and it's fascinating to consider his description in more detail, especially from the brain perspective. He speaks about the feelings; he speaks about the "nothingness" and the marvelous order; and ultimately, perceiving the universe as a single significant whole. But how do these descriptors relate to the brain?

In our last lecture, we looked at the neurophysiology of mystical experiences and we saw that the autonomic nervous system, the limbic system, and the parietal lobe are going to be involved. When we're talking about feelings, we're talking about what's going on in the limbic system and how that ultimately relates to the autonomic nervous system allowing us to feel it all the way through our entire body. When we're talking about a sense of oneness and wholeness, we're talking about the holistic processes of the brain that reside in large part in the parietal lobe, in which we lose our sense of self and feel that intimate connectedness to everything around us and a sense of oneness of everything around us.

But in addition to these basic brain functions, we can also think about how the other brain processes such as abstract thought, perceptual ideas, the holistic process, and others play a role in these kinds of very profound experiences. Today, I'd like to build on what we've learned by exploring mystical experiences in more detail. We'll try to better understand the subjective nature of the experiences themselves—what the person feels, what they think, and what they're perceiving—and we'll see how these experiences relate to some of the universal processes of the human brain. I'd call them universal because, as we've discussed, the brain of all people appear to have these basic processes; and perhaps we'll come to understand the universality of the experiences, both in terms of different spiritual traditions as well as the brain itself.

The spiritual brain is capable of a wide range of perceptions and experiences; but of all these experiences, the mystical experience is surely the most intense. Mystics describe an experience in which the distinctions between self and other, the barriers between the inside and outside, are completely broken down. These distinctions and barriers are replaced by a perception of the oneness and unity of all things. Moreover, the perception itself tends to be associated with a sense of tranquility and peace. As the famous Lakota holy man Black Elk put it, he said: "Peace comes within the souls of men / When they realize their oneness with the universe."

Here, we see in this very simple statement that the most important aspect of the experience is the experience of oneness, the holistic process of the brain. But there's also the notion of peace; and remember that peace is likely associated with the calming part, the parasympathetic system, which is part of the autonomic nervous system. Black Elk's words are also echoed in the mystical writings from numerous other religious traditions, and this ultimately leads to a very important question from both a spiritual and a neurophysiological point of view: Are different mystical experiences truly different, or are they the same and then described differently depending on the person's prevailing belief system?

Before addressing this question in more detail, let's look at a few other mystical descriptions from different traditions; and we're going to focus on some of the specific similarities and differences in their descriptions as well as consider the possible brain processes that might underlie these experiences.

For example, the Dominican theologian and mystic Meister Eckhart had this to say about our relationship to God. He asked the question: "How then am I to love the Godhead? Thou shalt not love him as he is: not as a God, not as a spirit, not as a Person, not [even] as an image, but as sheer, pure One." How do I as a neuroscientist approach this perception; this experience of the absolute unity of all things? What is it about the spiritual brain that makes it capable of even conceptualizing a notion like the oneness of the cosmos?

We can see his initial question is actually about love; this is actually about an emotion. There are very interesting brain scan studies that tell us a little bit about where love is in the brain. Love appears to be experienced in several areas of the brain including the reward system of the brain; and this includes some of the areas that are involved with dopamine. We spoke about dopamine before when we talked about various aspects of religious experience and other ways in which we feel better about ourselves, and that's why it's part of the reward systems. The insula is part of our brain that's between the limbic system and the upper parts of the cortex and it helps us to actually perceive and think about our emotions. Of course, the social area of our brain is also relevant because it helps us to know how we connect and how we interact with others and other things around us. In addition, some studies have suggested that the parietal lobe is actually decreased when we feel an experience of love; and this may go back to our original notion of how we connect the self with another.

Ultimately, Meister Eckhart concludes that we must love God as a oneness, and this takes us back to the holistic processes of the brain; what's going on in our parietal lobe that may have made Meister Eckhart of someone else who has a mystical experience feel that sense of connectedness and feel that profound sense of oneness.

Let's turn to another perspective. Rabbi Eleazer, a Jewish Mystic, stated:

> Think of yourself as nothing and totally forget yourself as
> you pray. You may then enter the Universe of Thought, a
> state of consciousness which is beyond time. Everything
> in this realm is the same—life and death, land, and sea.

In this quote, we see some very interesting references. First of all, he's talking about the act of prayer; but we've already seen how prayer affects the brain. We know that when we studied Franciscan nuns that they activated their frontal lobes; they were engaged in the process, they were focusing on the notion of God or on a particular prayer. They also decreased the activity in that orientation part of the brain, their parietal lobe; and they also activated their limbic system, the areas involved in emotion. When Rabbi Eleazer is talking about prayer, he's tapping into all these different ways in which the brain actually works to engage that experience. Since we know that prayer can affect not only our perception of self but our perception of space and time, we can understand how this can lead to the kinds of mystical experiences that are described by Rabbi Eleazer.

These two quotes suggest that the brain may not only be spiritual insofar as it can have spiritual experiences, but it may actually be mystical because we can have mystical experiences. Why might we consider our brain to be mystical? In the first place, there are very good reasons for calling the brain "mystical" just by looking at the physical structure of the brain itself. The brain works by integrating biological, psychological, social, and spiritual elements all together; and all of these things together make up who we are via the brain. Thus, the brain is intensely integrated. It's a oneness made of billions of neurons and molecules working together to provide a generally unified view of reality. The brain is also intensely integrated with the world around us. In fact, we have trouble truly knowing where our brain ends and the world begins.

Consciousness and subjective experience are intimately tied to the biological workings of the brain, but we have no clear way of describing how this actually happens. To some degree, this indescribability of how a physical brain relates to a spiritual mind is very similar to the kinds of paradoxical and ineffable descriptions that we see arising from mystical experiences. In addition, since we're forever trapped within our own consciousness, trapped within our own brain, we may never be able to figure out how this relationship occurs; it remains a fundamental mystery, just like the nature and elements of mystical experiences.

Finally, and perhaps most obviously, we can call the brain "mystical" because the brain clearly is capable of having mystical experiences. Indeed, people have been having mystical experiences throughout time and across a wide range of cultures and religious and spiritual traditions.

There are two very interesting research examples that help to demonstrate this inherent ability of the brain to have these kinds of mystical experiences. A very recent study of approximately 30 patients who had traumatic brain injuries showed that those patients who had damage to the right parietal region were much more likely to express feelings of unity and oneness with the universe. Think about this: The parietal lobe is this orientation part of the brain we keep talking about. When people have damage to this area, something interesting happens: There seems to be a way of accessing this kind of transcendent experience, especially when this particular area of the brain is damaged.

The second example is from the neuroscientist Jill Bolte Taylor. When she had a stroke on the left side of her brain at a very young age—she was in her 30s—she actually started to have a very intense unitary kind of experience; a kind of mystical experience. She suggested that the effect of the stroke on the left side of her brain somehow released the more natural mystical process of the right side. Is a similar process occurring in the brain damaged subjects as well? Clearly, there's something going on, and we're trying to get at that. We can use this information—we can combine this information with all of the previous discussions we've had about meditation and prayer practices and their impact on the brain and spiritual experiences—to try to help us understand where these mystical experiences come from. It certainly seems that the brain has some very basic abilities to be spiritual and even mystical.

Throughout this course we've been applying science as a way of gaining new insights into the nature of religion and spirituality and, of course, in this lecture, mysticism. If this is possible, then the scientific study of the spiritual brain could have some tremendous implications for how religious ideas and even theological ideas arise from or are associated with these kinds of profound spiritual experiences such as the mystical ones. This is one area in which the exciting new field that we spoke about a little bit before called neurotheology may contribute. As we explore the potential links between mystical experiences and the human brain, we might be able to understand better the nature of these experiences and also how the brain interprets and incorporates such an experience into a belief system. After all, it's not just enough that we have the experience, but what do we do with it?

In addition, such an analysis may provide a unique perspective on philosophical and theological concepts that pertain to morality, causality, ontology, and even epistemology; and we'll talk about this a little later in this lecture and in the last lecture. In fact, remember that experiences that we talked about before in our lecture on revelation—such as John's conversion on the road to Damascus, Ezekiel's revelations, Mohammed's visions, and Joseph Smith's revelations—all led to the development of an entire religion, or at least some very critical components of the doctrines of particular religions.

How do these experiences turn into ideas that comprise religions? Again, in previous lectures, we considered a variety of the different cognitive processes that are associated with religious and spiritual phenomena. These cognitive processes are involved in much of how religious and spiritual experiences are perceived and interpreted subjectively. But as in our discussion about beliefs, these experiences are then converted along with our memories, sensations, emotions, and even our social interactions into a set of beliefs that we can use throughout our lives. Let's think about this a little bit more and consider how this happens in more detail.

Remember, back, we talked about the causal process of the brain: our brain's way of looking at the world, trying to understand the causal relationships of things. If someone has a mystical experience and they have this powerful notion of oneness, how does that oneness cause something to go on in the material universe? Does it actually cause the material universe to come into existence? Of course, if the mystical experience is perceived as being connected to God or as God itself, then the mystical understanding of God is that God actually causes the universe to come into existence. This is now a way in which we can understand how that causal process of the brain can interpret that experience into a doctrine, into a belief system.

Not only is the universe experienced as a oneness, but the notion can become the prevailing tenet of a particular spiritual tradition. If we think about the holistic process of the brain—that involves our parietal lobes; that enables us to feel that sense of oneness and connectedness—maybe it's not just the experience itself but it becomes part of the doctrine; it becomes part of the belief system itself. Has this happened? Certainly when we look at Buddhist and Hindu philosophies we see this notion of the oneness of the universe and the oneness of the Buddha or enlightenment that binds all things together. When that happens, that's part of what an individual who subscribes to those particular traditions believes in as the way in which they should act about life, understand the world, and actually engage in their particular spiritual tradition.

In the past we've also talked about the binary process of the brain that helps to differentiate objects from each other and contrast objects as opposites, good and bad, right and wrong. This also helps us to differentiate the mystical reality, the mystical experience, from the experiences that we have in everyday reality. Of course, this also requires us to somehow address these two different perspectives. When somebody has this profound mystical experience and they now suddenly have a new realization about how the world works, how do they relate that back to the everyday reality experience that the rest of us have? We'll talk about this a little bit more in terms of our perceptions of reality in the last lecture; but the binary process is part of what enables us to juxtapose those two different ways of looking at the world.

The emotions that we have that arise out of our limbic system are also of fundamental importance to the mystical experiences. We hear so many different ways of people describing mystical experiences as having different kinds of emotions, sometimes very positive and sometimes very negative. In fact, if we can actually understand how all of these different emotions arise within the context of the mystical experience, that may tell us something not only about the experience but how we incorporate a particular emotional standpoint when we look at the world or we look at God. If somebody has a mystical experience and experiences compassion and love, then maybe they'll have a doctrinal understanding of God as being compassionate and loving.

Let's look at a several descriptions of other mystical experiences to see again how such experiences relate to each other, how they relate to the various functions of the brain, and how they might be interpreted into the tenets of a particular spiritual tradition. Along the way, we should also focus on the similarities and the differences across these experiences and traditions. For example, Li Po, who was the Taoist sage, made this statement. He said:

The birds have vanished into the sky,

and now the last cloud drains away.

We sit together, the mountain and me,

until only the mountain remains.

What's going on here? This is the notion of the loss of the sense of self. He's sitting with the mountain until only the mountain is there. He himself has gone away; and this very profound sense of oneness, connectedness, and the actual loss of the sense of self is all part of the experience. But the concept, the tenet, which arises from this experience is that the goal of Taoism is to experience a state of enlightenment in which you lose yourself completely; and in doing so, you actually end all of your suffering.

Let's take a look at another tradition and another mystic. In the Sufi tradition, the mystic Mansur al Hallaj from the 10th century stated the following:

I am He Whom I love, and He whom I love is I:

We are two spirits dwelling in one body.

If thou seest me, thou seest Him,

And if thou seest Him, thou seest us both.

Isn't it interesting that yet again we have a sense of the relationship between the self and God and the sense of oneness, a profound sense of union and connectedness, between the self and God; and for him, he believed that God was within him, and that he and God had basically become one and the same? He argued that the ideal spiritual state was to be emptied of everything but God. Importantly, this places an emphasis on embracing the divine presence in this life, right here, rather than whatever comes after life, in death. Therefore it became part of the doctrine of Sufism, the notion of emptying your entire self with the exception of God and finding that mystical union, that connectedness and oneness, with God.

Even scientists like Einstein and another very famous scientist, Erwin Schrodinger, who was one of the founders of quantum mechanics, used their experiences in a way that guided their lives, their beliefs, and to some degree their scientific explorations. For example, Schrodinger once said:

> Inconceivable as it seems to ordinary reason, you—and all other conscious beings as such—are all in all. Hence, this life of yours you are living is not merely a piece of the entire existence, but is in a certain sense the whole. ... Thus, you can throw yourself flat on the ground, stretched out upon Mother Earth with a certain conviction [that] you are one with her and she with you.

Even for the scientist, there's a sense of wholeness and a sense of oneness with nature, with Earth; and to some degree, he felt that that was the relationship that he had to embrace; that was part of what his scientific perspective was all about. He felt that scientists should view themselves in relationship to the world around them as a oneness. Everything is connected, and science was a way of helping towards that connection. In fact, what's particularly interesting is the distinction that appears to arise between the mystical version of God and the more usual religious versions of God.

The conclusion of the mystics is that God is by nature unknowable. God isn't an objective fact or an actual being, God is, in fact, being itself; the absolute, undifferentiated oneness that's perceived to be the ground of all existence. To some degree, this is what's been described by the famous mystics, including the famous scientists who've all looked at the world as this oneness. When we understand this concept that the mystics claim regarding God, then we can understand how people can conceive of God using the extremes of their brain's functions. When we talked about the unitary continuum, this notion of an absolute unitary state where the parietal lobe is kind of working at some kind of extreme where we lose our sense of self and we have this intense feeling of oneness, we can see how that experience is part of the mystical experience that changes the way a person actually understands the world. But interestingly, the mystical experience, even though it's so indescribable, is for some reason experienced as deeply connecting the individual with their notion of God, even if it's a scientist whose notion of God is nature itself. One of the other really interesting pieces of this that is it makes the experience completely and wholly tangible and having an incredible feeling of realness.

If we turn to the notion of a comforting image of a personal and knowable God—a God that exists apart from the rest of creation as some kind of distinct, individual being—then we tend to conceive of God via the standard mechanisms of the brain, and that includes our emotions, our thoughts, and our behaviors. We conceive of God, we think about how God relates to the world, how God relates to us, we have feelings about that; but again, the mystic feels that they don't think about God but they have this intimate union with God; the notion that God is not around us, but within us.

As I alluded to a moment ago, there's this one other very fundamentally important aspect of these mystical experiences. For the person who has them, the mystical experience of reality is extremely real. What do I mean by this? When they compare that notion of reality to our everyday reality, not only does it feel real but it actually feels more real. Because of this, it changes the way they look at reality in general and it changes the way they think about things in their life in particular, the beliefs that they hold. Remember the near death experiences and how they dramatically changed the life of the person. Mystical experiences are known to result as well in a profound feeling of enlightenment, which changes the entire way a person thinks, it transforms them.

Here's a quote from our survey of a particular woman who had a transformative spiritual experience. She said:

> I was lost, I had no sense of God's direction. Everything was dark. I cried out, [and there was] nothing. Finally, God asked me if I would do anything He asked. I surrendered everything, including my faith and my salvation. In an instant, God returned everything to me, transformed. He liberated me. From that day forward, a new relationship existed between God and me. But I am not attached to doctrine, dogmas, rituals. I see God's action all around me. I cry easier at the joy of what I see, I sing spontaneously, and I have found myself and my beliefs continually expanding, becoming more inclusive, [and] more universal.

The realness and intensity of this experience, combined with the emotions that she had and the sense of connectedness, brought this individual to a very different and new way of conceiving of herself, her relationship with what she perceived of as God, and her relationship with the rest of the world. In this way, her beliefs were dramatically changed.

One can get a sense about how different religious or spiritual beliefs might actually come about as the result of such an experience. Her initial religious beliefs were of a distant and to some degree very critical God; she talked about everything was negative, everything was dark. But as the result of the experience, God was seen as a liberator and a liberator that connects with the person without religious doctrine or ritual in the way. Theologically, this would lead to a notion of God as directly interacting with a person's personal life in a very loving manner rather than being very distant. This reflects a shift in the function of that orientation part of the brain from a sense of distance to a sense of closeness. For her, God was also not viewed as critical but was now related to an emotion of joy and thus her limbic system changed; it changed its overall emotional perspective on the world. So the experience led her to a new set of beliefs that were related to changes in personal orientation, her feels of surrendering her own personal self, and her emotions.

Thus, understanding the brain provides new insights into how a person's beliefs and perhaps a religious system's beliefs or doctrines may be related to the profound spiritual or mystical experiences that people have. In fact, such insights may lead us to a new understanding of fundamental questions related to theology, philosophy, and epistemology. Where do those ideas come from? How do we derive them from our experiences? Of course, all of this information also tell us a lot about the human brain; a brain that apparently is far more complex and changeable than perhaps we ever imagined. But no matter how much the brain changes and can be transformed, the one fascinating constant is that the brain keeps telling us that it's seeing reality clearly. For the individual whose story we just heard, her initial reality was that of a distant God, and now it's of a close and intimate God. But the brain treated both of these ideas as if they were reality at the time.

How is all of this possible? How is it possible that a mystical experience can change one's view of reality and do it so quickly? How can the brain experience something that seems "more real" than our everyday world around us? Indeed, how does the brain even determine what reality really is? These are the intriguing questions that we'll address in our final lecture. I'll see you then.

Reality and Beyond
Lecture 24

In this course, you have learned that there are many limitations that are built into the human brain, but rather than feeling despondent about this, you should find great reason for optimism. Recognizing limitations can actually make people more open to new ways of seeing and exploring reality. In addition, the idea of integrating the perspectives of science and religion would perhaps give people new lenses for looking at the world. Whether you are religious or not—a scientist or not—as a human being, you have a passion for inquiry that allows you to see if you can ask the right questions and somehow find the new paths that will lead toward the answers.

Knowing States and Reality

- There are some fascinating things that arise from our brain's interaction with the world around us. For one, we almost always think or act as if we have a clear idea of what reality is. Furthermore, we almost always first assume that when reality does not work the way we expect it to, it is the fault of reality—not us. Only when we have a lot of evidence that reality is okay do we then start to think that our brain may be the problem.

- When it comes to judging between real and unreal, the brain is unfortunately not as good as you might think it is. In fact, we can miss a lot that occurs in reality. Sometimes, our brain even perceives things that are not there.

- From a philosophical and scientific perspective, we can argue that we use several attributes to characterize something as real. The first way our brain probably decides if something is real is in the subjective sense that it is real: What is real simply feels more real than what is not. This may seem to be an unsatisfyingly soft standard, but it may be the best guidance that the greatest minds and brains of experts have produced.

- We might also divide our perceptions of reality into particular states, many of which we have all experienced. These states can be called primary knowing states because whenever we are in one, we tend to feel that we know that it is real.

- The state of reality that you are in right now, for example, feels very real to you, and you have a very good sense that you know what is going on. In addition, there are no other experiences of reality that you have.

- When you are dreaming, you are also in a primary knowing state. Every other state of reality is relegated to an inferior experience of reality, and you deal with your dream as if it is unquestionably real. Of course, the moment you wake up and are back in baseline reality, your usual immediate reaction is to acknowledge that you have been dreaming, and then the dream state is immediately relegated to an inferior experience of reality.

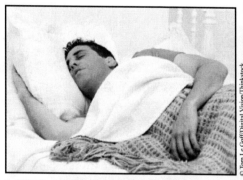

A dream state is an example of a knowing state that involves the perception of irregular relationships between multiple objects.

- How are these primary knowing states formed in the brain? It appears that they are experienced along three different dimensions that reflect three basic brain processes.

- The first brain process is our perceptual process, which enables us to perceive the world, or reality. Our perceptions can lead us to see the things or objects in the world in two very distinct ways. The first way is to perceive lots of different things in the world. In other words, we see multiple objects. The second way is to perceive no discrete objects. In this way, everything in reality is perceived as a unified oneness. This probably is associated with the quantitative function, which tells us that there are lots of things or only one thing.

- The second brain process is our causal process, which tells us how things in the world relate to each other—either in some kind of rational or regular way or in some type of illogical or bizarre way.

- The third brain process involved in primary knowing states is our emotional process. Broadly speaking, we can have either a positive, negative, or neutral emotional view of reality. It is our limbic system that prompts us to have one of these emotional set points.

- If you combine these three processes, there are a number of possible knowing states. For example, we might have a knowing state in which we perceive a reality with multiple objects, that are logically connected to each other, and we might have a neutral emotional attitude toward that reality. On the other hand, we might perceive a reality with multiple objects, but they are illogically related to one another, and we have a negative emotional attitude.

Possible Knowing States and the Brain

- The first group of knowing states involves a perception of reality with multiple discrete objects. These objects, such as your room or house, can be related to each other through the causal process of the brain in regular ways. This regularity is what allows science to work toward an understanding of what is typically called our baseline reality, which is the state that most of us are in most of the time. We typically perceive this reality as having an overall neutral emotional value. Overall, we see the world as simply existing.

- There are two knowing states, however, that are slightly different from baseline reality. They do involve the same multiple objects, and these objects do have logical relationships between them, but the individual takes either a very positive or a very negative emotional view of this reality.

- If the limbic system provides an individual with an overwhelmingly positive view of reality, the result is a perceptual state associated with an elated sense of being. The individual experiences joy because the universe is perceived as being fundamentally good.

- There is a sense of purposefulness to all things and to humankind's place within the universe. This purposefulness is not derived logically; it is simply intuited because of the positive emotional state.

- Although this state may have a sudden onset, it can last for many years and even for the rest of the person's life. People in this state are not psychotic—nor do they have any definite emotional or mental disorder. In most respects, they perceive reality in the same way as those of us in baseline reality, but they simply have a different emotional understanding of this perception.

- By contrast, some people experience a knowing state in which the common perception of multiple objects with regular relationships is associated with a profoundly negative emotional tone. It is a state of exquisite sadness and futility and involves the sense of the incredible smallness of humankind within the universe and the suffering inherent in the human condition.

- There are at least three different perceptions of reality. This experience of reality involves multiple objects that interact in a predictable causal fashion—but it can be perceived in a neutral, positive, or deeply negative emotional fashion.

- Because emotion is crucial to the way the brain constructs reality, it is accurate to say that these aren't just three different perceptions of reality; instead, they are three different realities in which the brain can live.

- There are the knowing states that involve the perception of multiple discrete objects that relate to one another in irregular or bizarre ways. Examples include dream states, drug-induced states, and diseases such as schizophrenia. The knowing states that involve irregular relationships can be associated with either negative, positive, or neutral emotion.

- There are the knowing states that involve the perception of a unitary reality—a reality in which everything is regarded as a singular oneness. When dealing with unitary reality, we need to drop the categories of regular and irregular relationships. There is only one object in this knowing state, so there are no relationships between multiple objects.

- While there may be many other states that have a significant feeling of unity, these are different from the state in which the person experiences the totality of everything as being completely unified.

- It is possible to have a mystical experience that is on the unitary continuum (from Lecture 22) but that doesn't attain the fullness of the absolute unitary state, which represents a state described in many religious traditions as nirvana, absolute reality, the oneness of God, or absolute unitary being.

- This unitary state probably has a neurophysiological correlate in that the areas of the brain that help to perceive objects, the self, and space and time probably have diminished function. Theoretically, the perception of a unitary reality might also be perceived in either a positive, negative, or neutral way.

- A knowing state that involves the perception of absolute oneness is clearly in the realm of the spiritual—and maybe the mystical—brain. Beyond this, more than any other knowing state, this particular state challenges our very notion of what is real.

- The absolute unitary state has a very peculiar aspect to it. Because there is no perception of any particular objects, there is no experience of the self. Because of this, those who experience this state have the perception of going beyond their own ego's thoughts and even beyond their own brain. However, such a notion seems highly contrary to the notion that the brain is what perceives our reality.

- Whenever you are in one primary knowing state, you perceive that state to represent reality above all other states. When you wake up from a dream, the dream seems less real. However, this is not the case with the absolute unitary state. When a person experiences this state, not only do they perceive it to be real when they are in it, but even when they are no longer in it, the brain keeps telling them that that experience represented the true reality. In fact, the experience is usually described as being more real than every other reality experience.

- We have this experience that seems to supersede all other experiences of reality. Is there a way we could scientifically prove what is real—or if whether what is inside our brain correlates with external reality? Perhaps, but science hasn't figured out how to do an experiment that would allow us observe the human brain observing its own function and, simultaneously, being aware of its own thought processes, for example.

- Up to this point, humanity seems to have taken one of two approaches: the scientific approach, which typically tries to reduce reality to measurable, material quantities; and the spiritual approach, which seems to culminate in this mystical experience that is beyond the reach of science.

- Perhaps, however, there's a third option. Maybe our best chance of understanding reality—indeed, of understanding ourselves—lies in taking an integrated approach to this problem that allows the spiritual perspective to inform the scientific perspective, and vice versa.

Suggested Reading

Beauregard and O'Leary, *The Spiritual Brain*.

d'Aquili and Newberg, *The Mystical Mind*.

Newberg, *Principles of Neurotheology*.

1. If we assume that the brain processes everything we perceive in reality, then scientifically and philosophically, can we ever really know if what we think inside our brains is accurate with what is real on the outside?

2. How might knowledge obtained through both science and spiritual approaches provide information about the true nature of reality?

Reality and Beyond

Lecture 24—Transcript

Right now, you're probably sitting at a computer table, maybe in your car or on your couch, and you've just turned on this lecture and started to hear my voice. Your brain is responding swiftly and easily as everything that's happening at this moment is real and can be interacted with in a predictable kind of way. For example, if you hit the start button on your DVD player and nothing happened, you would be surprised and your brain would start quickly trying to explain to you why reality isn't the way that you had anticipated.

But there are some fascinating things that arise from our brain's interaction with the world around us. For one, we almost always think or act as if we have a very clear idea of what reality is. Furthermore, we almost always first assume that when reality doesn't work the way we expect that it's the fault of reality and not us; not our brain. After all, if nothing happened when you turned the DVD or the CD player on, you would most likely conclude that there was a problem with the player, right? You usually wouldn't expect that your brain had misfired and somehow accidentally you tried to turn the sofa on, for example. Only when we have a lot of evidence that reality is really OK do we then start to think that maybe our brain really is the problem.

A more fundamental question that arises is: Why do we think that something, anything, is real in the first place? Why is it that your perception of me is treated by your brain as real? Why do you automatically dismiss certain claims as fundamentally unreal? For example, if I told you that my assistant during this entire lecture series was a friendly gorilla that was standing right next to me, no matter how much I tried to convince you and no matter how convincing I sounded, you would probably conclude fairly quickly that there was no gorilla there and you might even begin to suspect my own mental stability.

But when it comes to judging between what's real and what's unreal, the brain is unfortunately not as good as you might think. In fact, the evidence suggests that your brain might actually miss an entire gorilla. A number of years ago, there was a wonderful study that was designed in which people were asked to sit in front of a television screen, and they watched about four or five different people throwing different-colored balls back and forth. What the test subject was then asked to do was to count the number of throws and catches of these different people for one of the colored balls, the white ball for example; how many times did they throw the white ball back and forth to each other? As the person's counting it, they do this very diligently; and at one point in the midst of this video that only runs about 5 or 10 minutes, there's a person who walks in in a gorilla costume, walks into the center of the video, waves his arms around for a few minute, and then walks off the video.

What's amazing is that a huge percentage of people never see the gorilla; they're so focused, so concentrating on counting how many times that ball goes back and forth, that an entire gorilla goes completely out of their consciousness and out of their perceptions of reality. In fact, they're usually amazed when they actually see it. I love showing this video in large lecture halls because you start to slowly hear the laughter after a little while when people finally start to realize what's going on. So it appears that we can miss quite a lot that occurs in our reality.

On the other hand, sometimes our brain perceives things that aren't there in the first place. This is what happens to all of us when we may hear something that we really don't. For example, have you ever been in your house at night, it always seems to be when you're alone, you hear all kinds of noises? A lot of them aren't even real noises; and even when your brain actually does hear a noise, it starts to interpret it and you begin to react to the possibility— maybe it's an intruder—and then you listen for other noises, you hear little creaks and so forth. Even though ultimately it's probably just the wind blowing through the curtains or maybe even nothing at all, your brain is perceiving these things; and sometimes they're real, but sometimes they're not. In fact, studies of viewers watching different crime scenes show how erroneous our brain's perceptions of reality actually can be. For example, usually if you have five different people watching a video of a crime scene, you'll get five different descriptions of what actually happened.

But what's always been particularly fascinating to me, especially in the context of this entire course, is how our ability to perceive reality plays out in terms of religion or God. Why do some see God everywhere and some see God nowhere? This was one of the questions that led me into this field in the first place. When I talked in my first lecture about how I used to stay up nights when I was a kid thinking about this, this was one of those questions: How is it possible that some can believe and others don't? Remember in our discussion about believers and nonbelievers, there appear to be very specific brain differences between the types of people who believe and those who don't; but does that brain difference actually explain their different perceptions of reality? Perhaps the more important question is: How do we know whose reality is actually right?

Remember the study in which believers and nonbelievers looked at these kinds of distorted pictures and they were asked to describe the things that they saw. If you remember, the religious believers sometimes saw things that weren't really there even though they usually could find the things that were there. On the other hand, the nonbelievers almost never saw things that weren't there, but sometimes didn't see the things that were there. They both made mistakes about reality and they made them in different ways, but which way was really the correct way?

I think this leads us to an even more basic question. We might wonder: How do we evaluate reality in the first place? How do we decide what actually is real? To address these questions, let's return to the example I gave at the beginning of the lecture. What is it about your room, or house, or the CD or DVD player that makes you think they're real? What characteristics about them do you rely on to tell you that they actually exist and are real and you can interact with them? From a philosophical and scientific perspective, we might argue that we use several specific attributes to characterize something as being real.

The first way our brain probably decides if something is real is just the subjective sense that it's real: What's real simply feels more real than what's not. Of course, this is probably a very unsatisfying and very soft standard, but it may be the best guidance that the greatest minds and brains of experts has produced. We might look at other possibilities; maybe we'd ask other people around us about what's real and what isn't. But remember we've talked about so many ways in which our brains and the ways in which we think are affected by what other people tell us; so how do we know if just because somebody else says that's something real that we should go along with it? There's even the more problematic issue that all these other people exist within our perception; and therefore, if you're a schizophrenic and you hear people telling you things about reality, how do you know you can trust them?

Another way of thinking about what's real is a characteristic we might call persistence over time. For example, if you put this CD or DVD into the player and then you go away and come back an hour later, you'd except to find the CD or DVD still in the player; and that tells you something about its existence, that it's still there.

I actually think that there may be a better, more subtle way of talking about our perceptions of reality, and I think that we can actually divide our perceptions of reality into some very particular kinds of states, many of which we all have experienced at one point or another in our lives. I like to sometimes refer to these states as primary knowing states, and I call them that because whenever we're in one, we tend to feel that we know that it's real. Take the state of reality that you're in right now, listening to me give this lecture. It feels very real to you and you have a very good sense that you know what's going on and you know that it feels real. There are no other experiences of reality that you're having at this time, and this is your primary knowing state.

But what happens when you go to sleep tonight? Maybe you'll have a dream, and maybe it'll be a very real-feeling dream. When I was a kid, I had a recurring dream that felt incredibly real to me; it was actually of a dinosaur chasing me. I'm not sure why I had this dream, but the one thing that I do know is that when I perceived that dinosaur chasing me, there wasn't another part of my brain that said, "Stay calm, don't worry about the dinosaur, this is just a dream." In my dream, when that dinosaur came at me, I ran in my dream and I ran fast. My reality at that moment was the dream reality. My everyday reality was completely ignored; so in this case, while I was in the dream, the dream became my primary knowing state.

Think about a particularly vivid dream that you may have had, maybe recently, maybe a long time ago when you were a kid. Did you react in the dream as if it was the total reality? Even when obviously illogical things appear to be happening, the brain just keeps on going as if that's the reality. Maybe one minute you're at your school and the next minute you're in

Antarctica, but somehow that seems ok. Once more, when you're in the dream, that's your primary knowing state. Every other state of reality is relegated to an inferior experience of reality and you deal with your dream as if it's unquestionably real in the dream itself. Of course, the moment you wake up and you're back in our everyday, what we refer to as your baseline reality, your usual and immediate reaction is, "Thank goodness, that was just a dream." The dream state itself is immediately relegated to an inferior experience of reality.

How are these primary knowing states formed in the brain? Given all the different parts of the brain that we've talked about, the different processes, it appears to me that these knowing states are experienced along three different dimensions that reflect three basic brain processes. The first brain process is our perceptual process. This enables us to perceive the world or reality. Our perceptions lead us to see the things or objects in the world in two very distinct ways: The first way is to perceive lots of different things in the world. The CD player, the cars, the sofa, the house, these are all different things; there are multiple objects in the world. The second way is to perceive reality is one in which there are no discrete objects. In this way, everything in reality is perceived as a unified oneness. This is the kind of reality that's described when we discussed the mystical mind and the mystical experiences in our previous lecture. So our primary knowing states appear to be able to perceive reality either as containing lots of individual things or no individual things. I should add that this is probably somewhat associated with the quantitative function in the brain that we also have talked about in the past. This is the part of the brain that tells us there are lots of things, or maybe there's only one.

The second brain process that's involved in our knowing state is our causal process. This is the process, if you remember, which tells us how things in the world relate to each other; that one thing causes another thing. Things can relate to each other either in some kind of very rational or regular way, or in some kind of illogical or bizarre way, at least according to our causal process of the brain.

I'll expand on this in just a moment, but I want to move on to the third brain process involved in primary knowing states, and that's our emotional processes. Broadly speaking, we have either a very positive, a very negative, or a neutral emotional view on reality. Where do our emotions come from? You got it right; it's our limbic system that prompts us to have one of these different emotional set points within which we begin to look at reality.

If you combine these three basic processes together, there are a group of possible knowing states that we can be in. For example, we may have a knowing state in which we perceive reality with lots of objects that are all logically connected to each other, and we might have an overall neutral emotional attitude towards that reality. On the other hand, we might perceive a reality with lots of objects, but they're illogically related, they're irregularly related, to each another and maybe we have a very negative emotional attitude. That's obviously a very different kind of knowing state; but just like the dream versus the reality state, when you're in it, it feels real.

Let's examine these various knowing states a bit more so that we can understand them in detail and try to think about how the brain and each of us ultimately perceives reality. The first group of knowing states all involve the perception of reality with lots of discrete objects. These objects—again like your room, house, your player—can be related to each other through the causal process of the brain in very regular ways. This regularity is what allows science to work toward an understanding of what's typically called our baseline or everyday reality. Science would have a very sizeable problem if the laws of nature weren't consistent everywhere in the universe; we wouldn't know how to react to that universe or even study it. This is the state that most of us are in most of the time, and we typically perceive this reality as having an overall neutral emotional value. Sure, we might be happy or sad at various times in our life; but overall, we see the world as simply existing.

There are two other knowing states that are slightly different from what we've called this baseline reality. These other two states involve the same multiple objects with lots of rational, logical relationships between them, but the individual takes on either a very positive or a very negative emotional view of this reality. If the limbic system provides an individual with this overwhelmingly positive view of reality, the result is a perceptual state—a state of realness—that's associated with an elated sense of being. The individual experiences joy because the universe—the reality that they're living in—is perceived as being fundamentally good. There's a sense of purpose to all things, and to humankind's place within the universe. This purposefulness isn't derived logically, they haven't come to this rationally; it's simply intuited because of this incredibly positive emotional state. This state may have a sudden onset, it may come on slowly, and it can last for years or even for a person's entire life. It's not a psychotic state, but it's a definite emotional state that's not a mental disorder and reflects the same basic perceptions of reality that all us do in our baseline reality, they just have a different emotional understanding of this perception.

By contrast, some people experience a knowing state in which they have the common perception of lots of objects with regular relationships, but it's associated with a profoundly negative emotional tone. It's a state of exquisite sadness and futility and involves the sense of the incredible smallness of humankind within the universe and the suffering that's inherent in the human condition and in the world. To some degree, a mild form of this state may occur in a lot of people as they go through high school, college students that are kind of dealing with the issues of growing up and asserting their own independence in a world that frequently appears very harsh and very capricious. In the full-blown state, people often seek psychiatric help; maybe they have major depression and they go to a psychiatrist because the extreme depression can be so overwhelming.

But it's important to realize that if they're still in this state, they're not typically denying the reality of their knowing state when they seek treatment. They're essentially asking to be taught to think in an illusory way so that the world will seem to have some meaningful framework. They're not asking to be restored to baseline reality per se because at that moment that's not their reality; their reality, their brain, is locked in this very negative knowing state. But hopefully for them, they'll ultimately find a real way out of that state and end up in a different knowing state that's at the very least neutral and maybe even positive.

We've talked about three different perceptions of reality already; the experience of reality involving multiple objects that can interact in very predictable, causal ways. But it can be perceived in a neutral, positive, or deeply negative emotional fashion; and we can see how all of this is related to the brain processes that help us to construct our experience of reality. In fact, it may be very accurate to say that these aren't just three different ideas of reality or even perceptions of reality, but they're for all intents and purposes three different realities in which the brain can live.

Next we have the knowing states that involve the perception of multiple discrete objects that relate to one another in irregular or bizarre ways. We've already encountered one of them; that was the dream state that we mentioned earlier. Other states that are like this could be drug-induced states. When we talked about that in a prior lecture, we could hear how there were so many weird perceptions going on, so many different ways; but for the person, that state was their state of reality at that time. Even diseases like schizophrenia, where so many bizarre ways of relating objects to each other come about, wind up changing that person's perception of reality. Of course, each of these states can also be associated with either a negative, positive, or neutral emotion. For example, the "trip" that one has with LSD or other hallucinogenic drugs can either be incredibly elating or profoundly disturbing. Quite literally, these states can be described as either heaven or hell. Schizophrenia, again, can have a lot of very bizarre relationships and can be associated with negative, positive, or neutral emotions. For some people, those hallucinations are terrifyingly frightening, and for others they're fine and they're not so bad.

But now let's turn our attention to the knowing states that involve the perception of a unitary reality; a reality in which everything is regarded as a singular oneness. When dealing with unitary reality, of course, we have to drop the categories of regular or irregular relationships; it seems to defy the causal function of the brain. There's only one thing there; there's only one object in this knowing state so to speak: that's everything. There's no relationship between lots of objects.

I also want to be clear that while there may be many other states that have a significant feeling of unity and a significant feeling of oneness, these are different from the state in which the person experiences the totality of everything as being completely unified. In the prior lecture when I talked about the unitary continuum, we discussed these different states. It's possible to have a variety of different spiritual states along this continuum that ultimately doesn't attain the fullness of what I'd refer to as the absolute unitary state. The absolute unitary state that I'm talking about now represents a state described in many religious traditions as Nirvana, Absolute Reality, the Oneness of God, or Absolute Unitary Being.

In fact, a very interesting person, Charles Lindbergh, actually appeared to describe a spontaneous experience of this type of knowing state. Of his solo trip across the Atlantic, Lindbergh wrote:

> While I'm staring at the instruments, during an unearthly age of time, both conscious and asleep. ... There's no limit to my sight: my skull is one great eye, seeing everywhere at once ... I'm not conscious of time's direction. All sense of substance leaves. There's no longer weight to my body, no longer hardness to the stick. The feeling of flesh is gone. I become independent of physical laws; of food, of shelter, of life.

> I'm almost ... less tangible than air, universal as aether. ... For 25 years, it's been surrounded by solid walls of bone, not perceiving the limitless expanse, the immortal existence that lies outside ... Death no longer seems the final end it used to be, but rather the entrance to a new and free existence which includes all space, all time.

Isn't that an incredible statement? Remember also that this kind of unitary experience has a lot to do with all the different parts of the brain coming together as he interprets that experience. That sense of oneness that's going on with regards to the parietal lobe, the emotions of the limbic system; all of these things are a part of this very intense experience that's a different state of reality altogether. Of course, this state does have a neurophysiological basis; and therefore, we can talk about how all of these different changes in the brain relate to that particular kind of experience. Theoretically, the perception of a unitary reality in and of itself isn't only perceived from that unitary state, but may actually have positive, negative, or even neutral emotions associated with it. For example, the positive experience of absolute unity might be one in which the oneness is perceived as having love and compassion. This actually sounds a lot like the mystical descriptions of God.

God is an absolute oneness that's loving and compassionate. If the emotions are neutral, we might perceive the universe as just being; in fact, it might feel more like a nothingness than a oneness. To my knowledge, there's never been a report of anyone experiencing absolute unity with a negative emotional perspective. Maybe it's just that the experience of unity so overwhelming that it can't be negative.

It might be argued that if it's in fact a total unitary state, then all of the emotions as well should be unified. While I'm not sure what that might feel like, it may be a state that actually exists; and I have several examples from the respondents of our online survey who related both positive and negative emotions as part of their intense mystical experiences. They felt love and fear at the same time; they felt terrified and calm at the same time.

When we talk about a knowing state that involves the perception of absolute oneness, we're clearly in the realm of the spiritual and maybe the mystical brain. But beyond this, we're also brought right up against the most important problem that we've faced throughout this course; because more than any other knowing state, this particular state challenges our very notion of what's real. Let me explain why.

The absolute unitary state has a very peculiar aspect to it. Since there's no perception of any particular objects, there's no experience of the self. It's a very strange and unusual primary knowing state indeed. This also suggests that for the experiencer, since they have no perception of the self, they have the perception of going beyond their own ego's thoughts and even going beyond their own brain. But such a notion seems very contrary to the position that we first started with: the notion that the brain is what perceives our reality.

But these experiences go even one further. I mentioned that whenever you are in one primary knowing state, you perceive that state to represent reality above all other states. When you wake up from a dream, the dream seems less real. But this isn't the case with the absolute unitary state. When a person experiences this state, not only do they perceive it to be real when they're in it, even when they're no longer in it the brain keeps telling them that that experience represented the true reality. In fact, the experience is usually described as being more real than every other reality experience we have. It's not like the dream; when the person wakes up from the unitary reality experience, it's not relegated to an inferior reality.

If this is the case, what are we to do with our brain, our everyday reality around us, and even our science, which is looking at that everyday reality? We have this experience that seems to somehow supersede all other experiences of reality. As a scientist, what am I supposed to make of this? Is there a way we could prove what's real, or if we can know whether what's going on inside our brain correlates with external reality so that we can tell if the unitary reality or the multiple discrete object reality really represents the true reality?

What kind of study could we design, what would it look like? Think about it for some time. If you ever figure it out, let me know. There are so many ways of thinking about such an experience, but I've never been able to figure it out completely. I can't think of any experiment in which, for example, we could somehow maybe observe the human brain observing its own function and simultaneously be aware of its own thought processes. Even if we could, would this lead to some kind of trailblazing insight about the seat of human consciousness? Would those insights in turn be a crucial step along the path of understanding what ultimate reality is? Perhaps; but the fact of the matter is that science hasn't figured out how to do an experiment like that.

Have we gotten to the point where we have limits to our knowledge? Is there no way to push through this knotty problem of what reality is? Up to this point, humanity seems to have taken one of two approaches: On the one hand, there's the scientific approach, which typically tries to reduce reality to measurable, material quantities. On the other hand, there's a spiritual approach, which seems to culminate in this mystical experience that's beyond the reach of science. Perhaps, however, there's a third option. Maybe our best shot at understanding reality—indeed, of understanding ourselves— lies in taking an integrated approach to the problem; an approach that allows the spiritual perspective to inform the scientific perspective, and vice versa.

It's my belief that such an integrated approach is possible, and in my own research I continue to think about how this might work. Whether I'm right about that or not, I don't know; but we certainly have embarked on a new way of thinking about spirituality and the brain. We've learned about the importance of keeping science rigorous, of developing good methods, and making sure that we keep religions religious and spiritual. We've seen the importance of being analytical and skeptical, but we've also been open minded so that we can determine the many fascinating ways that religion and spirituality affect human beings; and in doing so, I think we've achieved a richer understanding of the nature of all of our different kinds of beliefs. True, in some areas we may have ended up with more questions than answers; but to some extent, good science always leads us to new and better questions.

This paradox is echoed in the quote I offered a few lectures ago from the Sufi mystic, Ibn al-'Arabi. He said: "God deposited within man knowledge of all things, then prevented him from perceiving what He had deposited within him." Or to look at the situation from a neuroscientific perspective: As we've seen so often in these 24 lectures, there are many limitations that are built into the human brain. But rather than feeling despondent about this, I actually find a great reason for optimism. Recognizing limitations actually can make us more open to new ways of seeing and exploring reality.

That's why I personally am so excited by the idea of integrating the perspectives of science and religion. Perhaps this would give us a new lens for looking at the world; and whether you're religious or not, a scientist or not, as human beings, we're left with a passion for inquiry, to see if we can ask the right questions and somehow find the new paths that will lead us towards the answers.

I hope you've enjoyed this course as much as I've enjoyed talking about these wonderful topics. Overall, this course points to the fact that we've only begun this long and wondrous journey towards understanding the spiritual brain. We certainly have a very long way to go; but with the information we've covered, I hope that all of you, regardless of your brain's belief systems, are motivated to continue in your own personal endeavors to understand yourself and your universe, always being open to new data, new ideas, and new possibilities. Perhaps if each of us is steadfast in our own scientific and our own spiritual pursuits, we'll collectively help humanity arrive at a new level of enlightenment.

Bibliography

Andresen, Jensine, and Robert Forman, eds. *Cognitive Models and Spiritual Maps*. Bowling Green, Ohio: Imprint Academic, 2000. An excellent compilation of articles discussing how various cognitive models of brain function are related to specific aspects of spirituality.

Arzy, Shahar, Moshe Idel, Theodor Landis, and Olaf Blanke. "Why Revelations Have Occurred on Mountains: Linking Mystical Experiences and Cognitive Neuroscience." *Medical Hypotheses* 65, no. 5 (2005): 841–845. Reviews how current cognitive neuroscience ideas relate to various types and aspects of mystical experiences.

Ashbrook, James, and Carol Albright. *The Humanizing Brain: Where Religion and Neuroscience Meet*. Cleveland, OH: Pilgrim Press, 1997. One of the early works of neurotheology. Attempts to construct an approach in which religion and neuroscience are integrated from a primarily Christian perspective.

Austin, James. *Zen and the Brain*. Cambridge, MA: MIT Press, 1999. An excellent overview of brain function, particularly of neurotransmitters and how they relate to meditation and other types of spiritual practices.

Azari, Nina, Janpeter Nickel, Gilbert Wunderlich, Michael Niedeggen, Harald Hefter, Lutz Tellmann, Hans Herzog, Petra Stoerig, Dieter Birnbacher, and Rudiger Seitz. "Neural Correlates of Religious Experience." *European Journal of Neuroscience* 13, no. 8 (2001): 1649–1652. An interesting research study that shows differences in the brain between religious and nonreligious recitation.

Baylor Institute for Studies of Religion. "American Piety in the 21st Century: New Insights to the Depth and Complexity of Religion in the US." http://www.baylor.edu/content/services/document.php/33304.pdf. A very thorough and controversial evaluation of religious and spiritual attitudes among Americans, providing interesting data on the various concepts of God and religion.

Beauregard, Mario, and Denyse O'Leary. *The Spiritual Brain*. New York: HarperCollins, 2007. A book description of new neuroimaging studies of Carmelite nuns and their spiritual experiences. Explores the overall relationship between spirituality and the brain.

Beauregard, Mario, and Vincent Paquette. "Neural Correlates of a Mystical Experience in Carmelite Nuns." *Neuroscience Letters* 405, no. 3 (2006): 186–190. Describes a research study that found specific changes in the brain associated with the recollection of spiritual experiences in Carmelite nuns.

Beauregard, Mario, Jerome Courtemanche, and Vincent Paquette. "Brain Activity in Near-Death Experiencers during a Meditative State." *Resuscitation* 80, no. 9 (2009): 1006–1010. Describes a research study that found specific changes in the brain associated with the recollection of near-death experiences.

Benson, Herbert. *Timeless Healing: The Power and Biology of Belief.* New York: Scribner, 1996. Describes the more practical aspects of the relationship between beliefs and health.

Blackmore, Susan. *Dying to Live: Science and Near-Death Experiences.* London: HarperCollins, 1993. Describes some of the original research exploring the nature and elements of near-death experiences.

Boyer, Pascal. *Religion Explained*. New York: Basic Books, 2002. Provides an interesting perspective on the nature and explanation for religious and spiritual phenomena, particularly from an evolutionary and also neuroscientific perspective.

Campbell, Joseph, and Bill Moyers. *The Power of Myth*. New York: Anchor, 1991. A classic book on the elements and nature of myth and how myth has had an impact on humanity.

Cardena, Etzel, Steven Lynn, and Stanley Krippner, eds. *Varieties of Anomalous Experience: Examining the Scientific Evidence*. New York: American Psychological Association, 2004. An excellent edited book on the study of a vast array of different anomalous experiences, including mystical, drug-induced, out-of-body, and paranormal experiences.

d'Aquili, Eugene. "Human Ceremonial Ritual and the Modulation of Aggression." *Zygon* 20, no. 1 (1985): 21–30. An early attempt at understanding the nature of rituals and how their physiological effects may lead to an increase or decrease in aggression.

———. "Senses of Reality in Science and Religion." *Zygon* 17, no 4 (1982): 361–384. An early work on how the brain processes our experience of reality and how that relates to religious and spiritual beliefs as well as epistemology.

———. "The Biopsychological Determinants of Religious Ritual Behavior." *Zygon* 10, no. 1 (1975): 32–58. An early article on how biology and brain function are related to religious ritual and the effects of ritual on the human person.

———. "The Myth-Ritual Complex: A Biogenetic Structural Analysis." *Zygon* 18, no. 3 (1983): 247–269. Explores the relationship between the development of myth and the elaboration of myth into ritual practices in a variety of religious and spiritual traditions.

———. "The Neurobiological Bases of Myth and Concepts of Deity." *Zygon* 13, no. 4 (1978): 257–275. Explores the potential relationship between neuroscience and different concepts of God in an attempt to link specific brain functions to particular elements of the human understanding of God.

d'Aquili, Eugene, and Andrew Newberg. *The Mystical Mind: Probing the Biology of Religious Experience*. Minneapolis: Fortress Press, 1999. Describes some of the initial research on the brain and spiritual experiences in an attempt to integrate neuroscience and spirituality in the context of neurotheology.

d'Aquili, Eugene, Charles Lauglin, and John McManus. *The Spectrum of Ritual: A Biological Structural Analysis*. New York: Columbia University Press, 1979. An excellent edited volume on the nature of rituals—from animal to human and from simple to complex religious rituals.

Deacon, Terrance. *The Symbolic Species: The Co-Evolution of Language and the Brain.* New York: Norton, 1998. An excellent description of how language has evolved in human beings and how the development of language relates to the evolutionary development of the human brain.

Dennett, Daniel. *Breaking the Spell: Religion as a Natural Phenomenon.* New York: Penguin, 2007. Argues for the natural development of religions from an evolutionary perspective and cites evidence of possible scientific causes of religions.

Dewhurst, Kenneth, and A. W. Beard. "Sudden Religious Conversions in Temporal Lobe Epilepsy." *British Journal of Psychiatry* 117 (1970): 497–507. A case report of several patients with temporal lobe epilepsy and their religious conversion experiences in one of the first descriptions relating seizures to religious experience.

Duke University's Center for Spirituality, Theology, and Health. "Latest Religion and Health Research Outside Duke." http://www. spiritualityandhealth.duke.edu/resources/pdfs/Research%20-%20latest%20 outside%20Duke.pdf. An excellent repository of articles relating to spirituality and health, ranging in all aspects of mental and physical health studies.

Fowler, James. *Stages of Faith: The Psychology of Human Development.* San Francisco: HarperSanFrancisco, 1981. An excellent review of how spirituality develops in human beings throughout the lifespan by postulating a progression from childhood-oriented beliefs to more universal beliefs later in life.

Gay, Volney, ed. *Neuroscience and Religion.* Plymouth, UK: Lexington Books, 2009. An excellent edited volume of articles directly relating neuroscientific concepts to religion—including such concepts as causality, morality, and the soul.

Goodman, Neil. "The Serotonergic System and Mysticism: Could LSD and the Nondrug-Induced Mystical Experience Share Common Neural Mechanisms?" *Journal of Psychoactive Drugs* 34, no. 3 (Jul–Sep 2002):

263–272. Reviews current evidence linking the neurotransmitter serotonin to the hallucinogenic effects of LSD and elements of mystical experiences, arguing for a similar neurophysiological basis.

Grassie, William, ed. *Advanced Methodologies in the Scientific Study of Religion and Spirituality*. Philadelphia, PA: Metanexus Institute, 2010. A collection of articles regarding scientific method and its capabilities and limitations in evaluating different aspects of religious and spiritual phenomena.

Greyson, Bruce, and N. E. Bush. "Distressing Near-Death Experiences." Psychiatry 55 (1992): 95–110. Describes the reports of negative aspects of near-death experiences, including negative emotions and terrifying experiences during near-death experiences.

Hall, Daniel, Keith Meador, and Harold Koenig. "Measuring Religiousness in Health Research: Review and Critique." *Journal of Religion and Health* 47, no. 2 (2008):134–163. A review and critique of various measurement techniques currently in use in the study of the relationship between religion and health—pointing to their strengths, limitations, and future directions.

Harris, Sam, Jonas Kaplan, Ashley Curiel, Susan Bookheimer, Marco Iacoboni, and Mark Cohen. "The Neural Correlates of Religious and Nonreligious Belief." *PLoS One* 4, no. 10 (October 1, 2009): e0007272. A neuroimaging study showing that religious and nonreligious beliefs appear to involve the same brain areas, thus providing interesting data with regard to the nature of different types of belief systems.

Heller, David. *The Children's God*. Chicago: University of Chicago Press, 1988. An interesting review of children's experiences and concepts of God and religion, describing emotional, experiential, and cognitive elements.

Hill, D. R., and Michael Persinger. "Application of Transcerebral, Weak (1 microT) Complex Magnetic Fields and Mystical Experiences: Are They Generated by Field-Induced Dimethyltryptamine Release from the Pineal Organ?" *Perceptual and Motor Skills*, 97, no. 3, pt. 2 (December 2003): 1049–1050. An interesting research study describing how magnetic fields applied to different parts of the brain might trigger mystical-type experiences and whether these might also be related to the release of the hallucinogenic compound dimethyltryptamine.

Hofmann, Albert, and Charles Tart, eds. *Psychoactive Sacramentals: Essays on Entheogens and Religion.* San Francisco, CA: Council on Spiritual Practices, 2001. A compilation of articles describing the use and experience of using various psychoactive substances in the context of religious and spiritual traditions.

Holden, Janice, Bruce Greyson, and Debbie James, eds. *The Handbook of Near-Death Experiences: Thirty Years of Investigation.* Santa Barbara, CA: Praeger Publishers, 2009. An excellent review of the current research on near-death experiences, including studies on the nature and components of such experiences, their relationship to different near-death states, their associated anomalous experiences, and possible explanations for their existence.

Hood, Ralph, Peter Hill, and W. Paul Williamson. *The Psychology of Religious Fundamentalism.* New York: Guilford Press, 2005. Reviews a variety of issues pertaining to the psychology of religious fundamentalism—including how and why people migrate to such strong feelings—focusing on particular religious groups.

Horgan, John. "The God Experiments." *Discover Magazine* 27, no. 12 (December 2006): 52–57. Reviews current research that explores ways of understanding the relationship between the brain and religious and spiritual experiences, focusing on imaging studies and also studies in which such experiences are directly stimulated.

Kjaer, Troels, Camilla Bertelsen, Paola Piccini, David Brooks, Jorgen Alving, and Hans Lou. "Increased Dopamine Tone during Meditation-Induced Change of Consciousness." *Cognitive Brain Research* 13, no. 2 (April 2002): 255–259. One of the few neuroimaging studies that explores the relationship between a neurotransmitter and meditation practice, showing that meditation is associated with an increased release of dopamine.

Koenig, Harold. "Research on Religion, Spirituality, and Mental Health: A Review." *Canadian Journal of Psychiatry* 54, no. 5 (May 2009): 283–291. An updated review on a variety of aspects related to religion and mental health, including disorders, treatment implications, and specific religious traditions.

Koenig, Harold, ed. *Handbook of Religion and Mental Health*. San Diego, CA: Academic Press, 1998. An excellent review of all aspects related to religion and mental health, including disorders such as depression and schizophrenia, treatment implications, and specific religious traditions.

Koenig, Harold, Michael McCullough, and David Larson. *Handbook of Religion and Health*. New York: Oxford University Press, 2001. An excellent review of all aspects related to religion and physical health, including diseases such as cancer and heart disease, effects on health and mortality, treatment implications, and specific religious traditions.

Lauglin, Charles, John McManus, and Eugene d'Aquili. *Brain, Symbol, and Experience*. 2nd ed. New York: Columbia University Press, 1992. An earlier work relating brain function to the development of symbols, language, and myth in human history with particular emphasis on the relationship with religious and spiritual development.

Lee, Bruce, and Andrew Newberg. "Religion and Health: A Review and Critical Analysis." *Zygon* 40, no. 2 (June 2005): 443–468. A thorough review of the relationship between religion and health, including both positive and negative effects.

McCullough, Michael, Ken Pargament, and Carl Thoresen, eds. *Forgiveness: Theory, Practice, and Research*. New York: The Guilford Press, 2000. One of the first detailed reviews of forgiveness, including its nature, process, and effects as well as its relationship to religious and spiritual traditions.

McNamara, Patrick, ed. *Where God and Science Meet*. Westport, CT: Praeger, 2006. A three-volume set that includes a variety of topics related to the brain and religious and spiritual phenomena such as mystical experiences, the belief in God, rituals, and morality.

Bibliography

444

Mecklenburger, Ralph. *Our Religious Brains*. Woodstock, VT: Jewish Lights Publishing, 2012. Describes how religion is related to the brain—with an emphasis on religious experience, the need for religious community, and the importance of faith.

Mohr, Sylvia, and Philippe Huguelet. "The Relationship between Schizophrenia and Religion and Its Implications for Care." *Swiss Medicine Weekly* 134 (June 26, 2004): 369–376. Describes current research and ideas relating schizophrenia to religious and spiritual experiences and beliefs with a focus on potential implications for the management of these patients.

Moody, Raymond. *Life after Life*. New York: HarperCollins, 2001. One of the original books describing the research and nature of near-death experiences and the implications for both science and the afterlife.

Murphy, Nancey, George Ellis, and Timothy O'Connor, eds. *Downward Causation and the Neurobiology of Free Will*. Berlin and Heidelberg, Germany: Springer, 2009. Describes the relationship between causality, the brain, and free will—showing how the three might be related and in what causal direction as well as considering potential moral and religious implications.

Newberg, Andrew. *Principles of Neurotheology*. London: Ashgate, 2011. A thorough analysis of current neuroscientific methods and findings as they relate to religious and spiritual phenomena with the goal of creating a more integrated approach relating the brain and such phenomena.

Newberg, Andrew, and Jeremy Iversen. "The Neural Basis of the Complex Mental Task of Meditation: Neurotransmitter and Neurochemical Considerations." *Medical Hypotheses* 61, no. 2 (2003): 282–291. A thorough review and theory of the neurochemical basis of meditation practices, including the importance of different brain structures and neurotransmitters such as glutamate, serotonin, and dopamine.

Newberg, Andrew, and Mark Waldman. *How God Changes Your Brain*. New York: Ballantine, 2010. Describes current research on the relationship between the brain and religious beliefs—particularly those surrounding

God—with an emphasis on neuroscientific and other studies that evaluate the short- and long-term effects.

————. *Why We Believe What We Believe.* New York: Free Press, 2006. One of the few books that details the nature of the neurophysiological basis of different belief-making processes—such as sensory, emotional, and cognitive processes—with a focus on religious and spiritual beliefs.

Newberg, Andrew, and Stephanie Newberg. "A Neuropsychological Perspective on Spiritual Development." In *Handbook of Spiritual Development in Childhood and Adolescence*, edited by Eugene Roehlkepartain, Pamela King, Linda Wagener, and Peter Benson. London: Sage Publications, Inc., 2005. Describes a potential model of spiritual development based on the development of the human brain throughout the life cycle with an emphasis on how the differential development of brain processes and functions may relate directly to different religious and spiritual expressions.

Newberg, Andrew, Eugene d'Aquili, and Vince Rause. *Why God Won't Go Away.* New York: Ballantine, 2001. Describes initial brain-imaging studies of different religious and spiritual practices such as meditation and prayer and explores the evolutionary and neuroscientific correlates of religion.

Newberg, Andrew, Nancy Wintering, Dharma Khalsa, Hannah Roggenkamp, and Mark Waldman. "Meditation Effects on Cognitive Function and Cerebral Blood Flow in Subjects with Memory Loss: A Preliminary Study." *Journal of Alzheimer's Disease* 20, no. 2 (2010): 517–526. One of the first longitudinal neuroimaging studies showing an acquired, long-term effect of meditation practice on brain function and a subsequent effect on cognition.

Newberg, Andrew, Nancy Wintering, Mark Waldman, Daniel Amen, Dharma Khalsa, and Alavi Alavi. "Cerebral Blood Flow Differences between Long-Term Meditators and Non-Meditators." *Consciousness and Cognition* 19, no. 4 (2010): 899–905. A study that demonstrated a functional difference in the brain between those individuals who had practiced meditation or prayer for many years compared to those who had not.

Paloutzian, Ray, and Crystal Park, eds. *The Handbook of the Psychology of Religion*. New York: Guilford Publications, Inc., 2005. A thorough review of the psychological correlates of religion, including an evaluation of pathological conditions such as depression and anxiety, developmental issues, treatment applications, and potential implications for religion itself.

Schultes, Richard, Albert, Hofmann, and Christian Rätsch. *Plants of the Gods: Their Sacred, Healing, and Hallucinogenic Powers*. Rochester, VT: Healing Arts Press, 2001. A thorough description of the nature of psychoactive plant compounds used in various spiritual traditions, focusing on their potential use for eliciting spiritual experiences, hallucinatory experiences, and healing.

Shermer, Michael. *The Believing Brain: From Ghosts and Gods to Politics and Conspiracies—How We Construct Beliefs and Reinforce Them as Truths*. New York: Times Books, 2011. An interesting description of the various aspects of human belief and how they relate to the brain—with an emphasis on religious and spiritual beliefs. Also, a discussion on political, moral, and social beliefs.

Streeter, Chris, J. Eric Jensen, Ruth Perlmutter, Howard Cabral, Hua Tian, Devin Terhune, Domenic Ciraulo, and Perry Renshaw. "Yoga Asana Sessions Increase Brain GABA Levels: A Pilot Study." *Journal of Alternative and Complementary Medicine* 13, no. 4 (May 2007): 419–426. A study that demonstrated that yoga meditation practice was associated with an increase in GABA, a primary inhibitory neurotransmitter in the brain.

Wilson, David Sloan. *Darwin's Cathedral: Evolution, Religion, and the Nature of Society*. Chicago: Chicago University Press, 2003. Describes the relationship between religion and society from an evolutionary perspective, discussing the possible adaptive advantage of religious beliefs and practices.

Notes